Table of Contents

CASE CLOSED

CONFIDEN

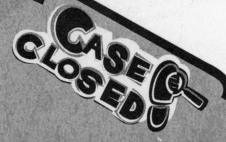

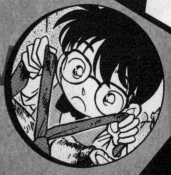

CASE CLOSED

Volume 14 • VIZ Media Edition

GOSHO AOYAMA

Translation
Naoko Amemiya

Touch-up & Lettering
Walden Wong

Cover & Graphics Design
Andrea Rice

Editor
Joel Enos

Managing Editor **Annette Roman**
Editorial Director **Elizabeth Kawasaki**
Editor in Chief **Alvin Lu**
Sr. Director of Acquisitions **Rika Inouye**
Sr. VP of Marketing **Liza Coppola**
Exec. VP of Sales & Marketing **John Easum**
Publisher **Hyoe Narita**

store.viz.com

www.viz.com

Printed in the U.S.A.
Published by VIZ Media, LLC
P.O. Box 77010
San Francisco, CA 94107

10 9 8 7 6 5 4 3 2 1
First printing, November 2006

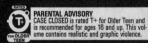

FILE 1:
THAT OLD PHOTO!!

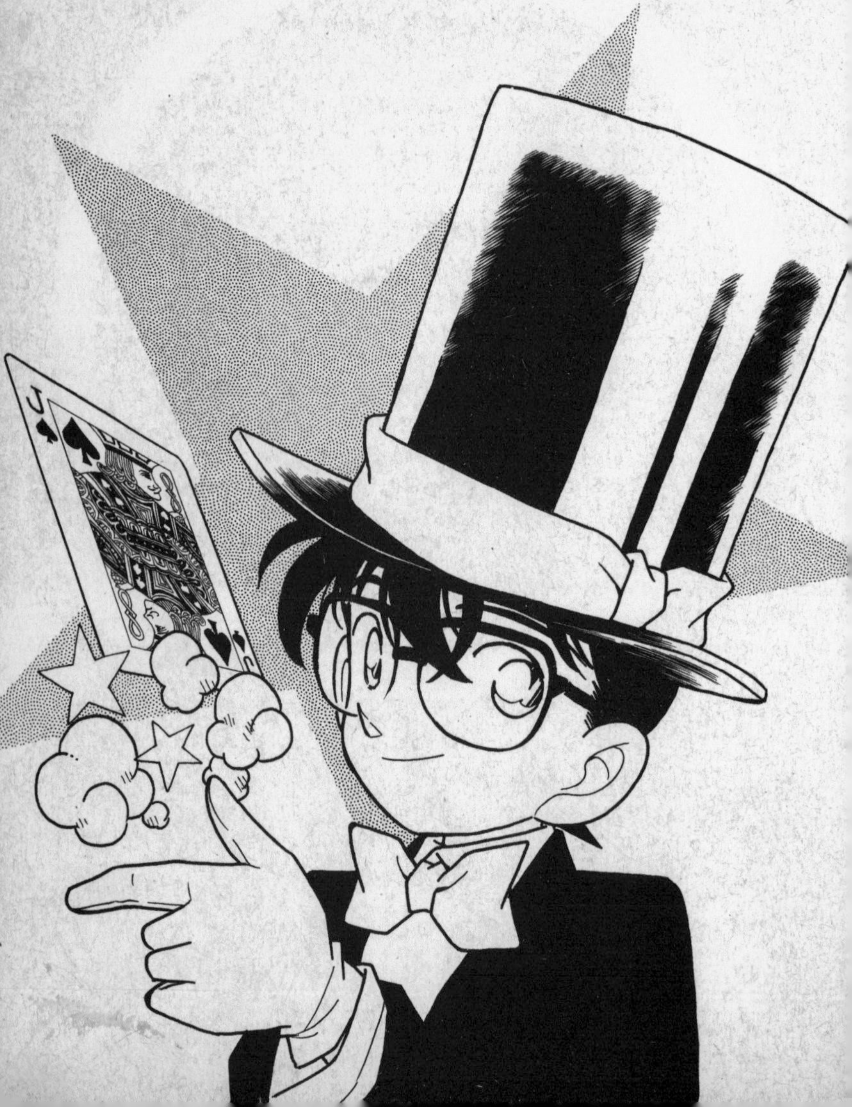

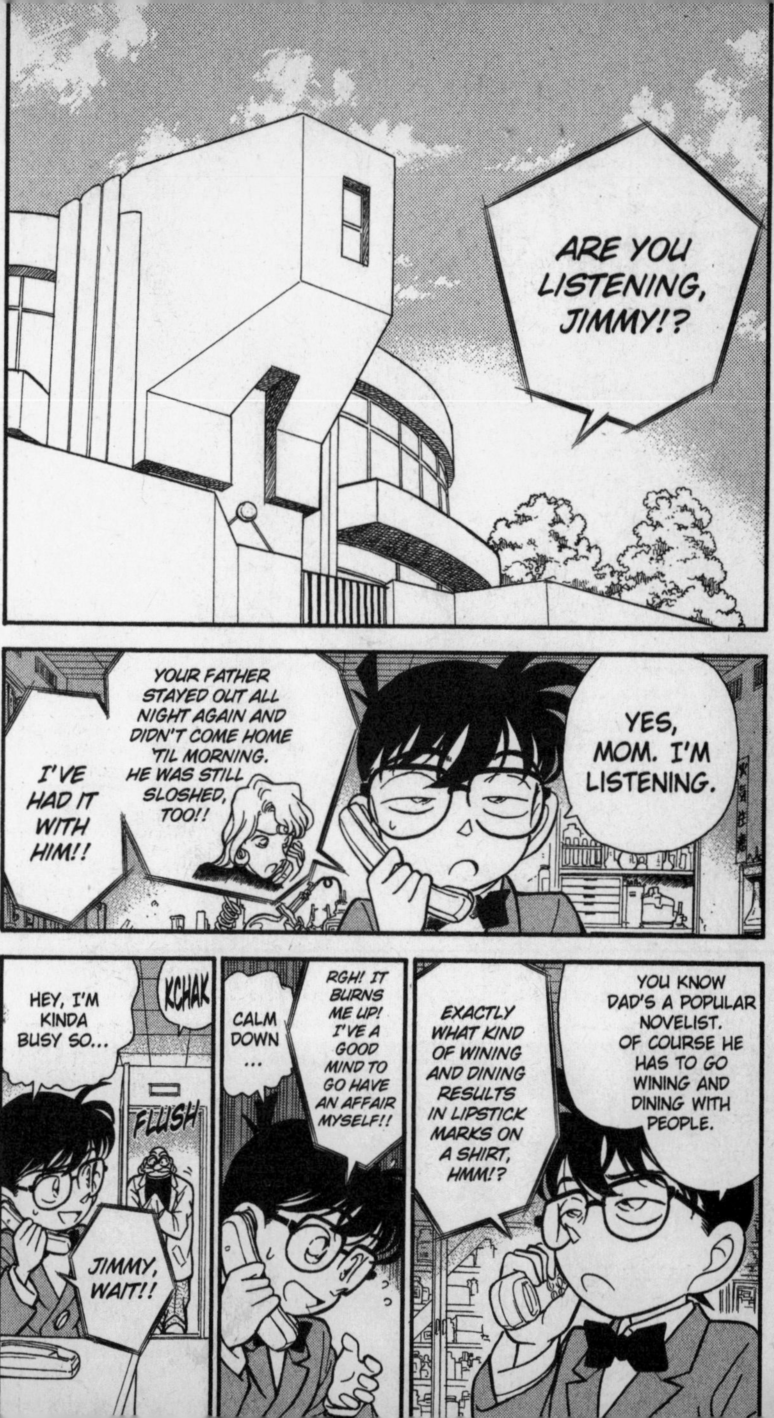
ARE YOU LISTENING, JIMMY!?
YES, MOM. I'M LISTENING.
YOUR FATHER STAYED OUT ALL NIGHT AGAIN AND DIDN'T COME HOME 'TIL MORNING. HE WAS STILL SLOSHED, TOO!!
I'VE HAD IT WITH HIM!!
YOU KNOW DAD'S A POPULAR NOVELIST. OF COURSE HE HAS TO GO WINING AND DINING WITH PEOPLE.
EXACTLY WHAT KIND OF WINING AND DINING RESULTS IN LIPSTICK MARKS ON A SHIRT, HMM!?
RGH! IT BURNS ME UP! I'VE A GOOD MIND TO GO HAVE AN AFFAIR MYSELF!!
CALM DOWN ...
KCHAK
HEY, I'M KINDA BUSY SO...
FLUSH
JIMMY, WAIT!!

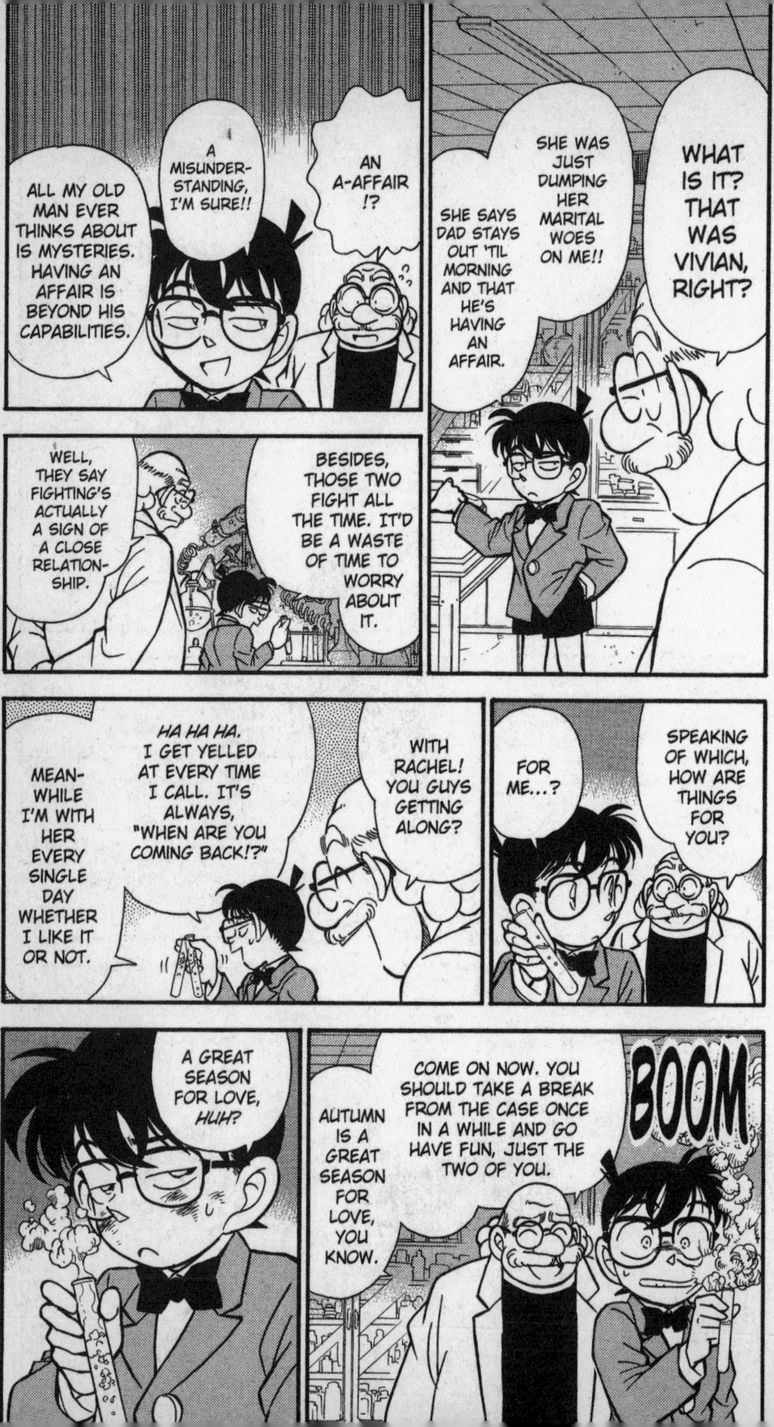
WHAT IS IT? THAT WAS VIVIAN, RIGHT?
SHE WAS JUST DUMPING HER MARITAL WOES ON ME!!
SHE SAYS DAD STAYS OUT 'TIL MORNING AND THAT HE'S HAVING AN AFFAIR.
AN A-AFFAIR !?
A MISUNDER-STANDING, I'M SURE!!
ALL MY OLD MAN EVER THINKS ABOUT IS MYSTERIES. HAVING AN AFFAIR IS BEYOND HIS CAPABILITIES.
BESIDES, THOSE TWO FIGHT ALL THE TIME. IT'D BE A WASTE OF TIME TO WORRY ABOUT IT.
WELL, THEY SAY FIGHTING'S ACTUALLY A SIGN OF A CLOSE RELATION-SHIP.
SPEAKING OF WHICH, HOW ARE THINGS FOR YOU?
FOR ME...?
WITH RACHEL! YOU GUYS GETTING ALONG?
HA HA HA. I GET YELLED AT EVERY TIME I CALL. IT'S ALWAYS, "WHEN ARE YOU COMING BACK!?"
MEAN-WHILE I'M WITH HER EVERY SINGLE DAY WHETHER I LIKE IT OR NOT.
BOOM
COME ON NOW. YOU SHOULD TAKE A BREAK FROM THE CASE ONCE IN A WHILE AND GO HAVE FUN, JUST THE TWO OF YOU.
AUTUMN IS A GREAT SEASON FOR LOVE, YOU KNOW.
A GREAT SEASON FOR LOVE, HUH?

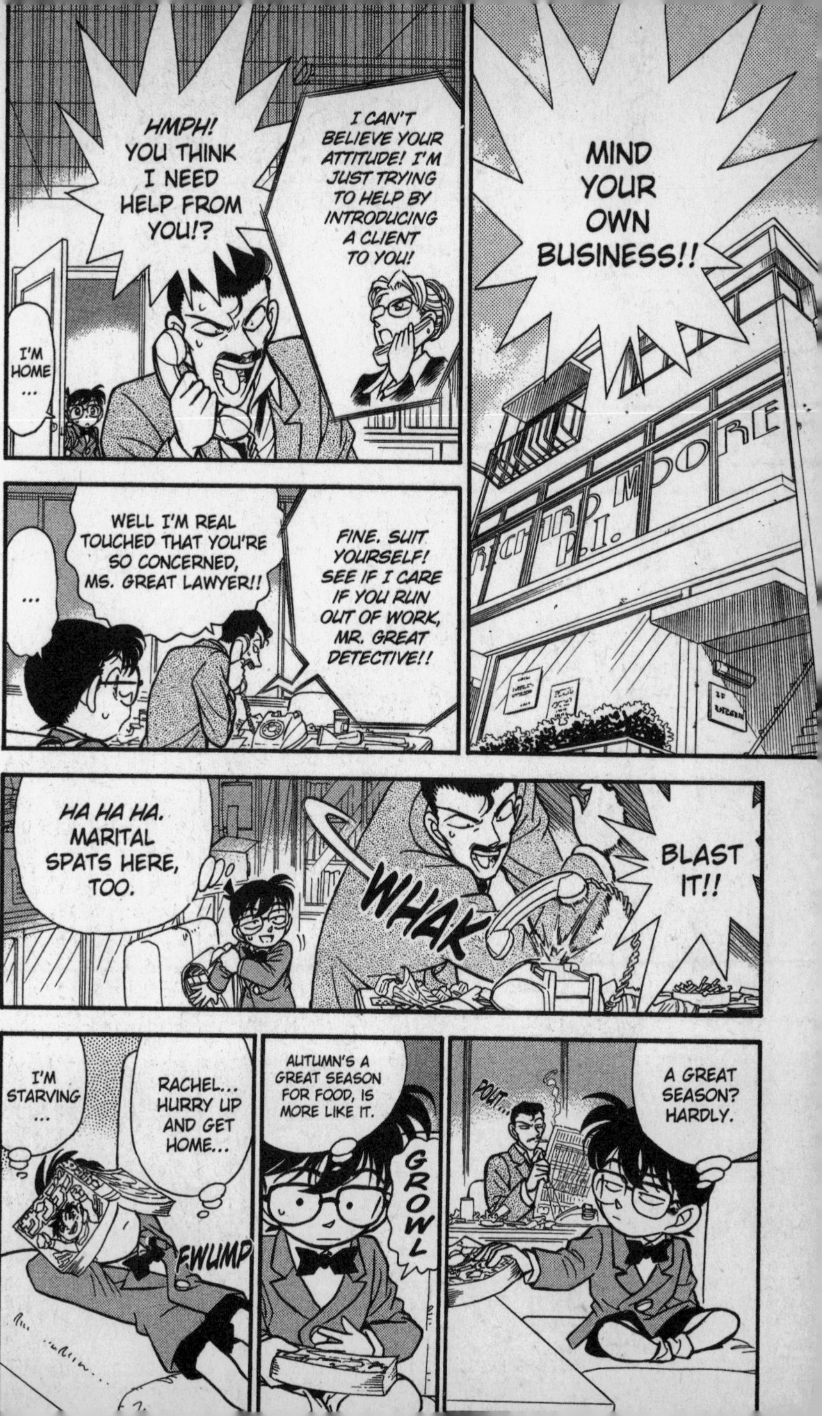
MIND YOUR OWN BUSINESS!!
RICHARD MOORE P.I.
I CAN'T BELIEVE YOUR ATTITUDE! I'M JUST TRYING TO HELP BY INTRODUCING A CLIENT TO YOU!
HMPH! YOU THINK I NEED HELP FROM YOU!?
I'M HOME ...
FINE. SUIT YOURSELF! SEE IF I CARE IF YOU RUN OUT OF WORK, MR. GREAT DETECTIVE!!
WELL I'M REAL TOUCHED THAT YOU'RE SO CONCERNED, MS. GREAT LAWYER!!
...
BLAST IT!!
WHAK
HA HA HA. MARITAL SPATS HERE, TOO.
A GREAT SEASON? HARDLY.
POUT...
AUTUMN'S A GREAT SEASON FOR FOOD, IS MORE LIKE IT.
GROWL
RACHEL... HURRY UP AND GET HOME...
I'M STARVING ...
FWUMP

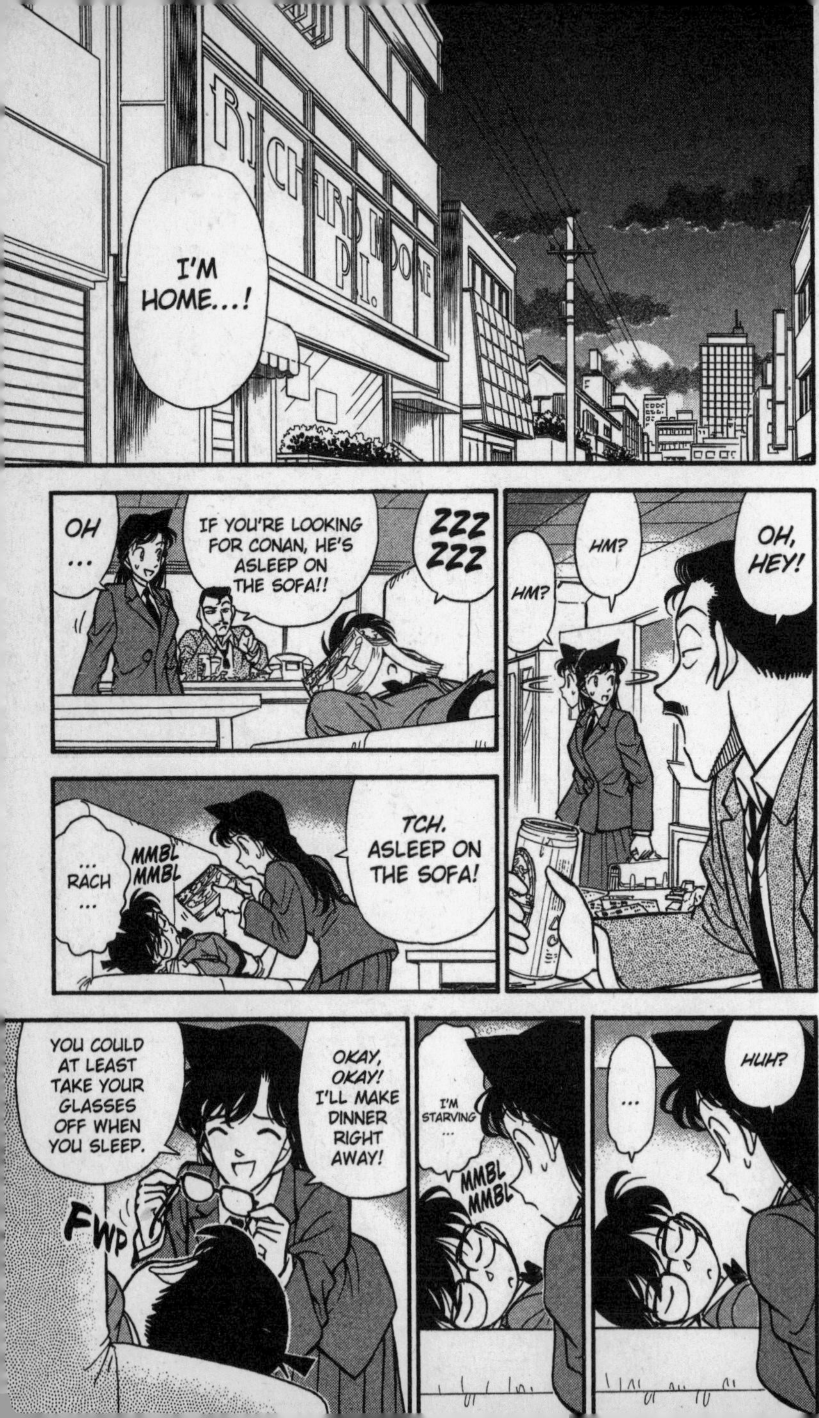
I'M HOME...!
OH, HEY!
HM?
HM?
ZZZ ZZZ
IF YOU'RE LOOKING FOR CONAN, HE'S ASLEEP ON THE SOFA!!
OH ...
TCH. ASLEEP ON THE SOFA!
MMBL MMBL
... RACH ...
HUH?
...
I'M STARVING ...
MMBL MMBL
OKAY, OKAY! I'LL MAKE DINNER RIGHT AWAY!
YOU COULD AT LEAST TAKE YOUR GLASSES OFF WHEN YOU SLEEP.
FWP

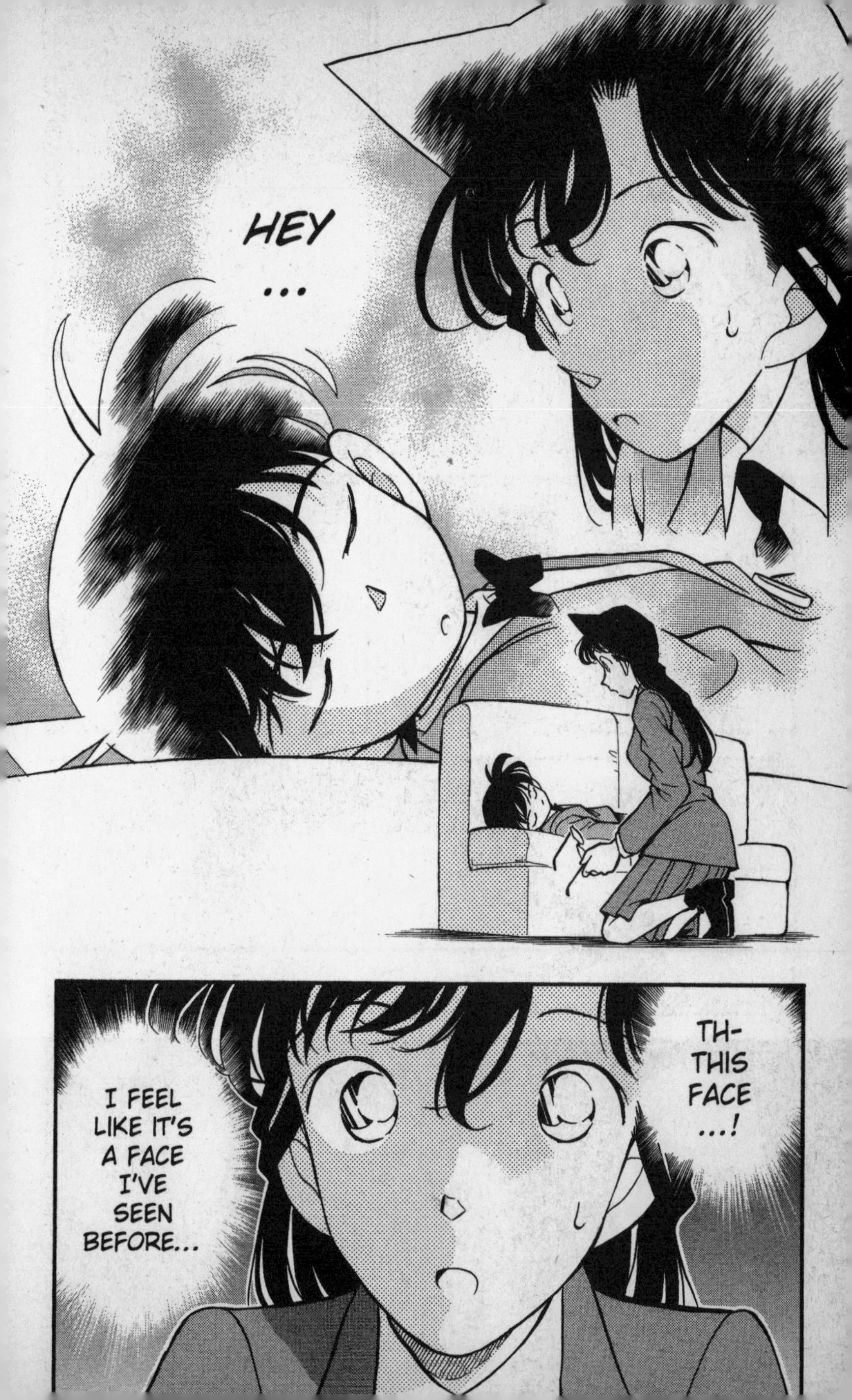
HEY
...
TH-
THIS
FACE
...!
I FEEL
LIKE IT'S
A FACE
I'VE
SEEN
BEFORE...

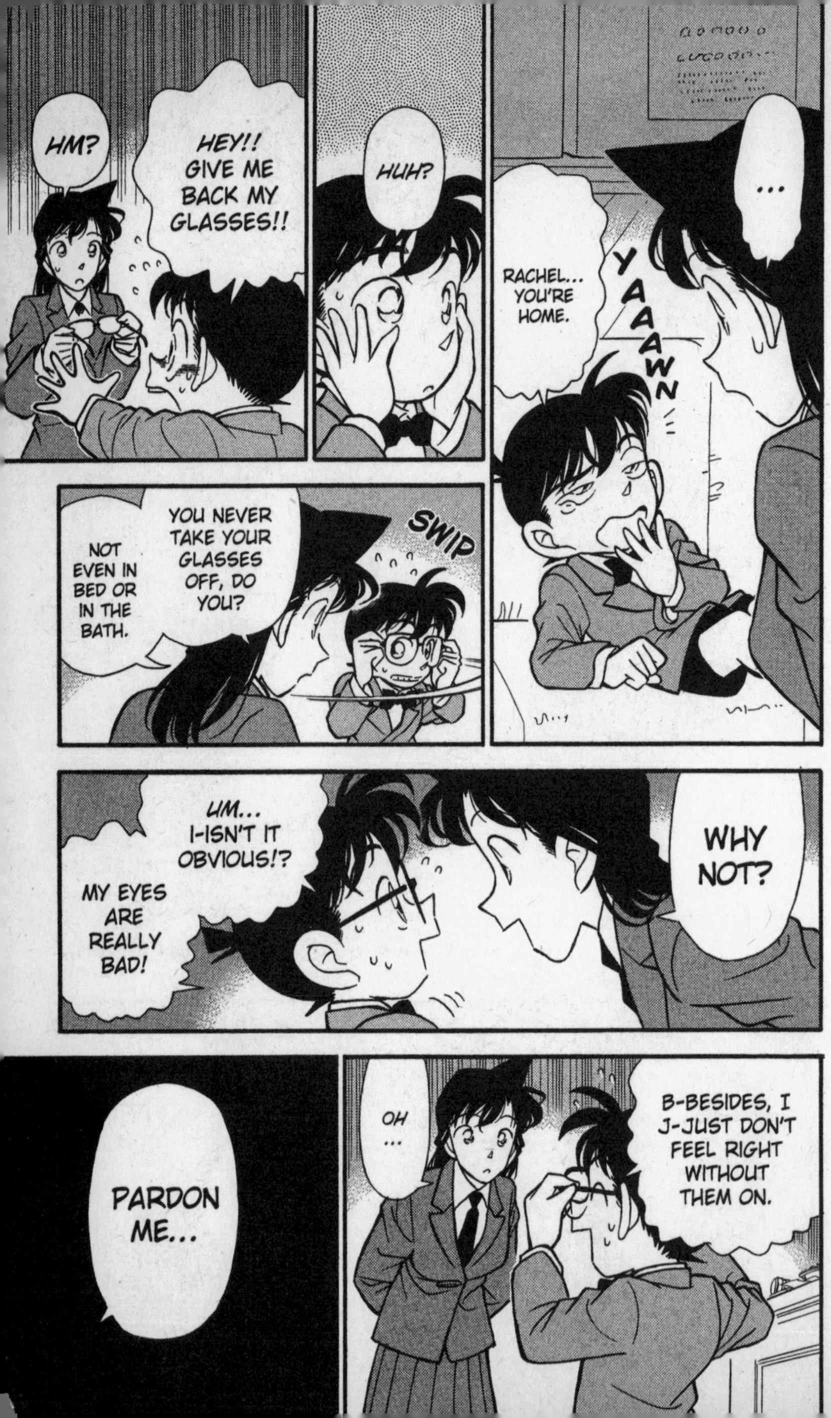
...
RACHEL... YOU'RE HOME.
YAAAAWN
HUH?
HEY!! GIVE ME BACK MY GLASSES!!
HM?
SWIP
YOU NEVER TAKE YOUR GLASSES OFF, DO YOU?
NOT EVEN IN BED OR IN THE BATH.
WHY NOT?
UM... I-ISN'T IT OBVIOUS!?
MY EYES ARE REALLY BAD!
B-BESIDES, I J-JUST DON'T FEEL RIGHT WITHOUT THEM ON.
OH ...
PARDON ME...

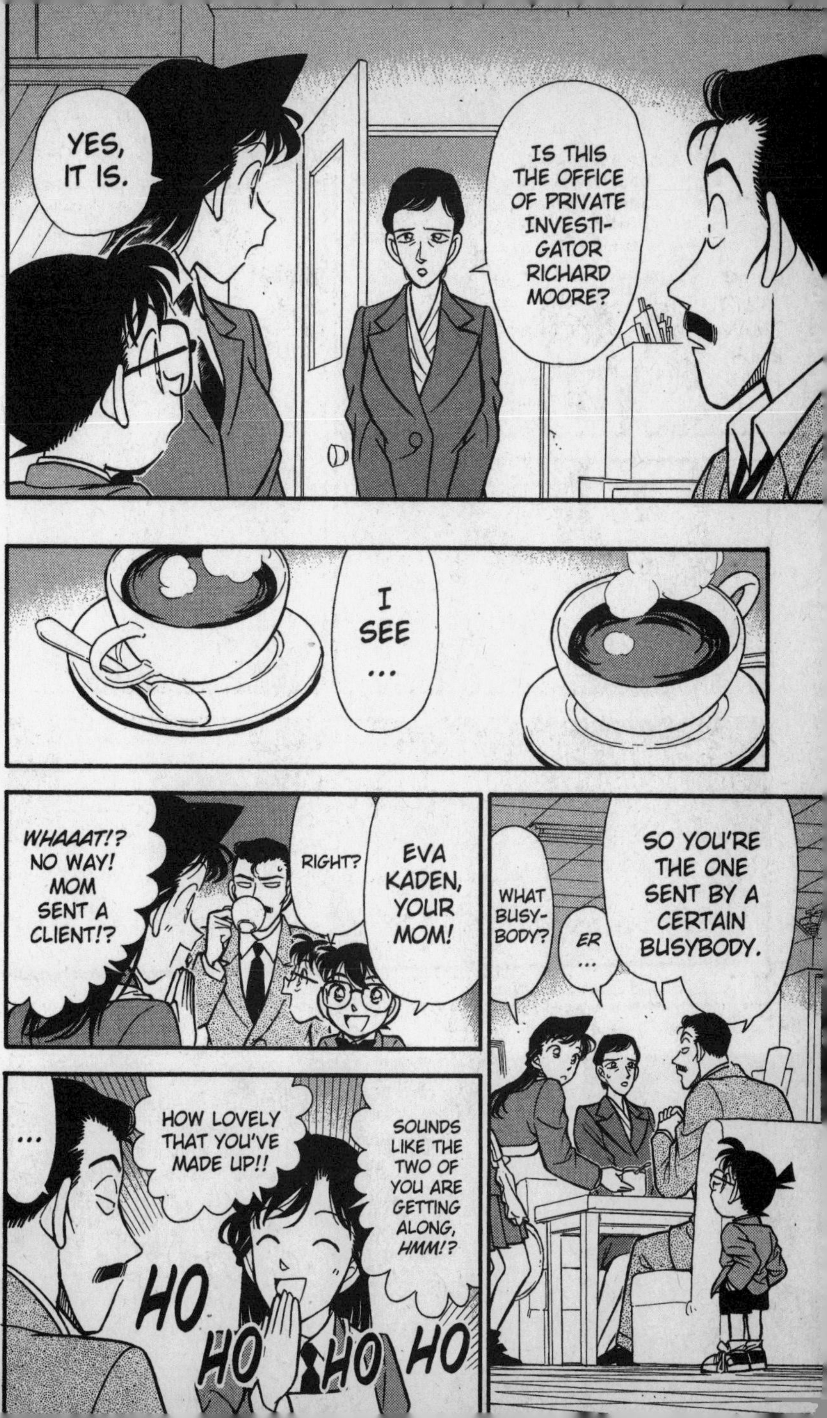
IS THIS THE OFFICE OF PRIVATE INVESTIGATOR RICHARD MOORE?
YES, IT IS.
I SEE ...
SO YOU'RE THE ONE SENT BY A CERTAIN BUSYBODY.
ER ...
WHAT BUSYBODY?
EVA KADEN, YOUR MOM!
RIGHT?
WHAAAT!? NO WAY! MOM SENT A CLIENT!?
SOUNDS LIKE THE TWO OF YOU ARE GETTING ALONG, HMM!?
HOW LOVELY THAT YOU'VE MADE UP!!
...
HO HO HO HO

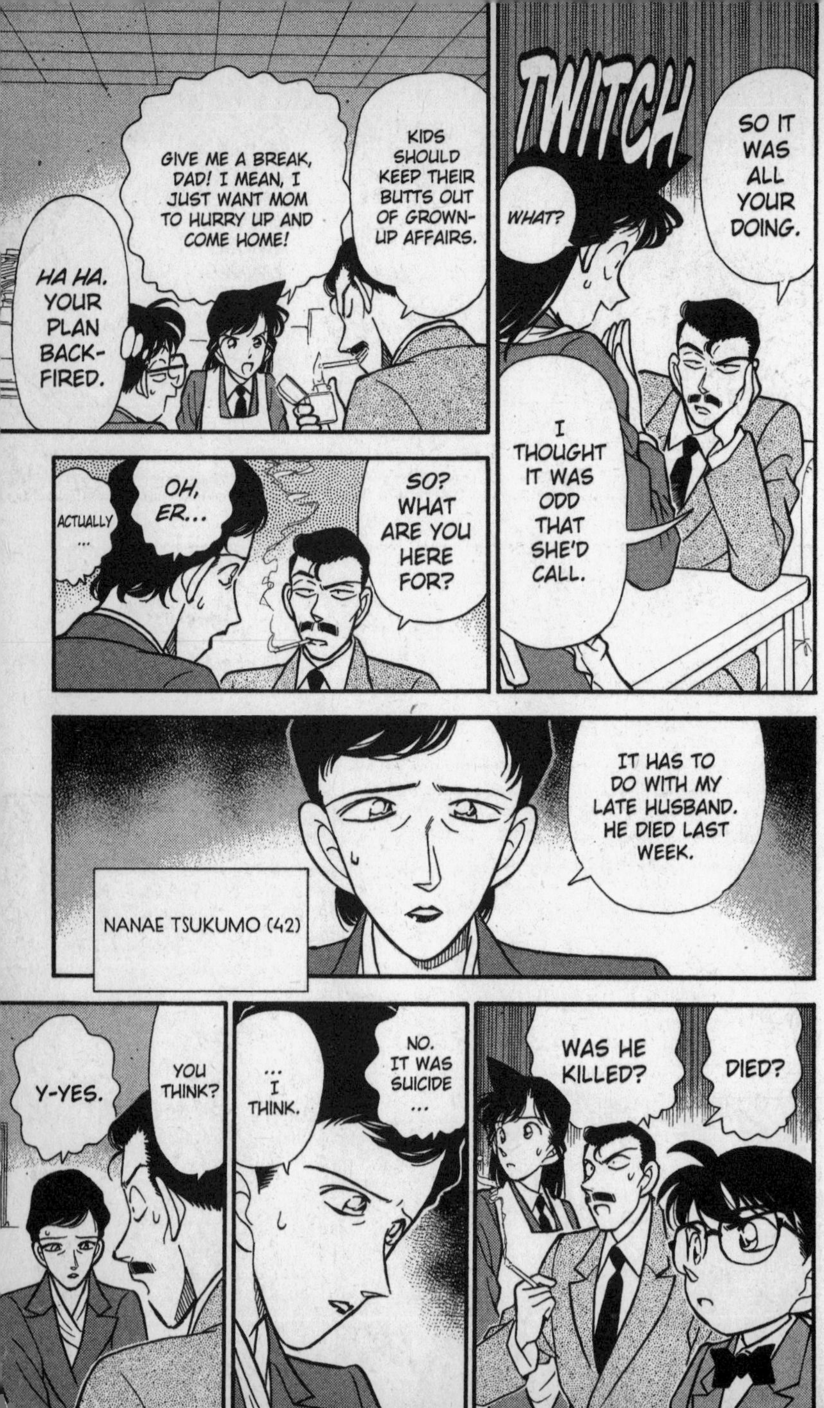
TWITCH
SO IT WAS ALL YOUR DOING.
WHAT?
I THOUGHT IT WAS ODD THAT SHE'D CALL.
KIDS SHOULD KEEP THEIR BUTTS OUT OF GROWN-UP AFFAIRS.
GIVE ME A BREAK, DAD! I MEAN, I JUST WANT MOM TO HURRY UP AND COME HOME!
HA HA. YOUR PLAN BACK-FIRED.
SO? WHAT ARE YOU HERE FOR?
OH, ER...
ACTUALLY ...
IT HAS TO DO WITH MY LATE HUSBAND. HE DIED LAST WEEK.
NANAE TSUKUMO (42)
DIED?
WAS HE KILLED?
NO. IT WAS SUICIDE ...
... I THINK.
YOU THINK?
Y-YES.

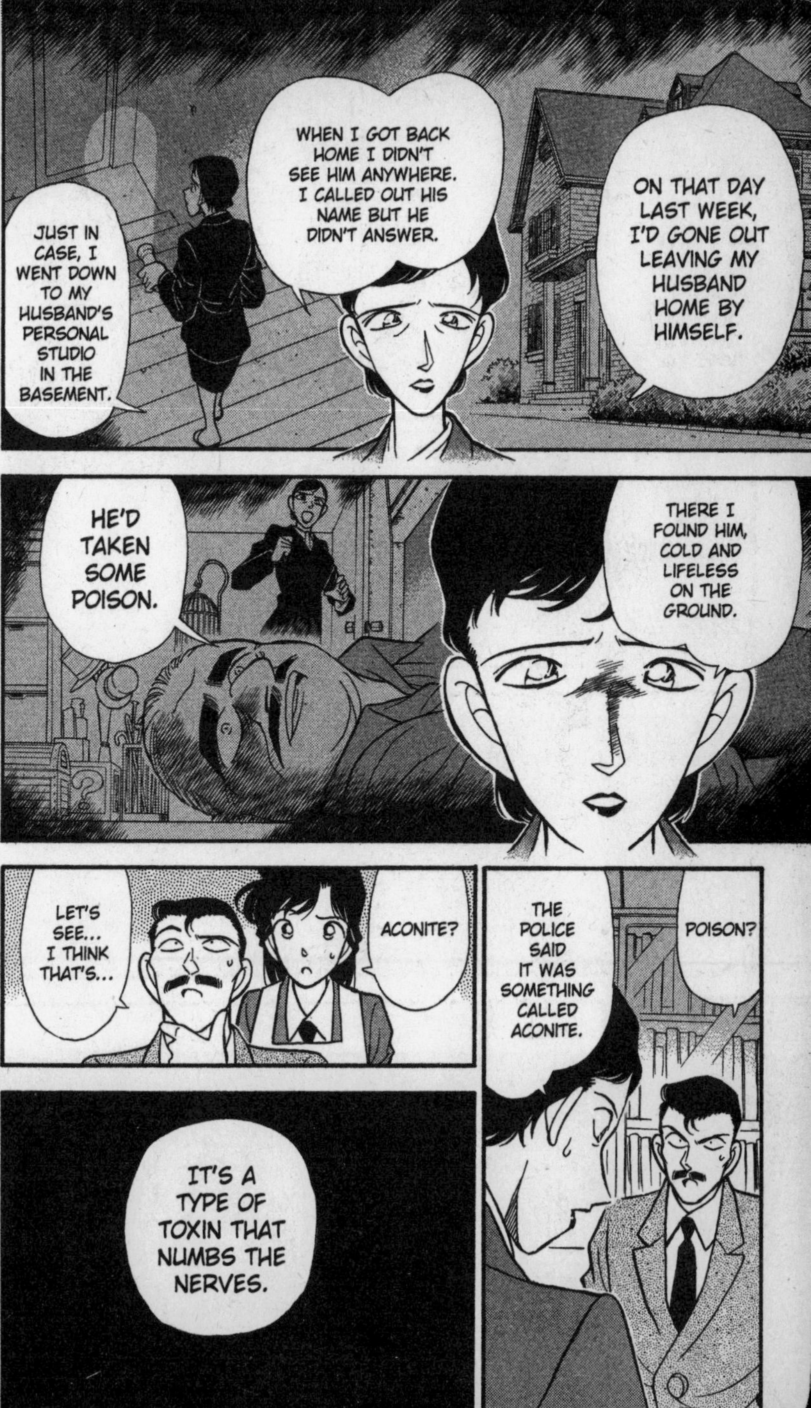
ON THAT DAY LAST WEEK, I'D GONE OUT LEAVING MY HUSBAND HOME BY HIMSELF.
WHEN I GOT BACK HOME I DIDN'T SEE HIM ANYWHERE. I CALLED OUT HIS NAME BUT HE DIDN'T ANSWER.
JUST IN CASE, I WENT DOWN TO MY HUSBAND'S PERSONAL STUDIO IN THE BASEMENT.
THERE I FOUND HIM, COLD AND LIFELESS ON THE GROUND.
HE'D TAKEN SOME POISON.
POISON?
THE POLICE SAID IT WAS SOMETHING CALLED ACONITE.
ACONITE?
LET'S SEE... I THINK THAT'S...
IT'S A TYPE OF TOXIN THAT NUMBS THE NERVES.

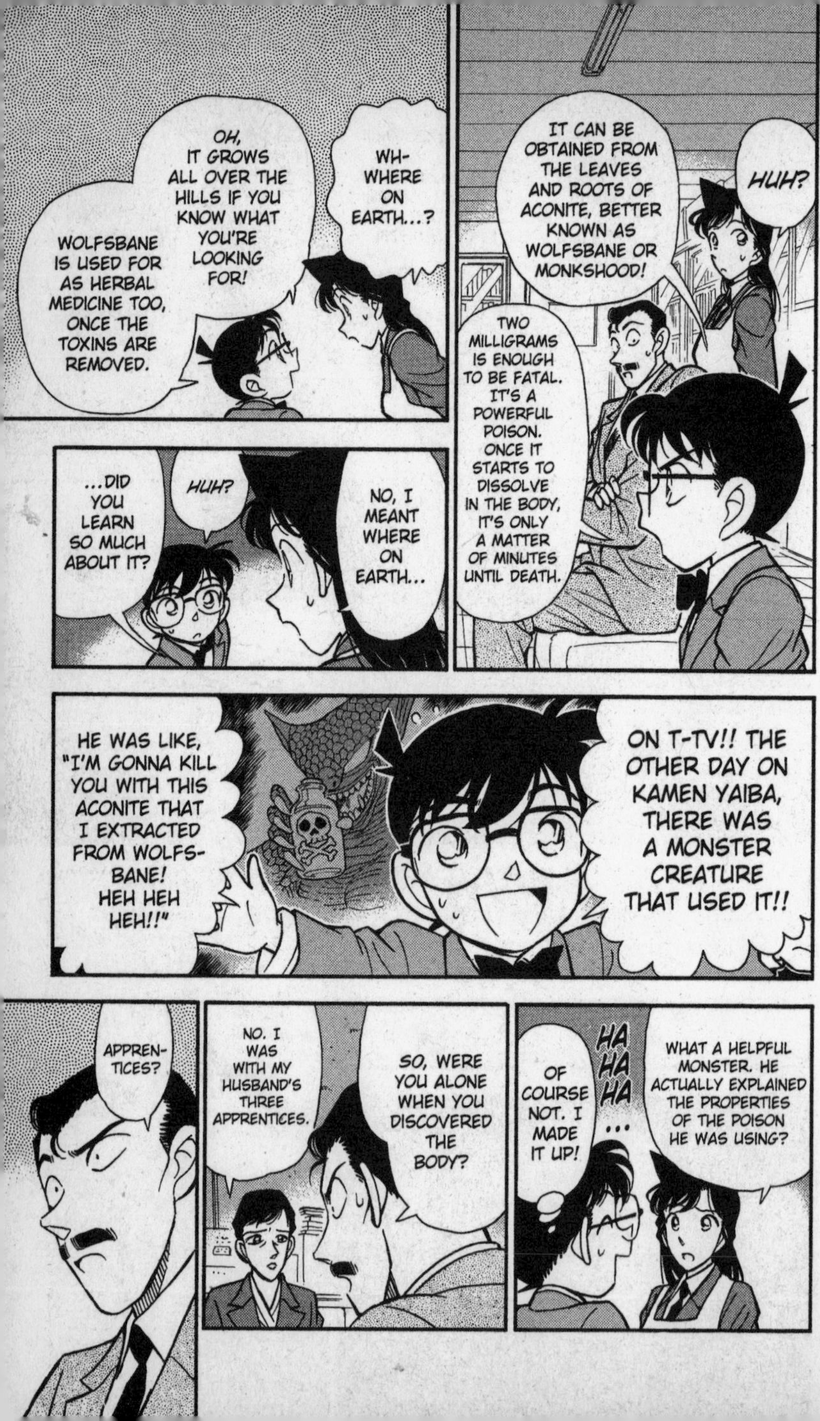
HUH?
IT CAN BE OBTAINED FROM THE LEAVES AND ROOTS OF ACONITE, BETTER KNOWN AS WOLFSBANE OR MONKSHOOD!
TWO MILLIGRAMS IS ENOUGH TO BE FATAL. IT'S A POWERFUL POISON. ONCE IT STARTS TO DISSOLVE IN THE BODY, IT'S ONLY A MATTER OF MINUTES UNTIL DEATH.
WH- WHERE ON EARTH...?
OH, IT GROWS ALL OVER THE HILLS IF YOU KNOW WHAT YOU'RE LOOKING FOR!
WOLFSBANE IS USED FOR AS HERBAL MEDICINE TOO, ONCE THE TOXINS ARE REMOVED.
NO, I MEANT WHERE ON EARTH...
HUH?
...DID YOU LEARN SO MUCH ABOUT IT?
ON T-TV!! THE OTHER DAY ON KAMEN YAIBA, THERE WAS A MONSTER CREATURE THAT USED IT!!
HE WAS LIKE, "I'M GONNA KILL YOU WITH THIS ACONITE THAT I EXTRACTED FROM WOLFS-BANE! HEH HEH HEH!!"
WHAT A HELPFUL MONSTER. HE ACTUALLY EXPLAINED THE PROPERTIES OF THE POISON HE WAS USING?
HA HA HA...
OF COURSE NOT. I MADE IT UP!
SO, WERE YOU ALONE WHEN YOU DISCOVERED THE BODY?
NO. I WAS WITH MY HUSBAND'S THREE APPRENTICES.
APPRENTI-CES?

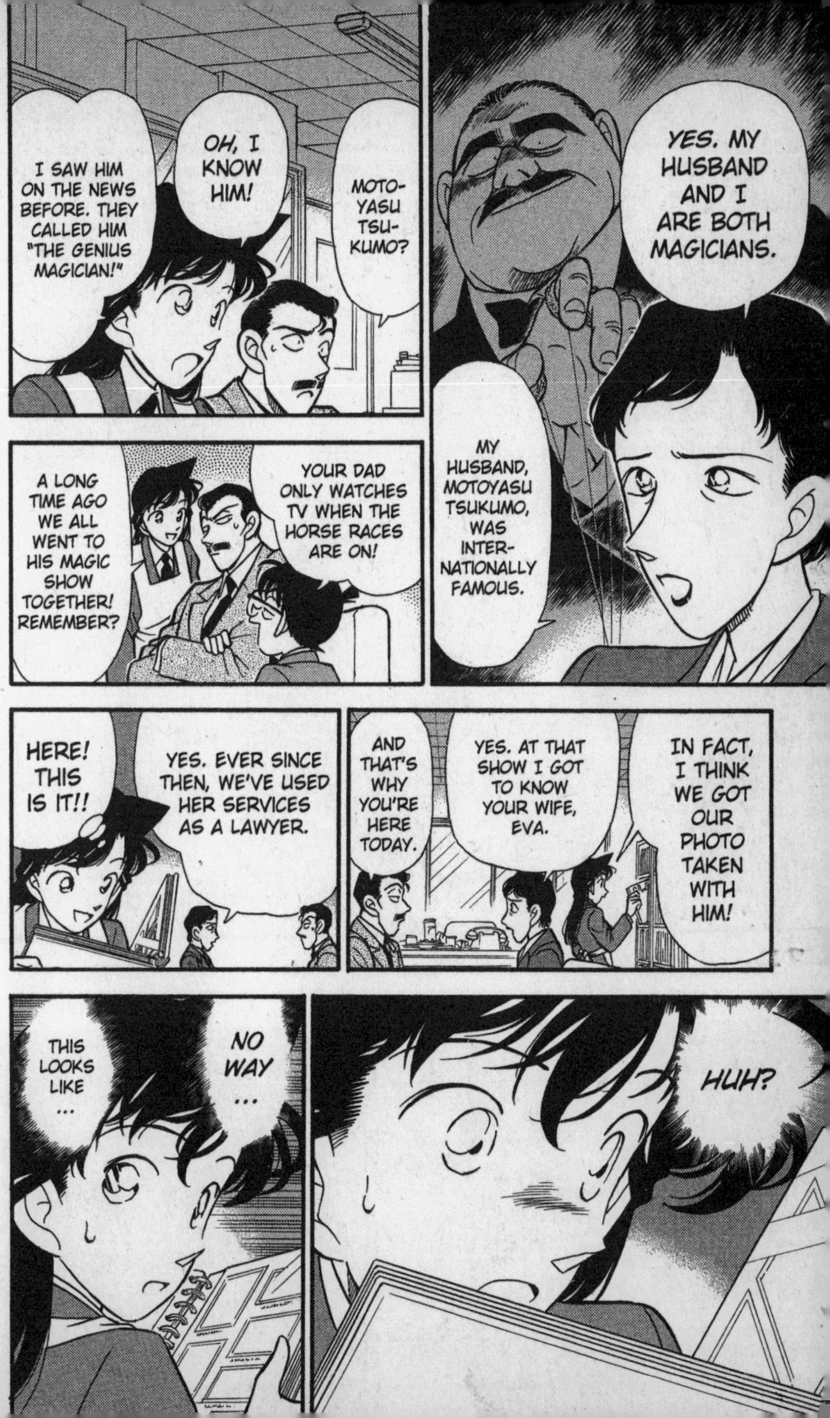
YES. MY HUSBAND AND I ARE BOTH MAGICIANS.
MY HUSBAND, MOTOYASU TSUKUMO, WAS INTER-NATIONALLY FAMOUS.
MOTO-YASU TSU-KUMO?
OH, I KNOW HIM!
I SAW HIM ON THE NEWS BEFORE. THEY CALLED HIM "THE GENIUS MAGICIAN!"
YOUR DAD ONLY WATCHES TV WHEN THE HORSE RACES ARE ON!
A LONG TIME AGO WE ALL WENT TO HIS MAGIC SHOW TOGETHER! REMEMBER?
IN FACT, I THINK WE GOT OUR PHOTO TAKEN WITH HIM!
YES. AT THAT SHOW I GOT TO KNOW YOUR WIFE, EVA.
AND THAT'S WHY YOU'RE HERE TODAY.
YES. EVER SINCE THEN, WE'VE USED HER SERVICES AS A LAWYER.
HERE! THIS IS IT!!
HUH?
NO WAY ...
THIS LOOKS LIKE ...

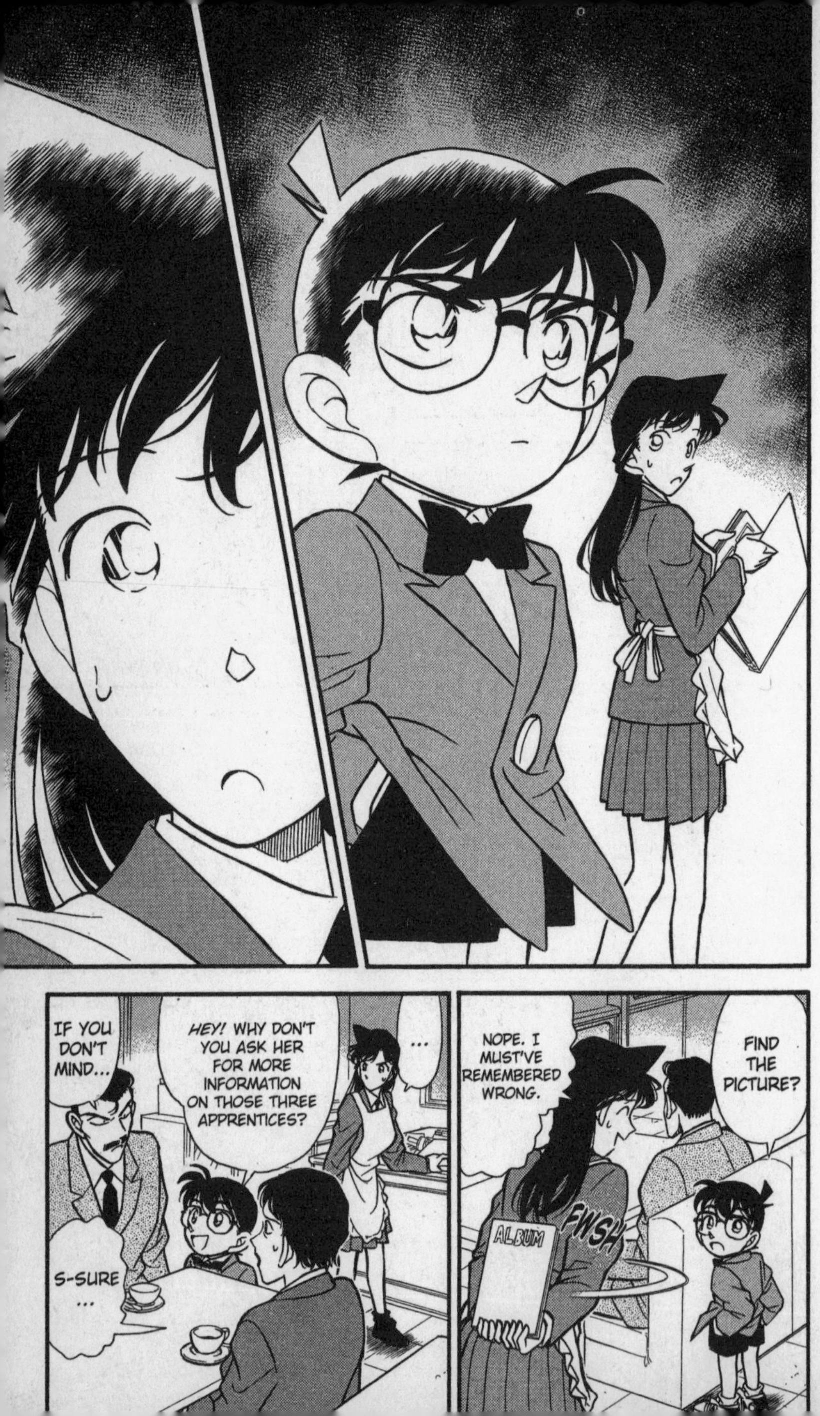
FIND THE PICTURE?
NOPE. I MUST'VE REMEMBERED WRONG.
FWSH
ALBUM
...
HEY! WHY DON'T YOU ASK HER FOR MORE INFORMATION ON THOSE THREE APPRENTICES?
IF YOU DON'T MIND...
S-SURE ...

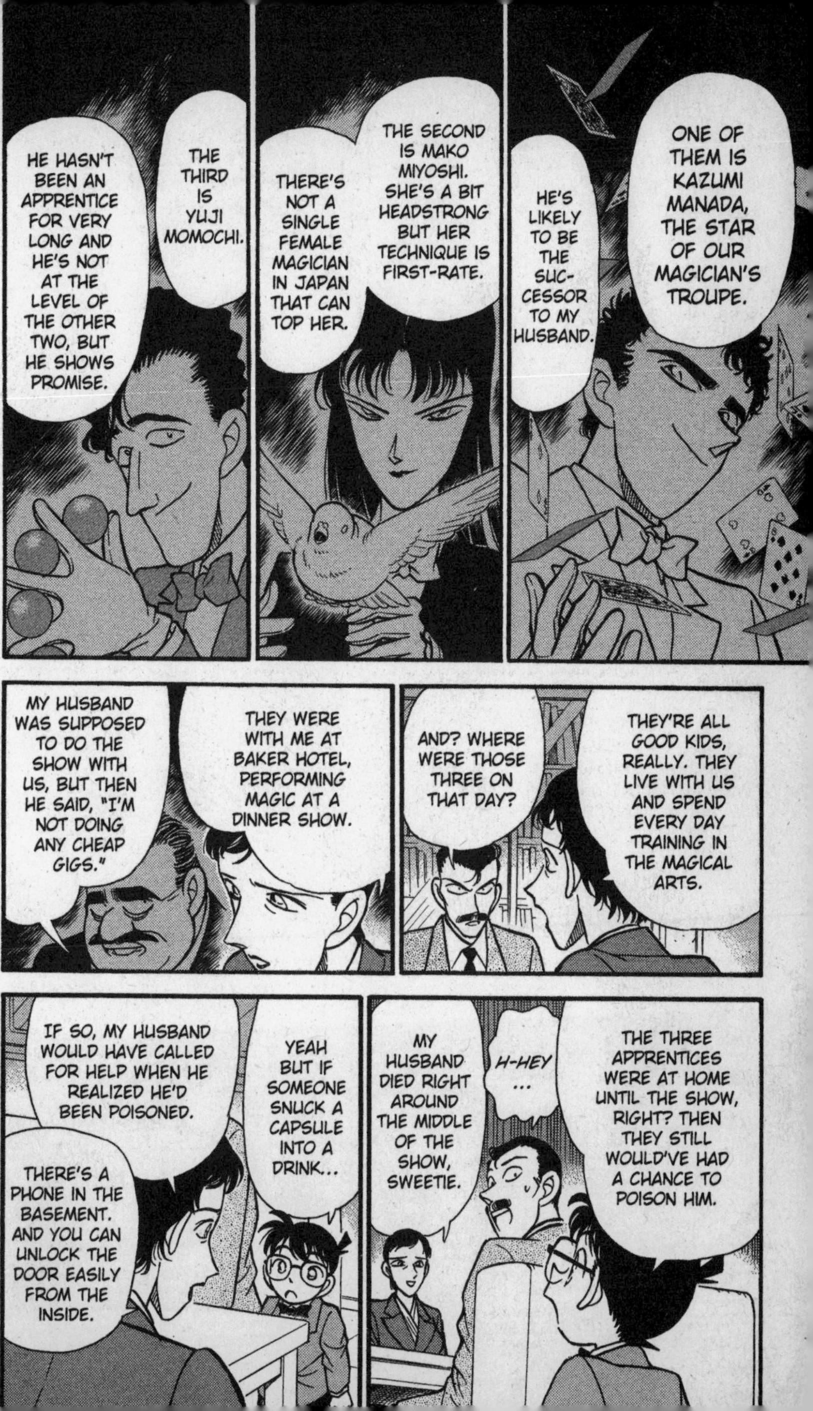
ONE OF THEM IS KAZUMI MANADA, THE STAR OF OUR MAGICIAN'S TROUPE.
HE'S LIKELY TO BE THE SUCCESSOR TO MY HUSBAND.
THE SECOND IS MAKO MIYOSHI. SHE'S A BIT HEADSTRONG BUT HER TECHNIQUE IS FIRST-RATE.
THERE'S NOT A SINGLE FEMALE MAGICIAN IN JAPAN THAT CAN TOP HER.
THE THIRD IS YUJI MOMOCHI.
HE HASN'T BEEN AN APPRENTICE FOR VERY LONG AND HE'S NOT AT THE LEVEL OF THE OTHER TWO, BUT HE SHOWS PROMISE.
THEY'RE ALL GOOD KIDS, REALLY. THEY LIVE WITH US AND SPEND EVERY DAY TRAINING IN THE MAGICAL ARTS.
AND? WHERE WERE THOSE THREE ON THAT DAY?
THEY WERE WITH ME AT BAKER HOTEL, PERFORMING MAGIC AT A DINNER SHOW.
MY HUSBAND WAS SUPPOSED TO DO THE SHOW WITH US, BUT THEN HE SAID, "I'M NOT DOING ANY CHEAP GIGS."
THE THREE APPRENTICES WERE AT HOME UNTIL THE SHOW, RIGHT? THEN THEY STILL WOULD'VE HAD A CHANCE TO POISON HIM.
H-HEY...
MY HUSBAND DIED RIGHT AROUND THE MIDDLE OF THE SHOW, SWEETIE.
YEAH BUT IF SOMEONE SNUCK A CAPSULE INTO A DRINK...
IF SO, MY HUSBAND WOULD HAVE CALLED FOR HELP WHEN HE REALIZED HE'D BEEN POISONED.
THERE'S A PHONE IN THE BASEMENT. AND YOU CAN UNLOCK THE DOOR EASILY FROM THE INSIDE.

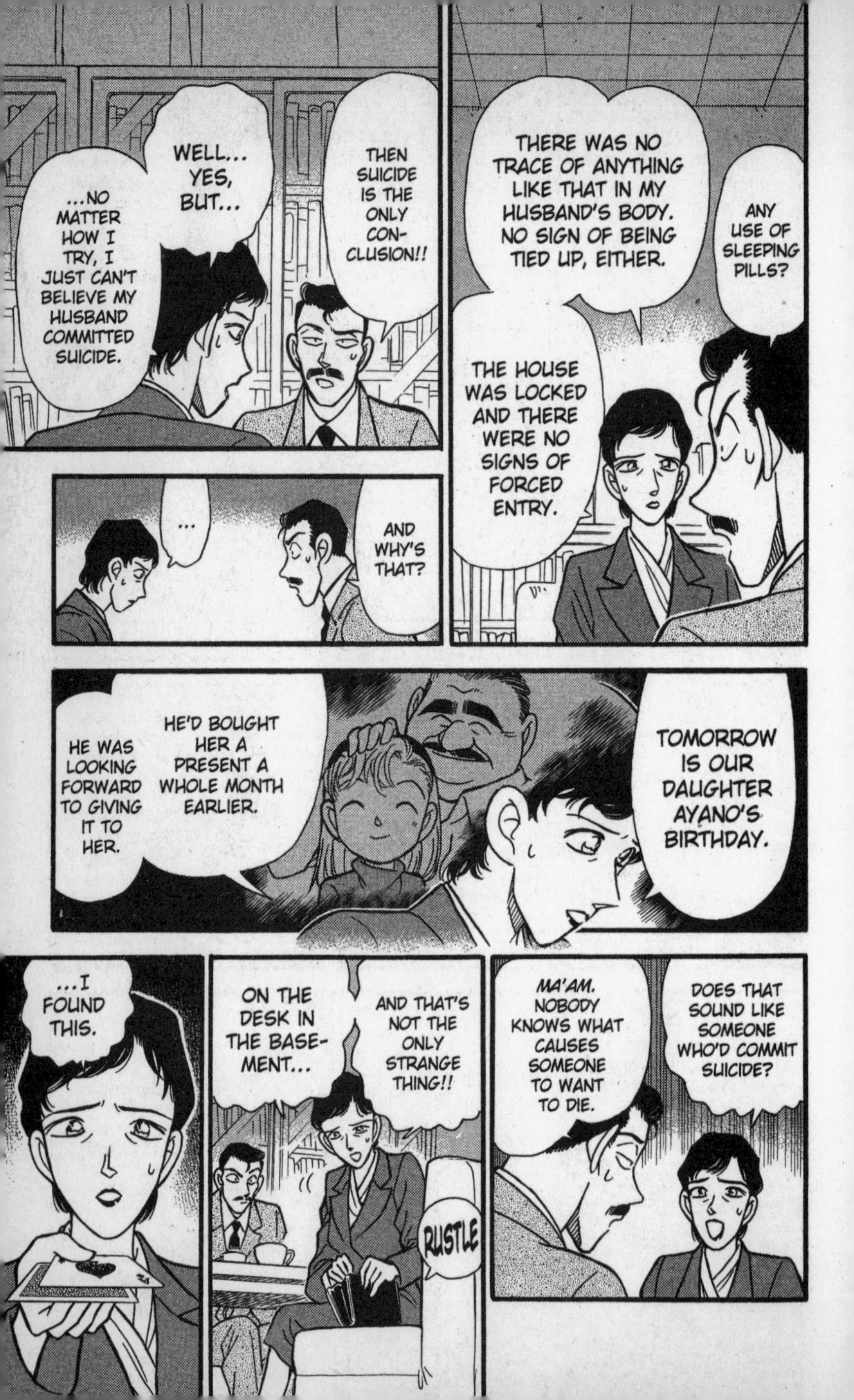
ANY USE OF SLEEPING PILLS?
THERE WAS NO TRACE OF ANYTHING LIKE THAT IN MY HUSBAND'S BODY. NO SIGN OF BEING TIED UP, EITHER.
THE HOUSE WAS LOCKED AND THERE WERE NO SIGNS OF FORCED ENTRY.
THEN SUICIDE IS THE ONLY CON-CLUSION!!
WELL... YES, BUT...
...NO MATTER HOW I TRY, I JUST CAN'T BELIEVE MY HUSBAND COMMITTED SUICIDE.
AND WHY'S THAT?
...
TOMORROW IS OUR DAUGHTER AYANO'S BIRTHDAY.
HE'D BOUGHT HER A PRESENT A WHOLE MONTH EARLIER.
HE WAS LOOKING FORWARD TO GIVING IT TO HER.
DOES THAT SOUND LIKE SOMEONE WHO'D COMMIT SUICIDE?
MA'AM. NOBODY KNOWS WHAT CAUSES SOMEONE TO WANT TO DIE.
AND THAT'S NOT THE ONLY STRANGE THING!!
ON THE DESK IN THE BASE-MENT...
RUSTLE
...I FOUND THIS.

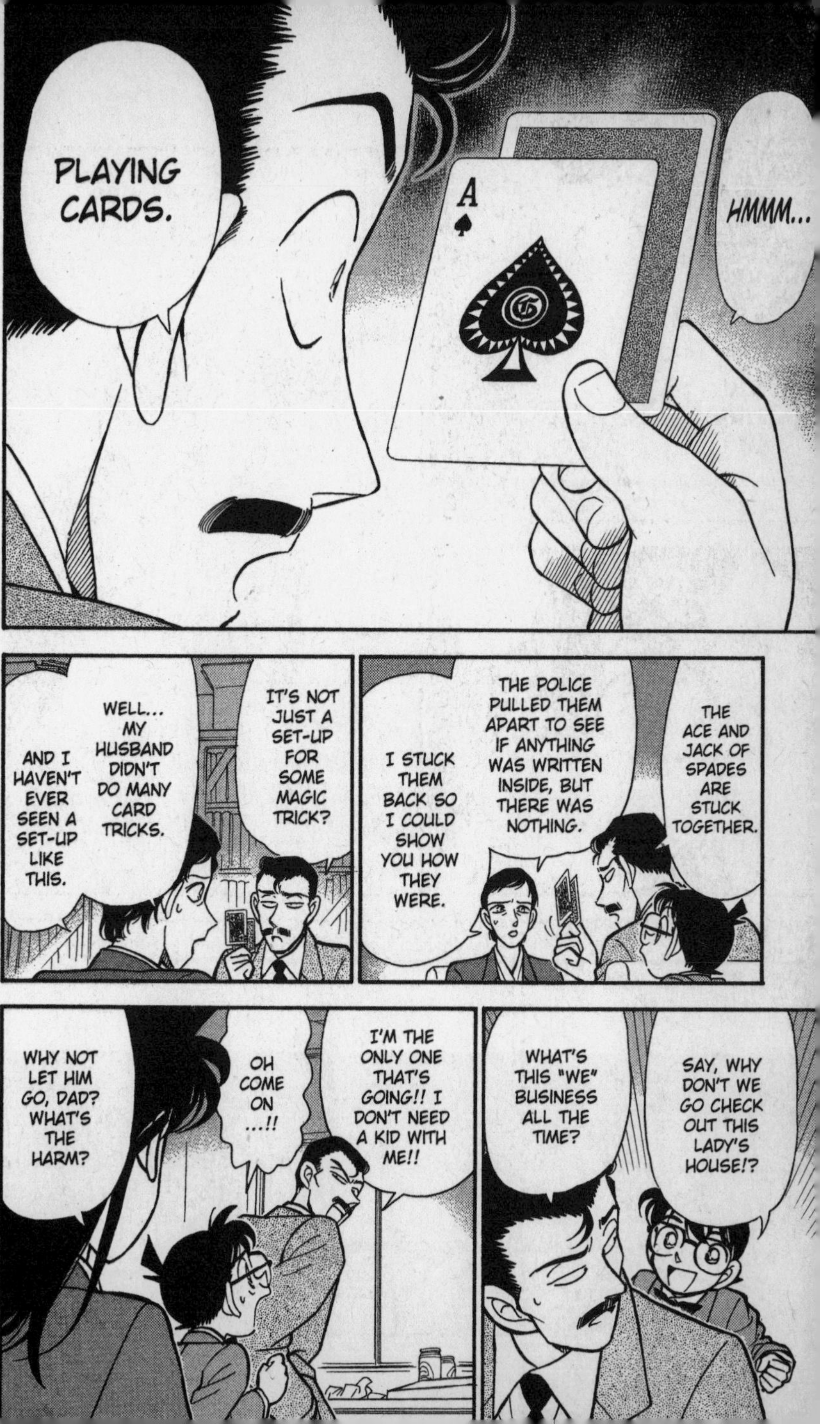
HMMM...
PLAYING CARDS.
THE ACE AND JACK OF SPADES ARE STUCK TOGETHER.
THE POLICE PULLED THEM APART TO SEE IF ANYTHING WAS WRITTEN INSIDE, BUT THERE WAS NOTHING.
I STUCK THEM BACK SO I COULD SHOW YOU HOW THEY WERE.
IT'S NOT JUST A SET-UP FOR SOME MAGIC TRICK?
WELL... MY HUSBAND DIDN'T DO MANY CARD TRICKS.
AND I HAVEN'T EVER SEEN A SET-UP LIKE THIS.
SAY, WHY DON'T WE GO CHECK OUT THIS LADY'S HOUSE!?
WHAT'S THIS "WE" BUSINESS ALL THE TIME?
I'M THE ONLY ONE THAT'S GOING!! I DON'T NEED A KID WITH ME!!
OH COME ON ...!!
WHY NOT LET HIM GO, DAD? WHAT'S THE HARM?

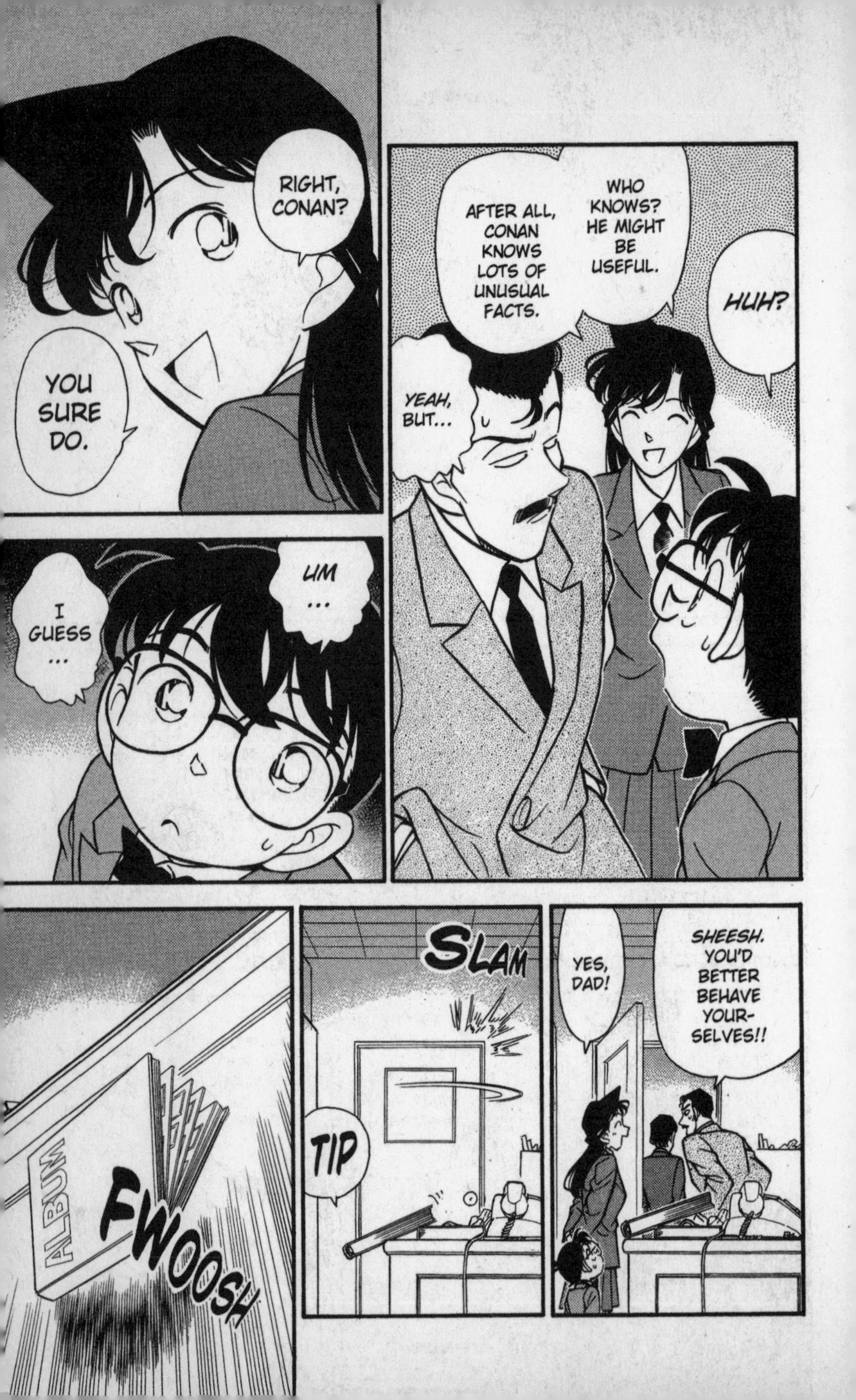
AFTER ALL, CONAN KNOWS LOTS OF UNUSUAL FACTS.
WHO KNOWS? HE MIGHT BE USEFUL.
HUH?
YEAH, BUT...
RIGHT, CONAN?
YOU SURE DO.
UM ...
I GUESS ...
SHEESH. YOU'D BETTER BEHAVE YOUR-SELVES!!
YES, DAD!
SLAM
TIP
ALBUM
FWOOSH

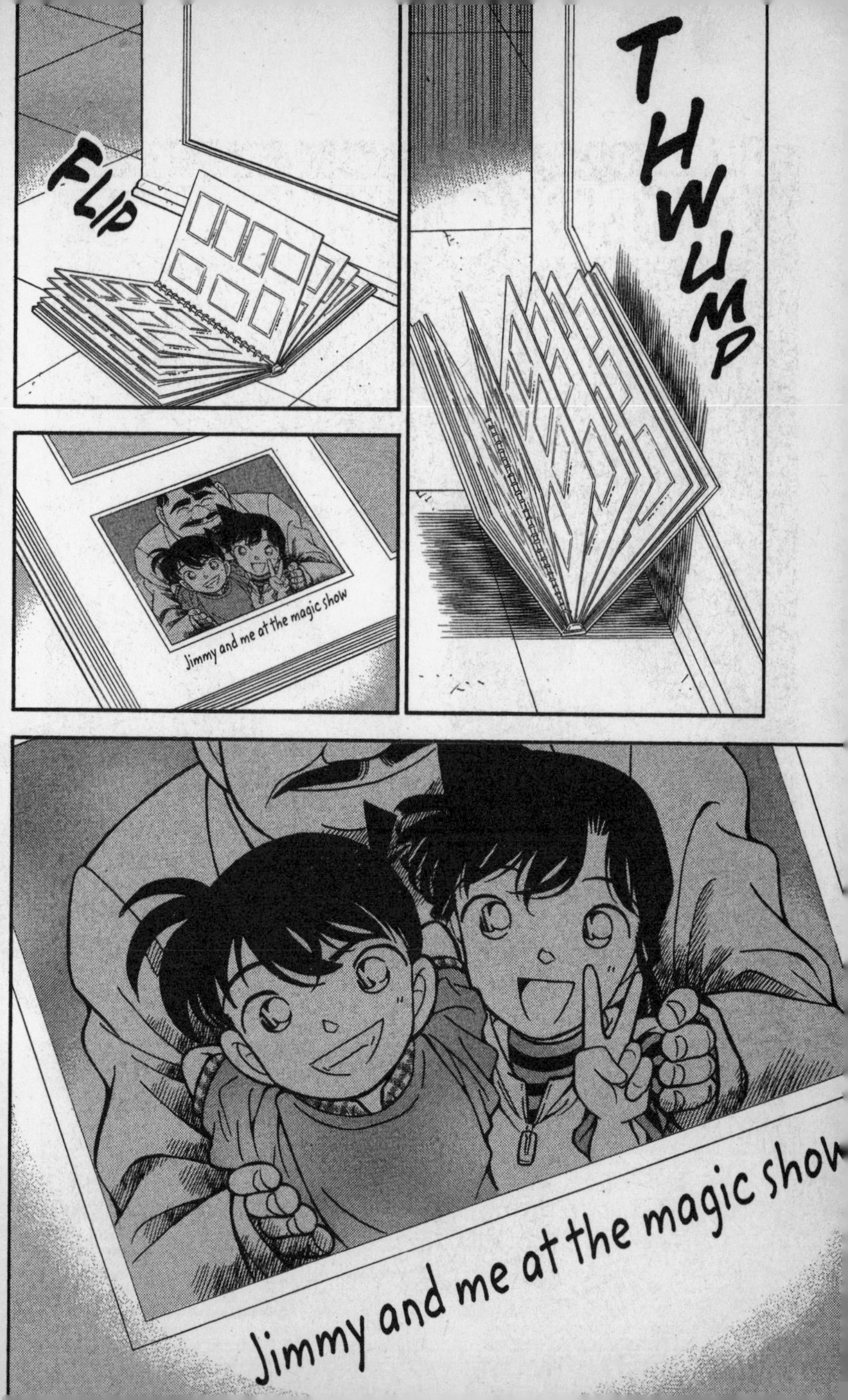
THWUMP
FLIP
Jimmy and me at the magic show
Jimmy and me at the magic show

FILE 2: NUMBERS ON THE PHONE

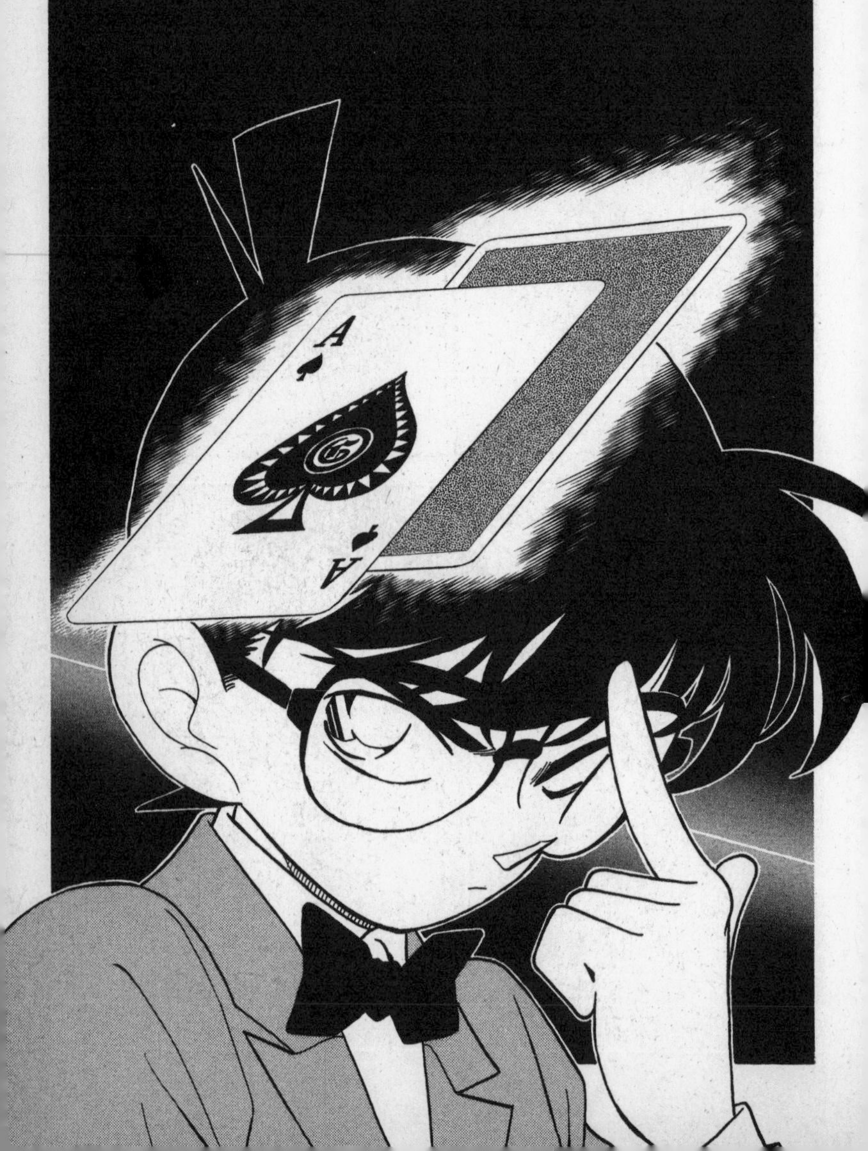

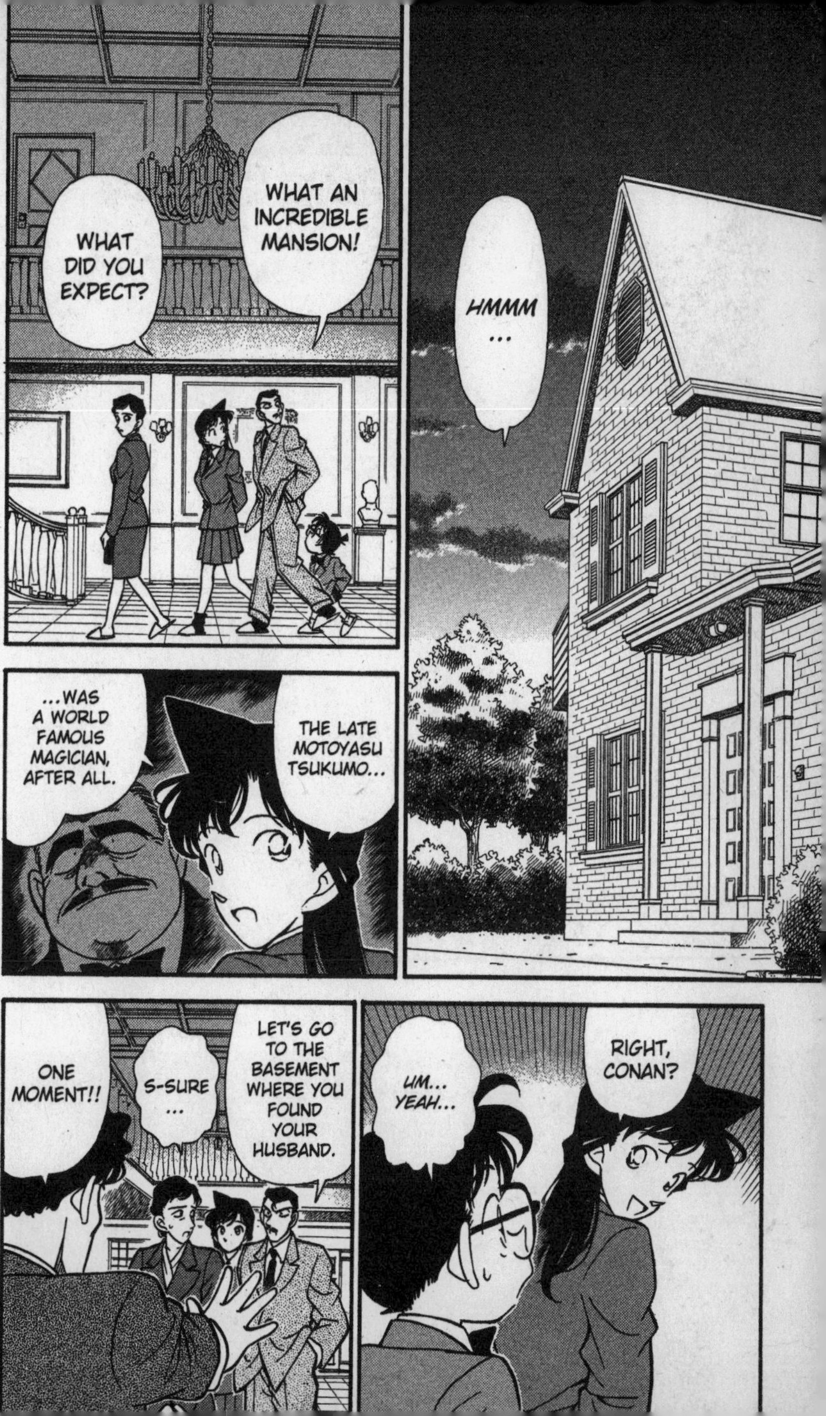
HMMM...
WHAT AN INCREDIBLE MANSION!
WHAT DID YOU EXPECT?
THE LATE MOTOYASU TSUKUMO...
...WAS A WORLD FAMOUS MAGICIAN, AFTER ALL.
RIGHT, CONAN?
UM... YEAH...
LET'S GO TO THE BASEMENT WHERE YOU FOUND YOUR HUSBAND.
S-SURE...
ONE MOMENT!!

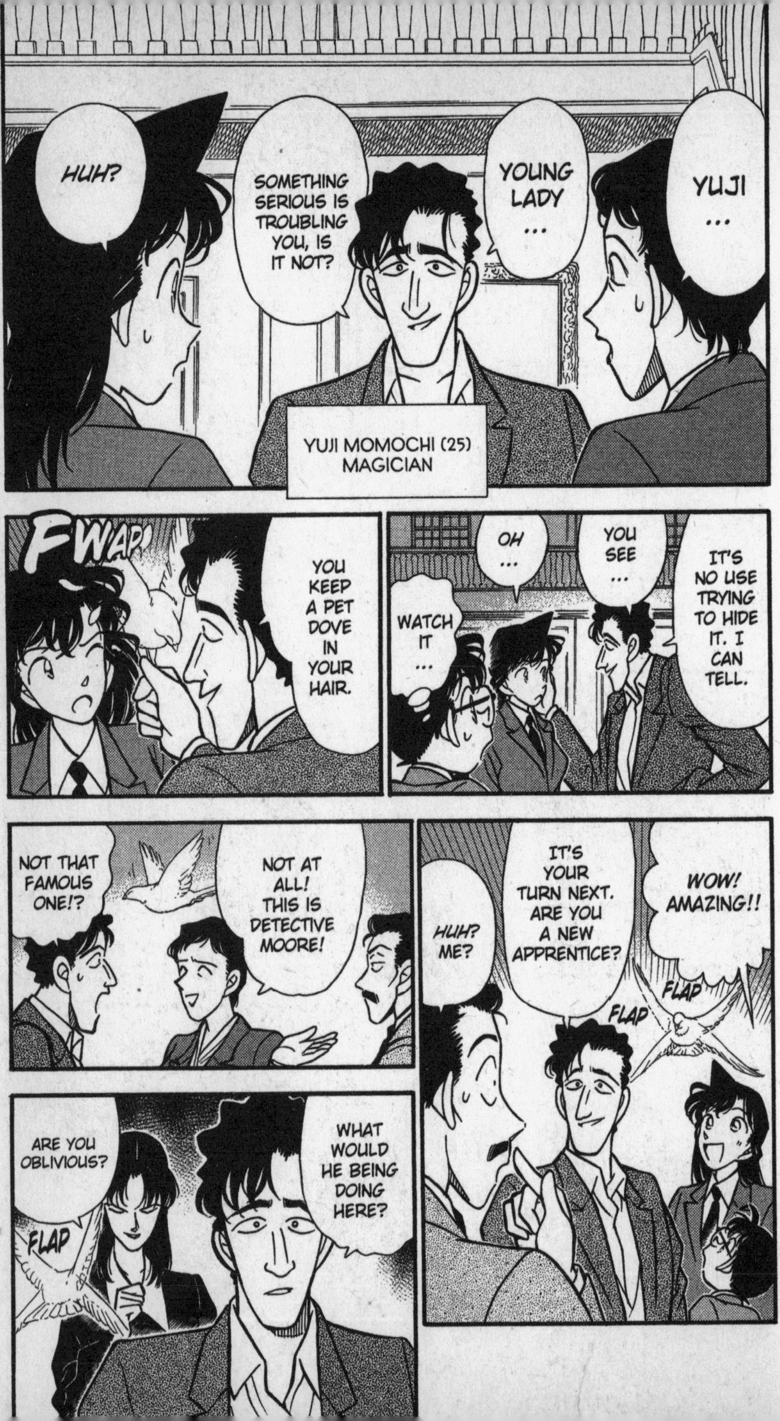
YUJI ...
YOUNG LADY ...
SOMETHING SERIOUS IS TROUBLING YOU, IS IT NOT?
HUH?
YUJI MOMOCHI (25) MAGICIAN
IT'S NO USE TRYING TO HIDE IT. I CAN TELL.
YOU SEE ...
OH ...
WATCH IT ...
FWAP
YOU KEEP A PET DOVE IN YOUR HAIR.
WOW! AMAZING!!
IT'S YOUR TURN NEXT. ARE YOU A NEW APPRENTICE?
HUH? ME?
FLAP
FLAP
NOT AT ALL! THIS IS DETECTIVE MOORE!
NOT THAT FAMOUS ONE!?
WHAT WOULD HE BEING DOING HERE?
ARE YOU OBLIVIOUS?
FLAP

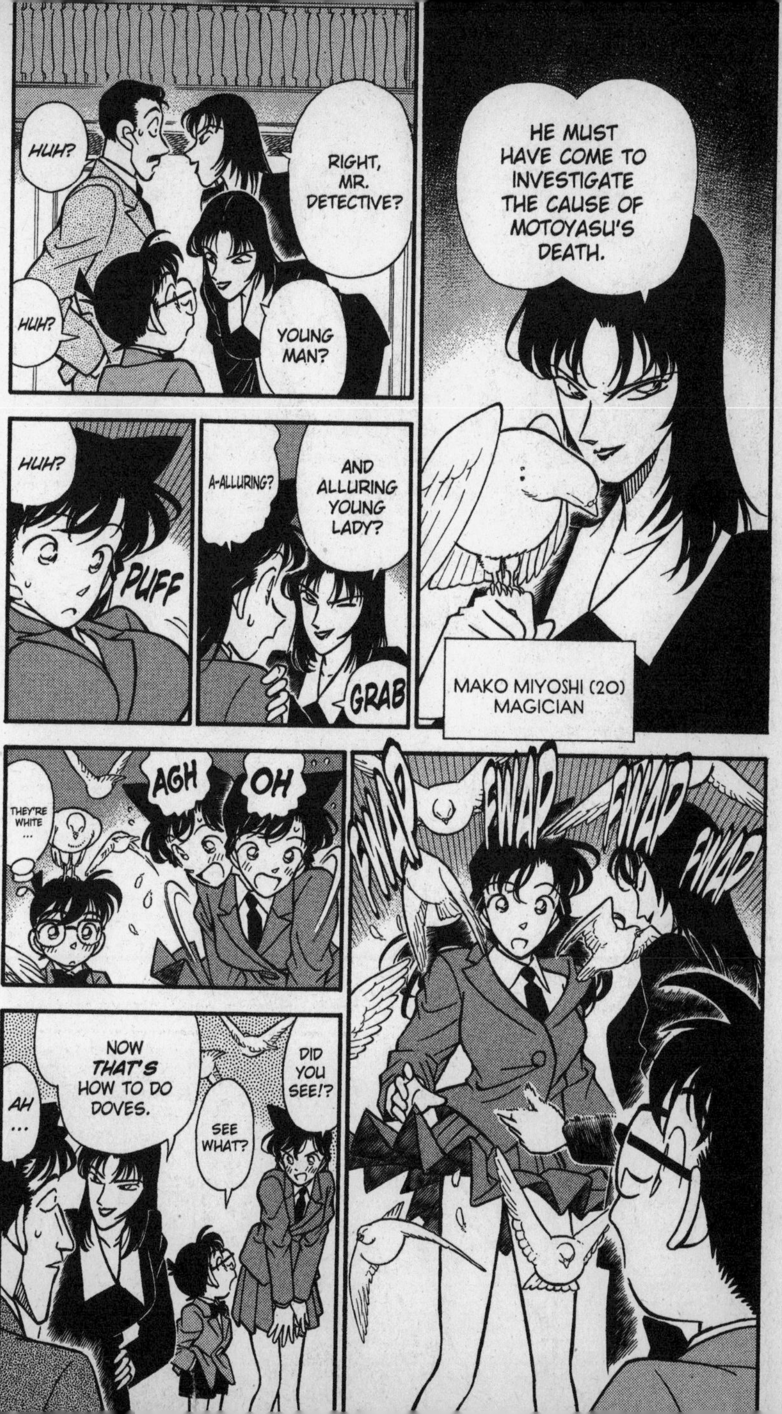
HE MUST HAVE COME TO INVESTIGATE THE CAUSE OF MOTOYASU'S DEATH.
MAKO MIYOSHI (20) MAGICIAN
RIGHT, MR. DETECTIVE?
HUH?
YOUNG MAN?
HUH?
AND ALLURING YOUNG LADY?
A-ALLURING?
GRAB
HUH?
PUFF
FWAP
FWAP
FWAP
FWAP
OH
AGH
THEY'RE WHITE ...
DID YOU SEE!?
NOW THAT'S HOW TO DO DOVES.
SEE WHAT?
AH ...

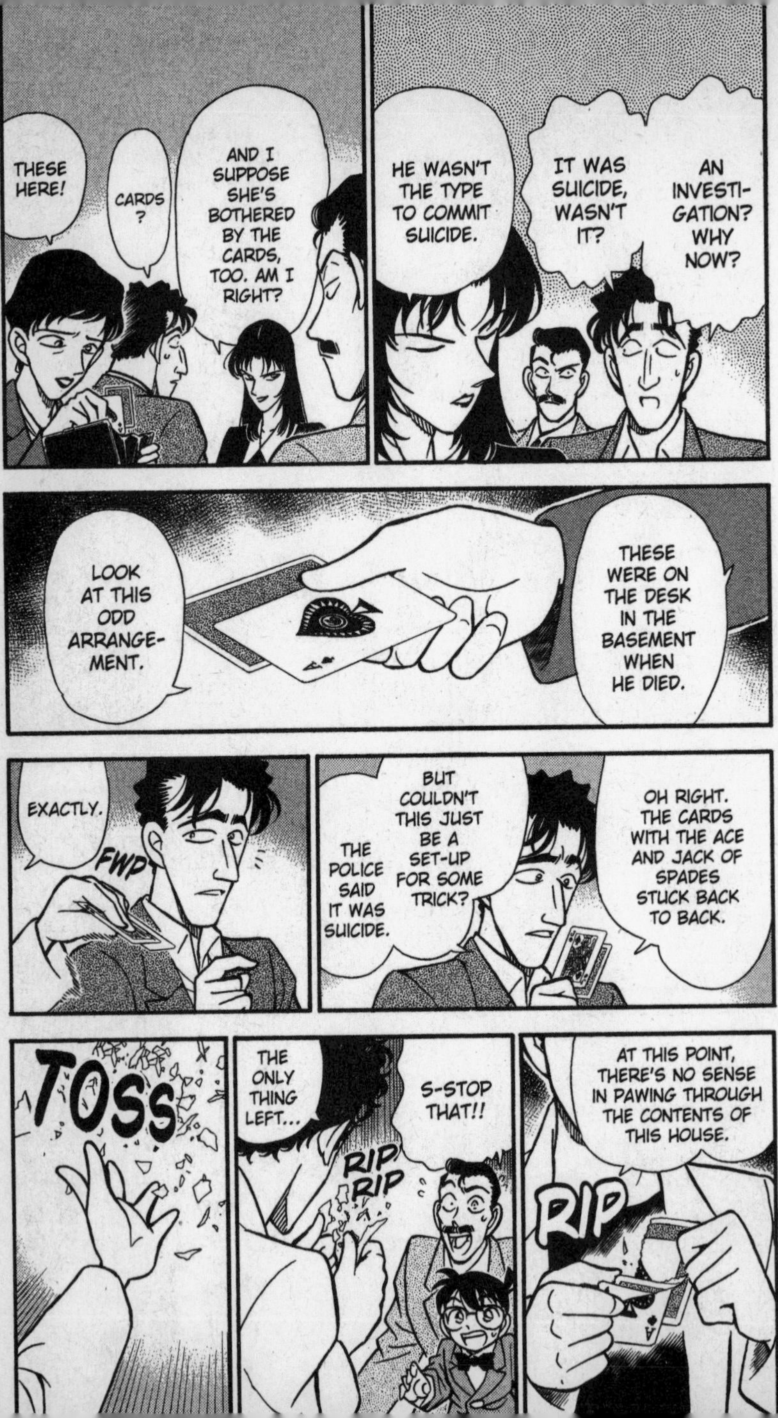
AN INVESTIGATION? WHY NOW?
IT WAS SUICIDE, WASN'T IT?
HE WASN'T THE TYPE TO COMMIT SUICIDE.
AND I SUPPOSE SHE'S BOTHERED BY THE CARDS, TOO. AM I RIGHT?
CARDS?
THESE HERE!
THESE WERE ON THE DESK IN THE BASEMENT WHEN HE DIED.
LOOK AT THIS ODD ARRANGE-MENT.
OH RIGHT. THE CARDS WITH THE ACE AND JACK OF SPADES STUCK BACK TO BACK.
BUT COULDN'T THIS JUST BE A SET-UP FOR SOME TRICK?
THE POLICE SAID IT WAS SUICIDE.
EXACTLY.
FWP
AT THIS POINT, THERE'S NO SENSE IN PAWING THROUGH THE CONTENTS OF THIS HOUSE.
RIP
S-STOP THAT!!
THE ONLY THING LEFT...
RIP RIP
TOSS

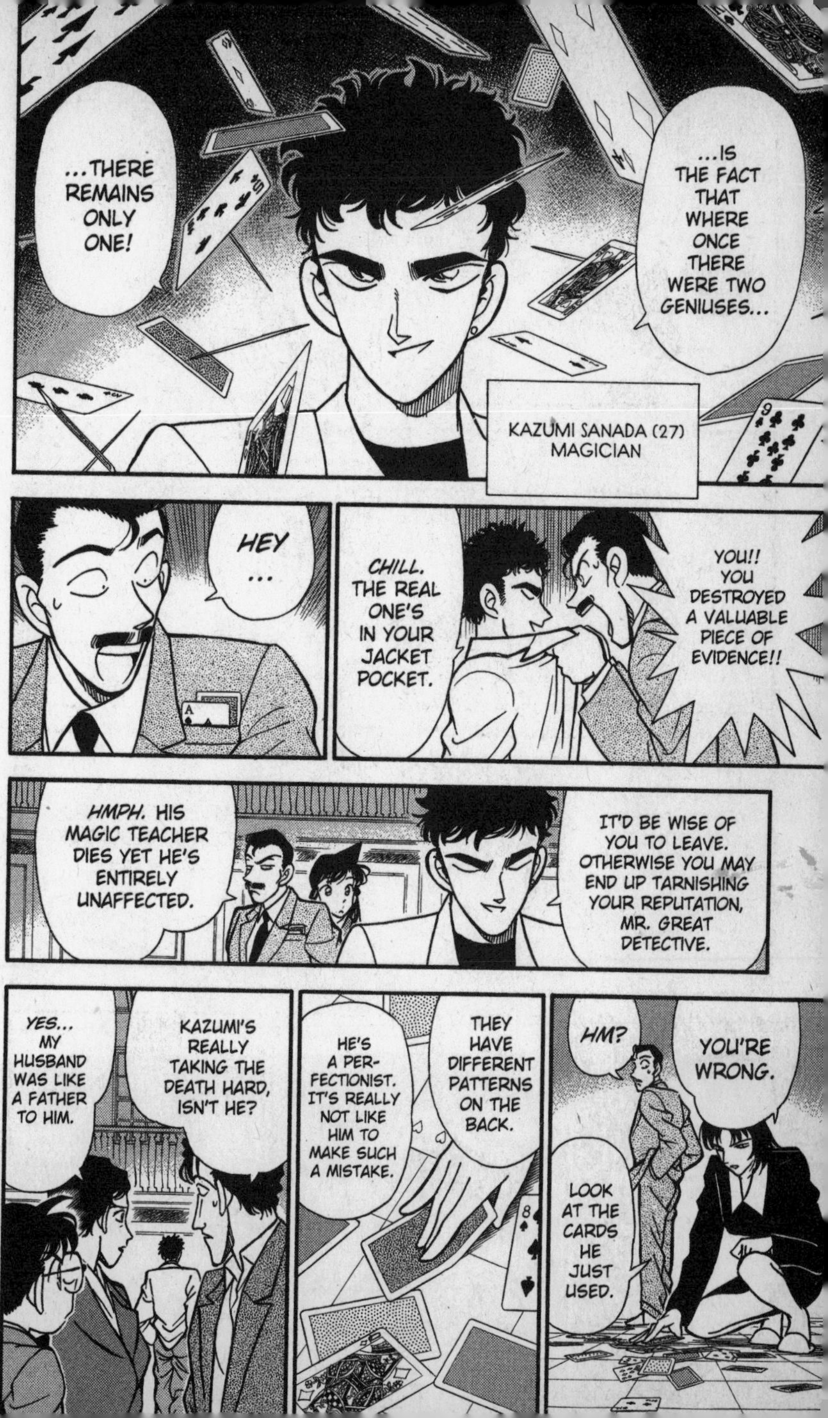
...IS THE FACT THAT WHERE ONCE THERE WERE TWO GENIUSES...
...THERE REMAINS ONLY ONE!
KAZUMI SANADA (27) MAGICIAN
YOU!! YOU DESTROYED A VALUABLE PIECE OF EVIDENCE!!
CHILL. THE REAL ONE'S IN YOUR JACKET POCKET.
HEY ...
IT'D BE WISE OF YOU TO LEAVE. OTHERWISE YOU MAY END UP TARNISHING YOUR REPUTATION, MR. GREAT DETECTIVE.
HMPH. HIS MAGIC TEACHER DIES YET HE'S ENTIRELY UNAFFECTED.
YOU'RE WRONG.
HM?
LOOK AT THE CARDS HE JUST USED.
THEY HAVE DIFFERENT PATTERNS ON THE BACK.
HE'S A PERFECTIONIST. IT'S REALLY NOT LIKE HIM TO MAKE SUCH A MISTAKE.
KAZUMI'S REALLY TAKING THE DEATH HARD, ISN'T HE?
YES... MY HUSBAND WAS LIKE A FATHER TO HIM.

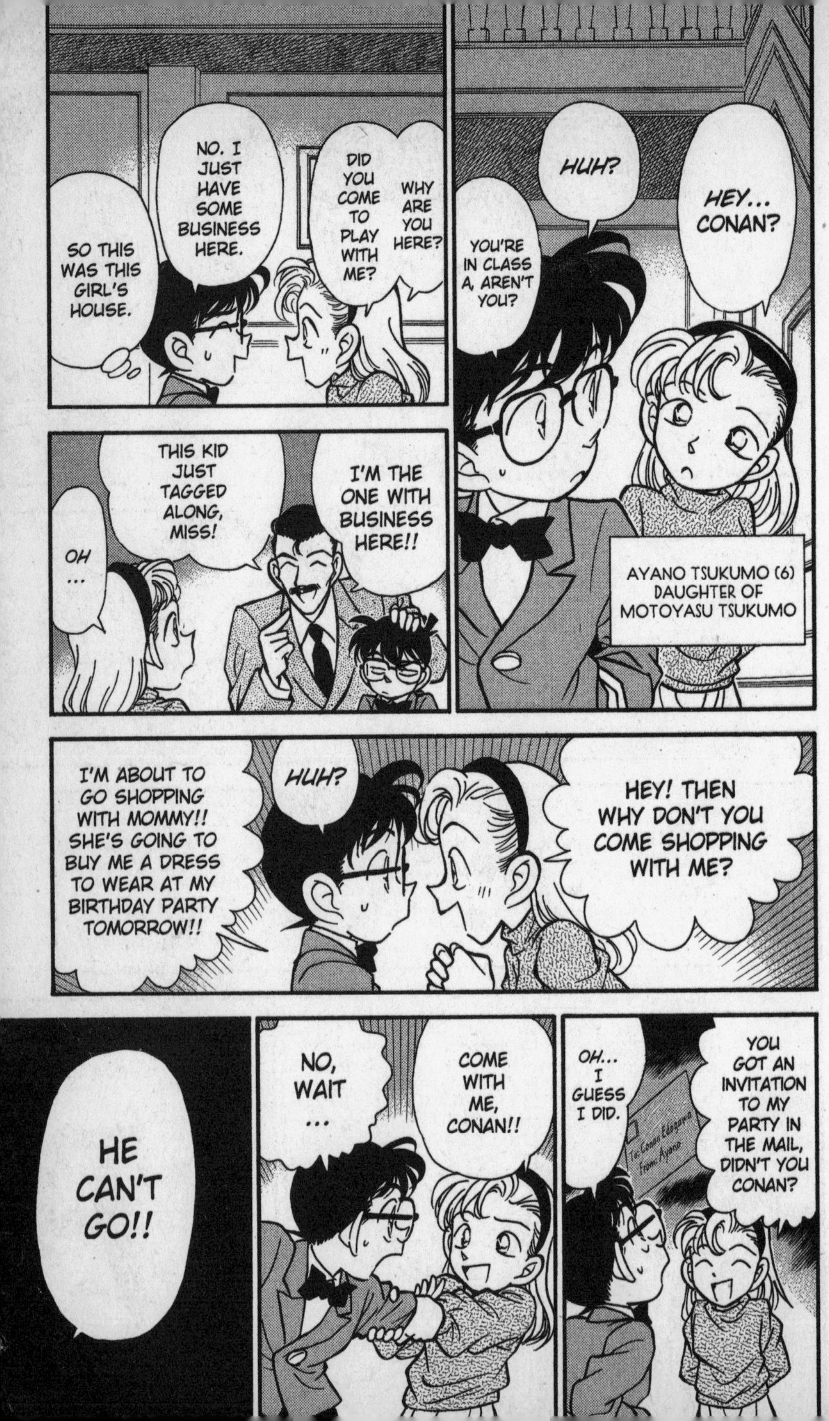
HEY... CONAN?
HUH?
YOU'RE IN CLASS A, AREN'T YOU?
AYANO TSUKUMO (6) DAUGHTER OF MOTOYASU TSUKUMO
WHY ARE YOU HERE?
DID YOU COME TO PLAY WITH ME?
NO. I JUST HAVE SOME BUSINESS HERE.
SO THIS WAS THIS GIRL'S HOUSE.
I'M THE ONE WITH BUSINESS HERE!!
THIS KID JUST TAGGED ALONG, MISS!
OH ...
HEY! THEN WHY DON'T YOU COME SHOPPING WITH ME?
HUH?
I'M ABOUT TO GO SHOPPING WITH MOMMY!! SHE'S GOING TO BUY ME A DRESS TO WEAR AT MY BIRTHDAY PARTY TOMORROW!!
YOU GOT AN INVITATION TO MY PARTY IN THE MAIL, DIDN'T YOU CONAN?
OH... I GUESS I DID.
To: Conan Edogawa From: Ayano
COME WITH ME, CONAN!!
NO, WAIT ...
HE CAN'T GO!!

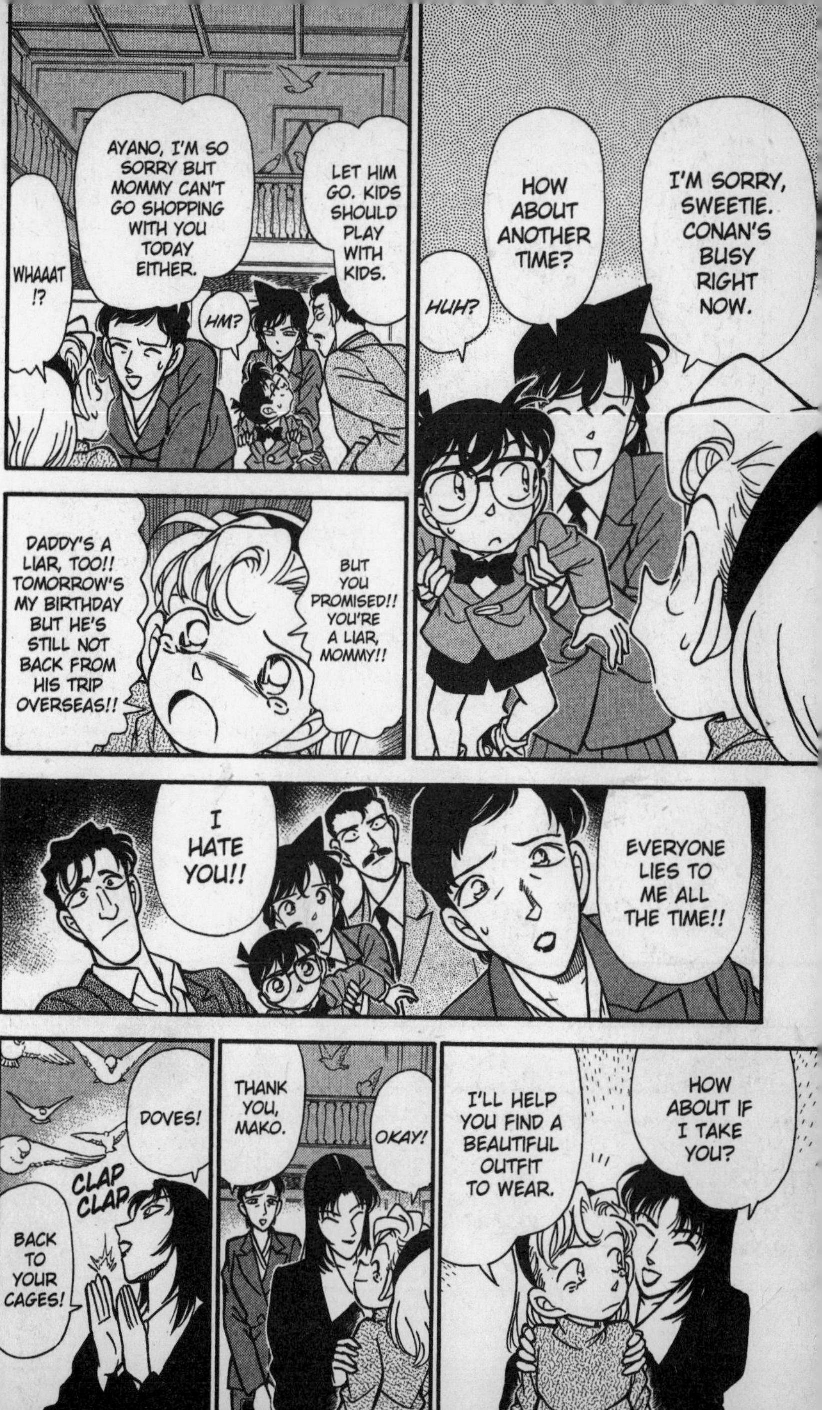
I'M SORRY, SWEETIE. CONAN'S BUSY RIGHT NOW.
HOW ABOUT ANOTHER TIME?
HUH?
LET HIM GO. KIDS SHOULD PLAY WITH KIDS.
AYANO, I'M SO SORRY BUT MOMMY CAN'T GO SHOPPING WITH YOU TODAY EITHER.
HM?
WHAAAT!?
BUT YOU PROMISED!! YOU'RE A LIAR, MOMMY!!
DADDY'S A LIAR, TOO!! TOMORROW'S MY BIRTHDAY BUT HE'S STILL NOT BACK FROM HIS TRIP OVERSEAS!!
EVERYONE LIES TO ME ALL THE TIME!!
I HATE YOU!!
HOW ABOUT IF I TAKE YOU?
I'LL HELP YOU FIND A BEAUTIFUL OUTFIT TO WEAR.
OKAY!
THANK YOU, MAKO.
DOVES!
CLAP CLAP
BACK TO YOUR CAGES!

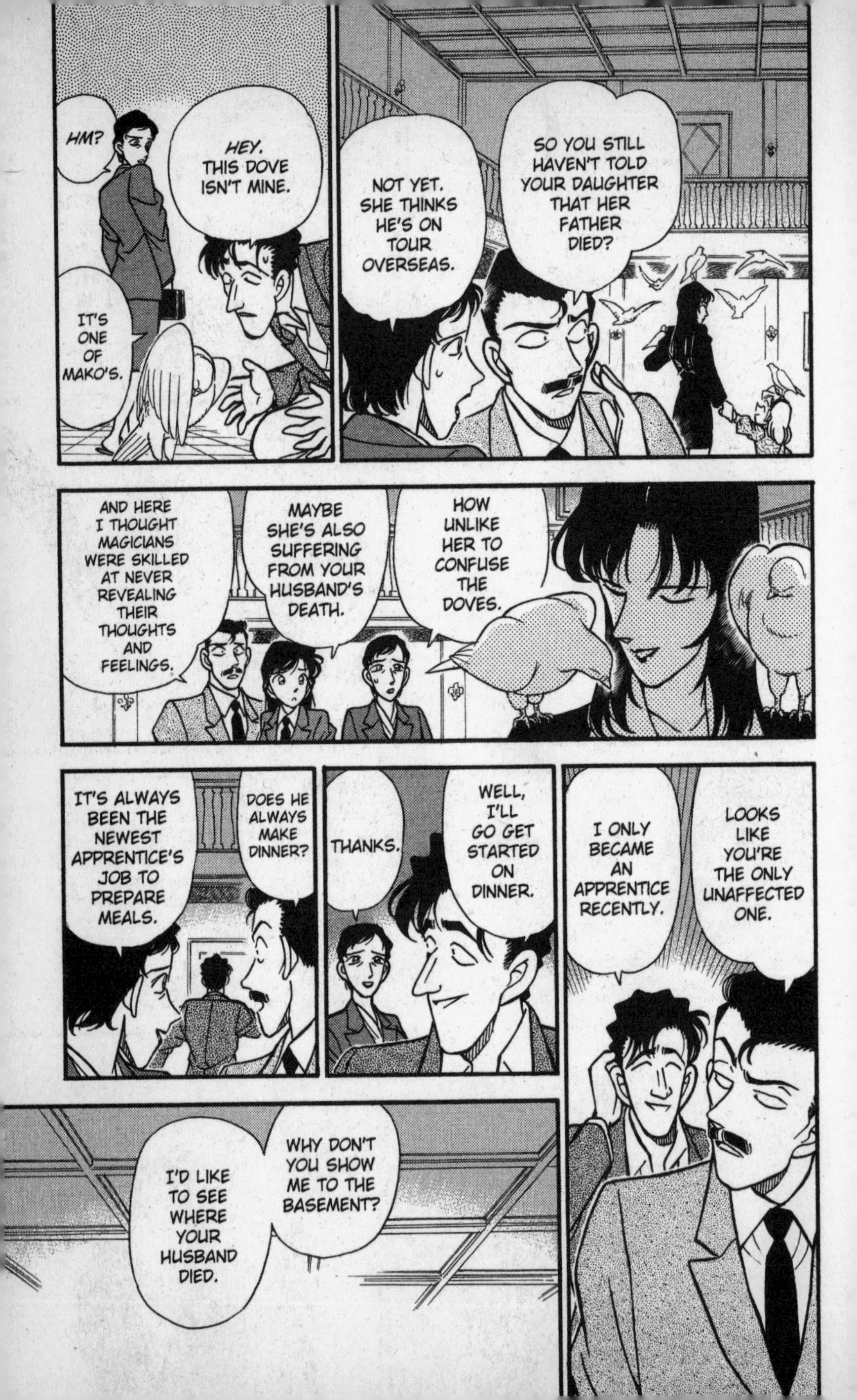
SO YOU STILL HAVEN'T TOLD YOUR DAUGHTER THAT HER FATHER DIED?
NOT YET. SHE THINKS HE'S ON TOUR OVERSEAS.
HEY. THIS DOVE ISN'T MINE.
HM?
IT'S ONE OF MAKO'S.
HOW UNLIKE HER TO CONFUSE THE DOVES.
MAYBE SHE'S ALSO SUFFERING FROM YOUR HUSBAND'S DEATH.
AND HERE I THOUGHT MAGICIANS WERE SKILLED AT NEVER REVEALING THEIR THOUGHTS AND FEELINGS.
LOOKS LIKE YOU'RE THE ONLY UNAFFECTED ONE.
I ONLY BECAME AN APPRENTICE RECENTLY.
WELL, I'LL GO GET STARTED ON DINNER.
THANKS.
DOES HE ALWAYS MAKE DINNER?
IT'S ALWAYS BEEN THE NEWEST APPRENTICE'S JOB TO PREPARE MEALS.
WHY DON'T YOU SHOW ME TO THE BASEMENT?
I'D LIKE TO SEE WHERE YOUR HUSBAND DIED.

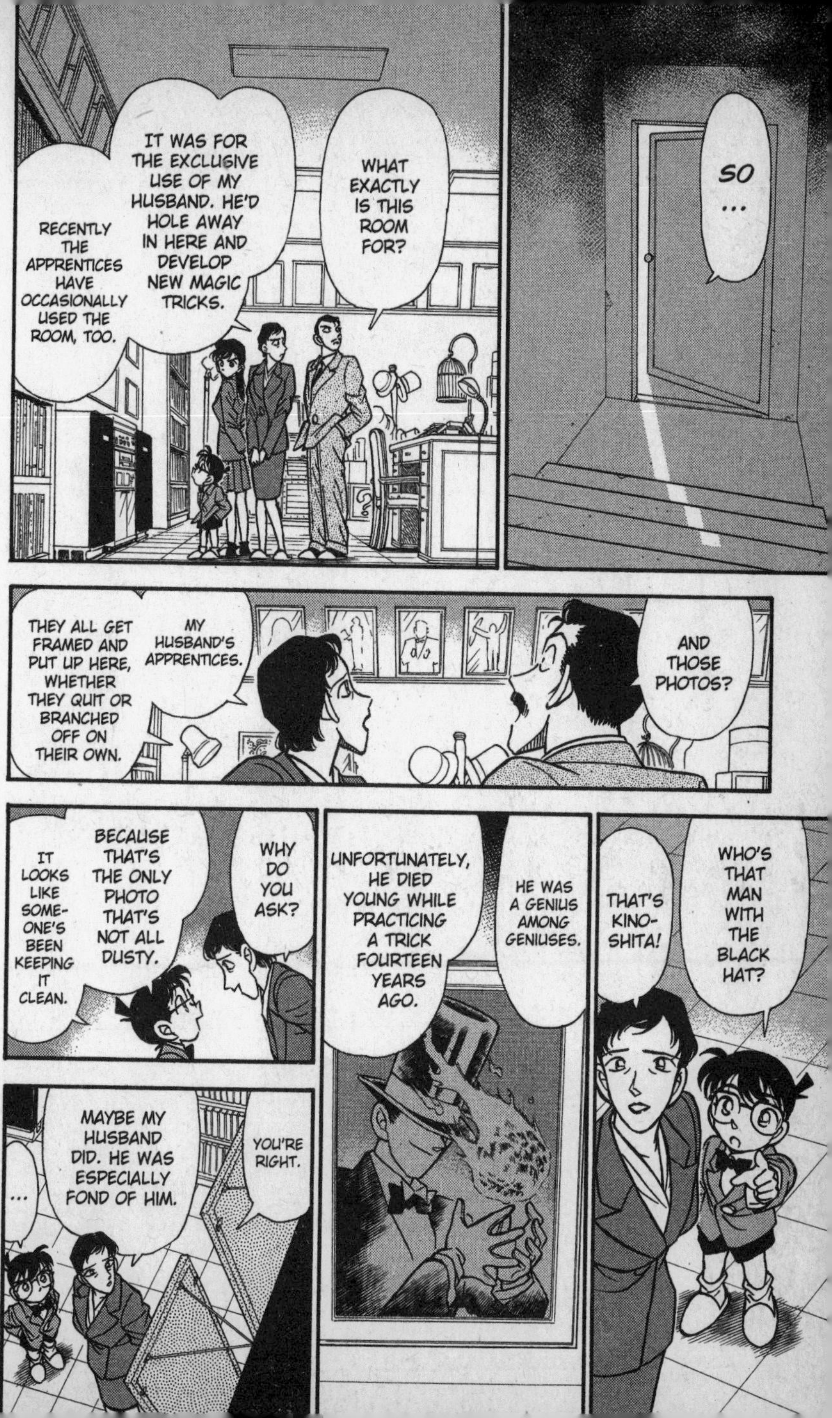
SO ...
WHAT EXACTLY IS THIS ROOM FOR?
IT WAS FOR THE EXCLUSIVE USE OF MY HUSBAND. HE'D HOLE AWAY IN HERE AND DEVELOP NEW MAGIC TRICKS.
RECENTLY THE APPRENTICES HAVE OCCASIONALLY USED THE ROOM, TOO.
AND THOSE PHOTOS?
MY HUSBAND'S APPRENTICES.
THEY ALL GET FRAMED AND PUT UP HERE, WHETHER THEY QUIT OR BRANCHED OFF ON THEIR OWN.
WHO'S THAT MAN WITH THE BLACK HAT?
THAT'S KINO-SHITA!
HE WAS A GENIUS AMONG GENIUSES.
UNFORTUNATELY, HE DIED YOUNG WHILE PRACTICING A TRICK FOURTEEN YEARS AGO.
WHY DO YOU ASK?
BECAUSE THAT'S THE ONLY PHOTO THAT'S NOT ALL DUSTY.
IT LOOKS LIKE SOME-ONE'S BEEN KEEPING IT CLEAN.
YOU'RE RIGHT.
MAYBE MY HUSBAND DID. HE WAS ESPECIALLY FOND OF HIM.
...

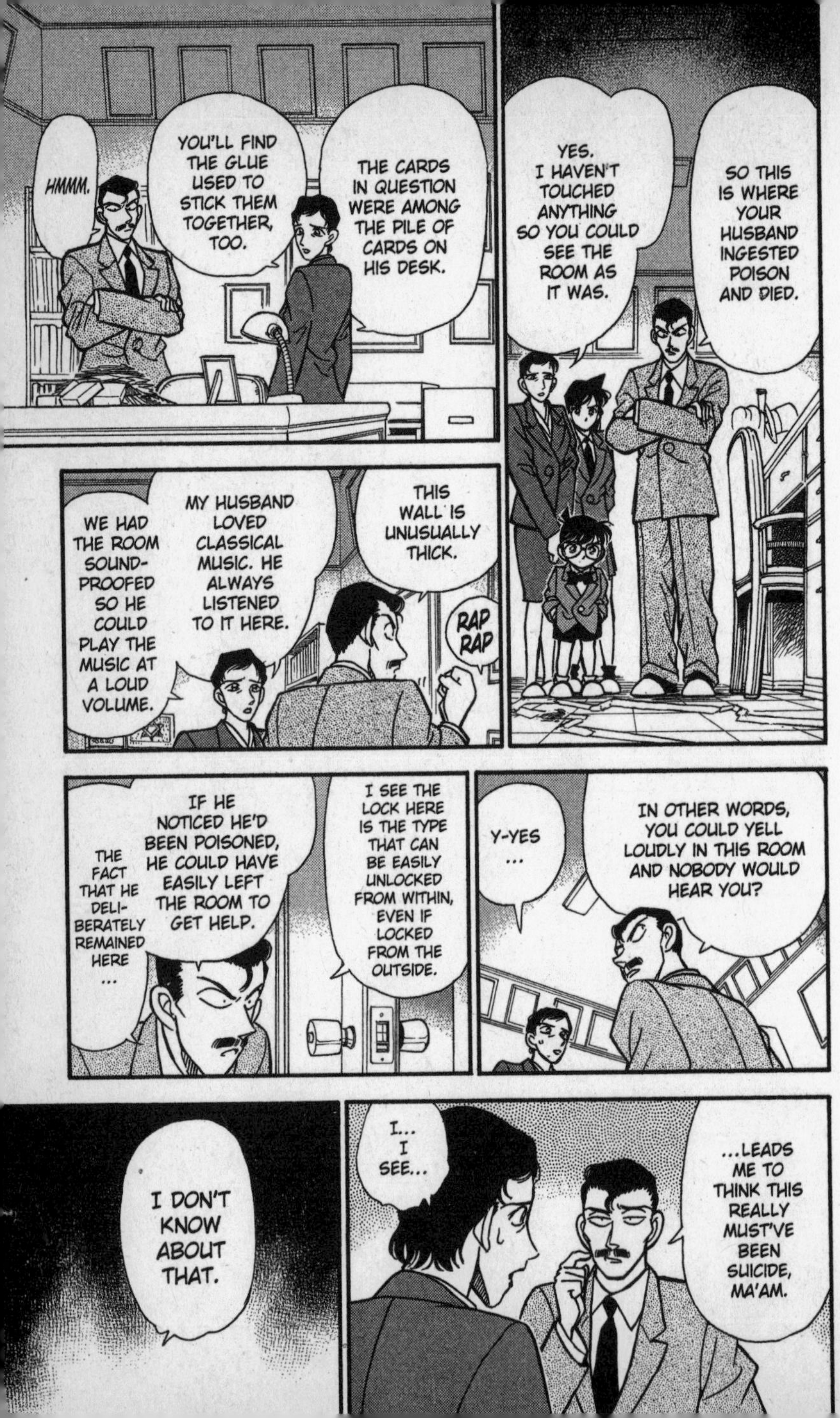
SO THIS IS WHERE YOUR HUSBAND INGESTED POISON AND DIED.
YES. I HAVEN'T TOUCHED ANYTHING SO YOU COULD SEE THE ROOM AS IT WAS.
THE CARDS IN QUESTION WERE AMONG THE PILE OF CARDS ON HIS DESK.
YOU'LL FIND THE GLUE USED TO STICK THEM TOGETHER, TOO.
HMMM.
THIS WALL IS UNUSUALLY THICK.
RAP RAP
MY HUSBAND LOVED CLASSICAL MUSIC. HE ALWAYS LISTENED TO IT HERE.
WE HAD THE ROOM SOUND-PROOFED SO HE COULD PLAY THE MUSIC AT A LOUD VOLUME.
IN OTHER WORDS, YOU COULD YELL LOUDLY IN THIS ROOM AND NOBODY WOULD HEAR YOU?
Y-YES ...
I SEE THE LOCK HERE IS THE TYPE THAT CAN BE EASILY UNLOCKED FROM WITHIN, EVEN IF LOCKED FROM THE OUTSIDE.
IF HE NOTICED HE'D BEEN POISONED, HE COULD HAVE EASILY LEFT THE ROOM TO GET HELP.
THE FACT THAT HE DELI-BERATELY REMAINED HERE ...
...LEADS ME TO THINK THIS REALLY MUST'VE BEEN SUICIDE, MA'AM.
I... I SEE...
I DON'T KNOW ABOUT THAT.

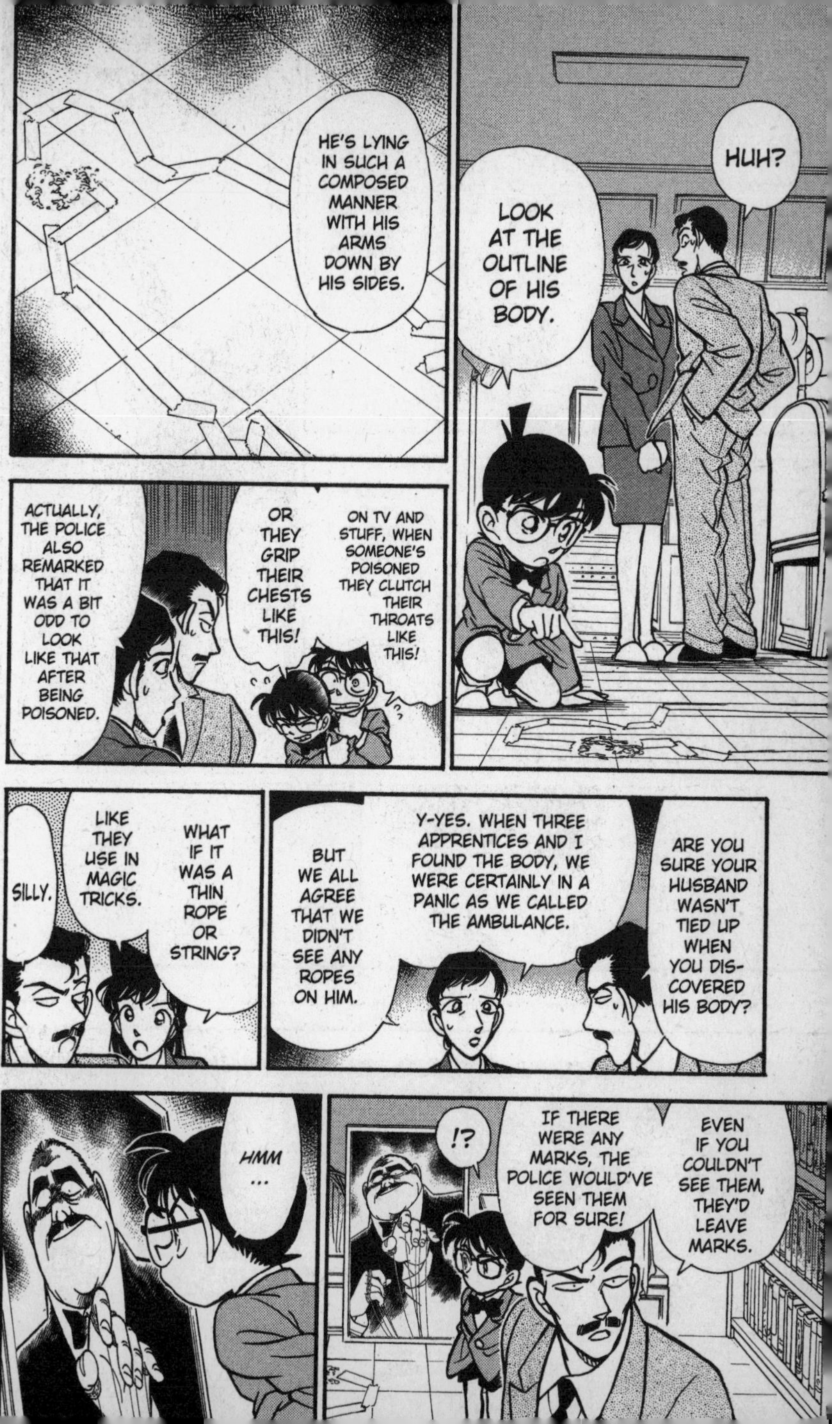
HUH?
LOOK AT THE OUTLINE OF HIS BODY.
HE'S LYING IN SUCH A COMPOSED MANNER WITH HIS ARMS DOWN BY HIS SIDES.
ON TV AND STUFF, WHEN SOMEONE'S POISONED THEY CLUTCH THEIR THROATS LIKE THIS!
OR THEY GRIP THEIR CHESTS LIKE THIS!
ACTUALLY, THE POLICE ALSO REMARKED THAT IT WAS A BIT ODD TO LOOK LIKE THAT AFTER BEING POISONED.
ARE YOU SURE YOUR HUSBAND WASN'T TIED UP WHEN YOU DIS-COVERED HIS BODY?
Y-YES. WHEN THREE APPRENTICES AND I FOUND THE BODY, WE WERE CERTAINLY IN A PANIC AS WE CALLED THE AMBULANCE.
BUT WE ALL AGREE THAT WE DIDN'T SEE ANY ROPES ON HIM.
WHAT IF IT WAS A THIN ROPE OR STRING?
LIKE THEY USE IN MAGIC TRICKS.
SILLY.
EVEN IF YOU COULDN'T SEE THEM, THEY'D LEAVE MARKS.
IF THERE WERE ANY MARKS, THE POLICE WOULD'VE SEEN THEM FOR SURE!
!?
HMM...

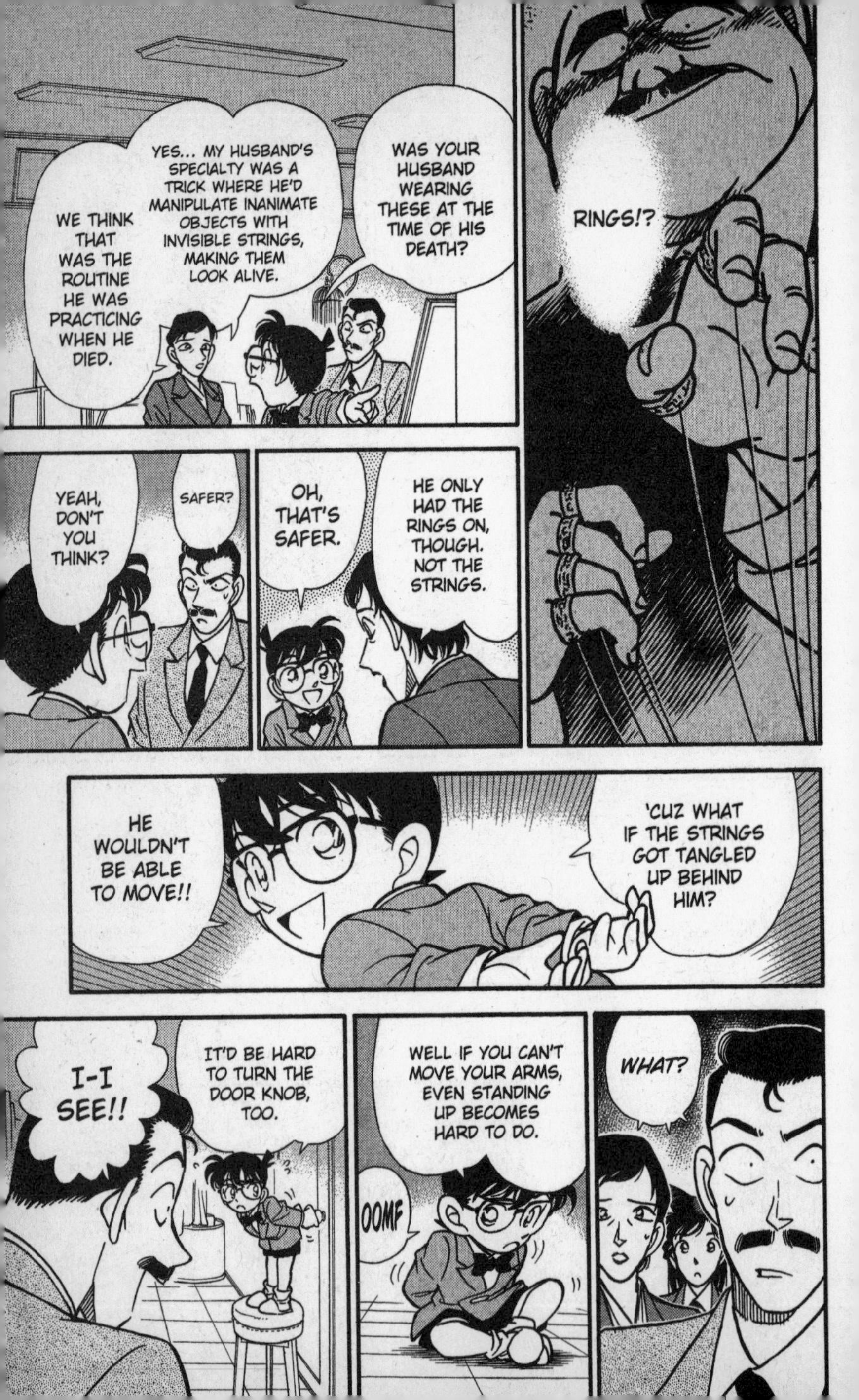

RINGS!?
WAS YOUR HUSBAND WEARING THESE AT THE TIME OF HIS DEATH?
YES... MY HUSBAND'S SPECIALTY WAS A TRICK WHERE HE'D MANIPULATE INANIMATE OBJECTS WITH INVISIBLE STRINGS, MAKING THEM LOOK ALIVE.
WE THINK THAT WAS THE ROUTINE HE WAS PRACTICING WHEN HE DIED.
HE ONLY HAD THE RINGS ON, THOUGH. NOT THE STRINGS.
OH, THAT'S SAFER.
SAFER?
YEAH, DON'T YOU THINK?
'CUZ WHAT IF THE STRINGS GOT TANGLED UP BEHIND HIM?
HE WOULDN'T BE ABLE TO MOVE!!
WHAT?
WELL IF YOU CAN'T MOVE YOUR ARMS, EVEN STANDING UP BECOMES HARD TO DO.
OOMF
IT'D BE HARD TO TURN THE DOOR KNOB, TOO.
I-I SEE!!

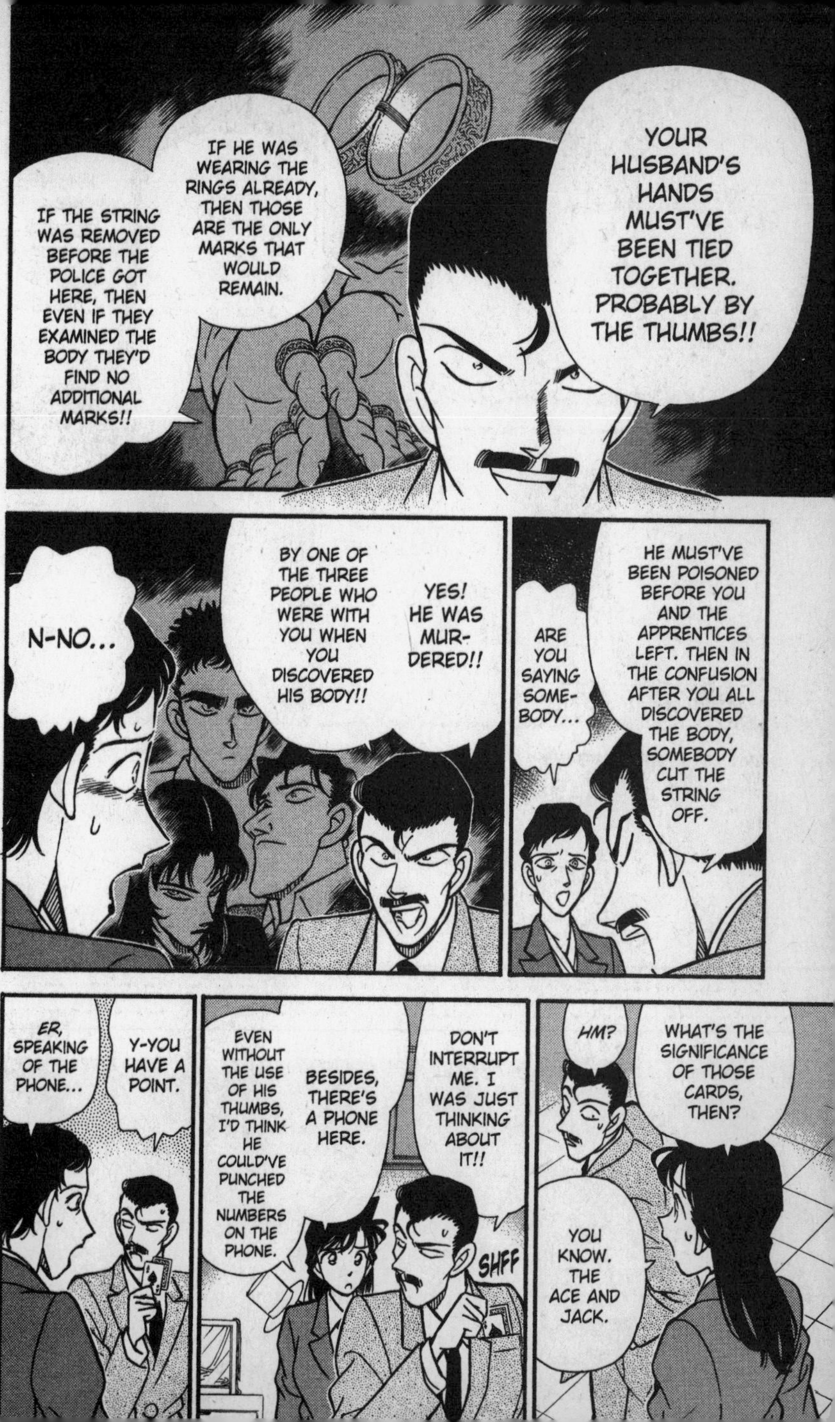
YOUR HUSBAND'S HANDS MUST'VE BEEN TIED TOGETHER. PROBABLY BY THE THUMBS!!
IF HE WAS WEARING THE RINGS ALREADY, THEN THOSE ARE THE ONLY MARKS THAT WOULD REMAIN.
IF THE STRING WAS REMOVED BEFORE THE POLICE GOT HERE, THEN EVEN IF THEY EXAMINED THE BODY THEY'D FIND NO ADDITIONAL MARKS!!
HE MUST'VE BEEN POISONED BEFORE YOU AND THE APPRENTICES LEFT. THEN IN THE CONFUSION AFTER YOU ALL DISCOVERED THE BODY, SOMEBODY CUT THE STRING OFF.
ARE YOU SAYING SOME-BODY...
YES! HE WAS MUR-DERED!!
BY ONE OF THE THREE PEOPLE WHO WERE WITH YOU WHEN YOU DISCOVERED HIS BODY!!
N-NO...
WHAT'S THE SIGNIFICANCE OF THOSE CARDS, THEN?
HM?
YOU KNOW. THE ACE AND JACK.
DON'T INTERRUPT ME. I WAS JUST THINKING ABOUT IT!!
SHFF
BESIDES, THERE'S A PHONE HERE.
EVEN WITHOUT THE USE OF HIS THUMBS, I'D THINK HE COULD'VE PUNCHED THE NUMBERS ON THE PHONE.
Y-YOU HAVE A POINT.
ER, SPEAKING OF THE PHONE...

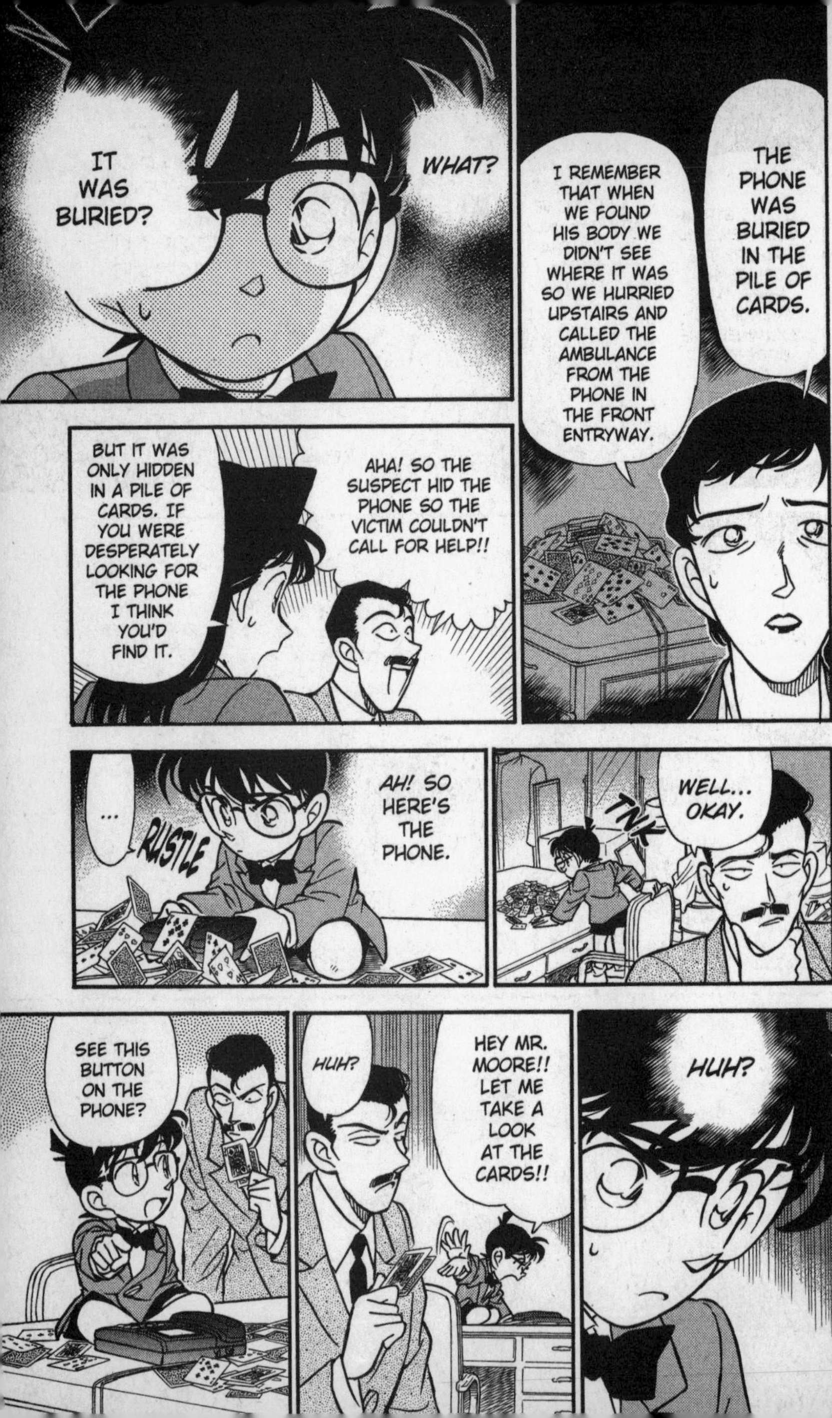
THE PHONE WAS BURIED IN THE PILE OF CARDS.
I REMEMBER THAT WHEN WE FOUND HIS BODY WE DIDN'T SEE WHERE IT WAS SO WE HURRIED UPSTAIRS AND CALLED THE AMBULANCE FROM THE PHONE IN THE FRONT ENTRYWAY.
WHAT?
IT WAS BURIED?
AHA! SO THE SUSPECT HID THE PHONE SO THE VICTIM COULDN'T CALL FOR HELP!!
BUT IT WAS ONLY HIDDEN IN A PILE OF CARDS. IF YOU WERE DESPERATELY LOOKING FOR THE PHONE I THINK YOU'D FIND IT.
WELL... OKAY.
TNK
AH! SO HERE'S THE PHONE.
RUSTLE
...
HUH?
HEY MR. MOORE!! LET ME TAKE A LOOK AT THE CARDS!!
HUH?
SEE THIS BUTTON ON THE PHONE?

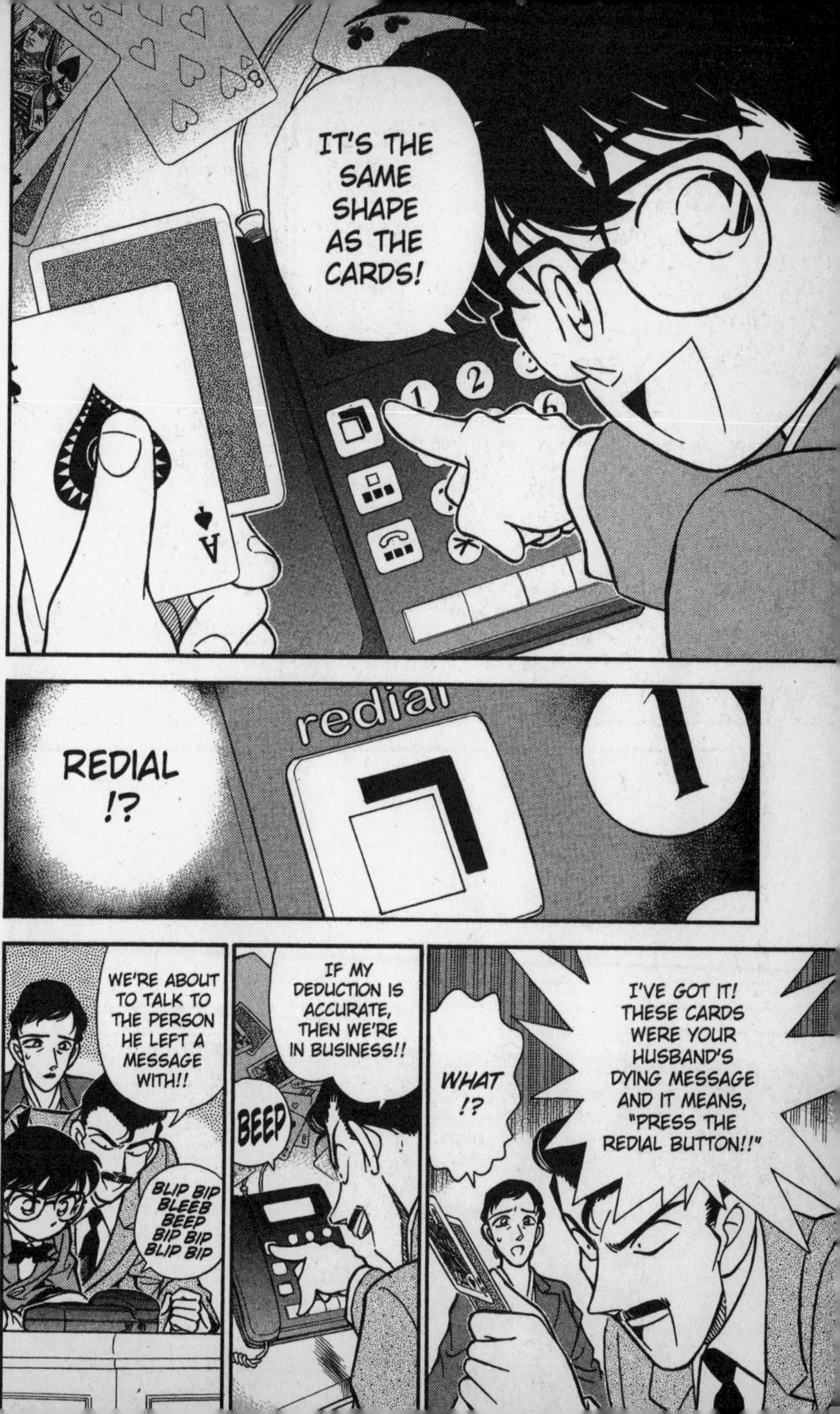

IT'S THE SAME SHAPE AS THE CARDS!
redial
REDIAL !?
I'VE GOT IT! THESE CARDS WERE YOUR HUSBAND'S DYING MESSAGE AND IT MEANS, "PRESS THE REDIAL BUTTON!!"
WHAT !?
IF MY DEDUCTION IS ACCURATE, THEN WE'RE IN BUSINESS!!
BEEP
WE'RE ABOUT TO TALK TO THE PERSON HE LEFT A MESSAGE WITH!!
BLIP BIP BLEEB BEEP BIP BIP BLIP BIP

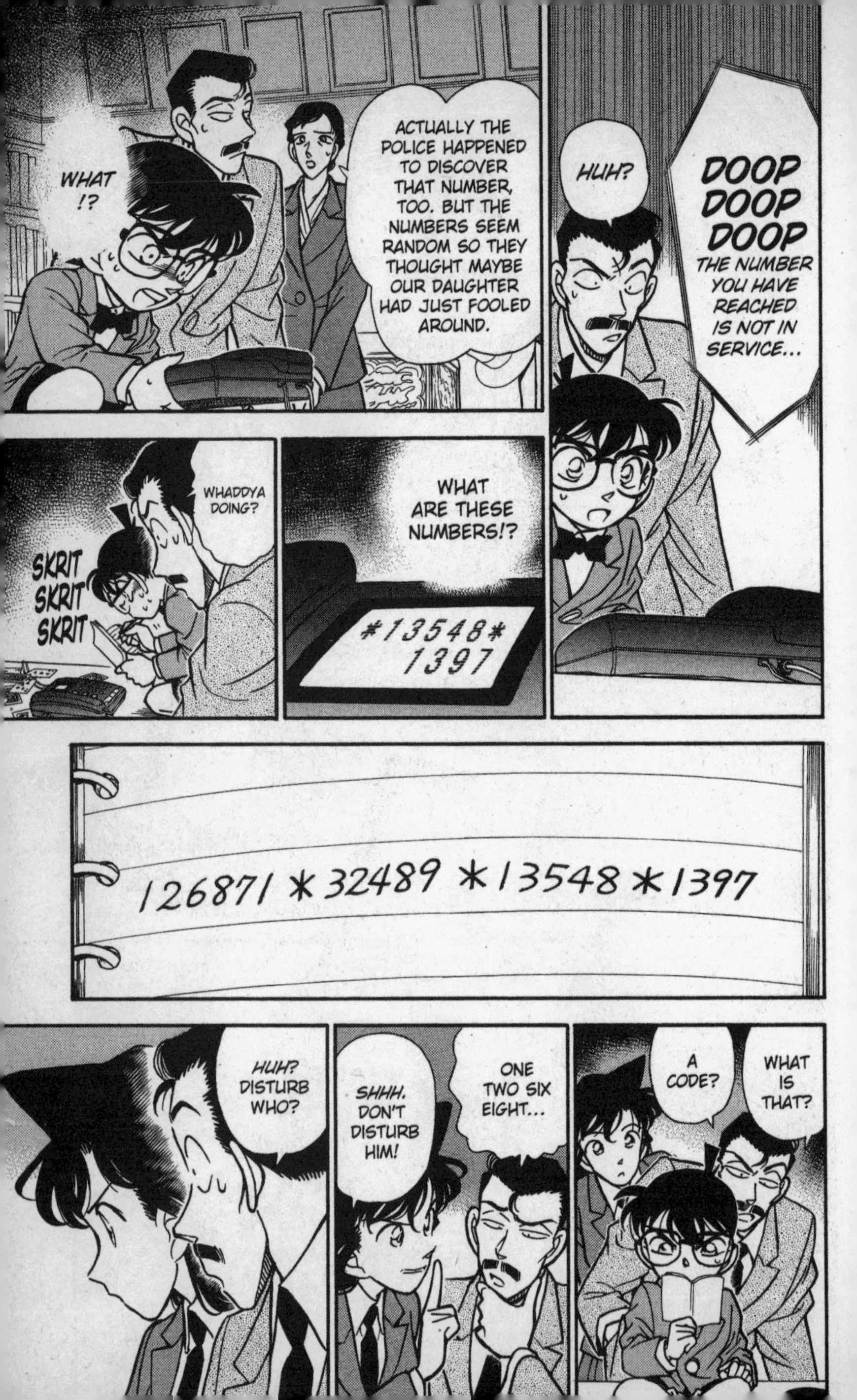
HUH?
DOOP DOOP DOOP
THE NUMBER YOU HAVE REACHED IS NOT IN SERVICE...
ACTUALLY THE POLICE HAPPENED TO DISCOVER THAT NUMBER, TOO. BUT THE NUMBERS SEEM RANDOM SO THEY THOUGHT MAYBE OUR DAUGHTER HAD JUST FOOLED AROUND.
WHAT !?
WHAT ARE THESE NUMBERS!?
13548 1397
WHADDYA DOING?
SKRIT SKRIT SKRIT
126871 *32489 *13548 *1397
WHAT IS THAT?
A CODE?
ONE TWO SIX EIGHT...
SHHH. DON'T DISTURB HIM!
HUH? DISTURB WHO?

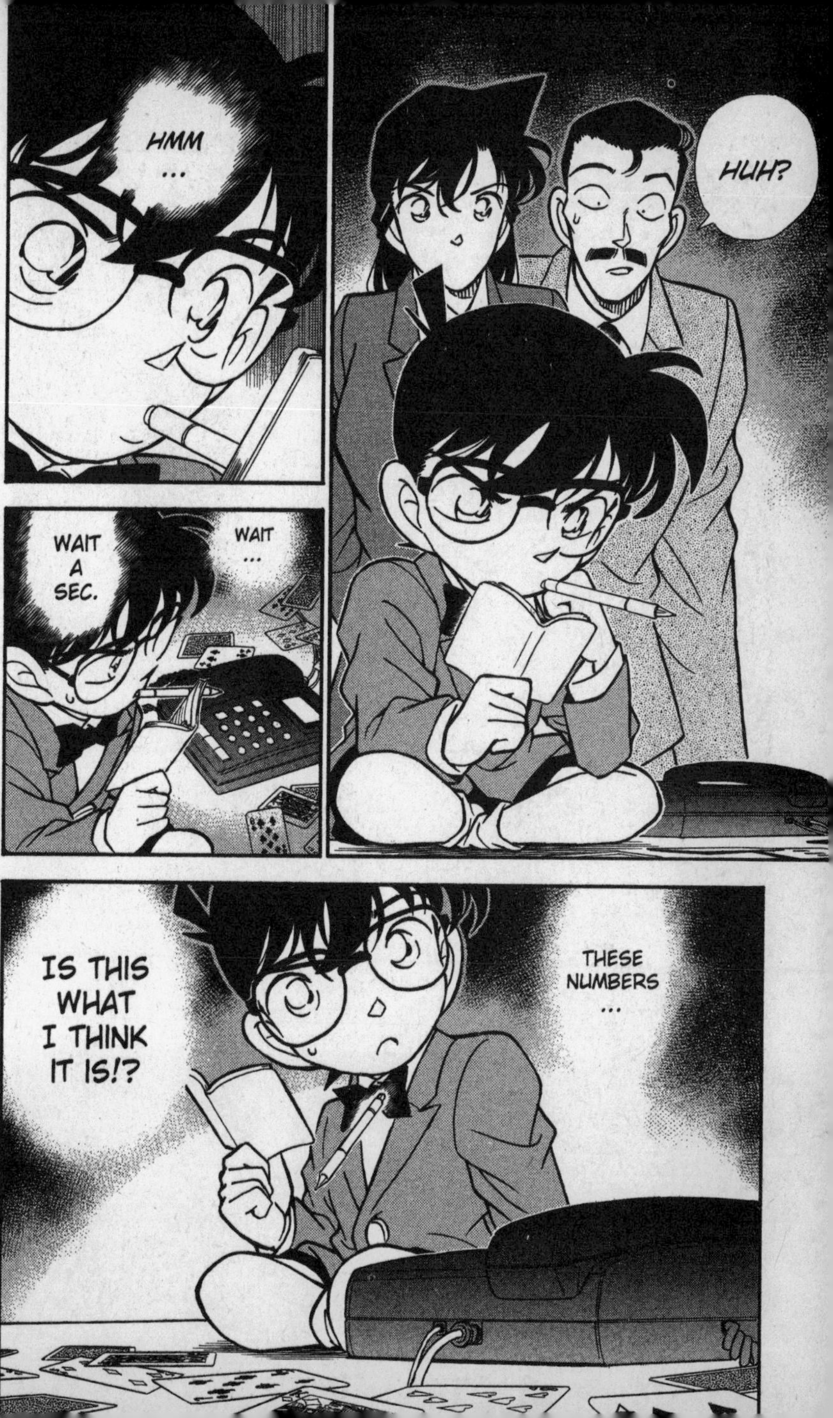
HUH?
HMM ...
WAIT ...
WAIT A SEC.
THESE NUMBERS ...
IS THIS WHAT I THINK IT IS!?

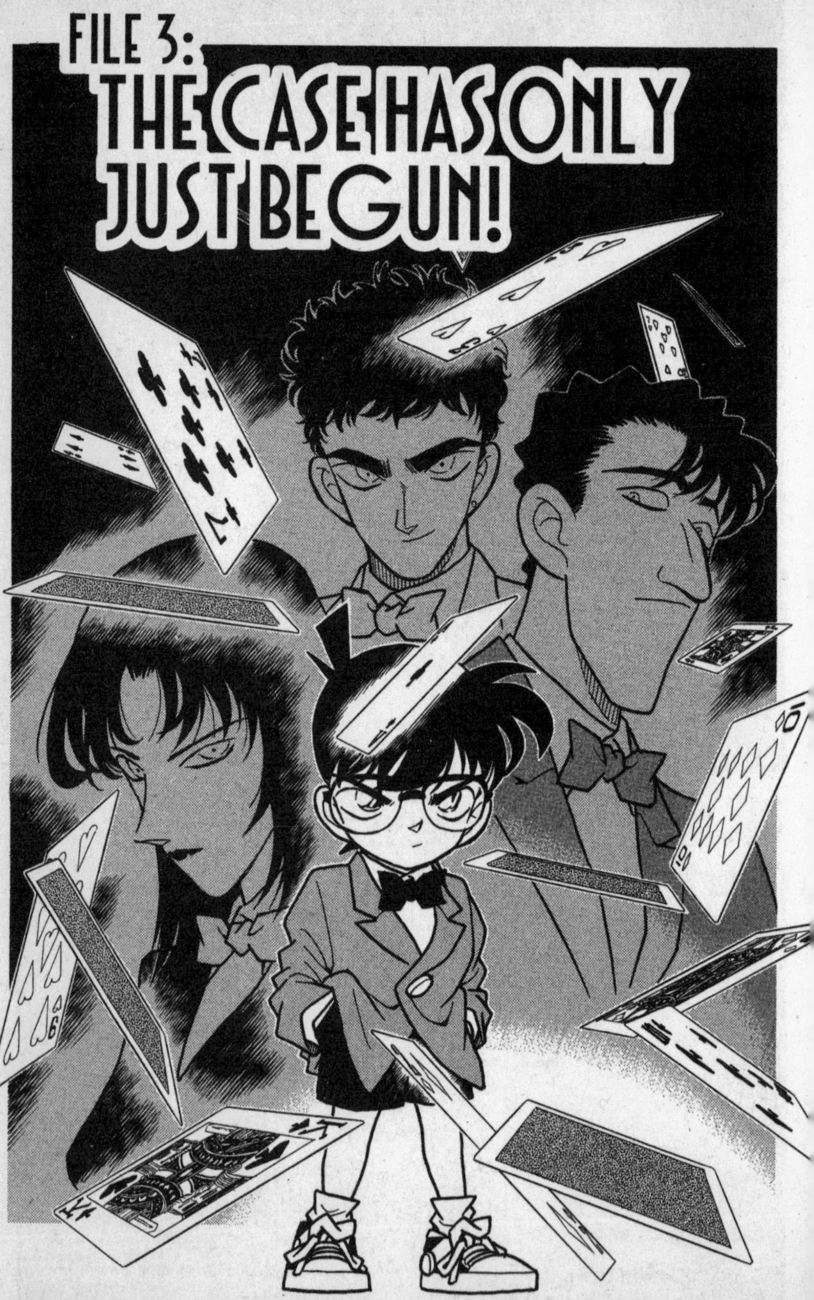
FILE 3:
THE CASE HAS ONLY JUST BEGUN!

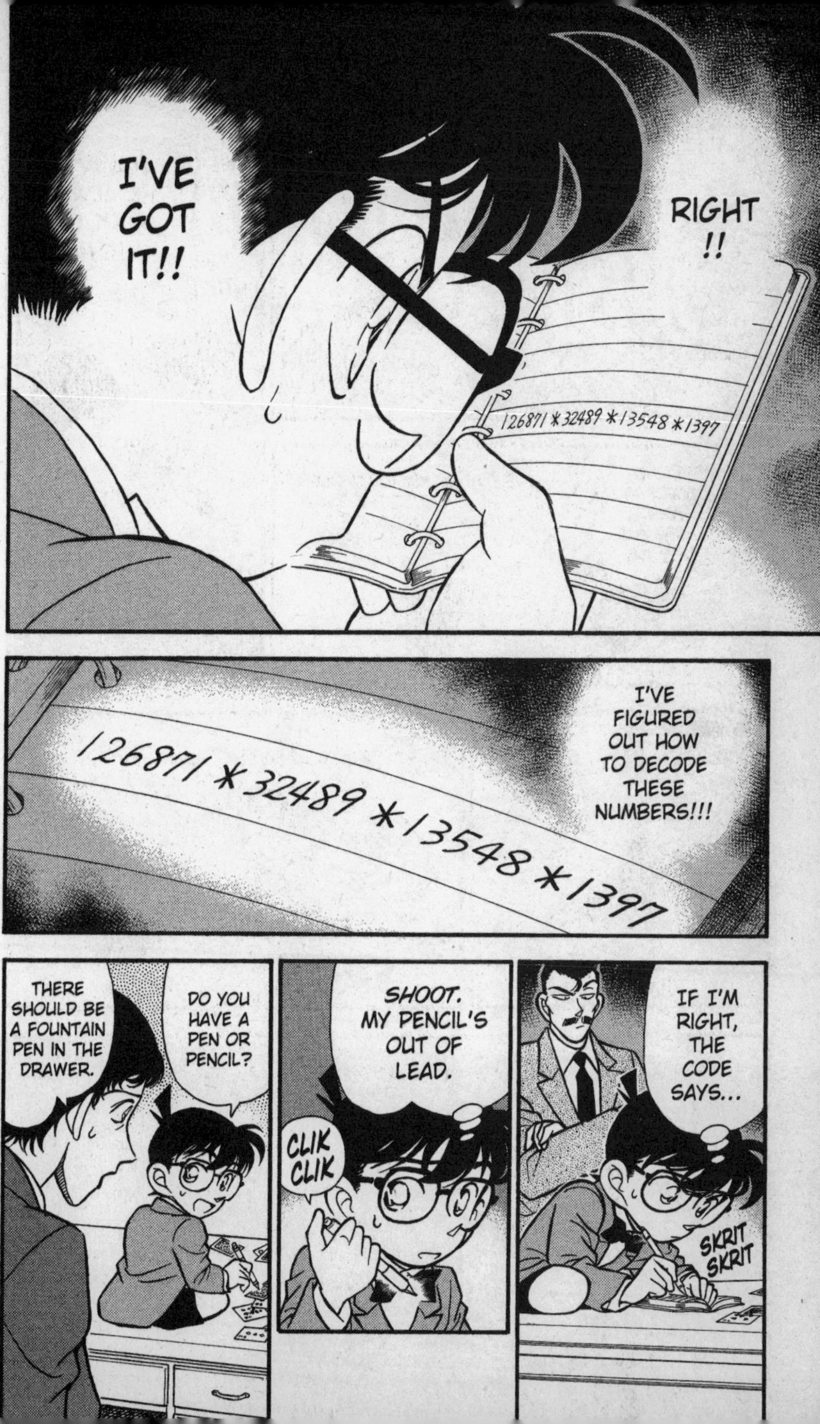
RIGHT !!
I'VE GOT IT!!
126871*32489*13548*1397
I'VE FIGURED OUT HOW TO DECODE THESE NUMBERS!!!
126871*32489*13548*1397
IF I'M RIGHT, THE CODE SAYS...
SKRIT SKRIT
SHOOT. MY PENCIL'S OUT OF LEAD.
CLIK CLIK
DO YOU HAVE A PEN OR PENCIL?
THERE SHOULD BE A FOUNTAIN PEN IN THE DRAWER.

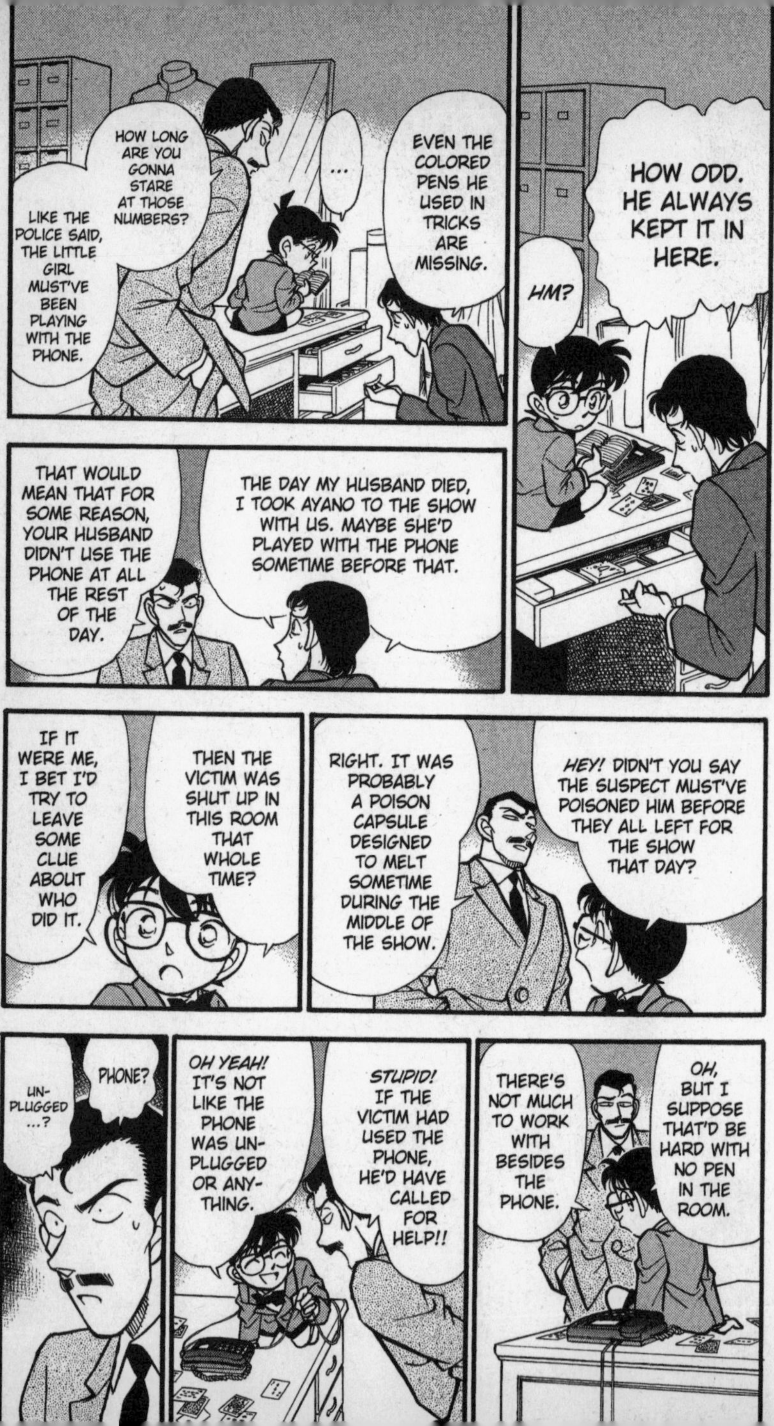
HOW ODD. HE ALWAYS KEPT IT IN HERE.
HM?
EVEN THE COLORED PENS HE USED IN TRICKS ARE MISSING.
...
HOW LONG ARE YOU GONNA STARE AT THOSE NUMBERS?
LIKE THE POLICE SAID, THE LITTLE GIRL MUST'VE BEEN PLAYING WITH THE PHONE.
THE DAY MY HUSBAND DIED, I TOOK AYANO TO THE SHOW WITH US. MAYBE SHE'D PLAYED WITH THE PHONE SOMETIME BEFORE THAT.
THAT WOULD MEAN THAT FOR SOME REASON, YOUR HUSBAND DIDN'T USE THE PHONE AT ALL THE REST OF THE DAY.
HEY! DIDN'T YOU SAY THE SUSPECT MUST'VE POISONED HIM BEFORE THEY ALL LEFT FOR THE SHOW THAT DAY?
RIGHT. IT WAS PROBABLY A POISON CAPSULE DESIGNED TO MELT SOMETIME DURING THE MIDDLE OF THE SHOW.
THEN THE VICTIM WAS SHUT UP IN THIS ROOM THAT WHOLE TIME?
IF IT WERE ME, I BET I'D TRY TO LEAVE SOME CLUE ABOUT WHO DID IT.
OH, BUT I SUPPOSE THAT'D BE HARD WITH NO PEN IN THE ROOM.
THERE'S NOT MUCH TO WORK WITH BESIDES THE PHONE.
STUPID! IF THE VICTIM HAD USED THE PHONE, HE'D HAVE CALLED FOR HELP!!
OH YEAH! IT'S NOT LIKE THE PHONE WAS UN-PLUGGED OR ANY-THING.
PHONE?
UN-PLUGGED ...?

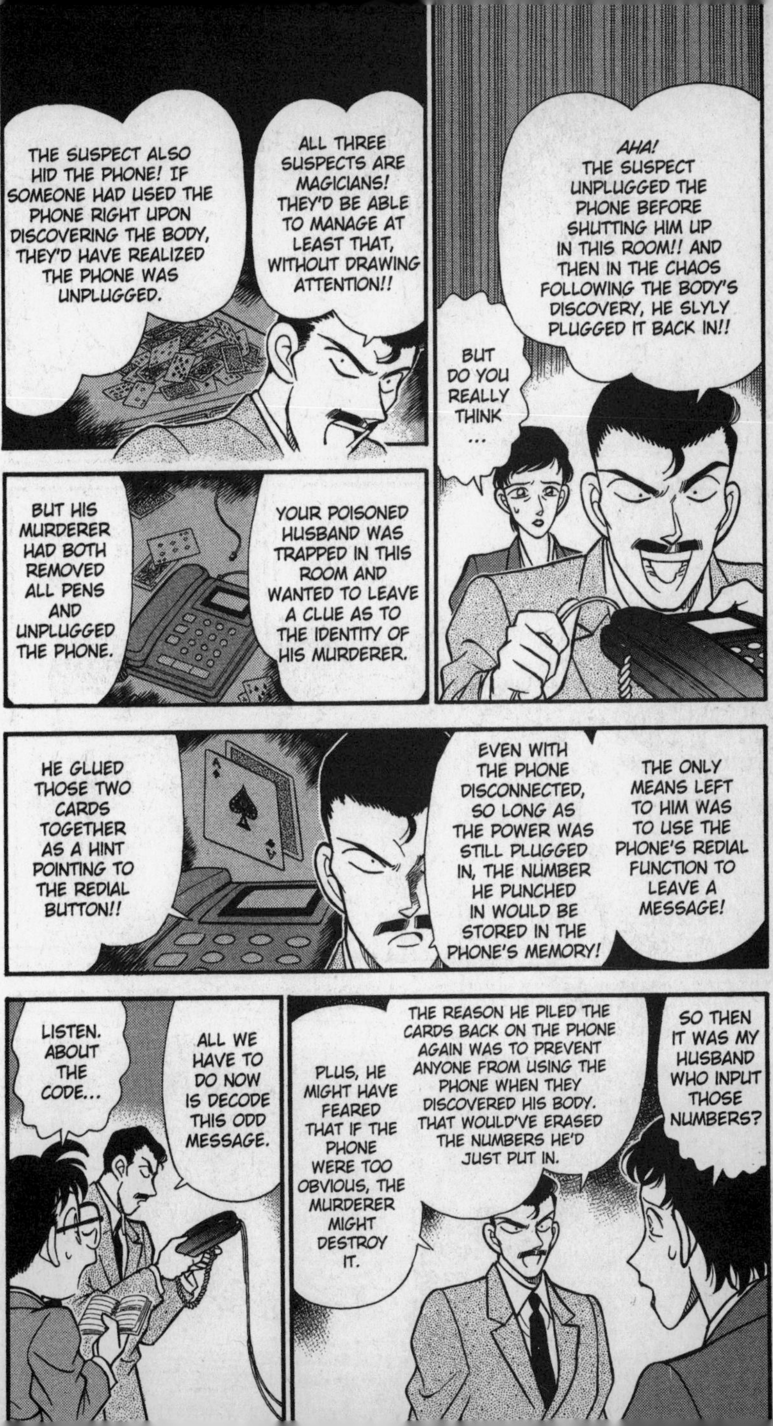
AHA! THE SUSPECT UNPLUGGED THE PHONE BEFORE SHUTTING HIM UP IN THIS ROOM!! AND THEN IN THE CHAOS FOLLOWING THE BODY'S DISCOVERY, HE SLYLY PLUGGED IT BACK IN!!
BUT DO YOU REALLY THINK ...
ALL THREE SUSPECTS ARE MAGICIANS! THEY'D BE ABLE TO MANAGE AT LEAST THAT, WITHOUT DRAWING ATTENTION!!
THE SUSPECT ALSO HID THE PHONE! IF SOMEONE HAD USED THE PHONE RIGHT UPON DISCOVERING THE BODY, THEY'D HAVE REALIZED THE PHONE WAS UNPLUGGED.
YOUR POISONED HUSBAND WAS TRAPPED IN THIS ROOM AND WANTED TO LEAVE A CLUE AS TO THE IDENTITY OF HIS MURDERER.
BUT HIS MURDERER HAD BOTH REMOVED ALL PENS AND UNPLUGGED THE PHONE.
THE ONLY MEANS LEFT TO HIM WAS TO USE THE PHONE'S REDIAL FUNCTION TO LEAVE A MESSAGE!
EVEN WITH THE PHONE DISCONNECTED, SO LONG AS THE POWER WAS STILL PLUGGED IN, THE NUMBER HE PUNCHED IN WOULD BE STORED IN THE PHONE'S MEMORY!
HE GLUED THOSE TWO CARDS TOGETHER AS A HINT POINTING TO THE REDIAL BUTTON!!
SO THEN IT WAS MY HUSBAND WHO INPUT THOSE NUMBERS?
THE REASON HE PILED THE CARDS BACK ON THE PHONE AGAIN WAS TO PREVENT ANYONE FROM USING THE PHONE WHEN THEY DISCOVERED HIS BODY. THAT WOULD'VE ERASED THE NUMBERS HE'D JUST PUT IN.
PLUS, HE MIGHT HAVE FEARED THAT IF THE PHONE WERE TOO OBVIOUS, THE MURDERER MIGHT DESTROY IT.
ALL WE HAVE TO DO NOW IS DECODE THIS ODD MESSAGE.
LISTEN. ABOUT THE CODE...

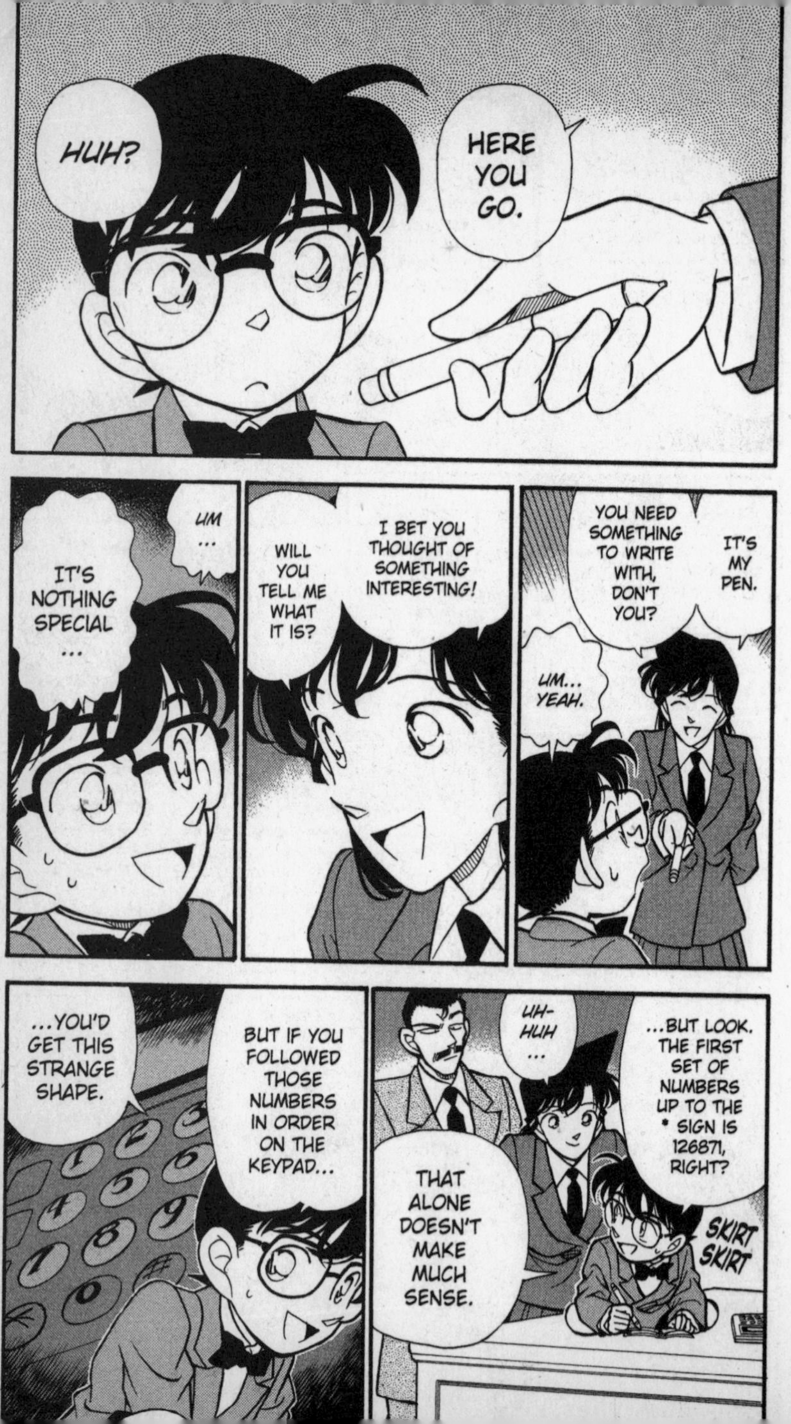
HERE YOU GO.
HUH?
IT'S MY PEN.
YOU NEED SOMETHING TO WRITE WITH, DON'T YOU?
UM... YEAH.
I BET YOU THOUGHT OF SOMETHING INTERESTING!
WILL YOU TELL ME WHAT IT IS?
UM ...
IT'S NOTHING SPECIAL ...
...BUT LOOK. THE FIRST SET OF NUMBERS UP TO THE * SIGN IS 126871, RIGHT?
UH-HUH ...
THAT ALONE DOESN'T MAKE MUCH SENSE.
SKIRT SKIRT
BUT IF YOU FOLLOWED THOSE NUMBERS IN ORDER ON THE KEYPAD...
...YOU'D GET THIS STRANGE SHAPE.

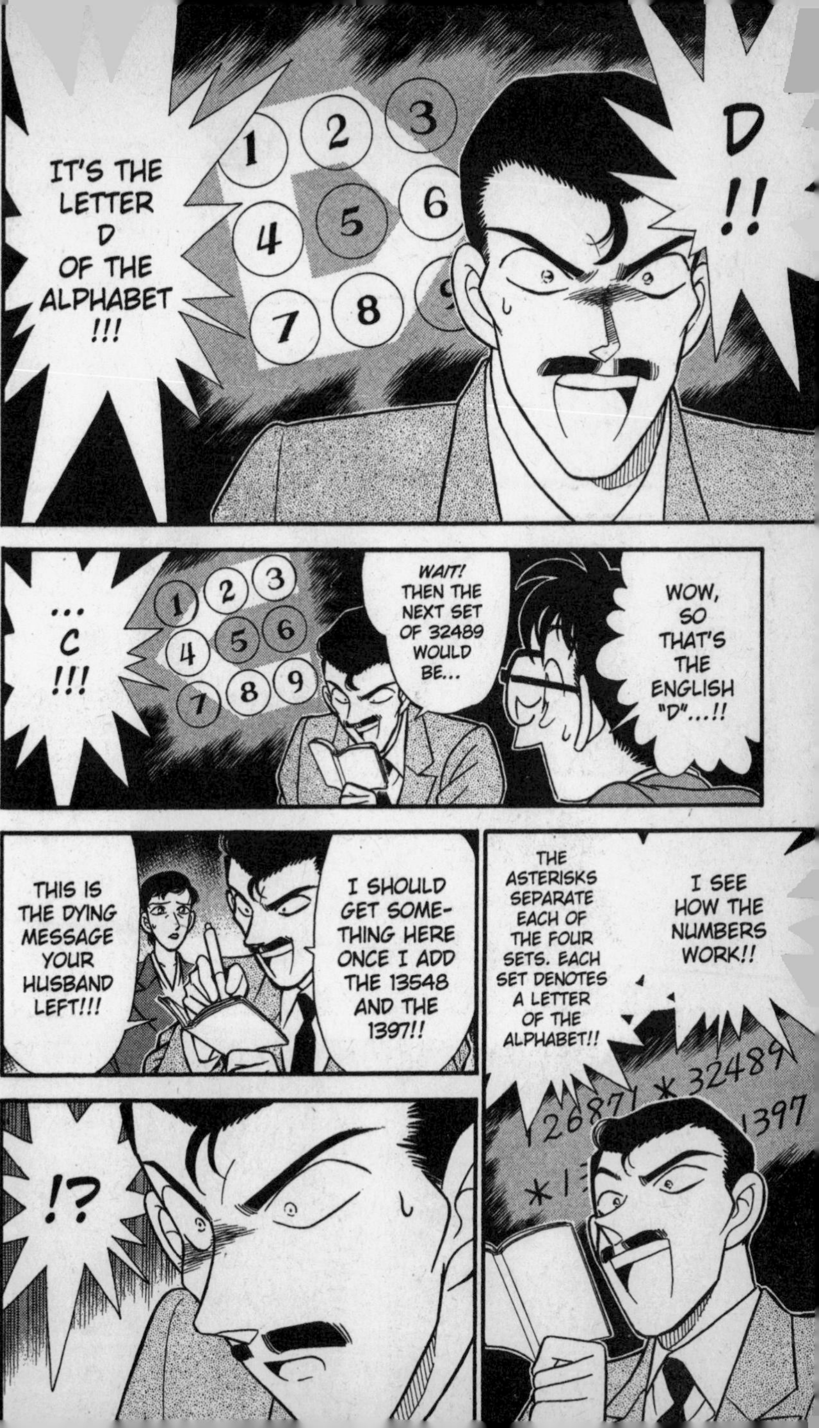
D !!
IT'S THE LETTER D OF THE ALPHABET !!!
WOW, SO THAT'S THE ENGLISH "D"...!!
WAIT! THEN THE NEXT SET OF 32489 WOULD BE...
... C !!!
I SEE HOW THE NUMBERS WORK!!
THE ASTERISKS SEPARATE EACH OF THE FOUR SETS. EACH SET DENOTES A LETTER OF THE ALPHABET!!
I SHOULD GET SOME-THING HERE ONCE I ADD THE 13548 AND THE 1397!!
THIS IS THE DYING MESSAGE YOUR HUSBAND LEFT!!!
!?

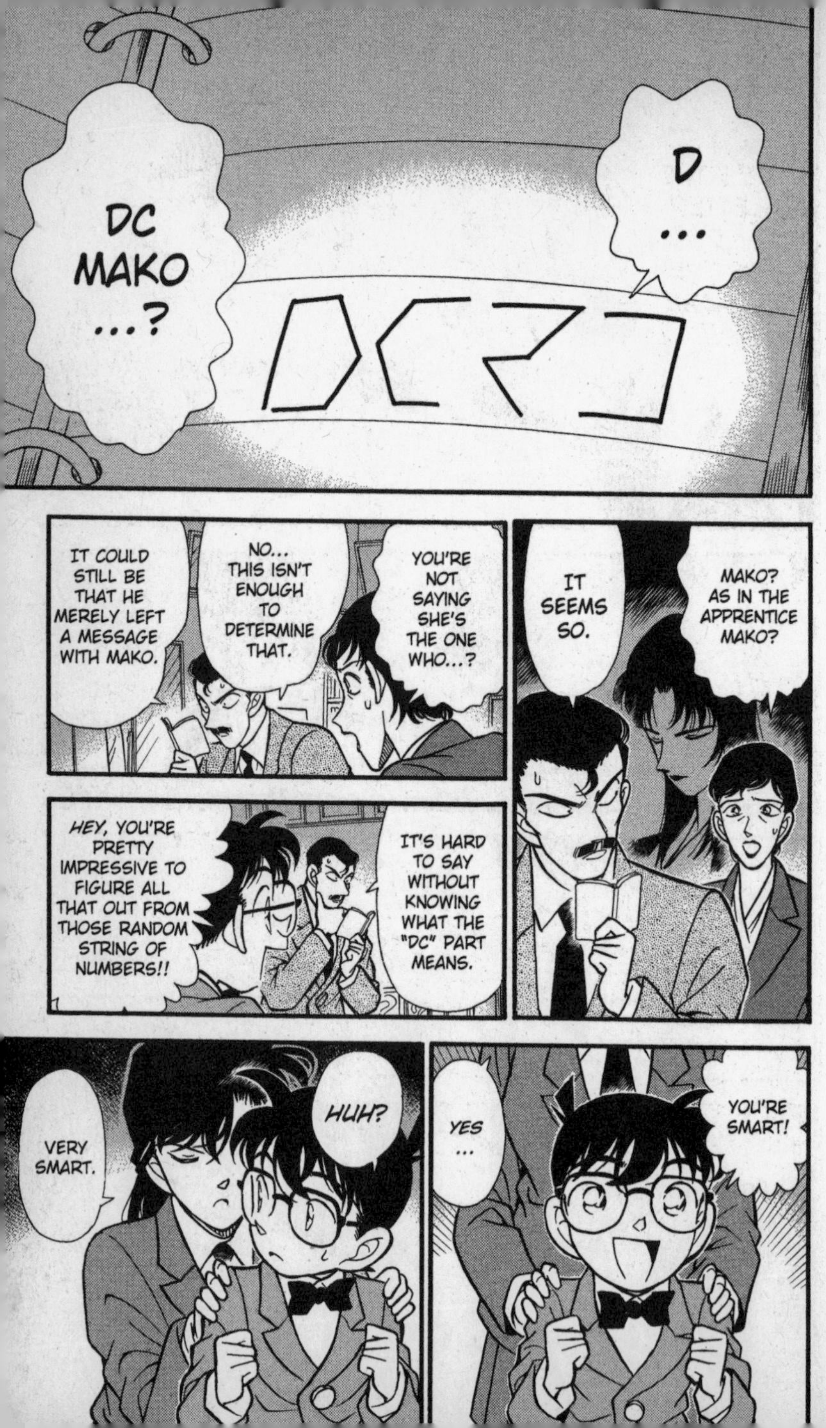
D ...
DC MAKO ...?
MAKO? AS IN THE APPRENTICE MAKO?
IT SEEMS SO.
YOU'RE NOT SAYING SHE'S THE ONE WHO...?
NO... THIS ISN'T ENOUGH TO DETERMINE THAT.
IT COULD STILL BE THAT HE MERELY LEFT A MESSAGE WITH MAKO.
IT'S HARD TO SAY WITHOUT KNOWING WHAT THE "DC" PART MEANS.
HEY, YOU'RE PRETTY IMPRESSIVE TO FIGURE ALL THAT OUT FROM THOSE RANDOM STRING OF NUMBERS!!
YOU'RE SMART!
YES ...
HUH?
VERY SMART.

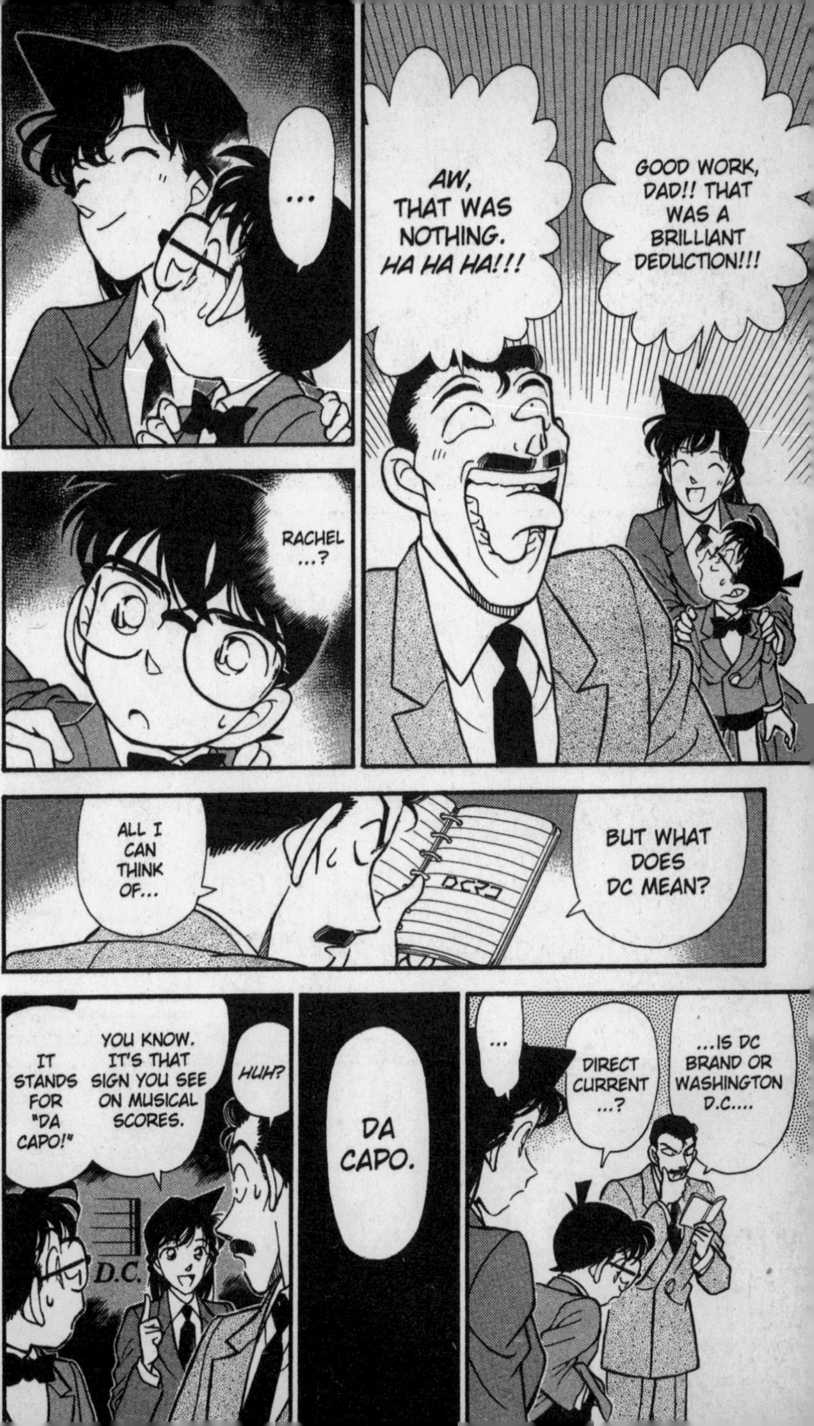
GOOD WORK, DAD!! THAT WAS A BRILLIANT DEDUCTION!!!
AW, THAT WAS NOTHING. HA HA HA!!!
...
RACHEL ...?
BUT WHAT DOES DC MEAN?
ALL I CAN THINK OF...
...IS DC BRAND OR WASHINGTON D.C....
DIRECT CURRENT ...?
...
DA CAPO.
HUH?
YOU KNOW. IT'S THAT SIGN YOU SEE ON MUSICAL SCORES.
IT STANDS FOR "DA CAPO!"
D.C.

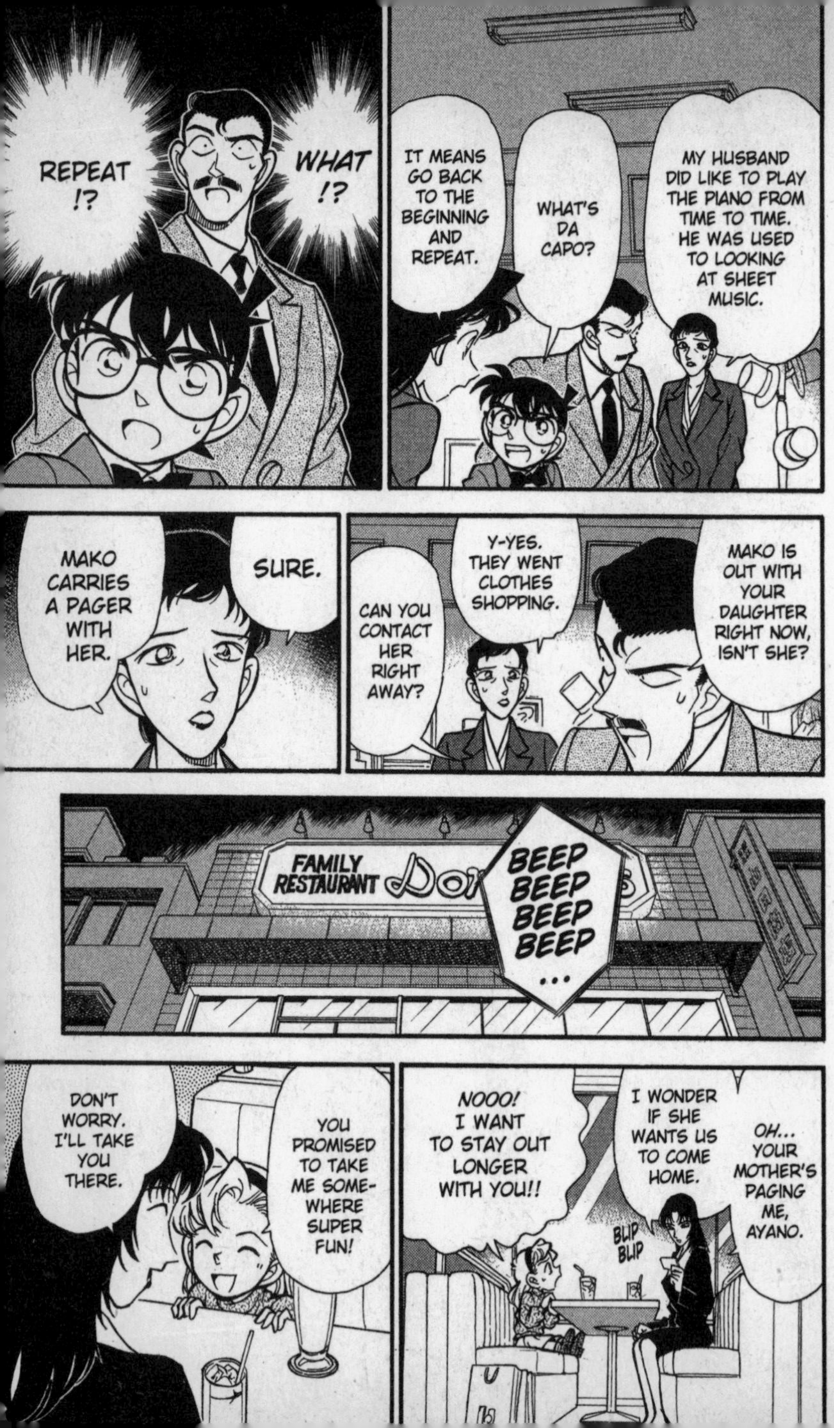
MY HUSBAND DID LIKE TO PLAY THE PIANO FROM TIME TO TIME. HE WAS USED TO LOOKING AT SHEET MUSIC.
WHAT'S DA CAPO?
IT MEANS GO BACK TO THE BEGINNING AND REPEAT.
WHAT !?
REPEAT !?
MAKO IS OUT WITH YOUR DAUGHTER RIGHT NOW, ISN'T SHE?
Y-YES. THEY WENT CLOTHES SHOPPING.
CAN YOU CONTACT HER RIGHT AWAY?
SURE.
MAKO CARRIES A PAGER WITH HER.
FAMILY RESTAURANT
BEEP BEEP BEEP BEEP ...
OH... YOUR MOTHER'S PAGING ME, AYANO.
I WONDER IF SHE WANTS US TO COME HOME.
BLIP BLIP
NOOO! I WANT TO STAY OUT LONGER WITH YOU!!
YOU PROMISED TO TAKE ME SOME-WHERE SUPER FUN!
DON'T WORRY. I'LL TAKE YOU THERE.

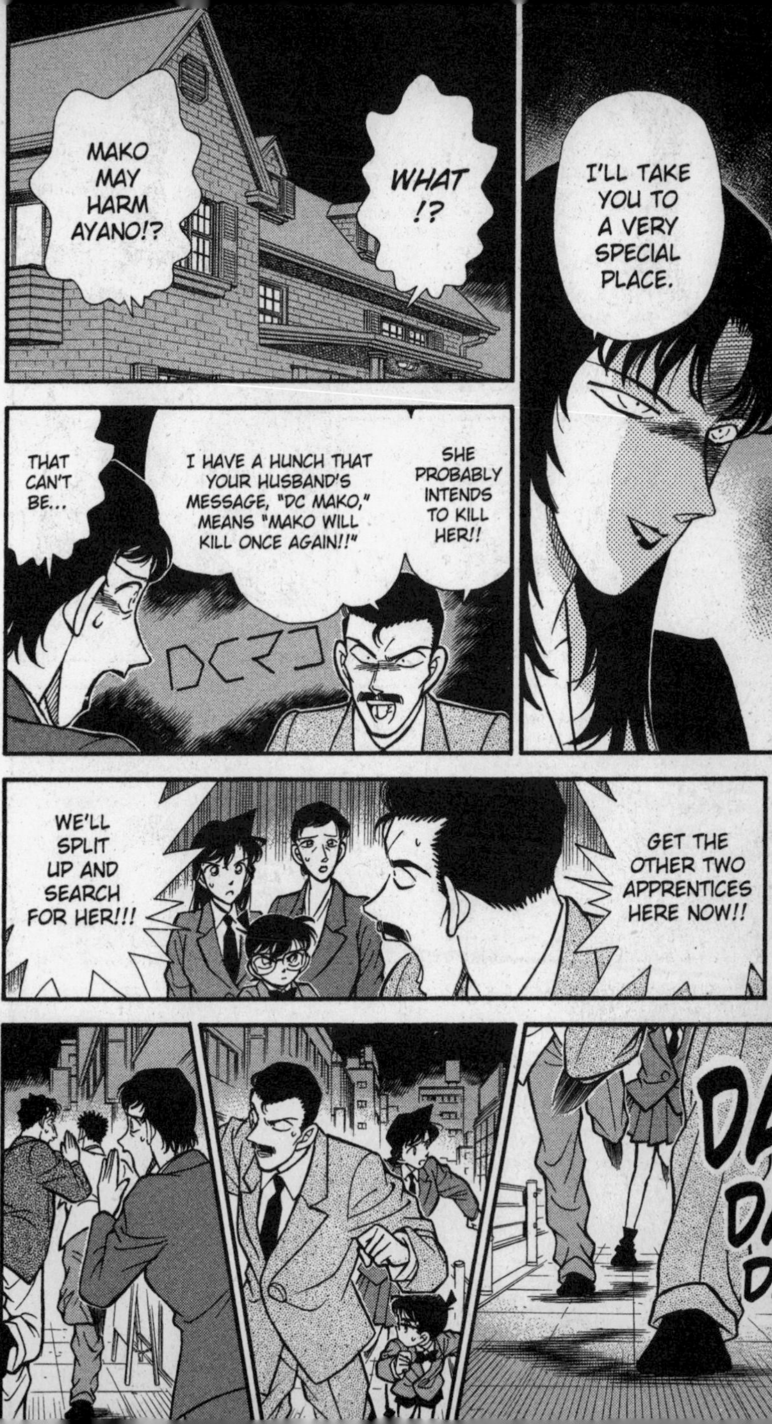
I'LL TAKE YOU TO A VERY SPECIAL PLACE.
WHAT!?
MAKO MAY HARM AYANO!?
SHE PROBABLY INTENDS TO KILL HER!!
I HAVE A HUNCH THAT YOUR HUSBAND'S MESSAGE, "DC MAKO," MEANS "MAKO WILL KILL ONCE AGAIN!!"
THAT CAN'T BE...
GET THE OTHER TWO APPRENTICES HERE NOW!!
WE'LL SPLIT UP AND SEARCH FOR HER!!!
DA DA DA DA

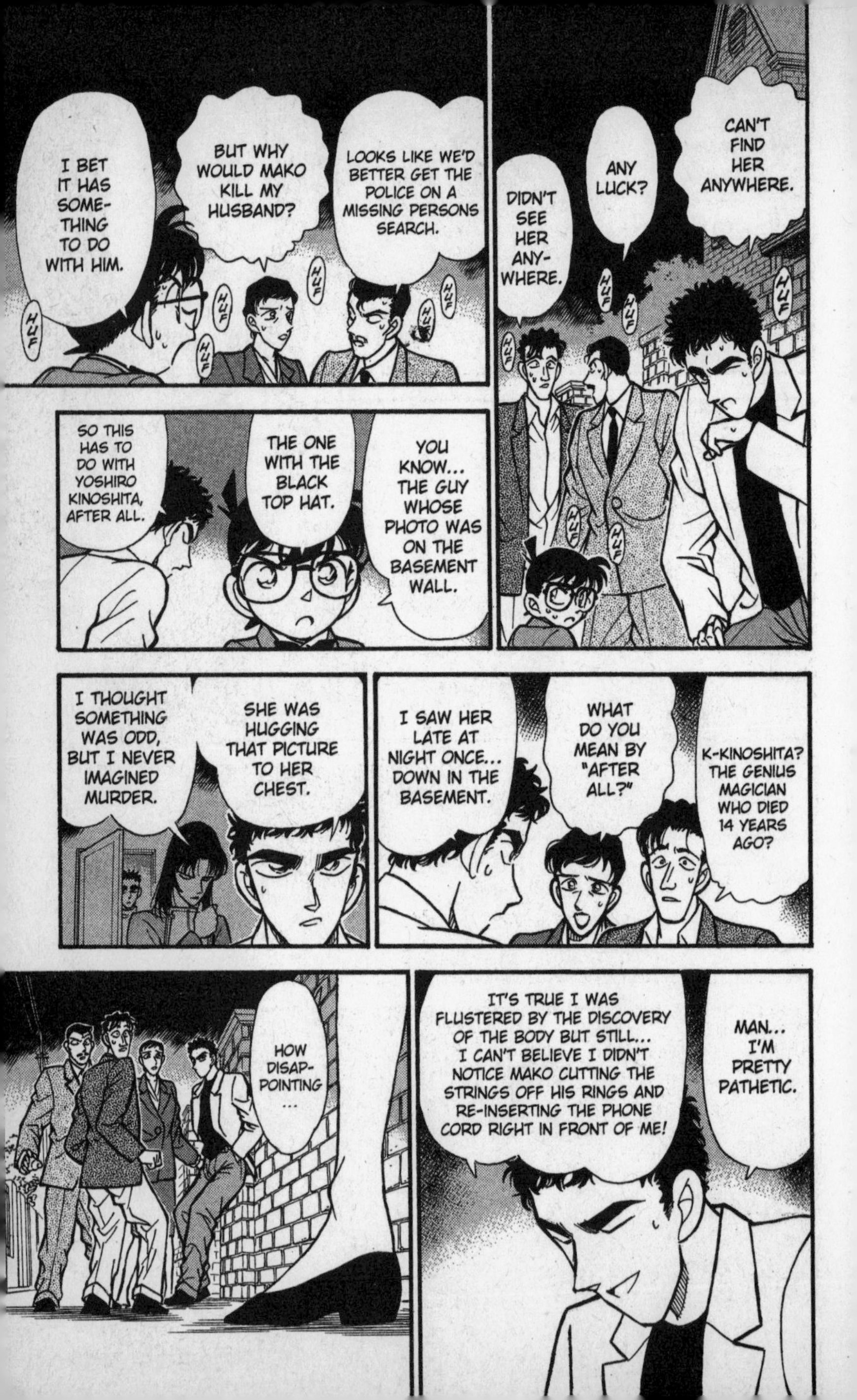
CAN'T FIND HER ANYWHERE.
ANY LUCK?
DIDN'T SEE HER ANYWHERE.
HUF
HUF
HUF
HUF
LOOKS LIKE WE'D BETTER GET THE POLICE ON A MISSING PERSONS SEARCH.
BUT WHY WOULD MAKO KILL MY HUSBAND?
I BET IT HAS SOMETHING TO DO WITH HIM.
HUF
HUF
HUF
HUF
YOU KNOW... THE GUY WHOSE PHOTO WAS ON THE BASEMENT WALL.
THE ONE WITH THE BLACK TOP HAT.
SO THIS HAS TO DO WITH YOSHIRO KINOSHITA, AFTER ALL.
K-KINOSHITA? THE GENIUS MAGICIAN WHO DIED 14 YEARS AGO?
WHAT DO YOU MEAN BY "AFTER ALL?"
I SAW HER LATE AT NIGHT ONCE... DOWN IN THE BASEMENT.
SHE WAS HUGGING THAT PICTURE TO HER CHEST.
I THOUGHT SOMETHING WAS ODD, BUT I NEVER IMAGINED MURDER.
MAN... I'M PRETTY PATHETIC.
IT'S TRUE I WAS FLUSTERED BY THE DISCOVERY OF THE BODY BUT STILL... I CAN'T BELIEVE I DIDN'T NOTICE MAKO CUTTING THE STRINGS OFF HIS RINGS AND RE-INSERTING THE PHONE CORD RIGHT IN FRONT OF ME!
HOW DISAPPOINTING...

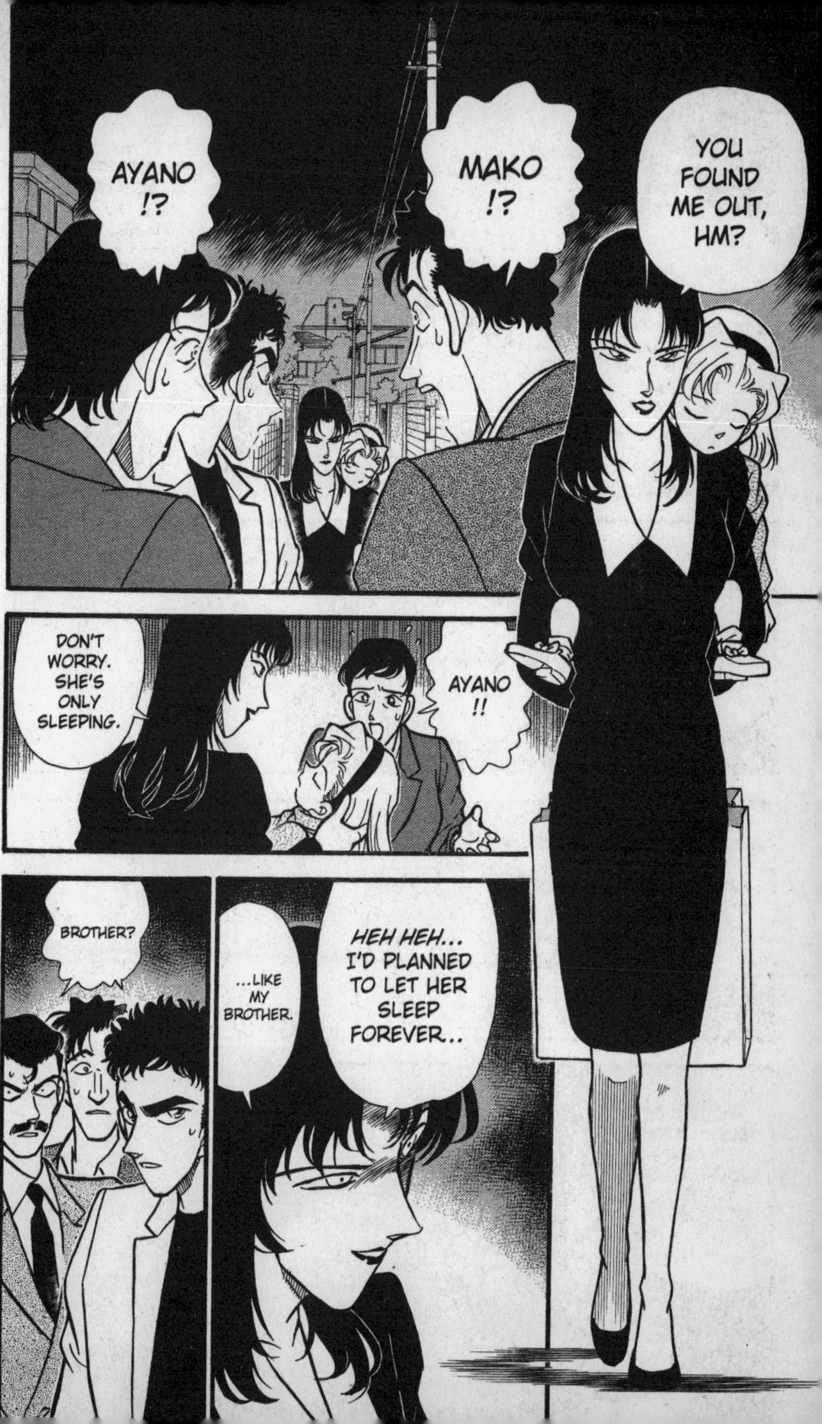
YOU FOUND ME OUT, HM?
MAKO !?
AYANO !?
AYANO !!
DON'T WORRY. SHE'S ONLY SLEEPING.
HEH HEH... I'D PLANNED TO LET HER SLEEP FOREVER...
...LIKE MY BROTHER.
BROTHER?

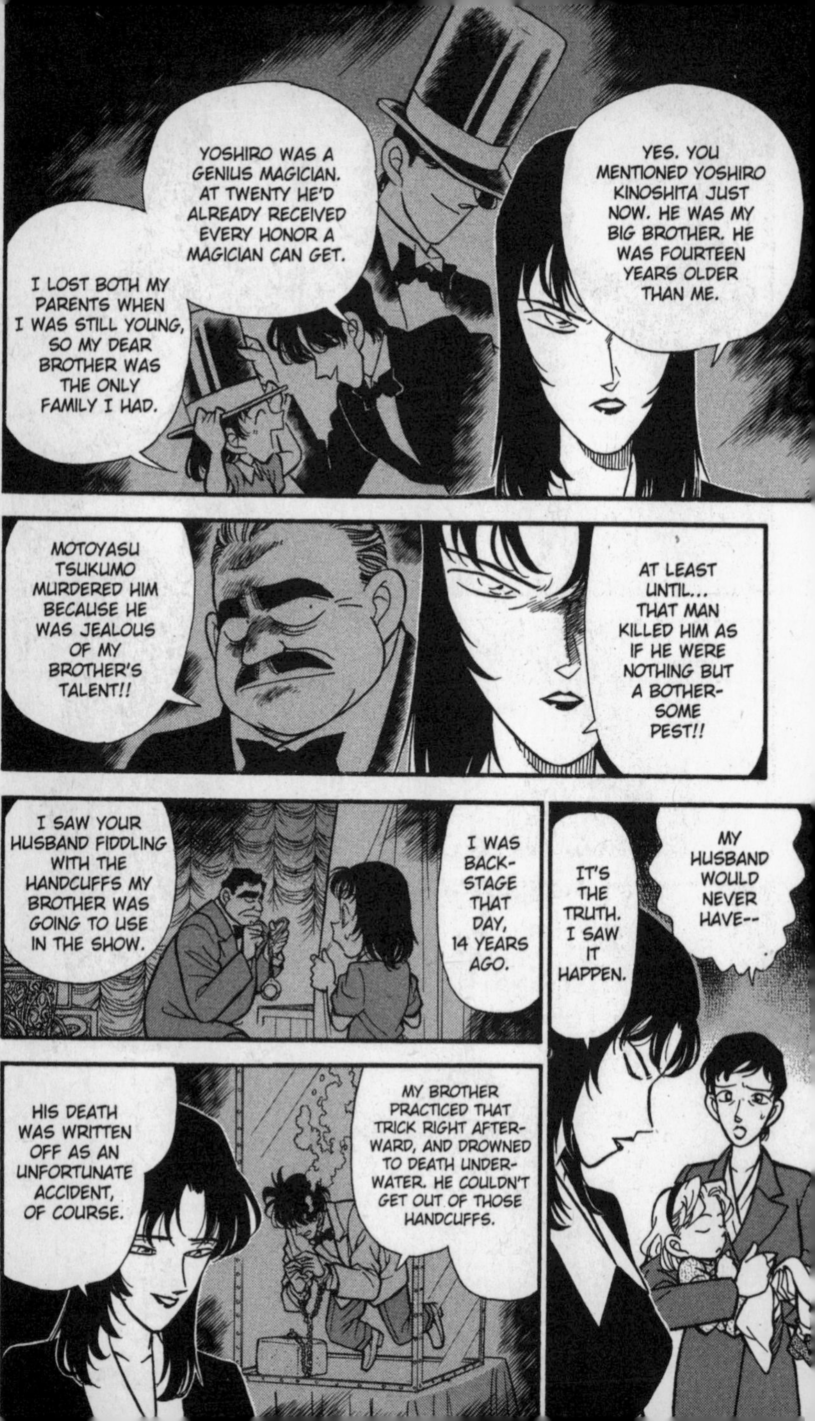
YES. YOU MENTIONED YOSHIRO KINOSHITA JUST NOW. HE WAS MY BIG BROTHER. HE WAS FOURTEEN YEARS OLDER THAN ME.
YOSHIRO WAS A GENIUS MAGICIAN. AT TWENTY HE'D ALREADY RECEIVED EVERY HONOR A MAGICIAN CAN GET.
I LOST BOTH MY PARENTS WHEN I WAS STILL YOUNG, SO MY DEAR BROTHER WAS THE ONLY FAMILY I HAD.
AT LEAST UNTIL... THAT MAN KILLED HIM AS IF HE WERE NOTHING BUT A BOTHER-SOME PEST!!
MOTOYASU TSUKUMO MURDERED HIM BECAUSE HE WAS JEALOUS OF MY BROTHER'S TALENT!!
MY HUSBAND WOULD NEVER HAVE--
IT'S THE TRUTH. I SAW IT HAPPEN.
I WAS BACK-STAGE THAT DAY, 14 YEARS AGO.
I SAW YOUR HUSBAND FIDDLING WITH THE HANDCUFFS MY BROTHER WAS GOING TO USE IN THE SHOW.
MY BROTHER PRACTICED THAT TRICK RIGHT AFTER-WARD, AND DROWNED TO DEATH UNDER-WATER. HE COULDN'T GET OUT OF THOSE HANDCUFFS.
HIS DEATH WAS WRITTEN OFF AS AN UNFORTUNATE ACCIDENT, OF COURSE.

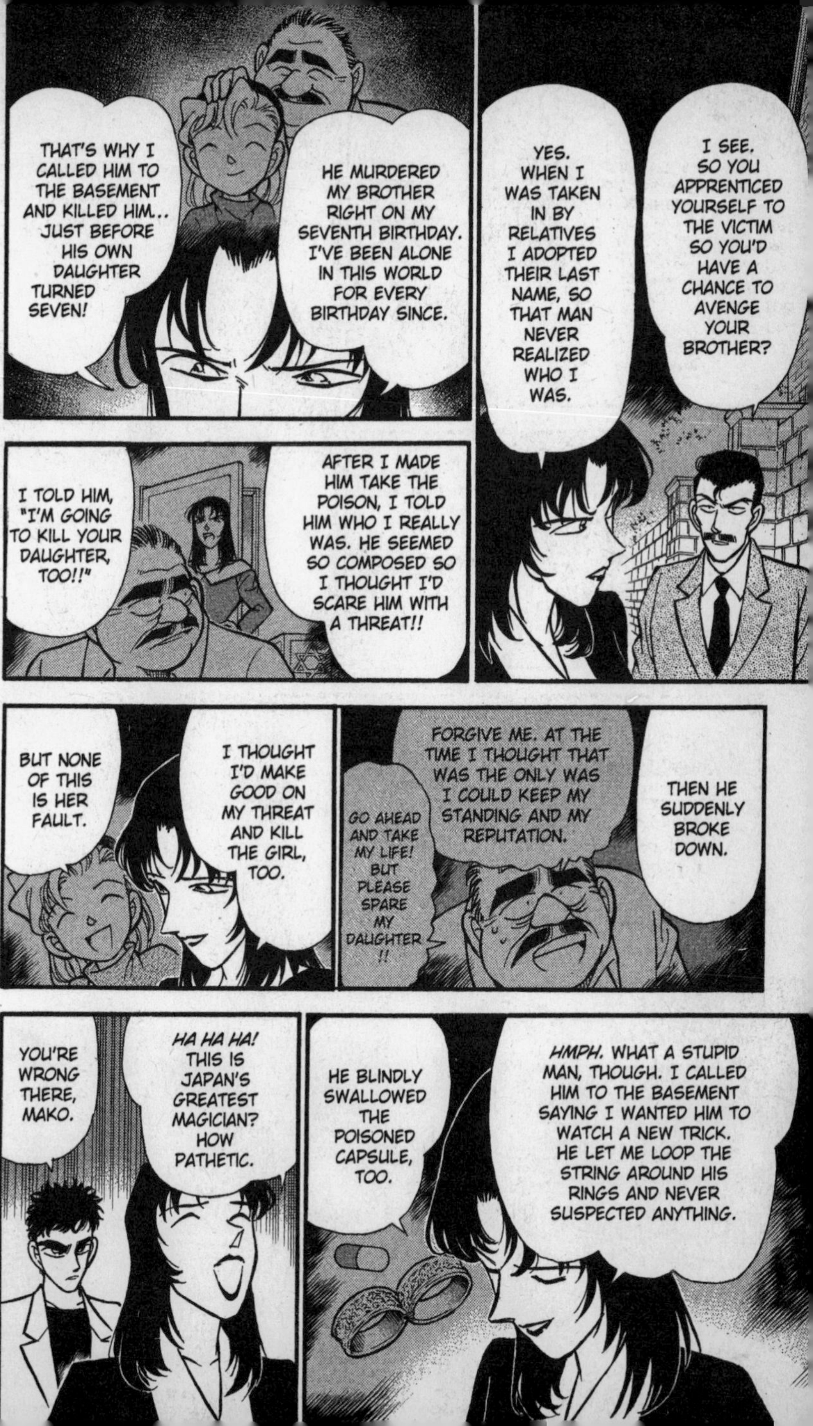
I SEE. SO YOU APPRENTICED YOURSELF TO THE VICTIM SO YOU'D HAVE A CHANCE TO AVENGE YOUR BROTHER?
YES. WHEN I WAS TAKEN IN BY RELATIVES I ADOPTED THEIR LAST NAME, SO THAT MAN NEVER REALIZED WHO I WAS.
HE MURDERED MY BROTHER RIGHT ON MY SEVENTH BIRTHDAY. I'VE BEEN ALONE IN THIS WORLD FOR EVERY BIRTHDAY SINCE.
THAT'S WHY I CALLED HIM TO THE BASEMENT AND KILLED HIM... JUST BEFORE HIS OWN DAUGHTER TURNED SEVEN!
AFTER I MADE HIM TAKE THE POISON, I TOLD HIM WHO I REALLY WAS. HE SEEMED SO COMPOSED SO I THOUGHT I'D SCARE HIM WITH A THREAT!!
I TOLD HIM, "I'M GOING TO KILL YOUR DAUGHTER, TOO!!"
THEN HE SUDDENLY BROKE DOWN.
FORGIVE ME. AT THE TIME I THOUGHT THAT WAS THE ONLY WAS I COULD KEEP MY STANDING AND MY REPUTATION.
GO AHEAD AND TAKE MY LIFE! BUT PLEASE SPARE MY DAUGHTER!!
I THOUGHT I'D MAKE GOOD ON MY THREAT AND KILL THE GIRL, TOO.
BUT NONE OF THIS IS HER FAULT.
HMPH. WHAT A STUPID MAN, THOUGH. I CALLED HIM TO THE BASEMENT SAYING I WANTED HIM TO WATCH A NEW TRICK. HE LET ME LOOP THE STRING AROUND HIS RINGS AND NEVER SUSPECTED ANYTHING.
HE BLINDLY SWALLOWED THE POISONED CAPSULE, TOO.
HA HA HA! THIS IS JAPAN'S GREATEST MAGICIAN? HOW PATHETIC.
YOU'RE WRONG THERE, MAKO.

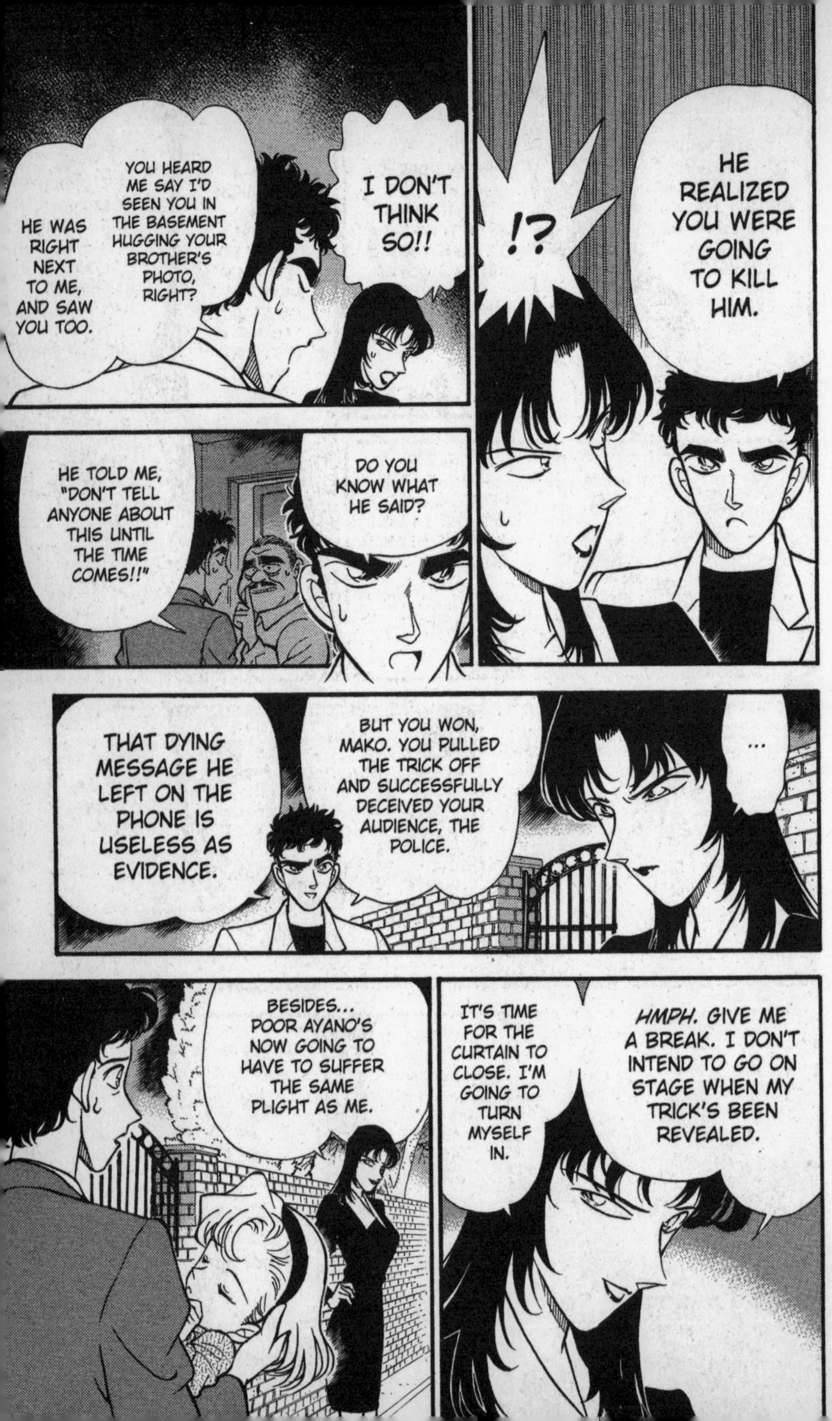
HE REALIZED YOU WERE GOING TO KILL HIM.
!?
I DON'T THINK SO!!
YOU HEARD ME SAY I'D SEEN YOU IN THE BASEMENT HUGGING YOUR BROTHER'S PHOTO, RIGHT?
HE WAS RIGHT NEXT TO ME, AND SAW YOU TOO.
DO YOU KNOW WHAT HE SAID?
HE TOLD ME, "DON'T TELL ANYONE ABOUT THIS UNTIL THE TIME COMES!!"
...
BUT YOU WON, MAKO. YOU PULLED THE TRICK OFF AND SUCCESSFULLY DECEIVED YOUR AUDIENCE, THE POLICE.
THAT DYING MESSAGE HE LEFT ON THE PHONE IS USELESS AS EVIDENCE.
HMPH. GIVE ME A BREAK. I DON'T INTEND TO GO ON STAGE WHEN MY TRICK'S BEEN REVEALED.
IT'S TIME FOR THE CURTAIN TO CLOSE. I'M GOING TO TURN MYSELF IN.
BESIDES... POOR AYANO'S NOW GOING TO HAVE TO SUFFER THE SAME PLIGHT AS ME.

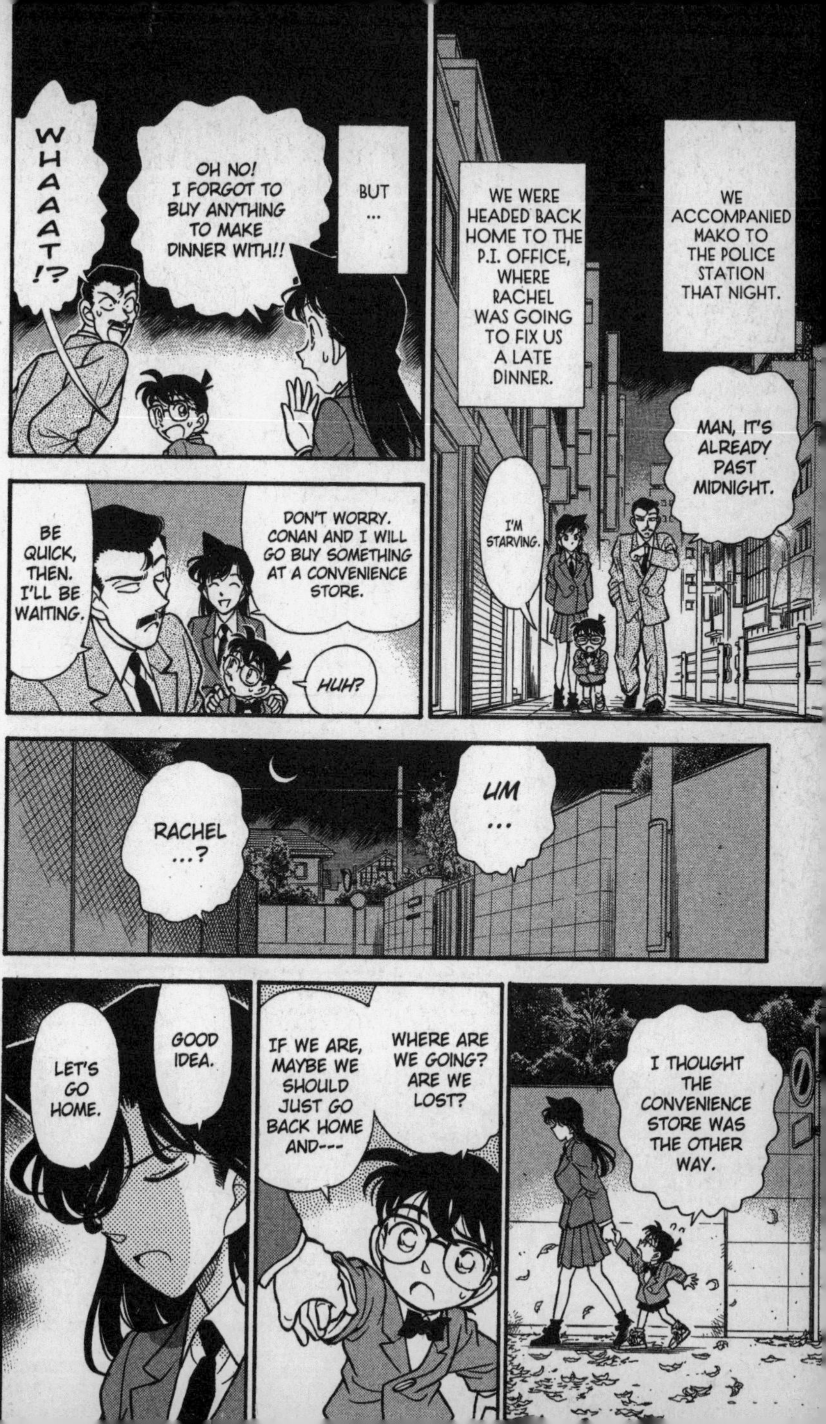
WE ACCOMPANIED MAKO TO THE POLICE STATION THAT NIGHT.
WE WERE HEADED BACK HOME TO THE P.I. OFFICE, WHERE RACHEL WAS GOING TO FIX US A LATE DINNER.
MAN, IT'S ALREADY PAST MIDNIGHT.
I'M STARVING.
BUT ...
OH NO! I FORGOT TO BUY ANYTHING TO MAKE DINNER WITH!!
WHAAAT!?
DON'T WORRY. CONAN AND I WILL GO BUY SOMETHING AT A CONVENIENCE STORE.
BE QUICK, THEN. I'LL BE WAITING.
HUH?
UM ...
RACHEL ...?
I THOUGHT THE CONVENIENCE STORE WAS THE OTHER WAY.
WHERE ARE WE GOING? ARE WE LOST?
IF WE ARE, MAYBE WE SHOULD JUST GO BACK HOME AND---
GOOD IDEA.
LET'S GO HOME.

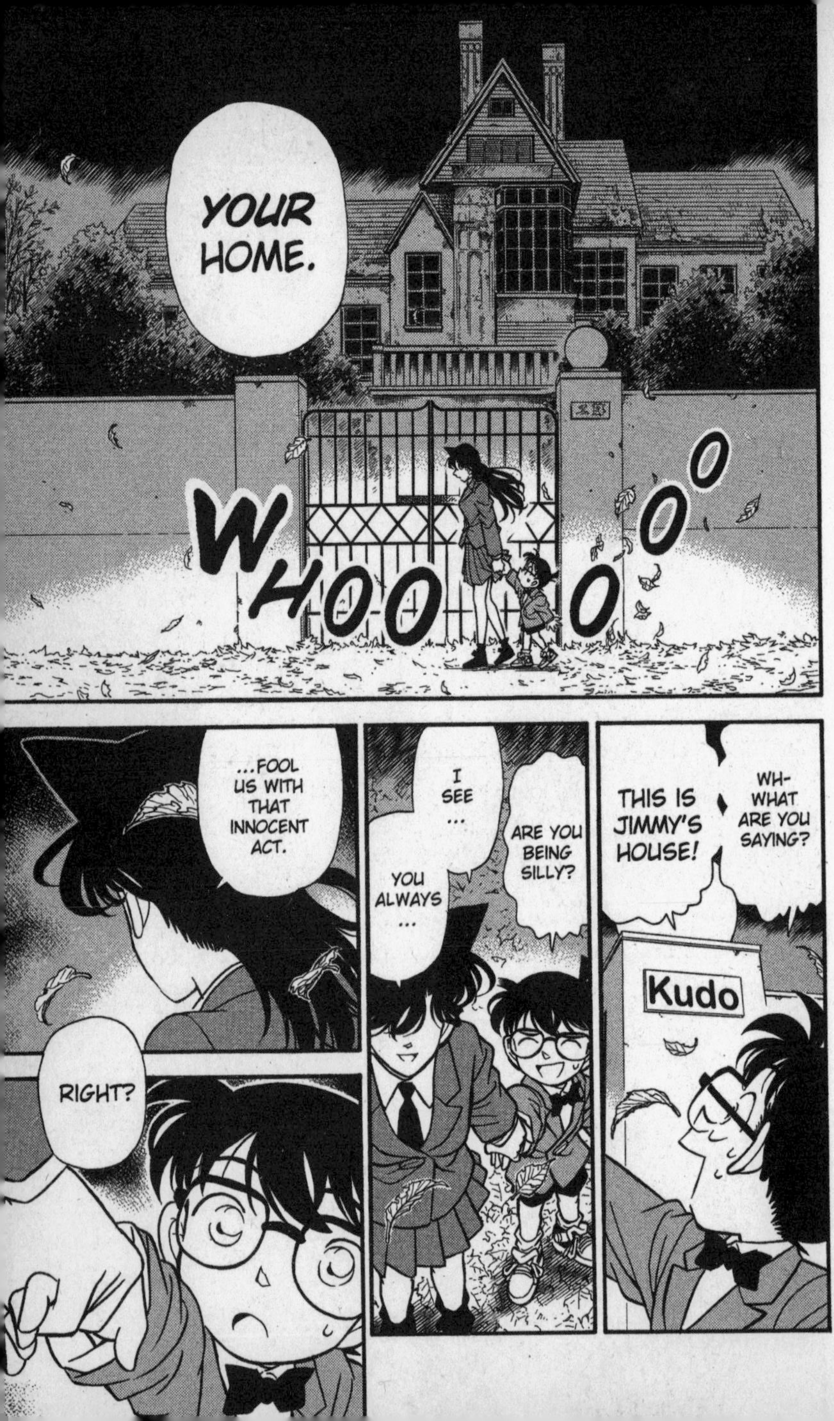
YOUR HOME.
WHOOOOOO
WH-WHAT ARE YOU SAYING?
THIS IS JIMMY'S HOUSE!
Kudo
ARE YOU BEING SILLY?
I SEE...
YOU ALWAYS...
...FOOL US WITH THAT INNOCENT ACT.
RIGHT?

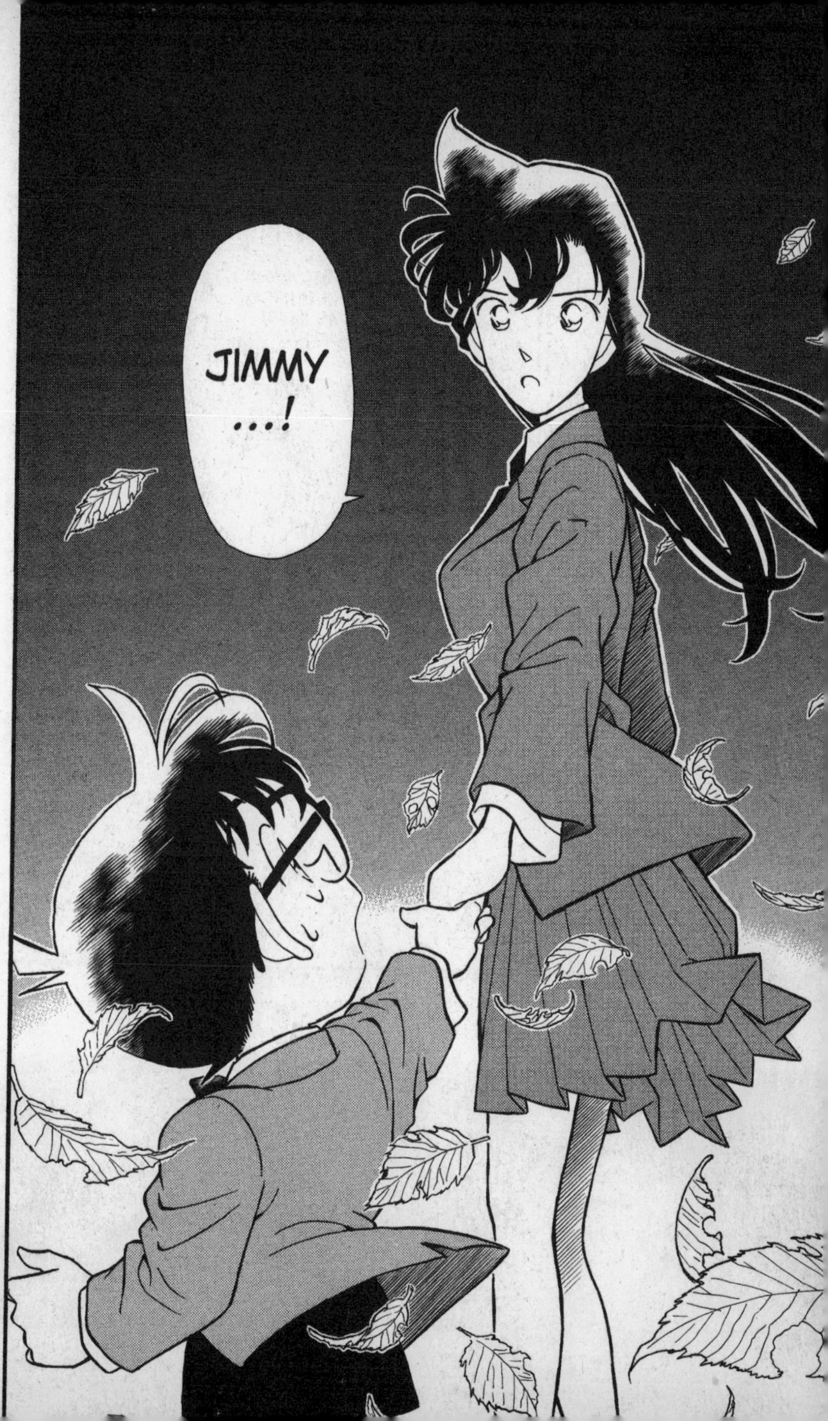
JIMMY ...!

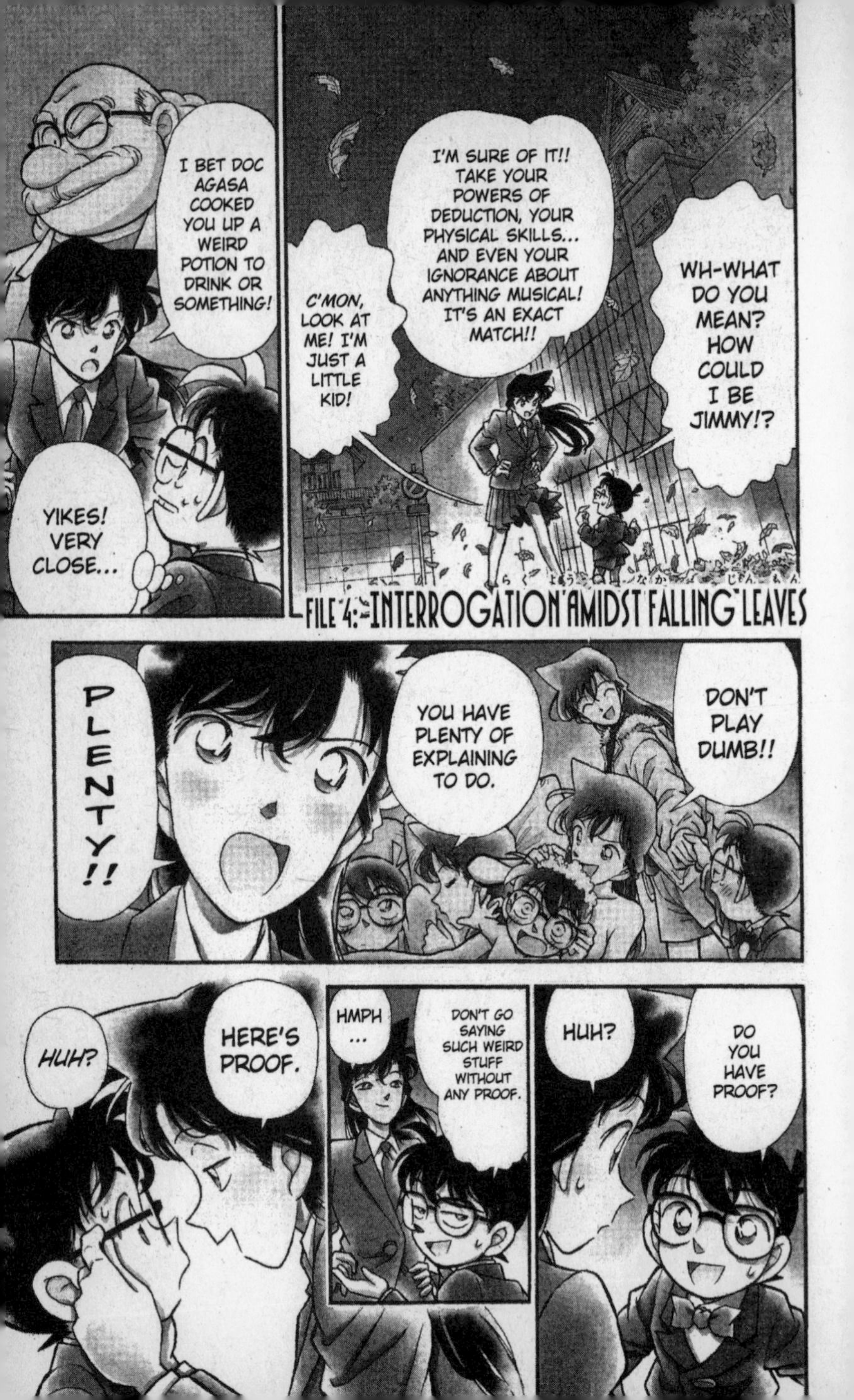
WH-WHAT DO YOU MEAN? HOW COULD I BE JIMMY!?
I'M SURE OF IT!! TAKE YOUR POWERS OF DEDUCTION, YOUR PHYSICAL SKILLS... AND EVEN YOUR IGNORANCE ABOUT ANYTHING MUSICAL! IT'S AN EXACT MATCH!!
C'MON, LOOK AT ME! I'M JUST A LITTLE KID!
I BET DOC AGASA COOKED YOU UP A WEIRD POTION TO DRINK OR SOMETHING!
YIKES! VERY CLOSE...
FILE 4: INTERROGATION AMIDST FALLING LEAVES
DON'T PLAY DUMB!!
YOU HAVE PLENTY OF EXPLAINING TO DO.
PLENTY!!
DO YOU HAVE PROOF?
HUH?
DON'T GO SAYING SUCH WEIRD STUFF WITHOUT ANY PROOF.
HMPH...
HERE'S PROOF.
HUH?

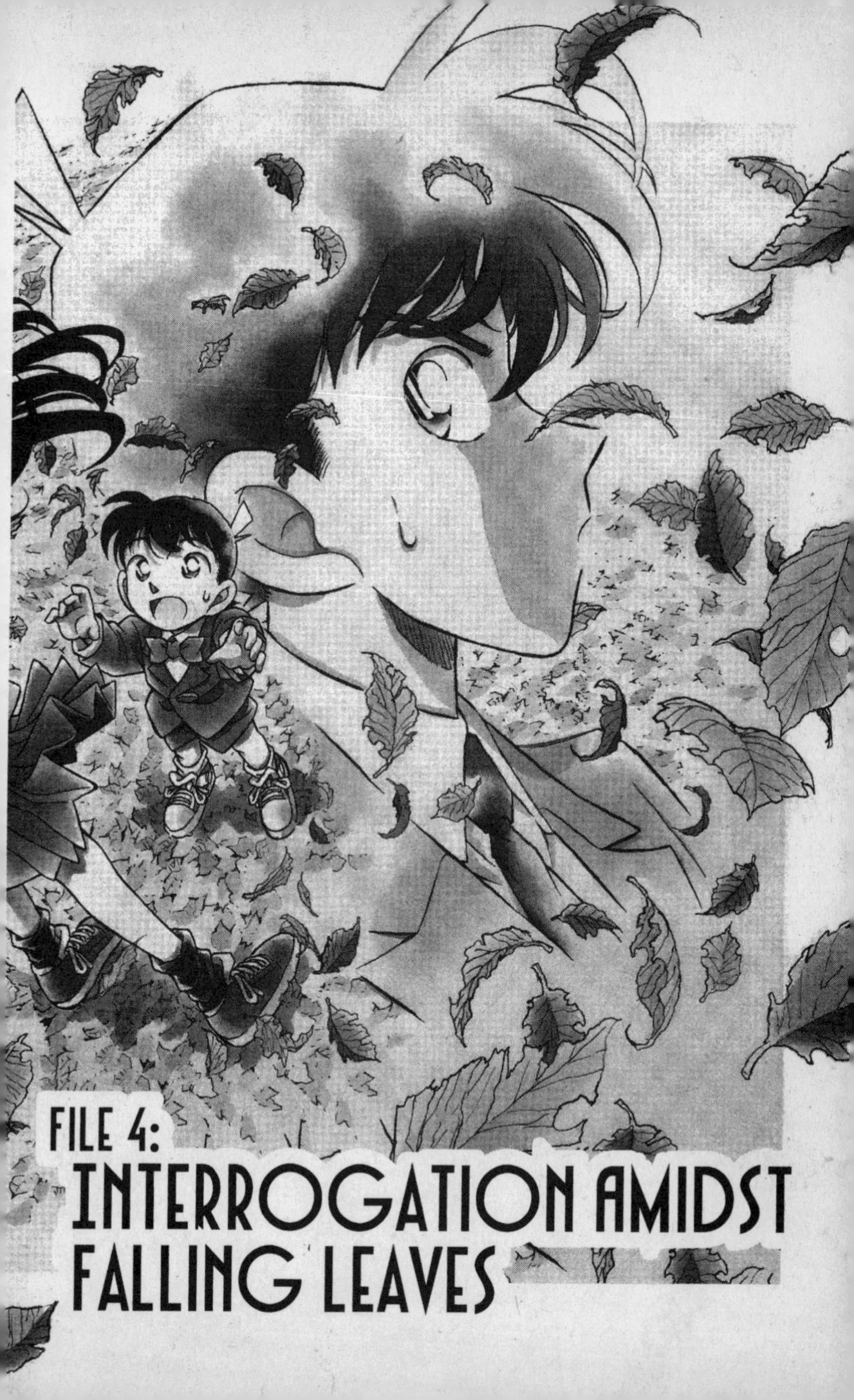
FILE 4:
INTERROGATION AMIDST FALLING LEAVES

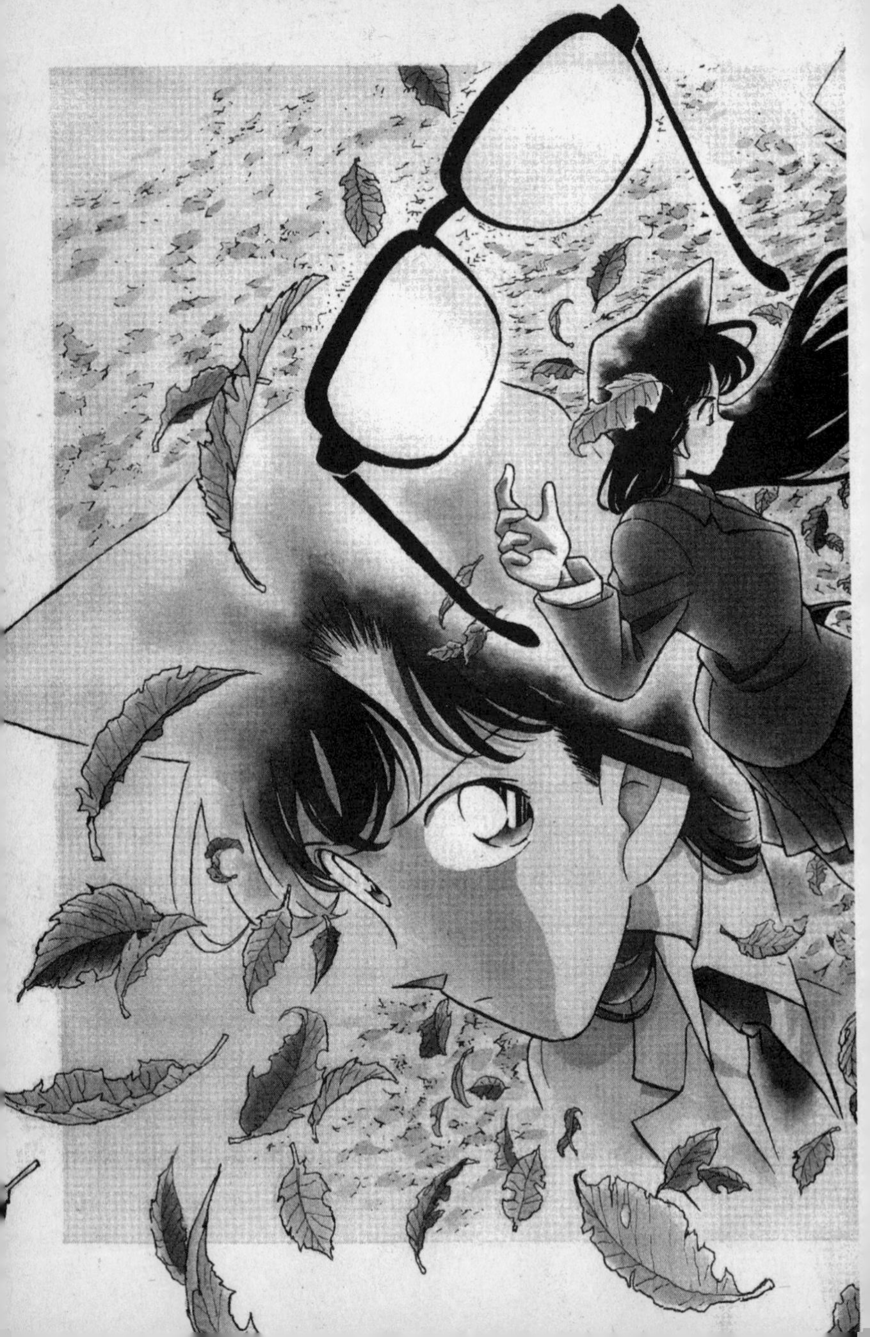

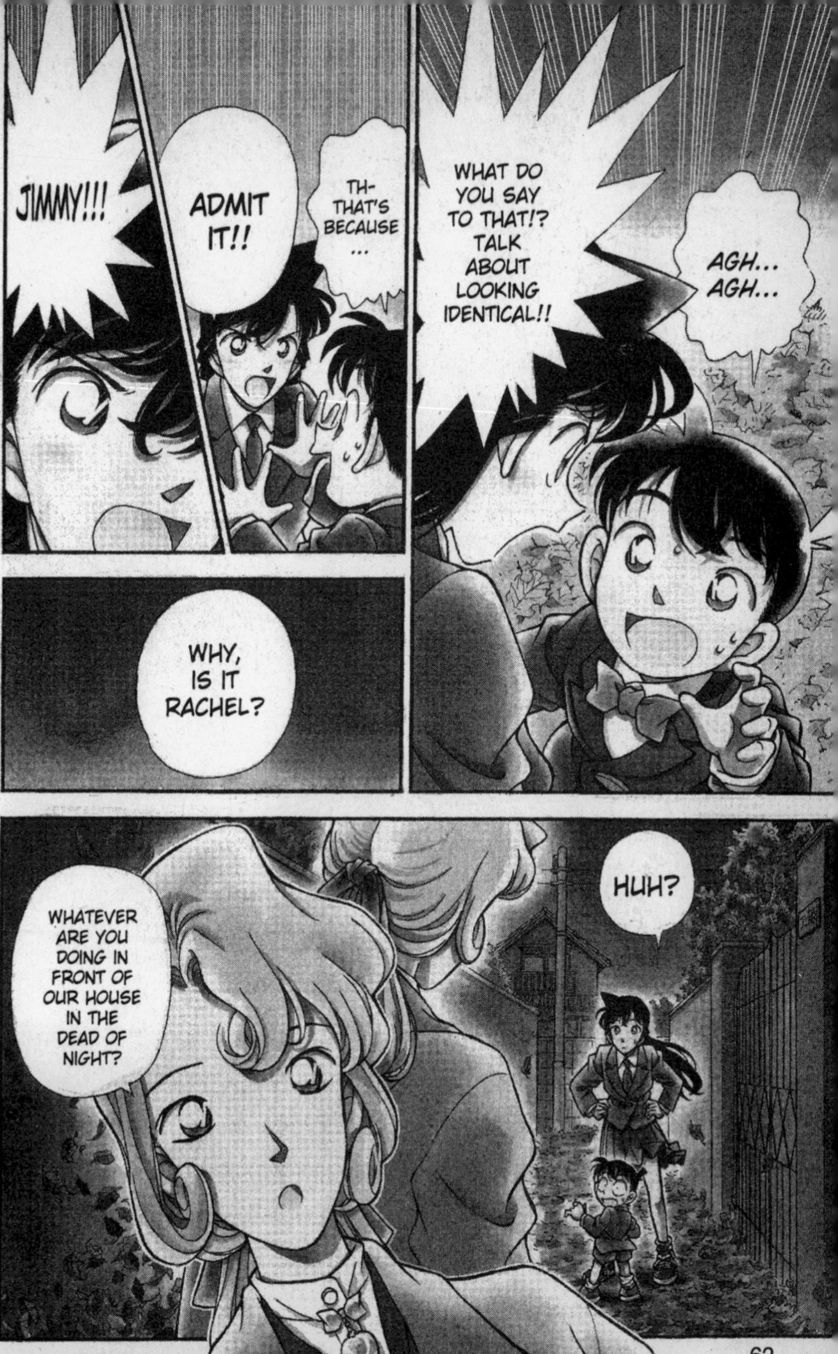
WHAT DO YOU SAY TO THAT!? TALK ABOUT LOOKING IDENTICAL!!
AGH... AGH...
ADMIT IT!!
TH- THAT'S BECAUSE ...
JIMMY!!!
WHY, IS IT RACHEL?
HUH?
WHATEVER ARE YOU DOING IN FRONT OF OUR HOUSE IN THE DEAD OF NIGHT?

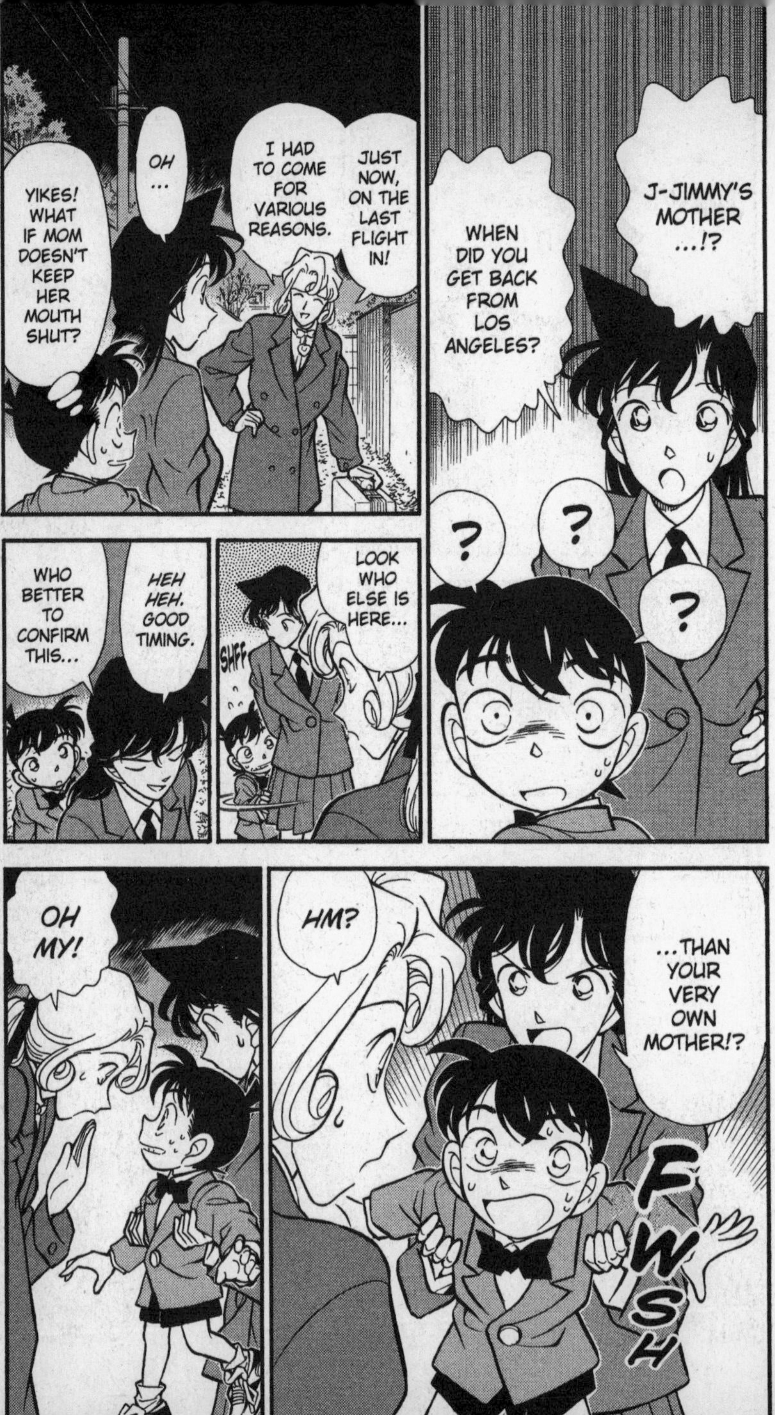
J-JIMMY'S MOTHER ...!?
WHEN DID YOU GET BACK FROM LOS ANGELES?
?
?
?
JUST NOW, ON THE LAST FLIGHT IN!
I HAD TO COME FOR VARIOUS REASONS.
OH ...
YIKES! WHAT IF MOM DOESN'T KEEP HER MOUTH SHUT?
LOOK WHO ELSE IS HERE...
SHFF
HEH HEH. GOOD TIMING.
WHO BETTER TO CONFIRM THIS...
...THAN YOUR VERY OWN MOTHER!?
HM?
FWSH
OH MY!

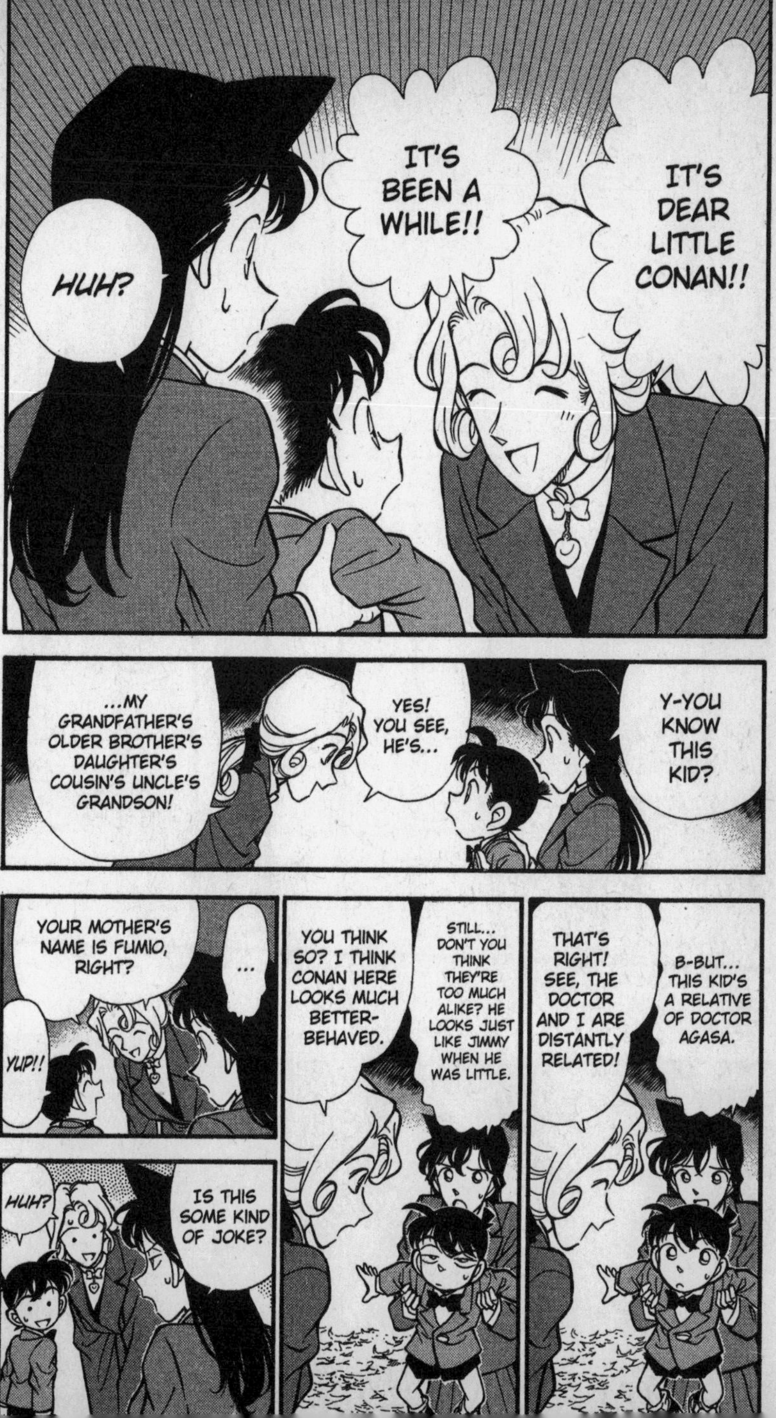
IT'S DEAR LITTLE CONAN!!
IT'S BEEN A WHILE!!
HUH?
Y-YOU KNOW THIS KID?
YES! YOU SEE, HE'S...
...MY GRANDFATHER'S OLDER BROTHER'S DAUGHTER'S COUSIN'S UNCLE'S GRANDSON!
B-BUT... THIS KID'S A RELATIVE OF DOCTOR AGASA.
THAT'S RIGHT! SEE, THE DOCTOR AND I ARE DISTANTLY RELATED!
STILL... DON'T YOU THINK THEY'RE TOO MUCH ALIKE? HE LOOKS JUST LIKE JIMMY WHEN HE WAS LITTLE.
YOU THINK SO? I THINK CONAN HERE LOOKS MUCH BETTER-BEHAVED.
...
YOUR MOTHER'S NAME IS FUMIO, RIGHT?
YUP!!
IS THIS SOME KIND OF JOKE?
HUH?

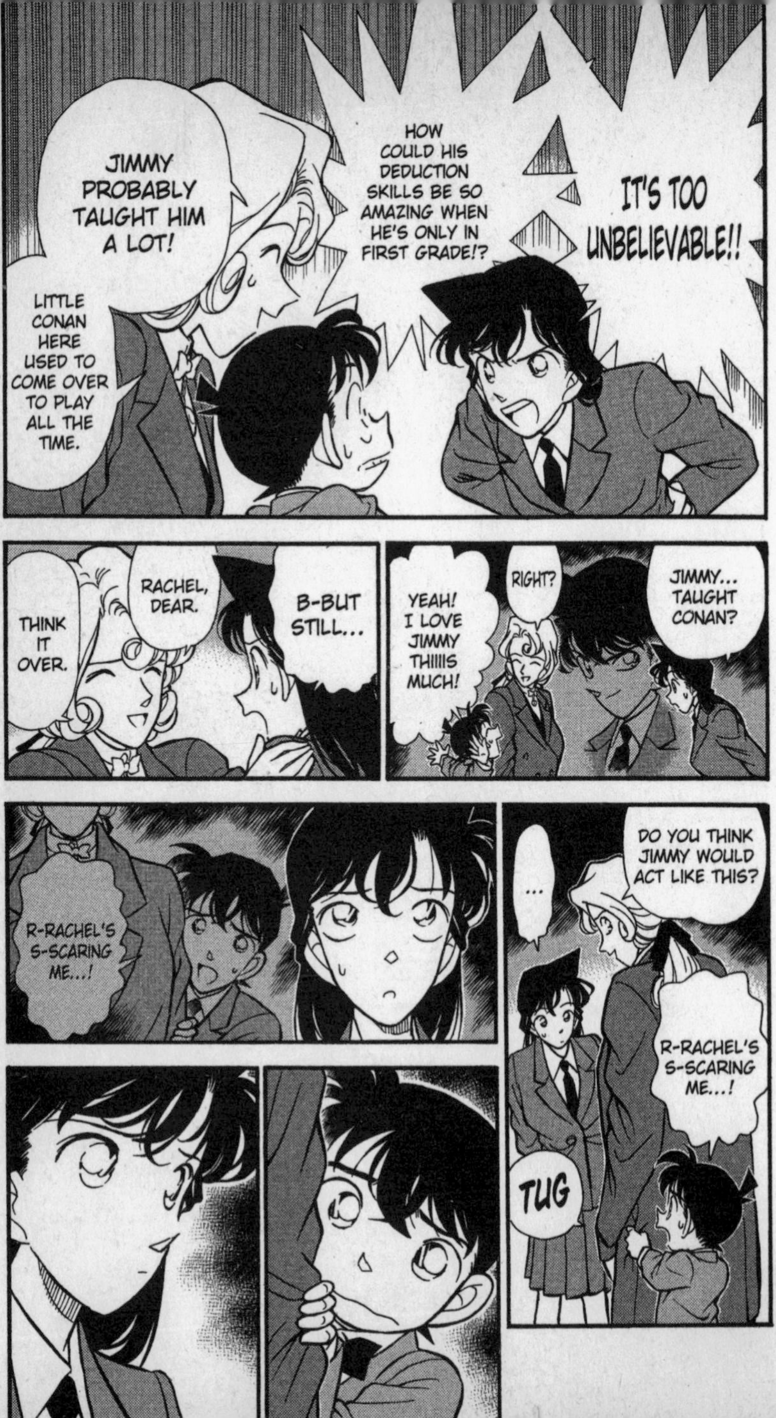
IT'S TOO UNBELIEVABLE!!
HOW COULD HIS DEDUCTION SKILLS BE SO AMAZING WHEN HE'S ONLY IN FIRST GRADE!?
JIMMY PROBABLY TAUGHT HIM A LOT!
LITTLE CONAN HERE USED TO COME OVER TO PLAY ALL THE TIME.
JIMMY... TAUGHT CONAN?
RIGHT?
YEAH! I LOVE JIMMY THIIIIS MUCH!
B-BUT STILL...
RACHEL, DEAR.
THINK IT OVER.
DO YOU THINK JIMMY WOULD ACT LIKE THIS?
...
R-RACHEL'S S-SCARING ME...!
TUG
R-RACHEL'S S-SCARING ME...!

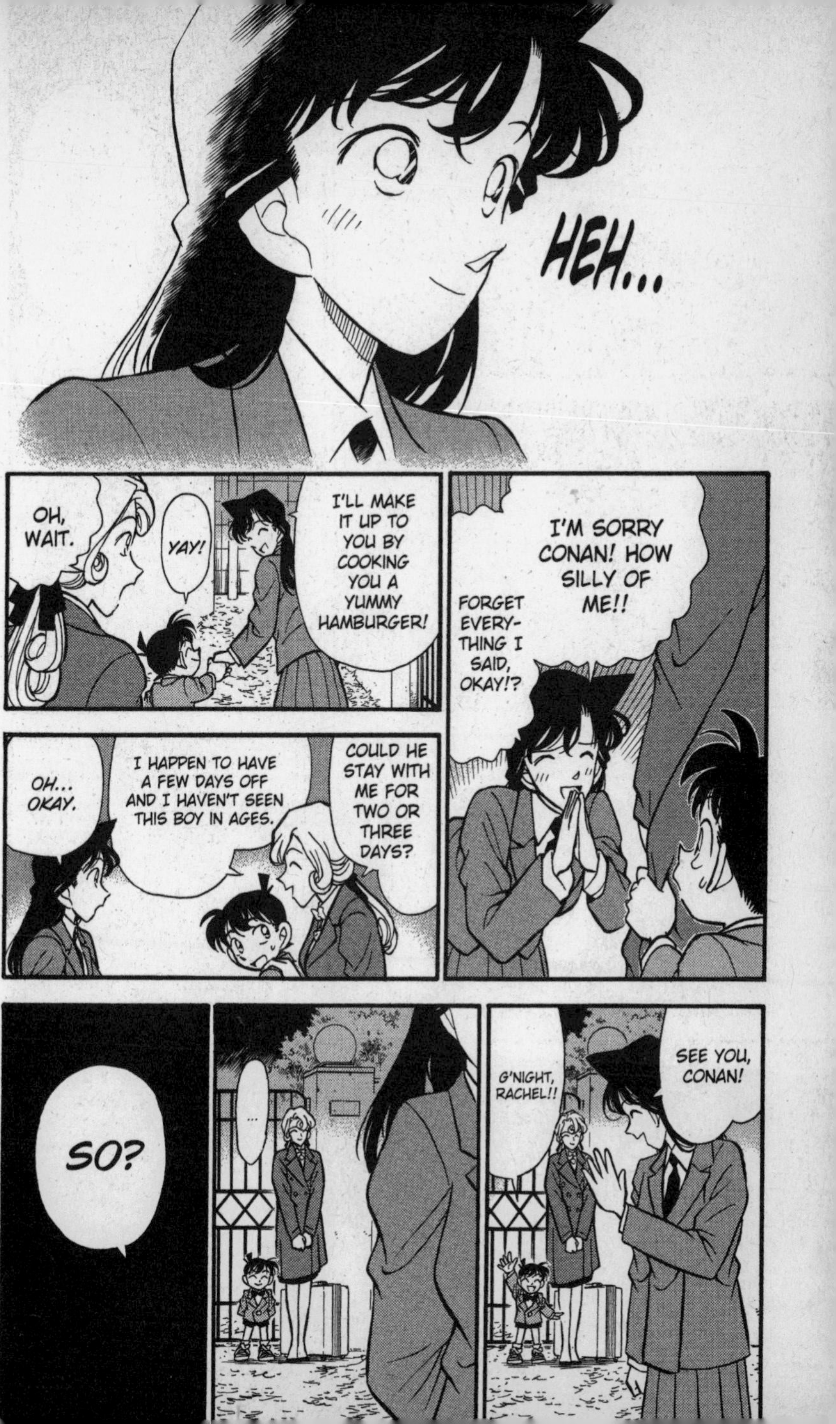
HEH...
I'M SORRY CONAN! HOW SILLY OF ME!!
FORGET EVERY-THING I SAID, OKAY!?
I'LL MAKE IT UP TO YOU BY COOKING YOU A YUMMY HAMBURGER!
YAY!
OH, WAIT.
COULD HE STAY WITH ME FOR TWO OR THREE DAYS?
I HAPPEN TO HAVE A FEW DAYS OFF AND I HAVEN'T SEEN THIS BOY IN AGES.
OH... OKAY.
SEE YOU, CONAN!
G'NIGHT, RACHEL!!
...
SO?

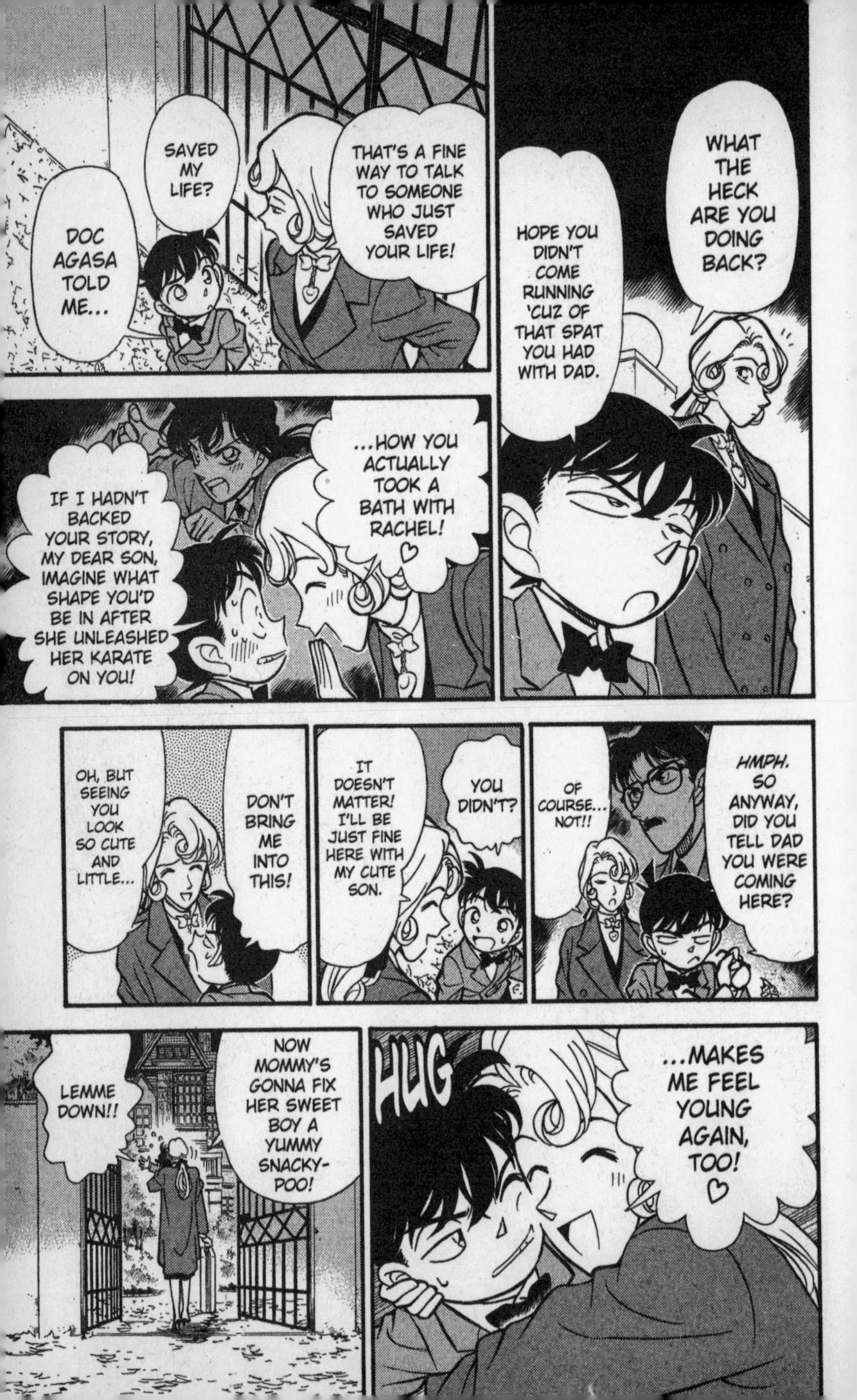
WHAT THE HECK ARE YOU DOING BACK?
HOPE YOU DIDN'T COME RUNNING 'CUZ OF THAT SPAT YOU HAD WITH DAD.
THAT'S A FINE WAY TO TALK TO SOMEONE WHO JUST SAVED YOUR LIFE!
SAVED MY LIFE?
DOC AGASA TOLD ME...
...HOW YOU ACTUALLY TOOK A BATH WITH RACHEL! ♡
IF I HADN'T BACKED YOUR STORY, MY DEAR SON, IMAGINE WHAT SHAPE YOU'D BE IN AFTER SHE UNLEASHED HER KARATE ON YOU!
HMPH. SO ANYWAY, DID YOU TELL DAD YOU WERE COMING HERE?
OF COURSE... NOT!!
YOU DIDN'T?
IT DOESN'T MATTER! I'LL BE JUST FINE HERE WITH MY CUTE SON.
DON'T BRING ME INTO THIS!
OH, BUT SEEING YOU LOOK SO CUTE AND LITTLE...
HUG
...MAKES ME FEEL YOUNG AGAIN, TOO! ♡
NOW MOMMY'S GONNA FIX HER SWEET BOY A YUMMY SNACKY-POO!
LEMME DOWN!!

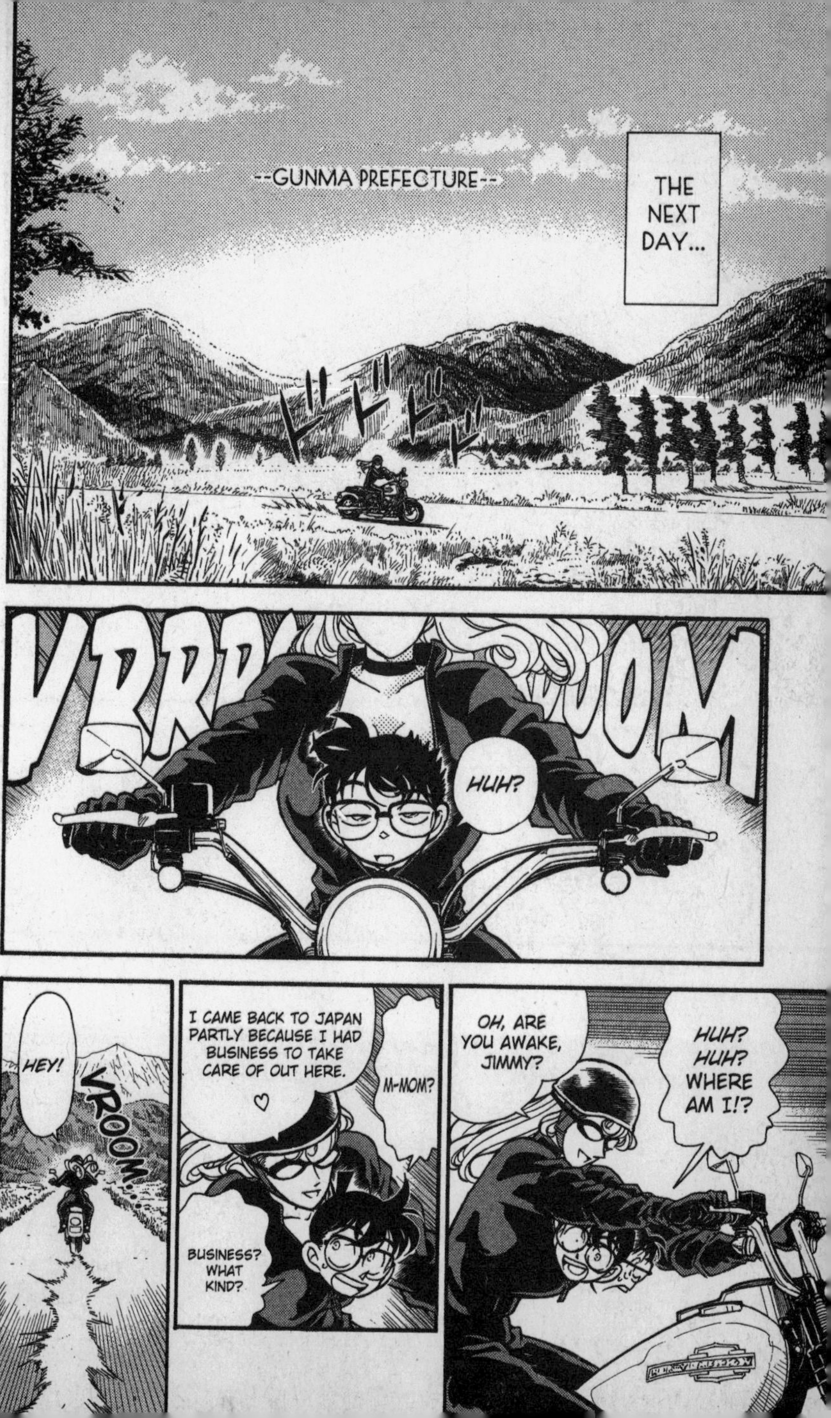
THE NEXT DAY...
--GUNMA PREFECTURE--
ドドドド
HUH?
HUH? HUH? WHERE AM I!?
OH, ARE YOU AWAKE, JIMMY?
M-MOM?
I CAME BACK TO JAPAN PARTLY BECAUSE I HAD BUSINESS TO TAKE CARE OF OUT HERE. ♡
BUSINESS? WHAT KIND?
HEY!
VROOOM!

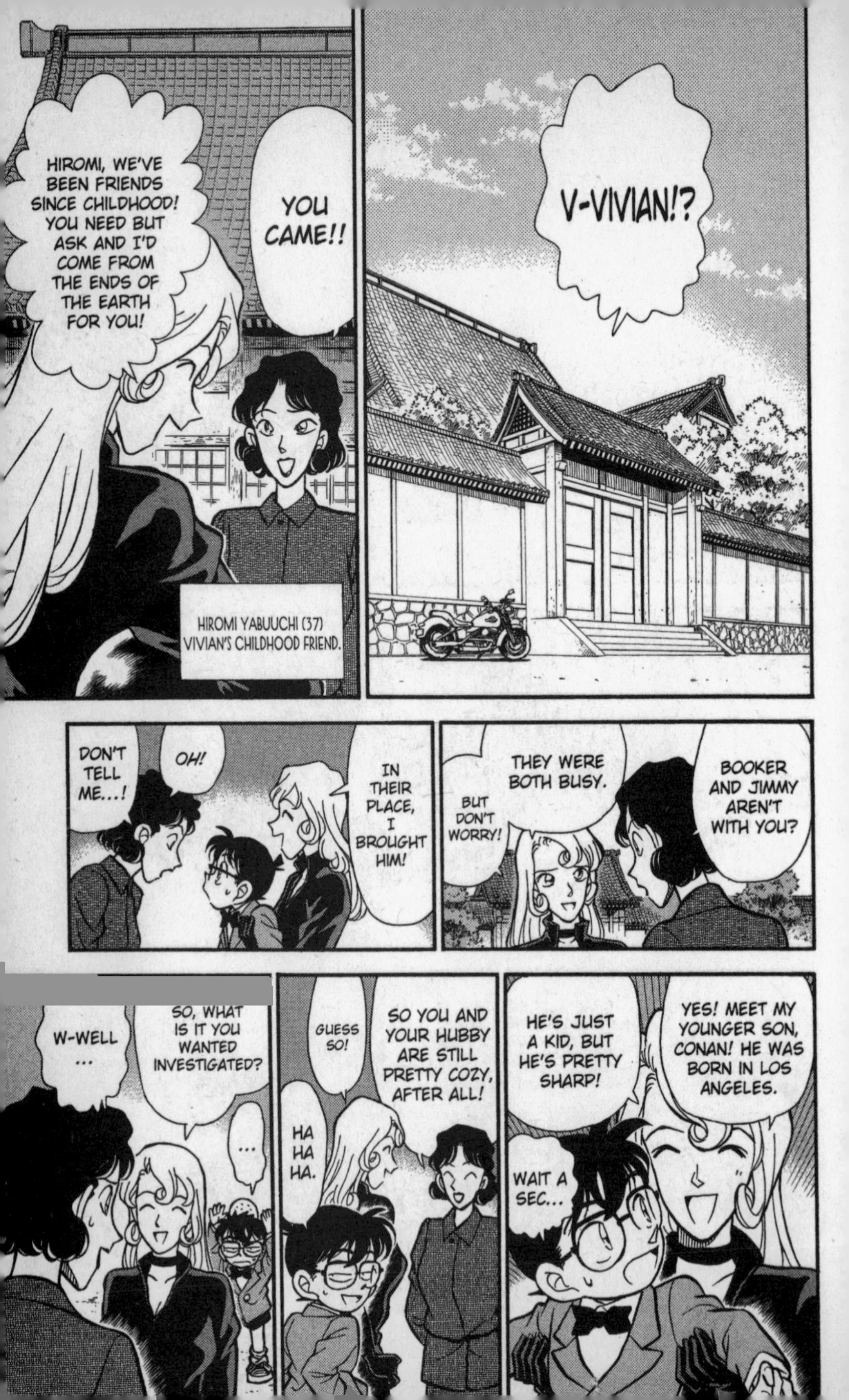
V-VIVIAN!?
YOU CAME!!
HIROMI, WE'VE BEEN FRIENDS SINCE CHILDHOOD! YOU NEED BUT ASK AND I'D COME FROM THE ENDS OF THE EARTH FOR YOU!
HIROMI YABUUCHI (37) VIVIAN'S CHILDHOOD FRIEND.
BOOKER AND JIMMY AREN'T WITH YOU?
THEY WERE BOTH BUSY.
BUT DON'T WORRY!
IN THEIR PLACE, I BROUGHT HIM!
OH!
DON'T TELL ME...!
YES! MEET MY YOUNGER SON, CONAN! HE WAS BORN IN LOS ANGELES.
HE'S JUST A KID, BUT HE'S PRETTY SHARP!
WAIT A SEC...
SO YOU AND YOUR HUBBY ARE STILL PRETTY COZY, AFTER ALL!
GUESS SO!
HA HA HA.
SO, WHAT IS IT YOU WANTED INVESTIGATED?
W-WELL ...
...

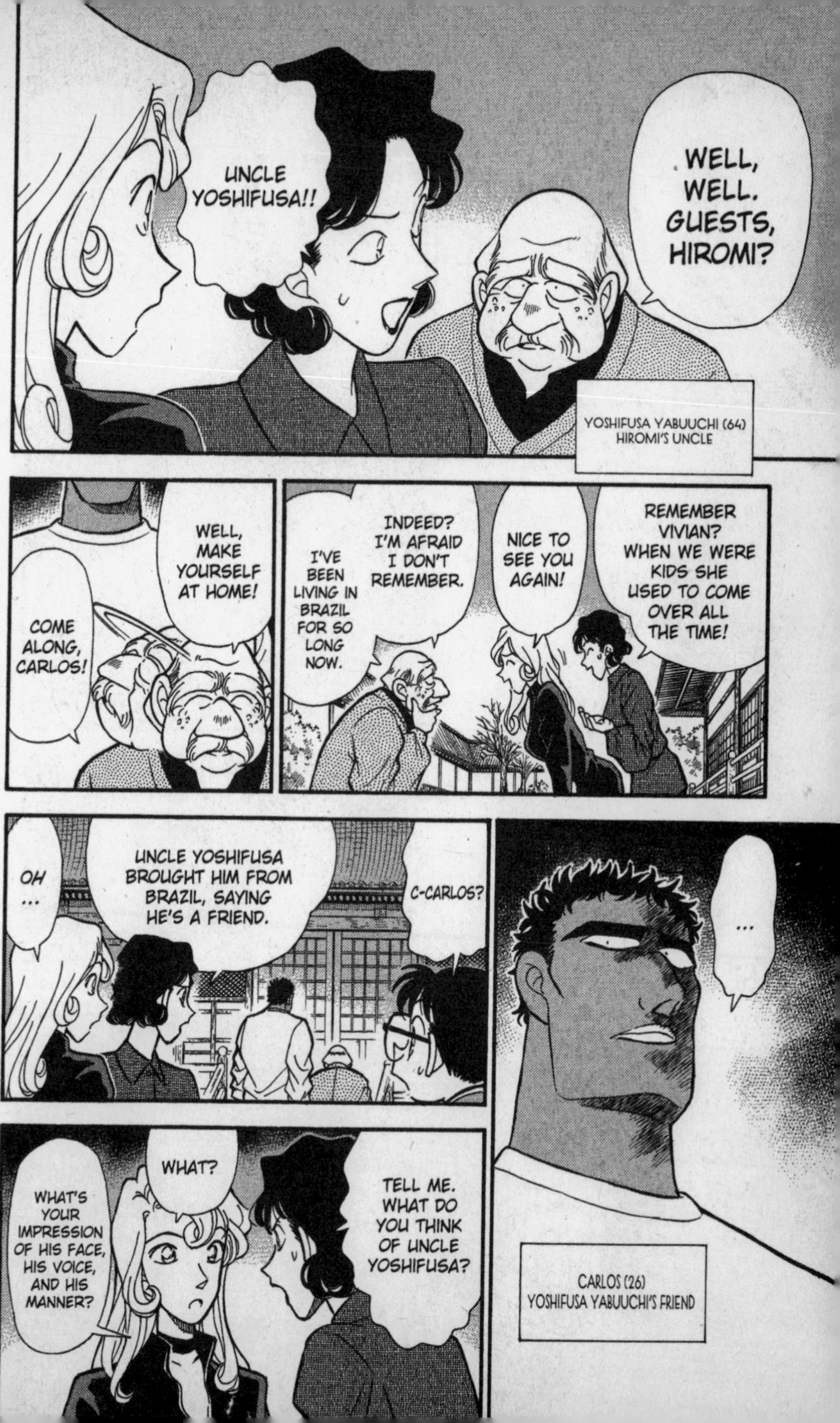
WELL, WELL. GUESTS, HIROMI?
UNCLE YOSHIFUSA!!
YOSHIFUSA YABUUCHI (64) HIROMI'S UNCLE
REMEMBER VIVIAN? WHEN WE WERE KIDS SHE USED TO COME OVER ALL THE TIME!
NICE TO SEE YOU AGAIN!
INDEED? I'M AFRAID I DON'T REMEMBER.
I'VE BEEN LIVING IN BRAZIL FOR SO LONG NOW.
WELL, MAKE YOURSELF AT HOME!
COME ALONG, CARLOS!
...
CARLOS (26) YOSHIFUSA YABUUCHI'S FRIEND
C-CARLOS?
UNCLE YOSHIFUSA BROUGHT HIM FROM BRAZIL, SAYING HE'S A FRIEND.
OH ...
TELL ME. WHAT DO YOU THINK OF UNCLE YOSHIFUSA?
WHAT?
WHAT'S YOUR IMPRESSION OF HIS FACE, HIS VOICE, AND HIS MANNER?

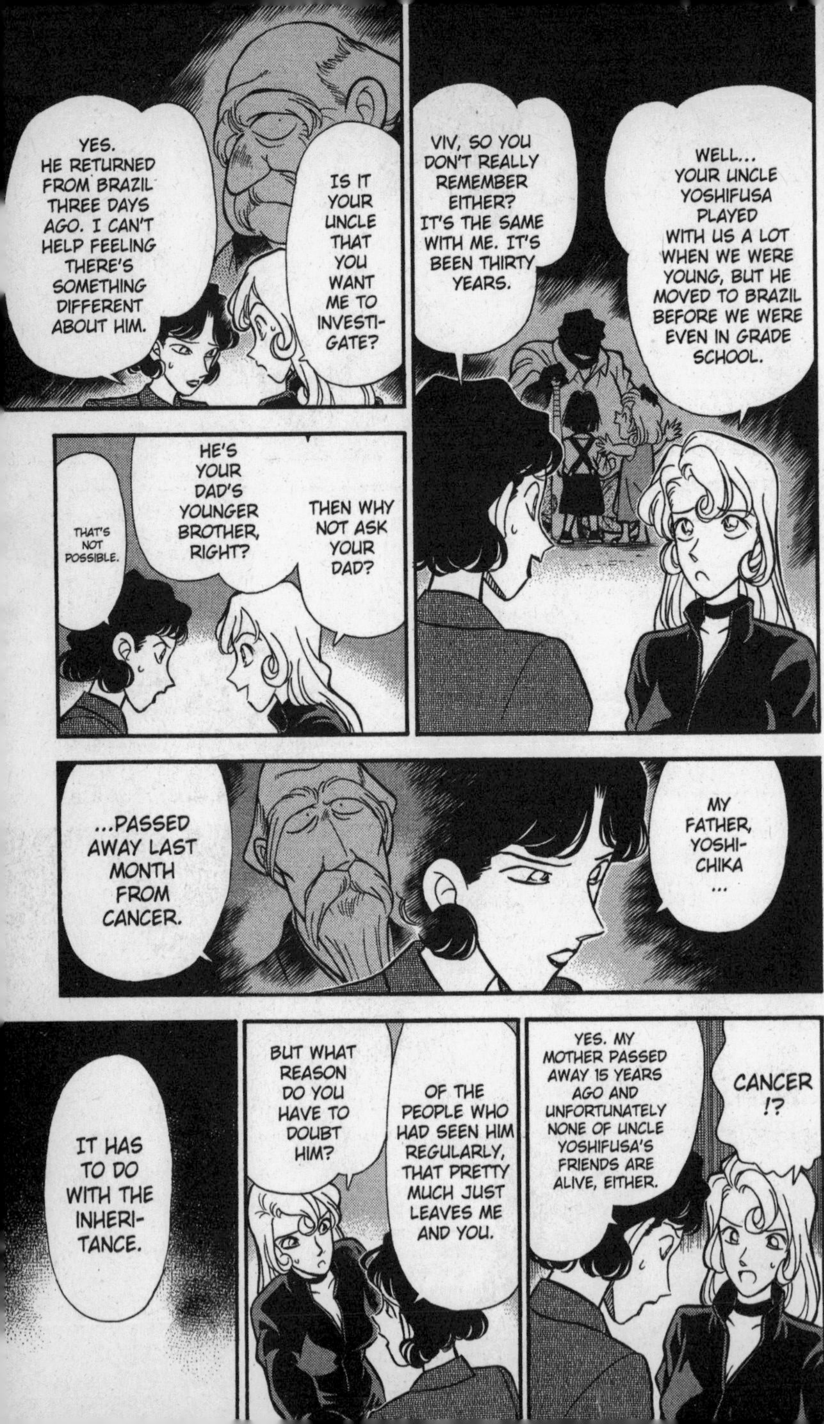
WELL... YOUR UNCLE YOSHIFUSA PLAYED WITH US A LOT WHEN WE WERE YOUNG, BUT HE MOVED TO BRAZIL BEFORE WE WERE EVEN IN GRADE SCHOOL.
VIV, SO YOU DON'T REALLY REMEMBER EITHER? IT'S THE SAME WITH ME. IT'S BEEN THIRTY YEARS.
IS IT YOUR UNCLE THAT YOU WANT ME TO INVESTIGATE?
YES. HE RETURNED FROM BRAZIL THREE DAYS AGO. I CAN'T HELP FEELING THERE'S SOMETHING DIFFERENT ABOUT HIM.
THEN WHY NOT ASK YOUR DAD?
HE'S YOUR DAD'S YOUNGER BROTHER, RIGHT?
THAT'S NOT POSSIBLE.
MY FATHER, YOSHICHIKA...
...PASSED AWAY LAST MONTH FROM CANCER.
CANCER!?
YES. MY MOTHER PASSED AWAY 15 YEARS AGO AND UNFORTUNATELY NONE OF UNCLE YOSHIFUSA'S FRIENDS ARE ALIVE, EITHER.
OF THE PEOPLE WHO HAD SEEN HIM REGULARLY, THAT PRETTY MUCH JUST LEAVES ME AND YOU.
BUT WHAT REASON DO YOU HAVE TO DOUBT HIM?
IT HAS TO DO WITH THE INHERITANCE.

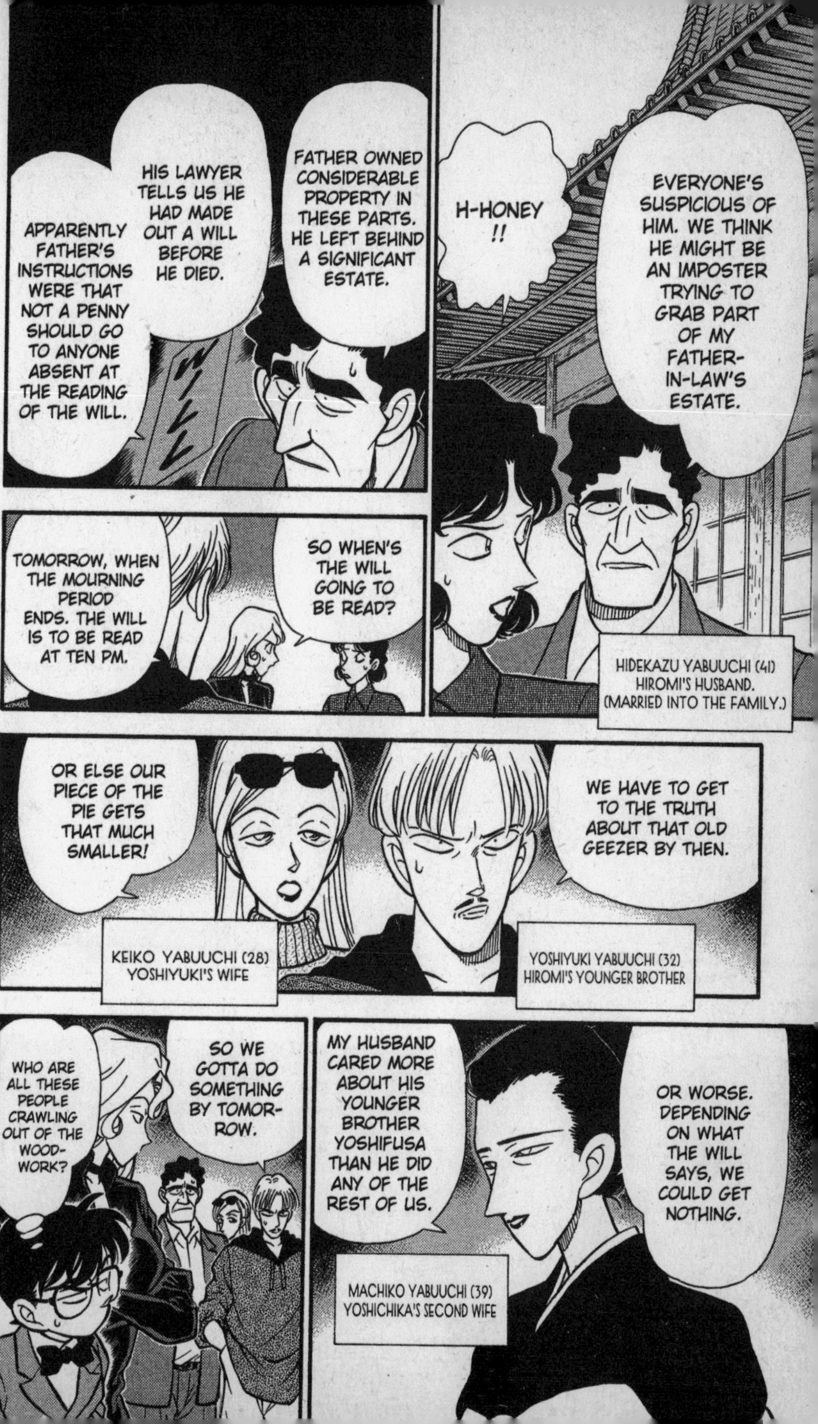
EVERYONE'S SUSPICIOUS OF HIM. WE THINK HE MIGHT BE AN IMPOSTER TRYING TO GRAB PART OF MY FATHER-IN-LAW'S ESTATE.
H-HONEY !!
HIDEKAZU YABUUCHI (41) HIROMI'S HUSBAND. (MARRIED INTO THE FAMILY.)
FATHER OWNED CONSIDERABLE PROPERTY IN THESE PARTS. HE LEFT BEHIND A SIGNIFICANT ESTATE.
HIS LAWYER TELLS US HE HAD MADE OUT A WILL BEFORE HE DIED.
APPARENTLY FATHER'S INSTRUCTIONS WERE THAT NOT A PENNY SHOULD GO TO ANYONE ABSENT AT THE READING OF THE WILL.
SO WHEN'S THE WILL GOING TO BE READ?
TOMORROW, WHEN THE MOURNING PERIOD ENDS. THE WILL IS TO BE READ AT TEN PM.
WE HAVE TO GET TO THE TRUTH ABOUT THAT OLD GEEZER BY THEN.
YOSHIYUKI YABUUCHI (32) HIROMI'S YOUNGER BROTHER
OR ELSE OUR PIECE OF THE PIE GETS THAT MUCH SMALLER!
KEIKO YABUUCHI (28) YOSHIYUKI'S WIFE
OR WORSE. DEPENDING ON WHAT THE WILL SAYS, WE COULD GET NOTHING.
MY HUSBAND CARED MORE ABOUT HIS YOUNGER BROTHER YOSHIFUSA THAN HE DID ANY OF THE REST OF US.
MACHIKO YABUUCHI (39) YOSHICHIKA'S SECOND WIFE
SO WE GOTTA DO SOMETHING BY TOMOR-ROW.
WHO ARE ALL THESE PEOPLE CRAWLING OUT OF THE WOOD-WORK?

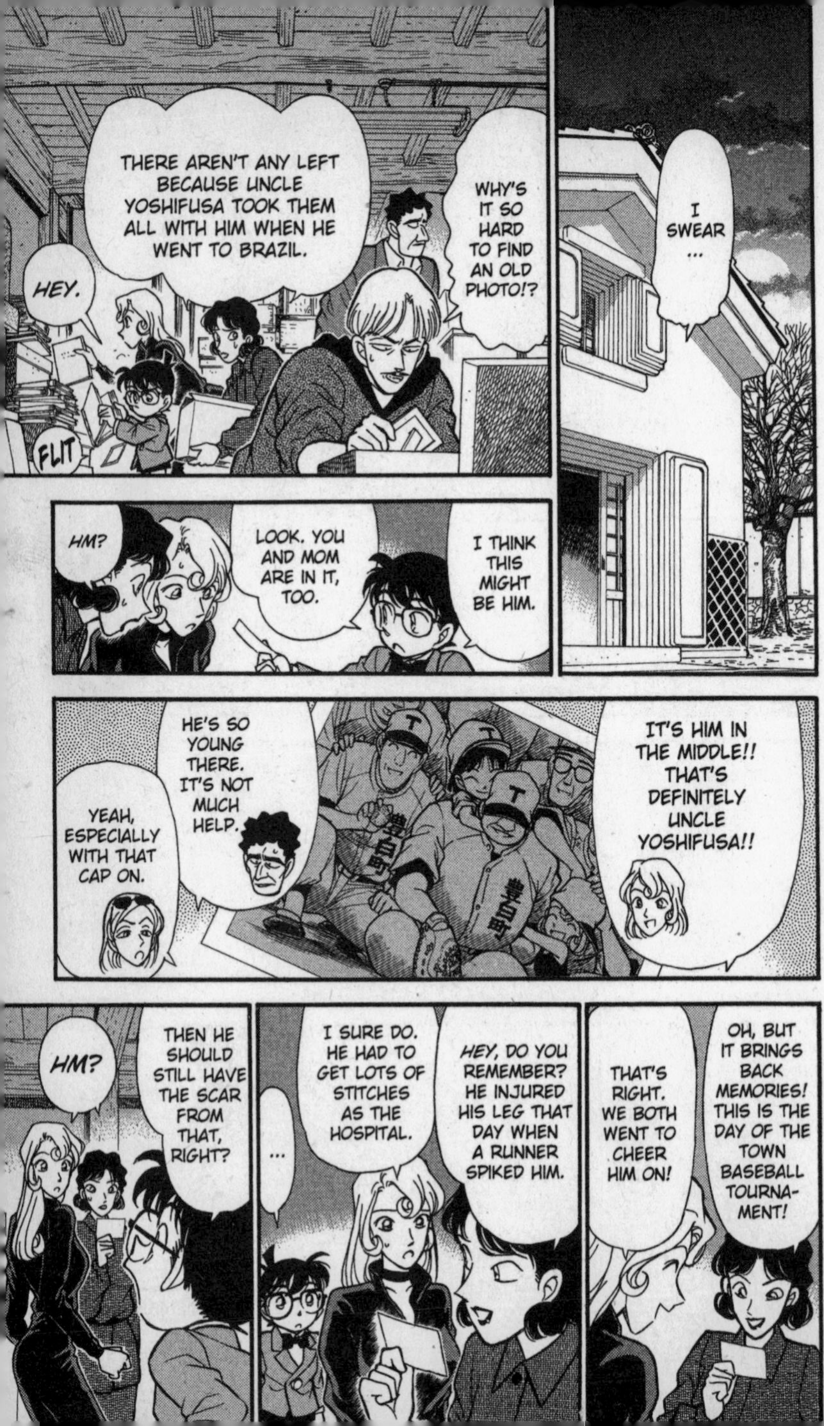
I SWEAR ...
WHY'S IT SO HARD TO FIND AN OLD PHOTO!?
THERE AREN'T ANY LEFT BECAUSE UNCLE YOSHIFUSA TOOK THEM ALL WITH HIM WHEN HE WENT TO BRAZIL.
HEY.
FLIT
I THINK THIS MIGHT BE HIM.
LOOK. YOU AND MOM ARE IN IT, TOO.
HM?
IT'S HIM IN THE MIDDLE!! THAT'S DEFINITELY UNCLE YOSHIFUSA!!
HE'S SO YOUNG THERE. IT'S NOT MUCH HELP.
YEAH, ESPECIALLY WITH THAT CAP ON.
OH, BUT IT BRINGS BACK MEMORIES! THIS IS THE DAY OF THE TOWN BASEBALL TOURNAMENT!
THAT'S RIGHT. WE BOTH WENT TO CHEER HIM ON!
HEY, DO YOU REMEMBER? HE INJURED HIS LEG THAT DAY WHEN A RUNNER SPIKED HIM.
I SURE DO. HE HAD TO GET LOTS OF STITCHES AS THE HOSPITAL.
...
THEN HE SHOULD STILL HAVE THE SCAR FROM THAT, RIGHT?
HM?

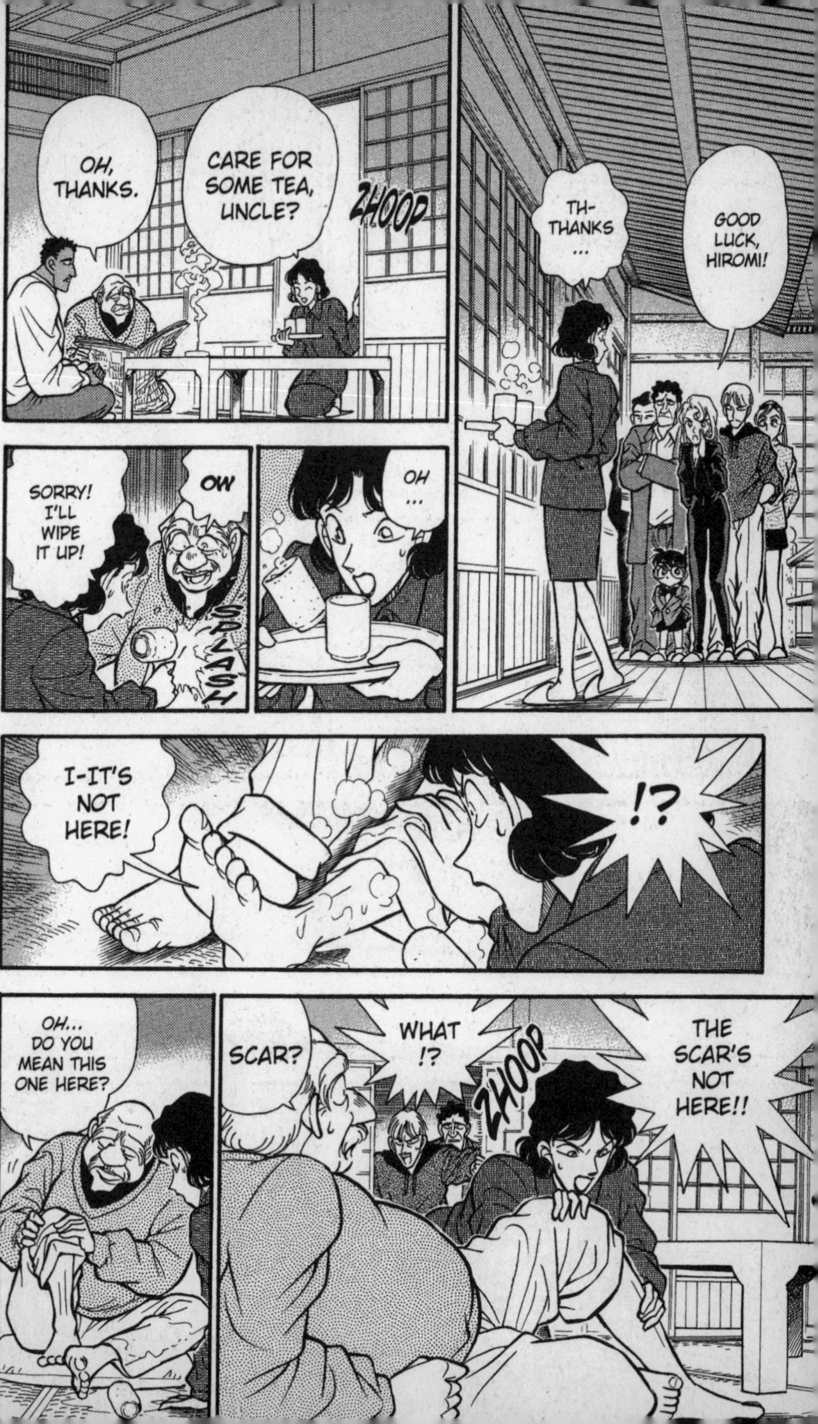
GOOD LUCK, HIROMI!
TH- THANKS ...
ZHOOP
CARE FOR SOME TEA, UNCLE?
OH, THANKS.
OH ...
OW
SPLASH
SORRY! I'LL WIPE IT UP!
!?
I-IT'S NOT HERE!
THE SCAR'S NOT HERE!!
ZHOOP
WHAT !?
SCAR?
OH... DO YOU MEAN THIS ONE HERE?

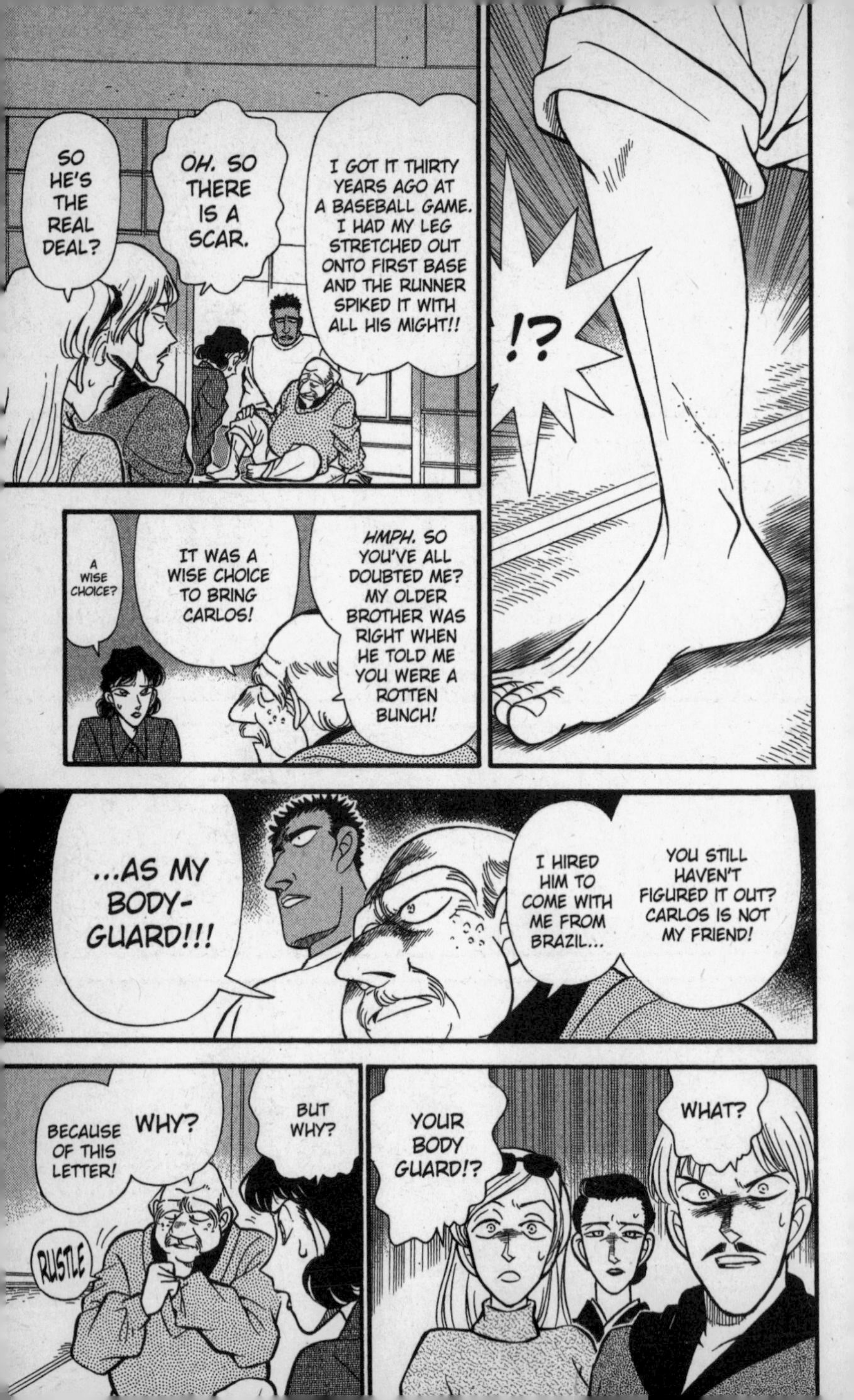
!?
I GOT IT THIRTY YEARS AGO AT A BASEBALL GAME. I HAD MY LEG STRETCHED OUT ONTO FIRST BASE AND THE RUNNER SPIKED IT WITH ALL HIS MIGHT!!
OH. SO THERE IS A SCAR.
SO HE'S THE REAL DEAL?
HMPH. SO YOU'VE ALL DOUBTED ME? MY OLDER BROTHER WAS RIGHT WHEN HE TOLD ME YOU WERE A ROTTEN BUNCH!
IT WAS A WISE CHOICE TO BRING CARLOS!
A WISE CHOICE?
YOU STILL HAVEN'T FIGURED IT OUT? CARLOS IS NOT MY FRIEND!
I HIRED HIM TO COME WITH ME FROM BRAZIL...
...AS MY BODY-GUARD!!!
WHAT?
YOUR BODY GUARD!?
BUT WHY?
WHY?
BECAUSE OF THIS LETTER!
RUSTLE

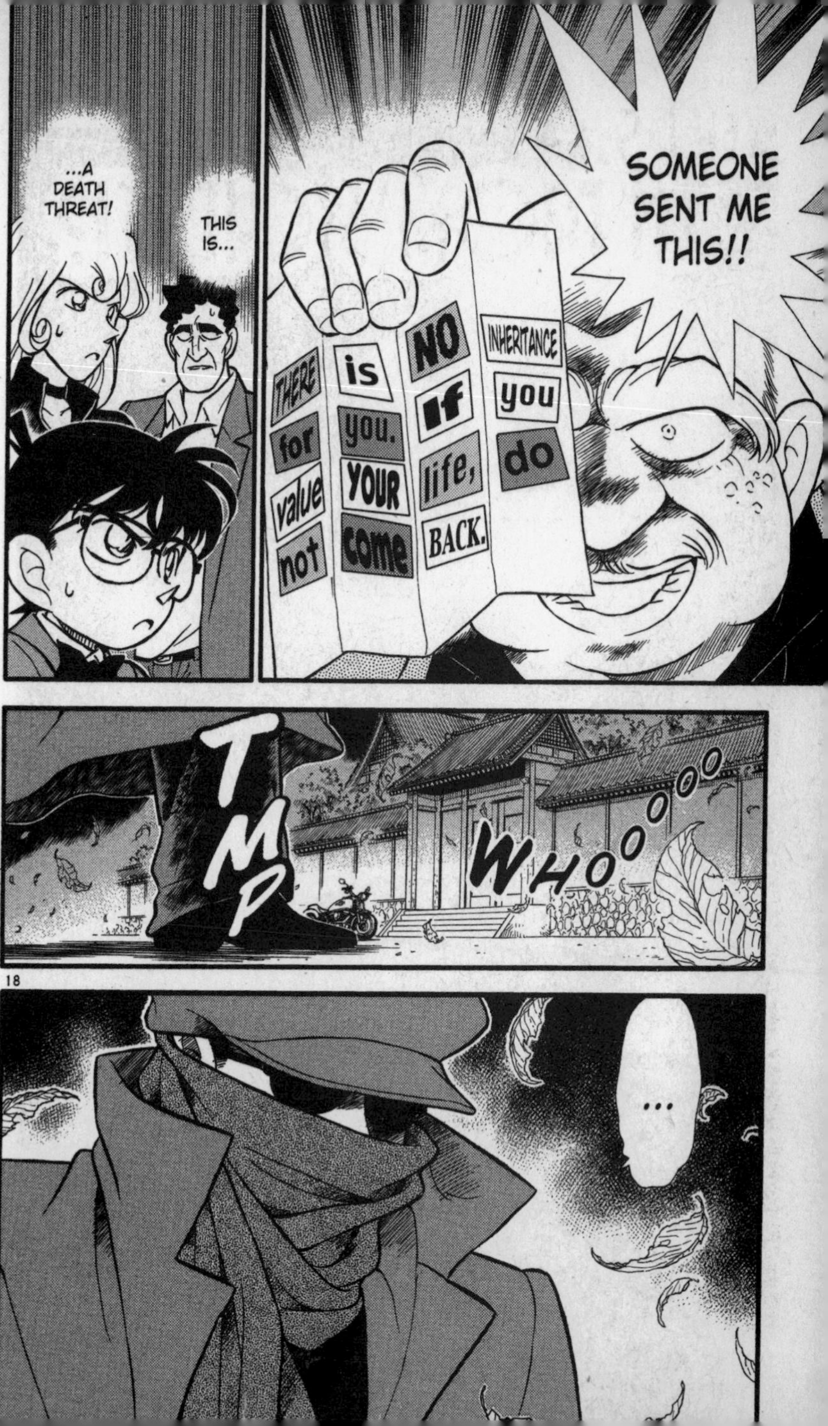
SOMEONE SENT ME THIS!!
THERE is NO INHERITANCE for you. If you value YOUR life, do not come BACK.
THIS IS...
...A DEATH THREAT!
WHOOOOOO
TMP
...

FILE 5: IN MOM'S CHEST!?

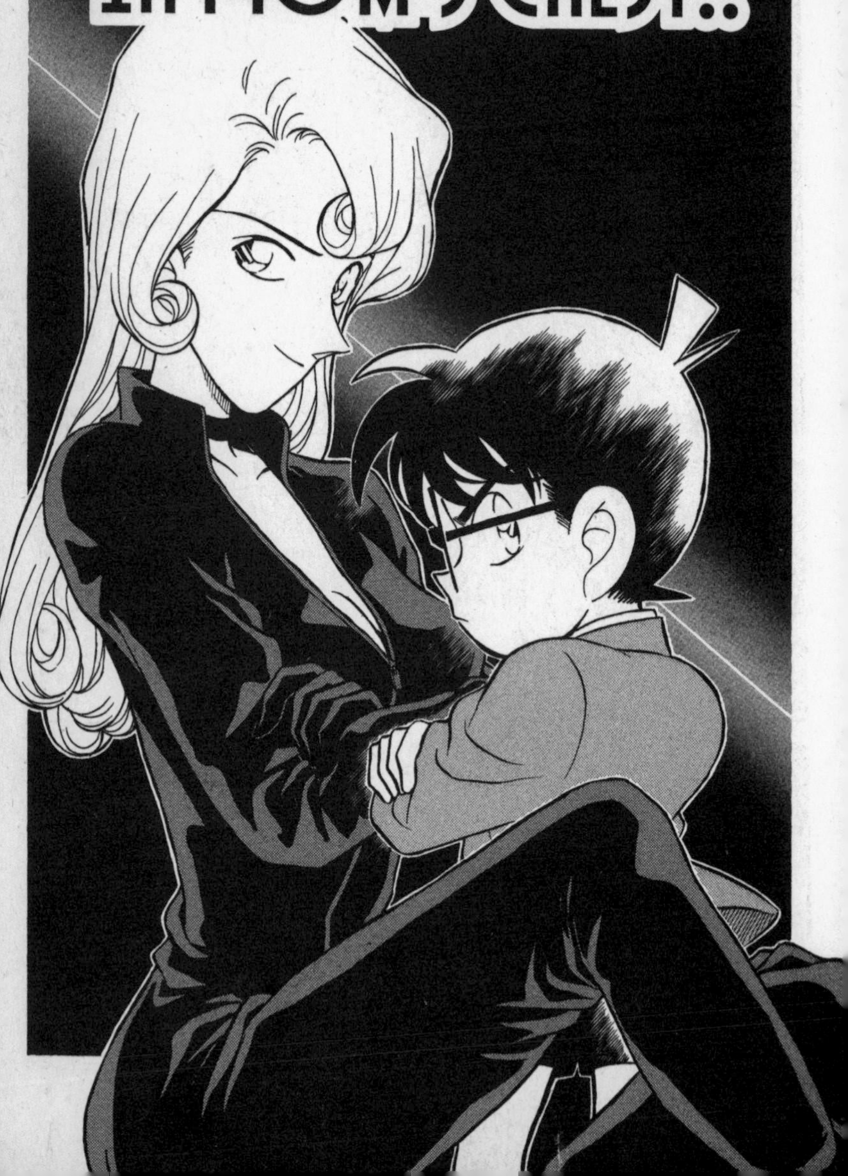

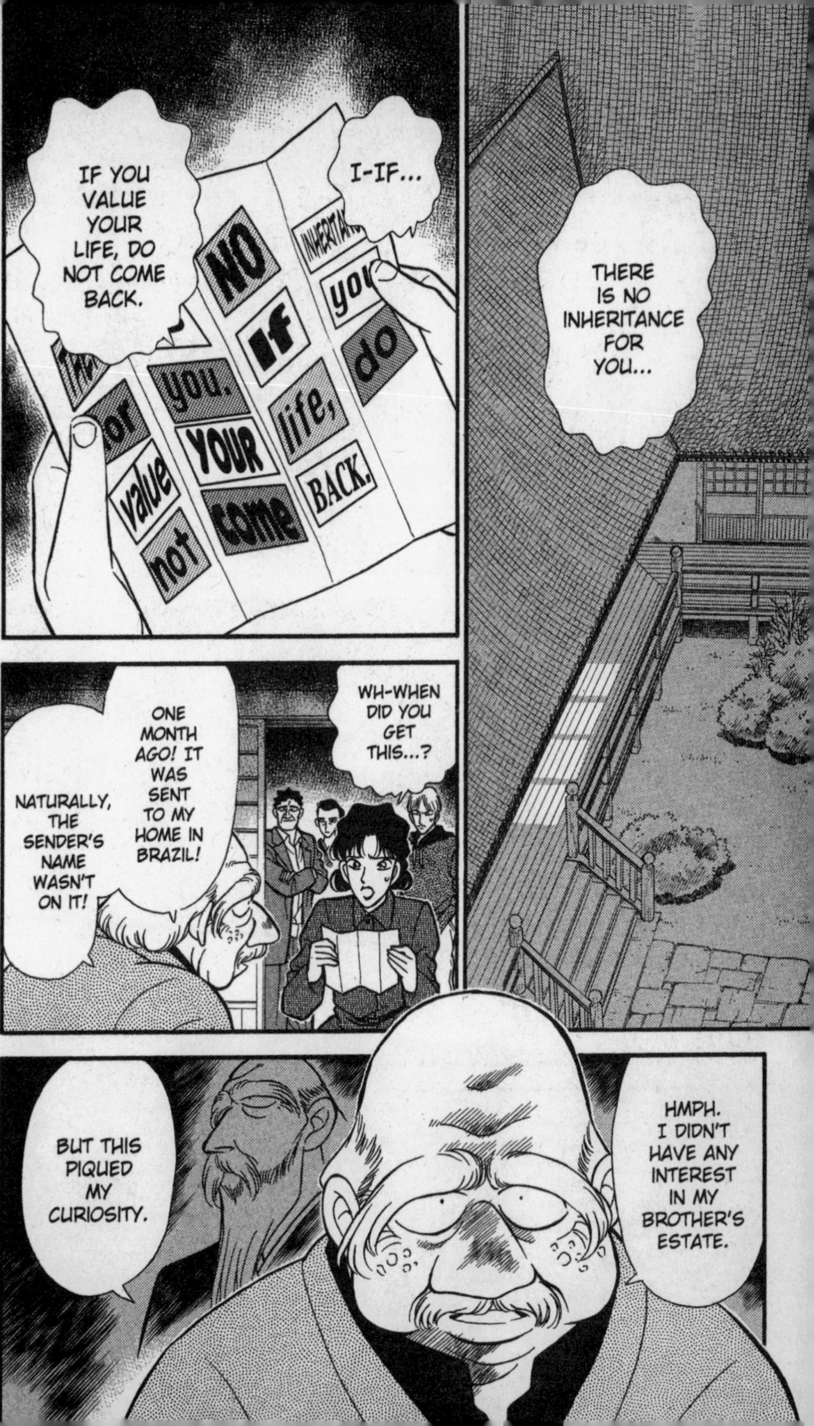
THERE IS NO INHERITANCE FOR YOU...
I-IF...
IF YOU VALUE YOUR LIFE, DO NOT COME BACK.
WH-WHEN DID YOU GET THIS...?
ONE MONTH AGO! IT WAS SENT TO MY HOME IN BRAZIL!
NATURALLY, THE SENDER'S NAME WASN'T ON IT!
HMPH. I DIDN'T HAVE ANY INTEREST IN MY BROTHER'S ESTATE.
BUT THIS PIQUED MY CURIOSITY.

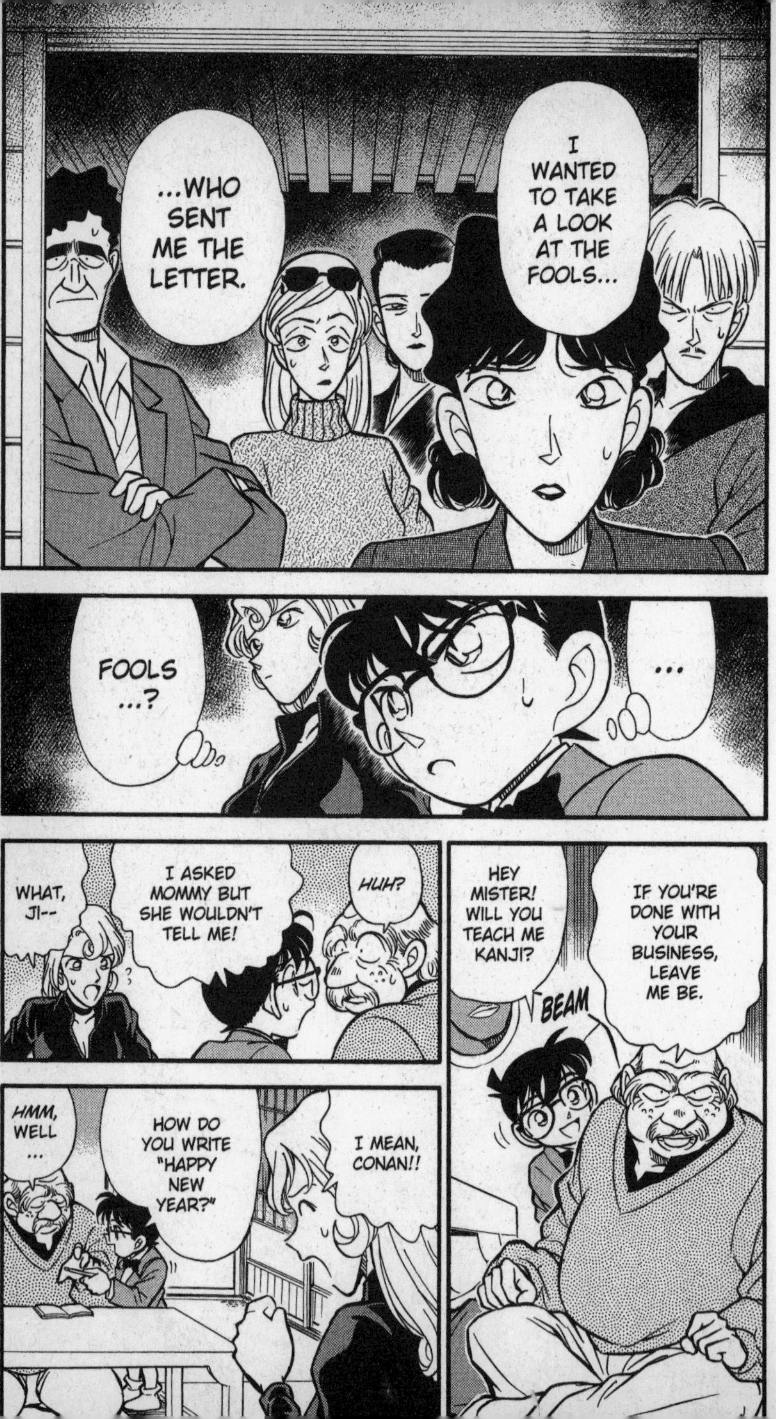
I WANTED TO TAKE A LOOK AT THE FOOLS...
...WHO SENT ME THE LETTER.
...
FOOLS ...?
IF YOU'RE DONE WITH YOUR BUSINESS, LEAVE ME BE.
HEY MISTER! WILL YOU TEACH ME KANJI?
BEAM
HUH?
I ASKED MOMMY BUT SHE WOULDN'T TELL ME!
WHAT, JI--
I MEAN, CONAN!!
HOW DO YOU WRITE "HAPPY NEW YEAR?"
HMM, WELL ...

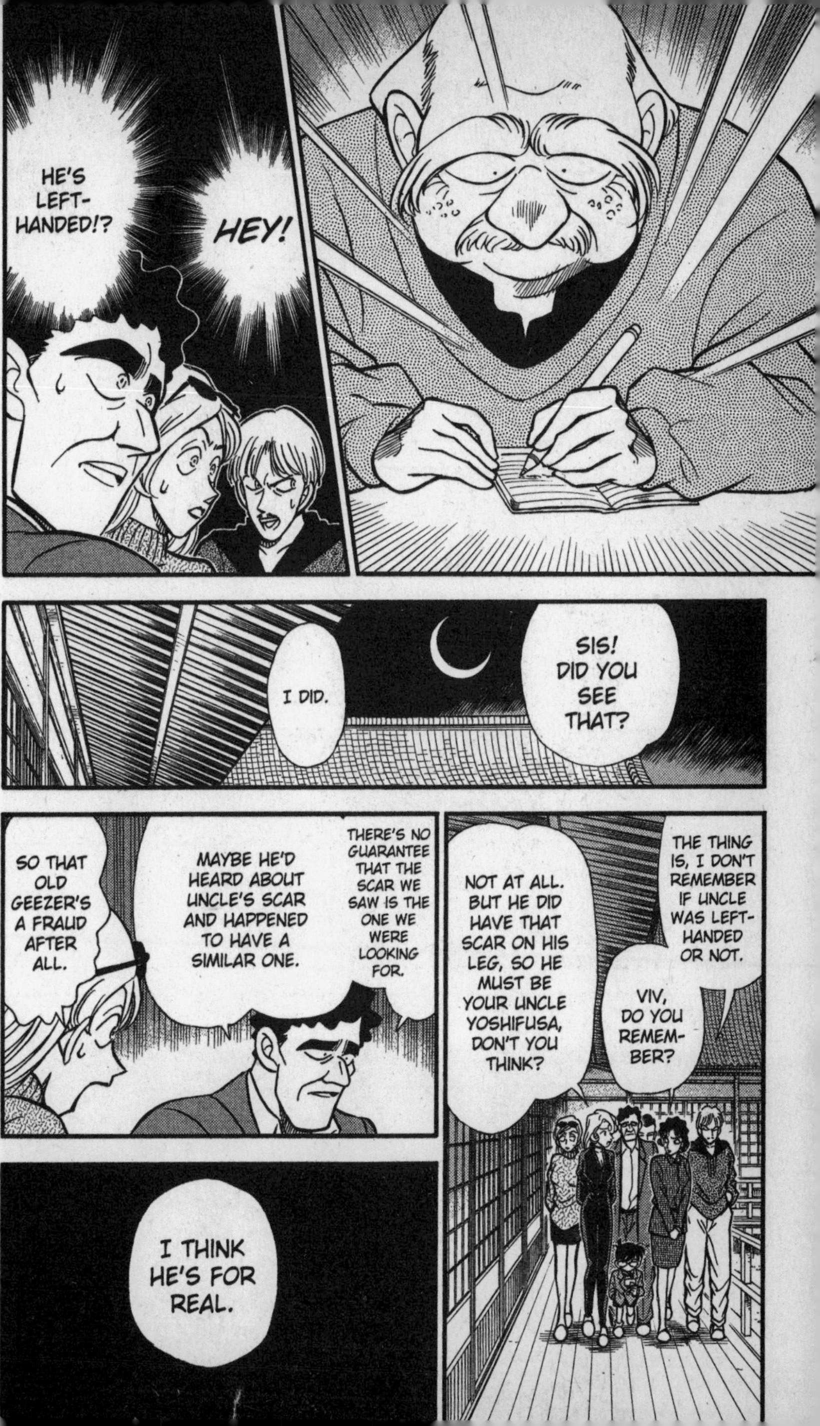
HEY!
HE'S LEFT-HANDED!?
SIS! DID YOU SEE THAT?
I DID.
THE THING IS, I DON'T REMEMBER IF UNCLE WAS LEFT-HANDED OR NOT.
VIV, DO YOU REMEMBER?
NOT AT ALL. BUT HE DID HAVE THAT SCAR ON HIS LEG, SO HE MUST BE YOUR UNCLE YOSHIFUSA, DON'T YOU THINK?
THERE'S NO GUARANTEE THAT THE SCAR WE SAW IS THE ONE WE WERE LOOKING FOR.
MAYBE HE'D HEARD ABOUT UNCLE'S SCAR AND HAPPENED TO HAVE A SIMILAR ONE.
SO THAT OLD GEEZER'S A FRAUD AFTER ALL.
I THINK HE'S FOR REAL.

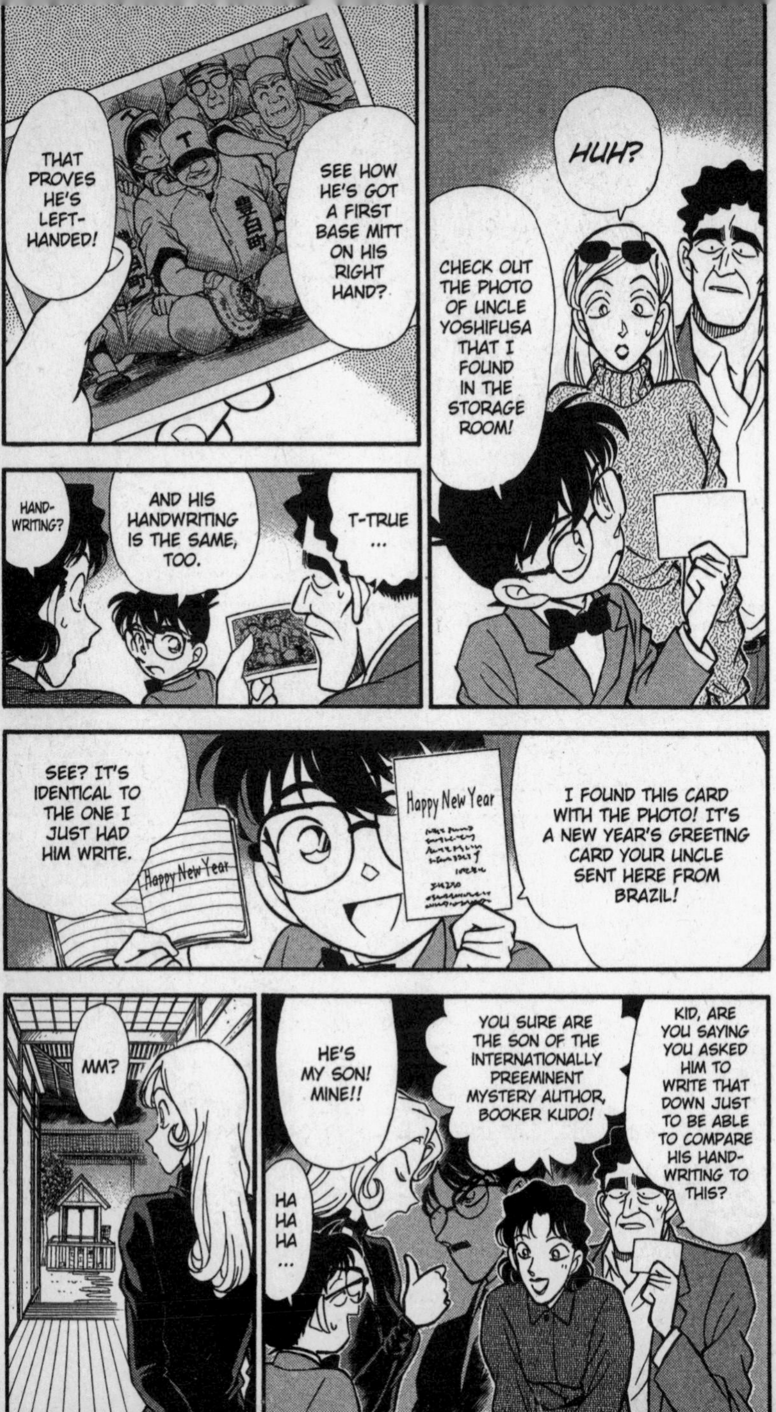
HUH?
CHECK OUT THE PHOTO OF UNCLE YOSHIFUSA THAT I FOUND IN THE STORAGE ROOM!
SEE HOW HE'S GOT A FIRST BASE MITT ON HIS RIGHT HAND?
THAT PROVES HE'S LEFT-HANDED!
T-TRUE ...
AND HIS HANDWRITING IS THE SAME, TOO.
HAND-WRITING?
I FOUND THIS CARD WITH THE PHOTO! IT'S A NEW YEAR'S GREETING CARD YOUR UNCLE SENT HERE FROM BRAZIL!
Happy New Year
SEE? IT'S IDENTICAL TO THE ONE I JUST HAD HIM WRITE.
Happy New Year
KID, ARE YOU SAYING YOU ASKED HIM TO WRITE THAT DOWN JUST TO BE ABLE TO COMPARE HIS HAND-WRITING TO THIS?
YOU SURE ARE THE SON OF THE INTERNATIONALLY PREEMINENT MYSTERY AUTHOR, BOOKER KUDO!
HE'S MY SON! MINE!!
HA HA HA ...
MM?

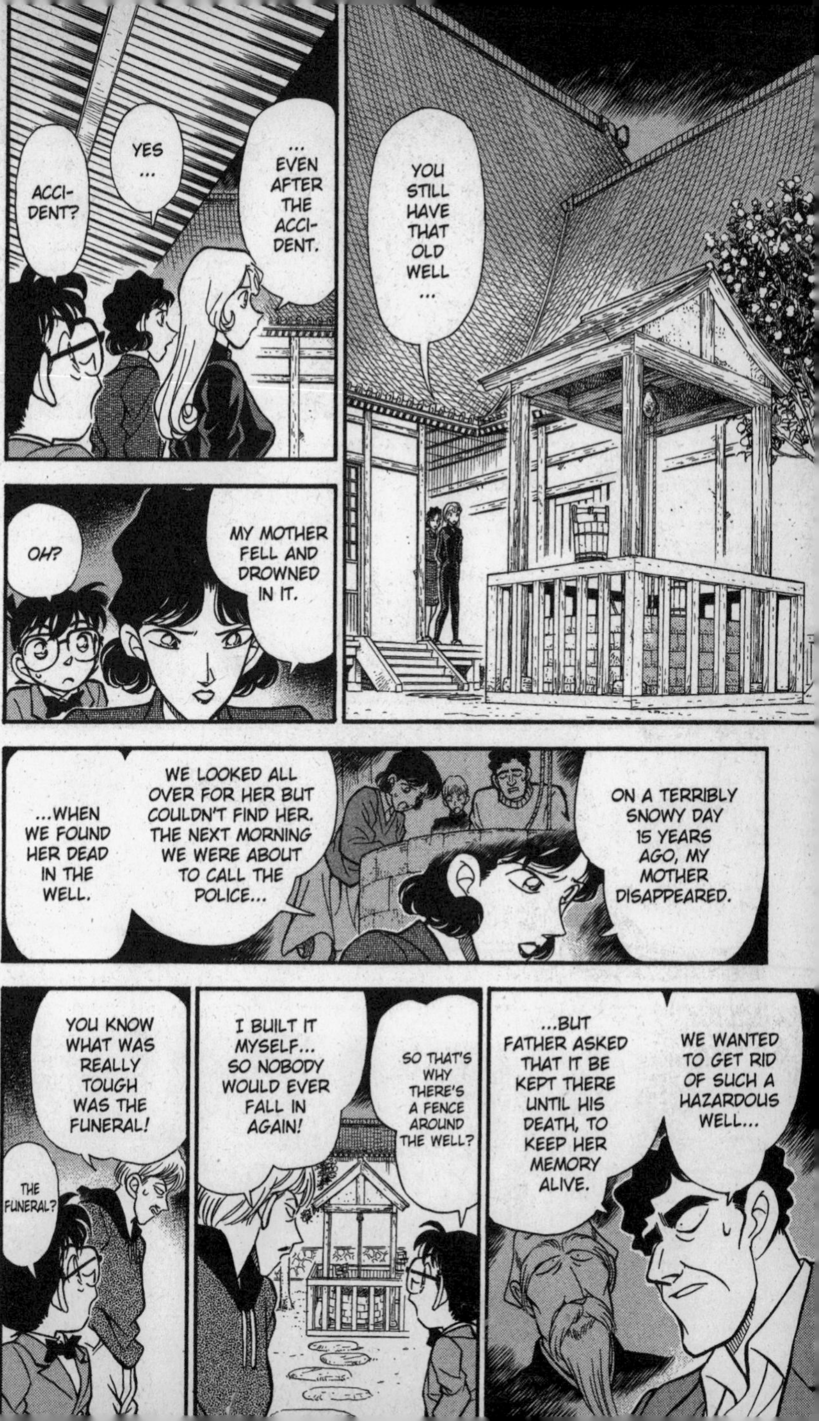
YOU STILL HAVE THAT OLD WELL ...
... EVEN AFTER THE ACCIDENT.
YES ...
ACCIDENT?
MY MOTHER FELL AND DROWNED IN IT.
OH?
ON A TERRIBLY SNOWY DAY 15 YEARS AGO, MY MOTHER DISAPPEARED.
WE LOOKED ALL OVER FOR HER BUT COULDN'T FIND HER. THE NEXT MORNING WE WERE ABOUT TO CALL THE POLICE...
...WHEN WE FOUND HER DEAD IN THE WELL.
WE WANTED TO GET RID OF SUCH A HAZARDOUS WELL...
...BUT FATHER ASKED THAT IT BE KEPT THERE UNTIL HIS DEATH, TO KEEP HER MEMORY ALIVE.
SO THAT'S WHY THERE'S A FENCE AROUND THE WELL?
I BUILT IT MYSELF... SO NOBODY WOULD EVER FALL IN AGAIN!
YOU KNOW WHAT WAS REALLY TOUGH WAS THE FUNERAL!
THE FUNERAL?

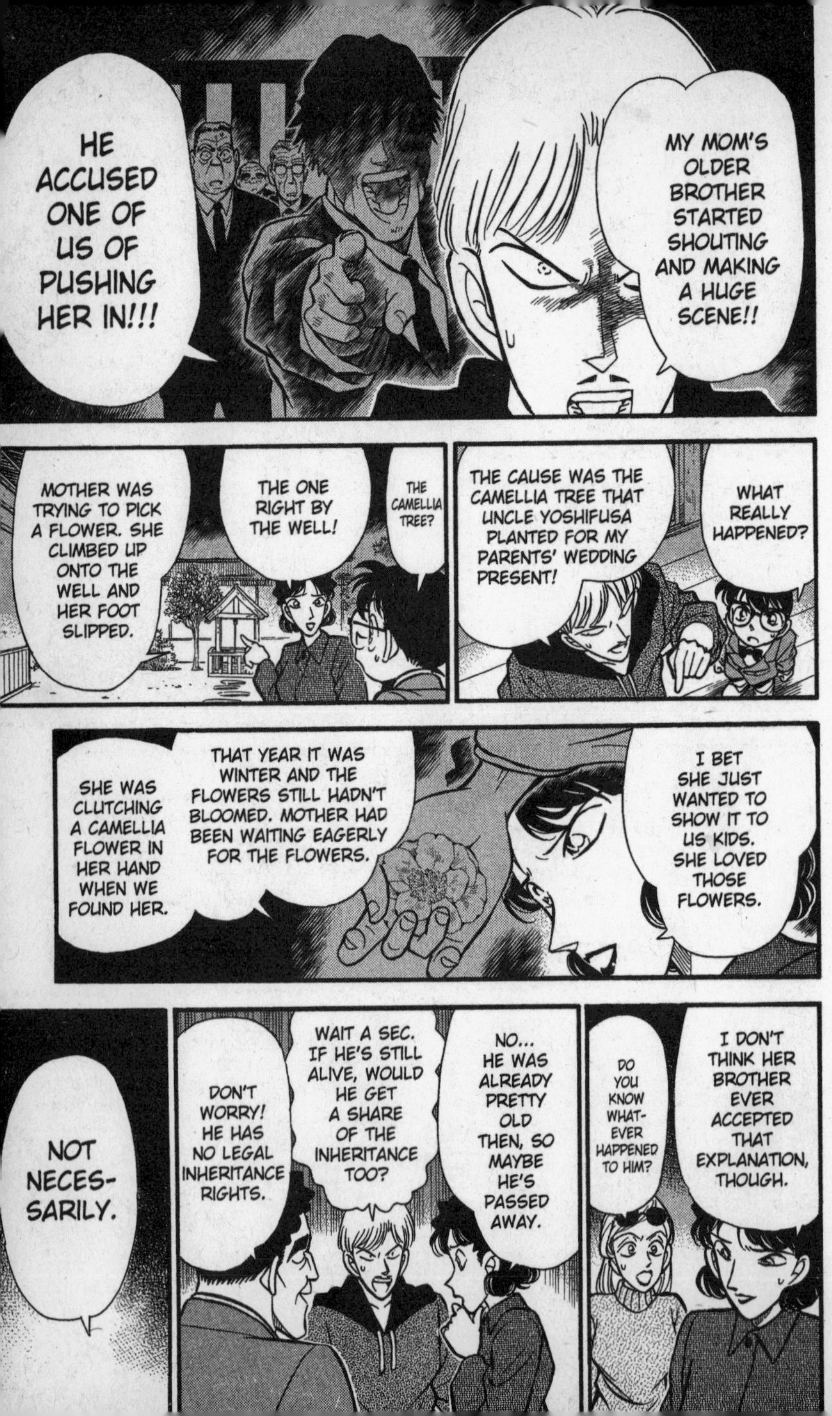
MY MOM'S OLDER BROTHER STARTED SHOUTING AND MAKING A HUGE SCENE!!
HE ACCUSED ONE OF US OF PUSHING HER IN!!!
WHAT REALLY HAPPENED?
THE CAUSE WAS THE CAMELLIA TREE THAT UNCLE YOSHIFUSA PLANTED FOR MY PARENTS' WEDDING PRESENT!
THE CAMELLIA TREE?
THE ONE RIGHT BY THE WELL!
MOTHER WAS TRYING TO PICK A FLOWER. SHE CLIMBED UP ONTO THE WELL AND HER FOOT SLIPPED.
I BET SHE JUST WANTED TO SHOW IT TO US KIDS. SHE LOVED THOSE FLOWERS.
THAT YEAR IT WAS WINTER AND THE FLOWERS STILL HADN'T BLOOMED. MOTHER HAD BEEN WAITING EAGERLY FOR THE FLOWERS.
SHE WAS CLUTCHING A CAMELLIA FLOWER IN HER HAND WHEN WE FOUND HER.
I DON'T THINK HER BROTHER EVER ACCEPTED THAT EXPLANATION, THOUGH.
DO YOU KNOW WHAT-EVER HAPPENED TO HIM?
NO... HE WAS ALREADY PRETTY OLD THEN, SO MAYBE HE'S PASSED AWAY.
WAIT A SEC. IF HE'S STILL ALIVE, WOULD HE GET A SHARE OF THE INHERITANCE TOO?
DON'T WORRY! HE HAS NO LEGAL INHERITANCE RIGHTS.
NOT NECES-SARILY.

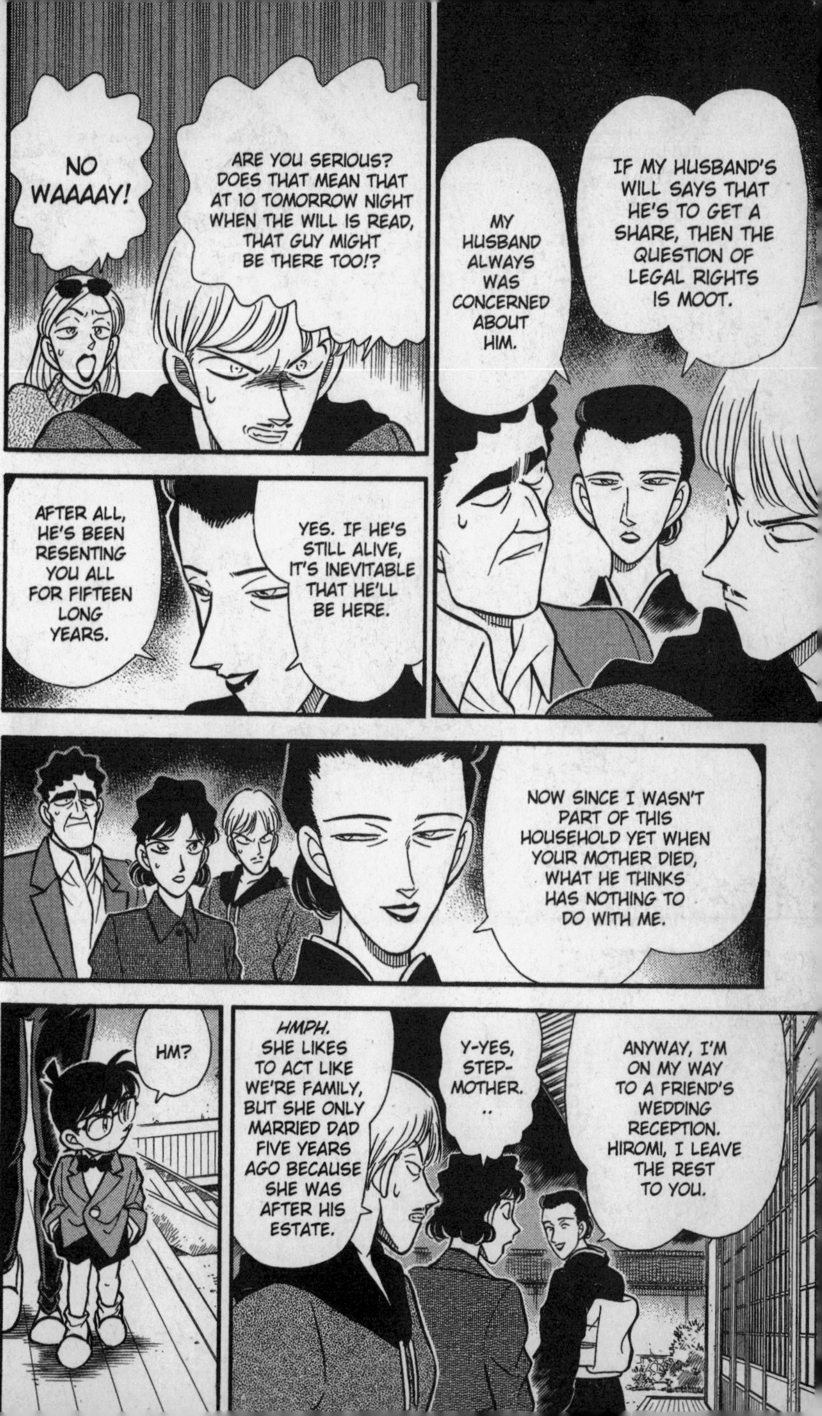
IF MY HUSBAND'S WILL SAYS THAT HE'S TO GET A SHARE, THEN THE QUESTION OF LEGAL RIGHTS IS MOOT.
MY HUSBAND ALWAYS WAS CONCERNED ABOUT HIM.
ARE YOU SERIOUS? DOES THAT MEAN THAT AT 10 TOMORROW NIGHT WHEN THE WILL IS READ, THAT GUY MIGHT BE THERE TOO!?
NO WAAAAY!
YES. IF HE'S STILL ALIVE, IT'S INEVITABLE THAT HE'LL BE HERE.
AFTER ALL, HE'S BEEN RESENTING YOU ALL FOR FIFTEEN LONG YEARS.
NOW SINCE I WASN'T PART OF THIS HOUSEHOLD YET WHEN YOUR MOTHER DIED, WHAT HE THINKS HAS NOTHING TO DO WITH ME.
ANYWAY, I'M ON MY WAY TO A FRIEND'S WEDDING RECEPTION. HIROMI, I LEAVE THE REST TO YOU.
Y-YES, STEP-MOTHER. ..
HMPH. SHE LIKES TO ACT LIKE WE'RE FAMILY, BUT SHE ONLY MARRIED DAD FIVE YEARS AGO BECAUSE SHE WAS AFTER HIS ESTATE.
HM?

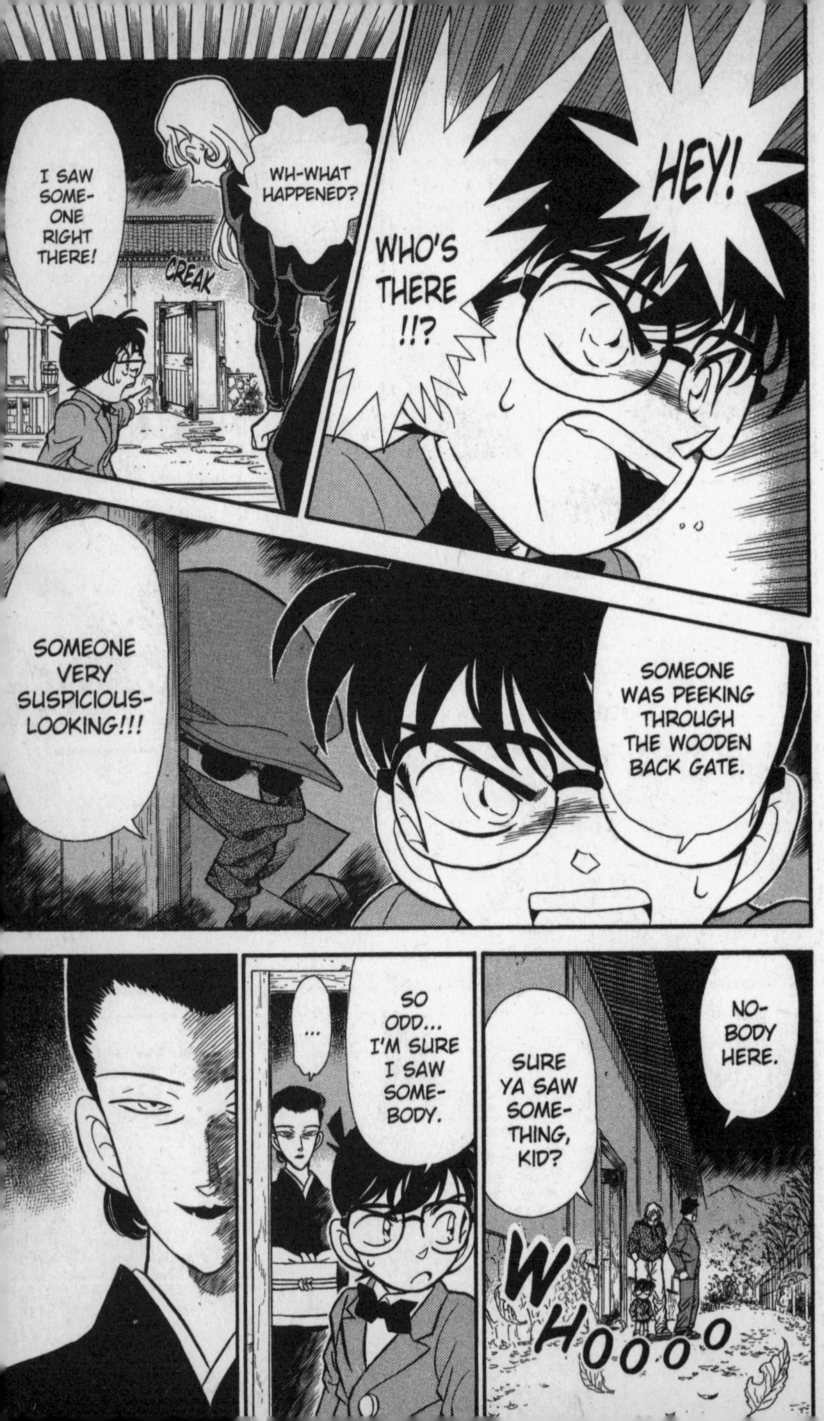
HEY!
WHO'S THERE!!?
WH-WHAT HAPPENED?
I SAW SOMEONE RIGHT THERE!
CREAK
SOMEONE WAS PEEKING THROUGH THE WOODEN BACK GATE.
SOMEONE VERY SUSPICIOUS-LOOKING!!!
NOBODY HERE.
SURE YA SAW SOMETHING, KID?
WHOOOOO
SO ODD... I'M SURE I SAW SOMEBODY.
...

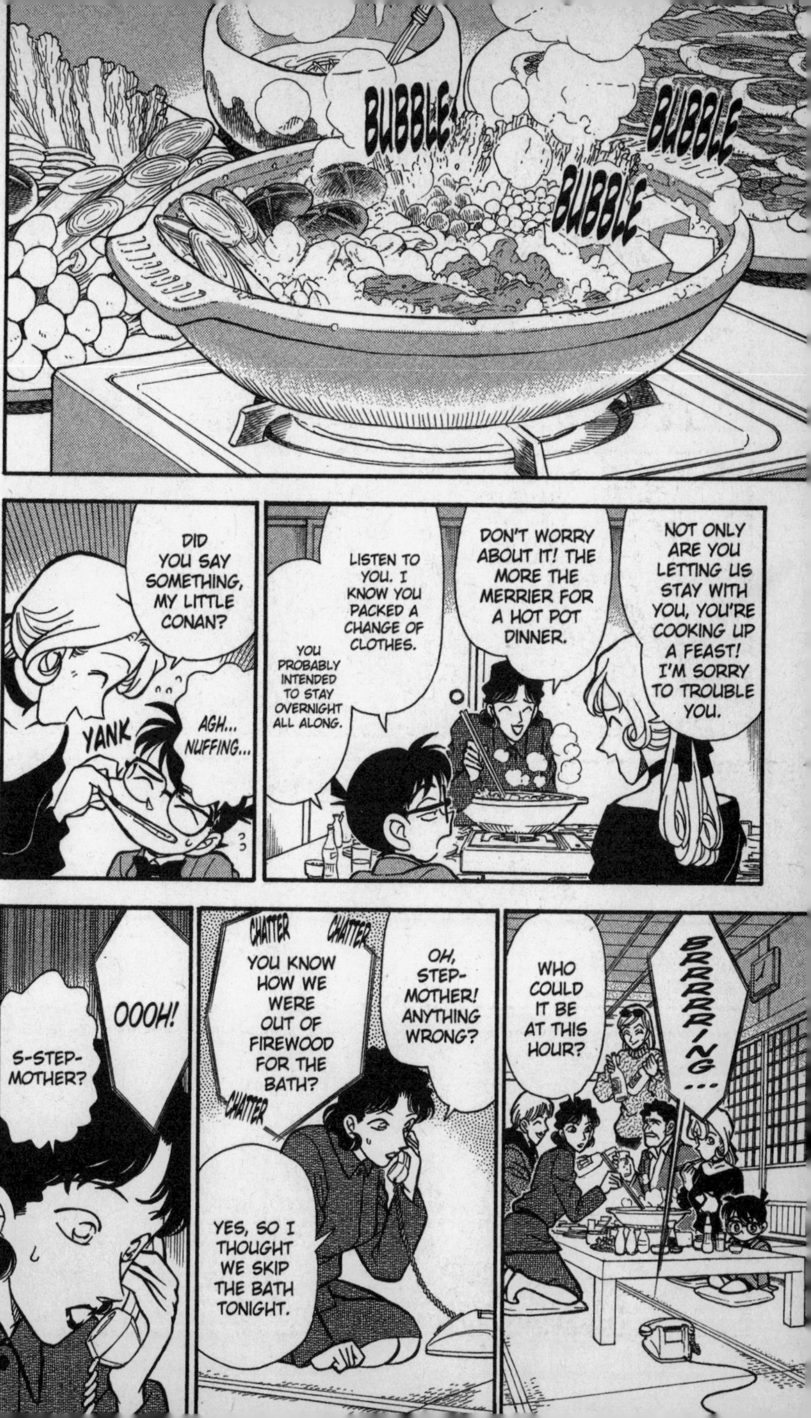
BUBBLE
BUBBLE
BUBBLE
NOT ONLY ARE YOU LETTING US STAY WITH YOU, YOU'RE COOKING UP A FEAST! I'M SORRY TO TROUBLE YOU.
DON'T WORRY ABOUT IT! THE MORE THE MERRIER FOR A HOT POT DINNER.
LISTEN TO YOU. I KNOW YOU PACKED A CHANGE OF CLOTHES.
YOU PROBABLY INTENDED TO STAY OVERNIGHT ALL ALONG.
DID YOU SAY SOMETHING, MY LITTLE CONAN?
AGH... NUFFING...
YANK
BRRRRRING...
WHO COULD IT BE AT THIS HOUR?
OH, STEP-MOTHER! ANYTHING WRONG?
CHATTER
CHATTER
YOU KNOW HOW WE WERE OUT OF FIREWOOD FOR THE BATH?
CHATTER
YES, SO I THOUGHT WE SKIP THE BATH TONIGHT.
OOOH!
S-STEP-MOTHER?

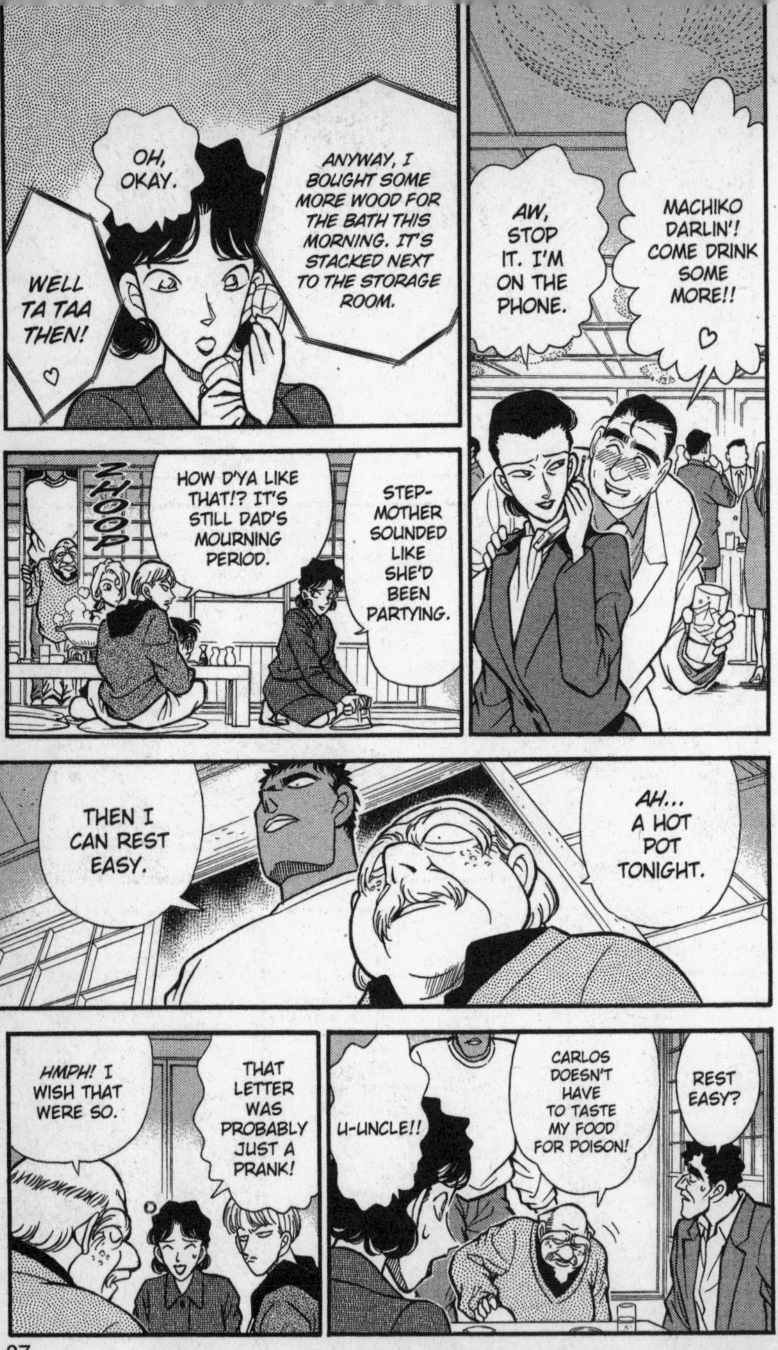
MACHIKO DARLIN'! COME DRINK SOME MORE!! ♡
AW, STOP IT. I'M ON THE PHONE.
ANYWAY, I BOUGHT SOME MORE WOOD FOR THE BATH THIS MORNING. IT'S STACKED NEXT TO THE STORAGE ROOM.
OH, OKAY.
WELL TA TAA THEN! ♡
STEP-MOTHER SOUNDED LIKE SHE'D BEEN PARTYING.
HOW D'YA LIKE THAT!? IT'S STILL DAD'S MOURNING PERIOD.
ZHOOP
AH... A HOT POT TONIGHT.
THEN I CAN REST EASY.
REST EASY?
CARLOS DOESN'T HAVE TO TASTE MY FOOD FOR POISON!
U-UNCLE!!
THAT LETTER WAS PROBABLY JUST A PRANK!
HMPH! I WISH THAT WERE SO.

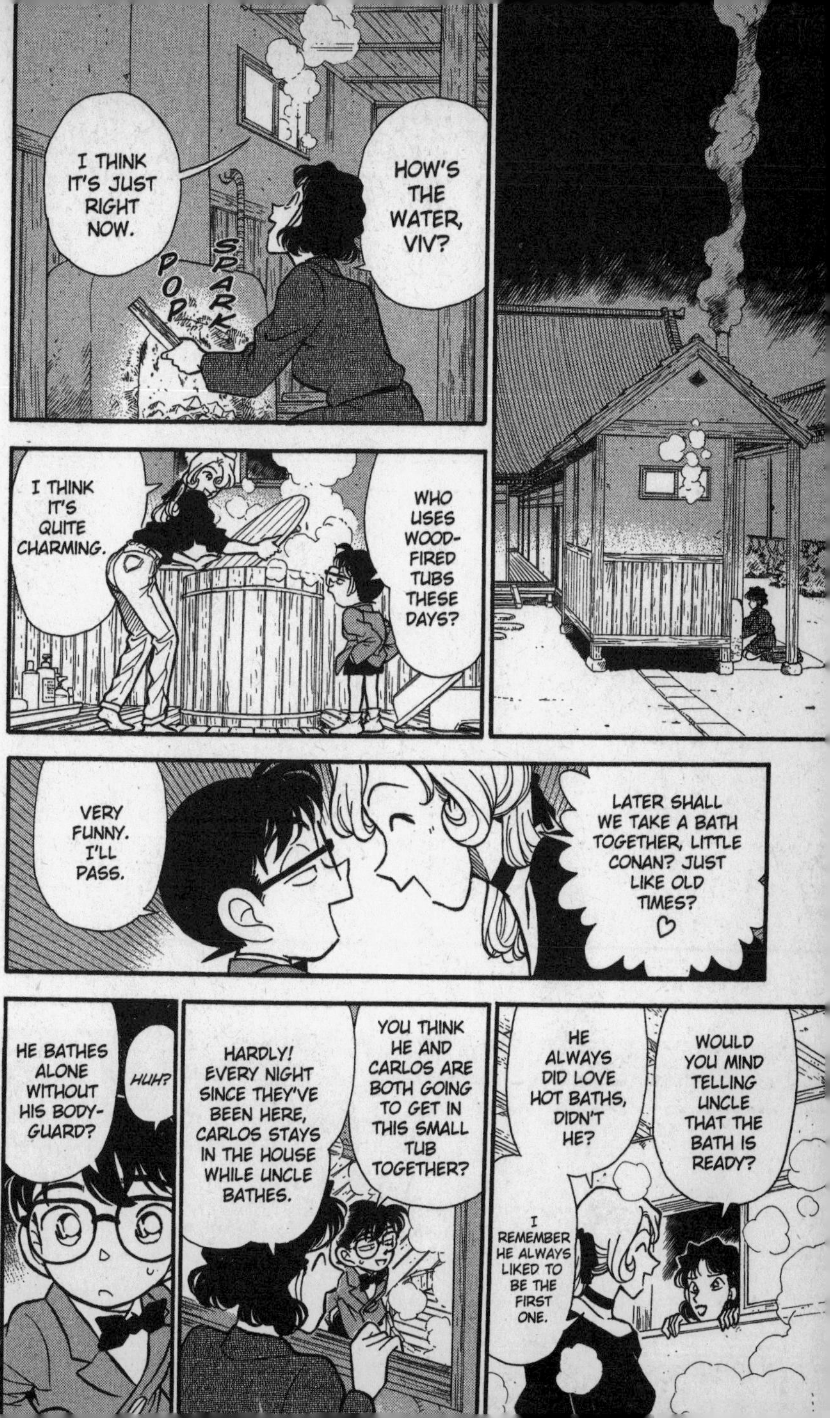
HOW'S THE WATER, VIV?
I THINK IT'S JUST RIGHT NOW.
SPARK
POP
WHO USES WOOD-FIRED TUBS THESE DAYS?
I THINK IT'S QUITE CHARMING.
LATER SHALL WE TAKE A BATH TOGETHER, LITTLE CONAN? JUST LIKE OLD TIMES? ♡
VERY FUNNY. I'LL PASS.
WOULD YOU MIND TELLING UNCLE THAT THE BATH IS READY?
HE ALWAYS DID LOVE HOT BATHS, DIDN'T HE?
I REMEMBER HE ALWAYS LIKED TO BE THE FIRST ONE.
YOU THINK HE AND CARLOS ARE BOTH GOING TO GET IN THIS SMALL TUB TOGETHER?
HARDLY! EVERY NIGHT SINCE THEY'VE BEEN HERE, CARLOS STAYS IN THE HOUSE WHILE UNCLE BATHES.
HUH?
HE BATHES ALONE WITHOUT HIS BODY-GUARD?

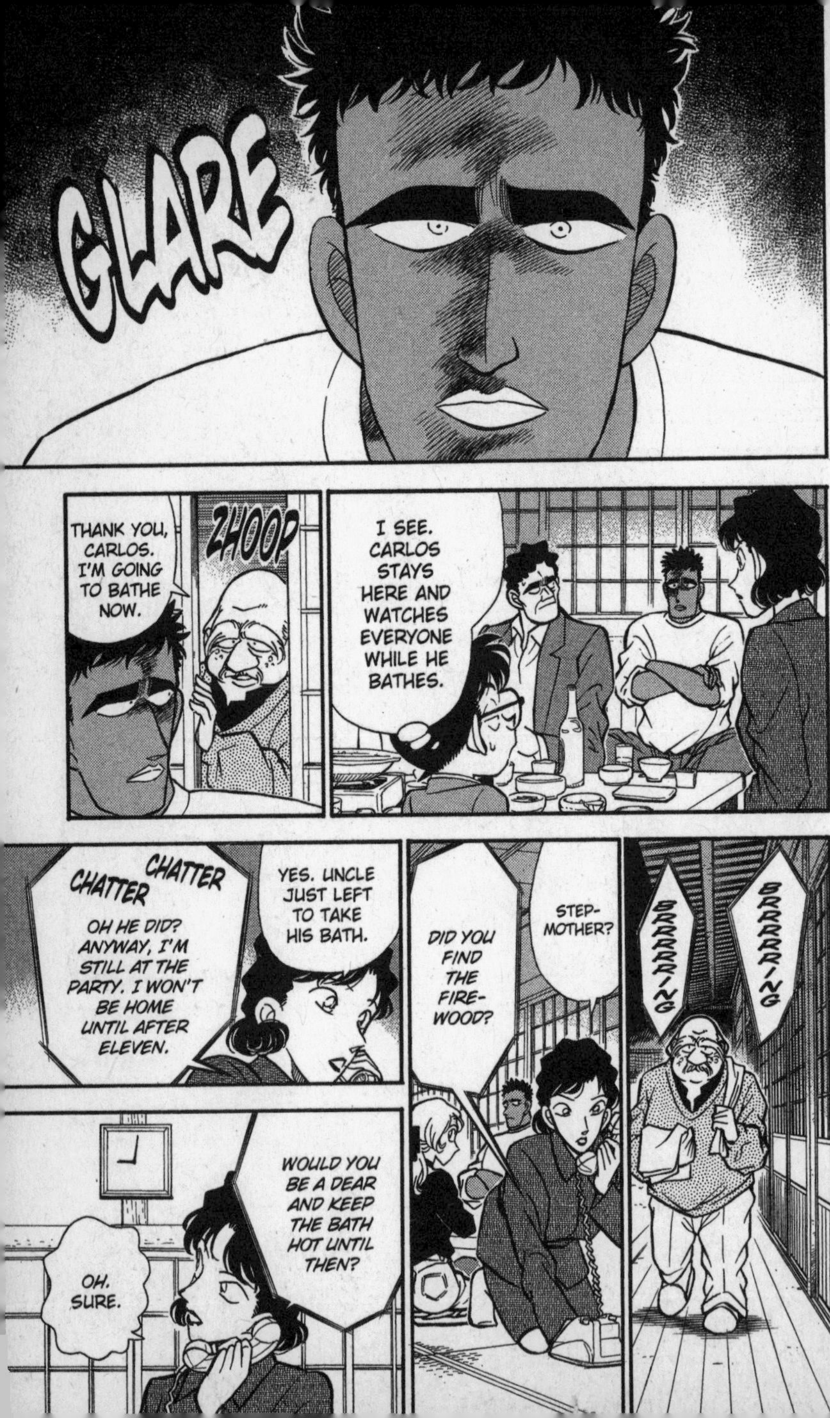
GLARE
I SEE. CARLOS STAYS HERE AND WATCHES EVERYONE WHILE HE BATHES.
ZHOOP
THANK YOU, CARLOS. I'M GOING TO BATHE NOW.
BRRRRING
BRRRRING
STEP-MOTHER?
DID YOU FIND THE FIRE-WOOD?
YES. UNCLE JUST LEFT TO TAKE HIS BATH.
CHATTER
CHATTER
OH HE DID? ANYWAY, I'M STILL AT THE PARTY. I WON'T BE HOME UNTIL AFTER ELEVEN.
WOULD YOU BE A DEAR AND KEEP THE BATH HOT UNTIL THEN?
OH. SURE.

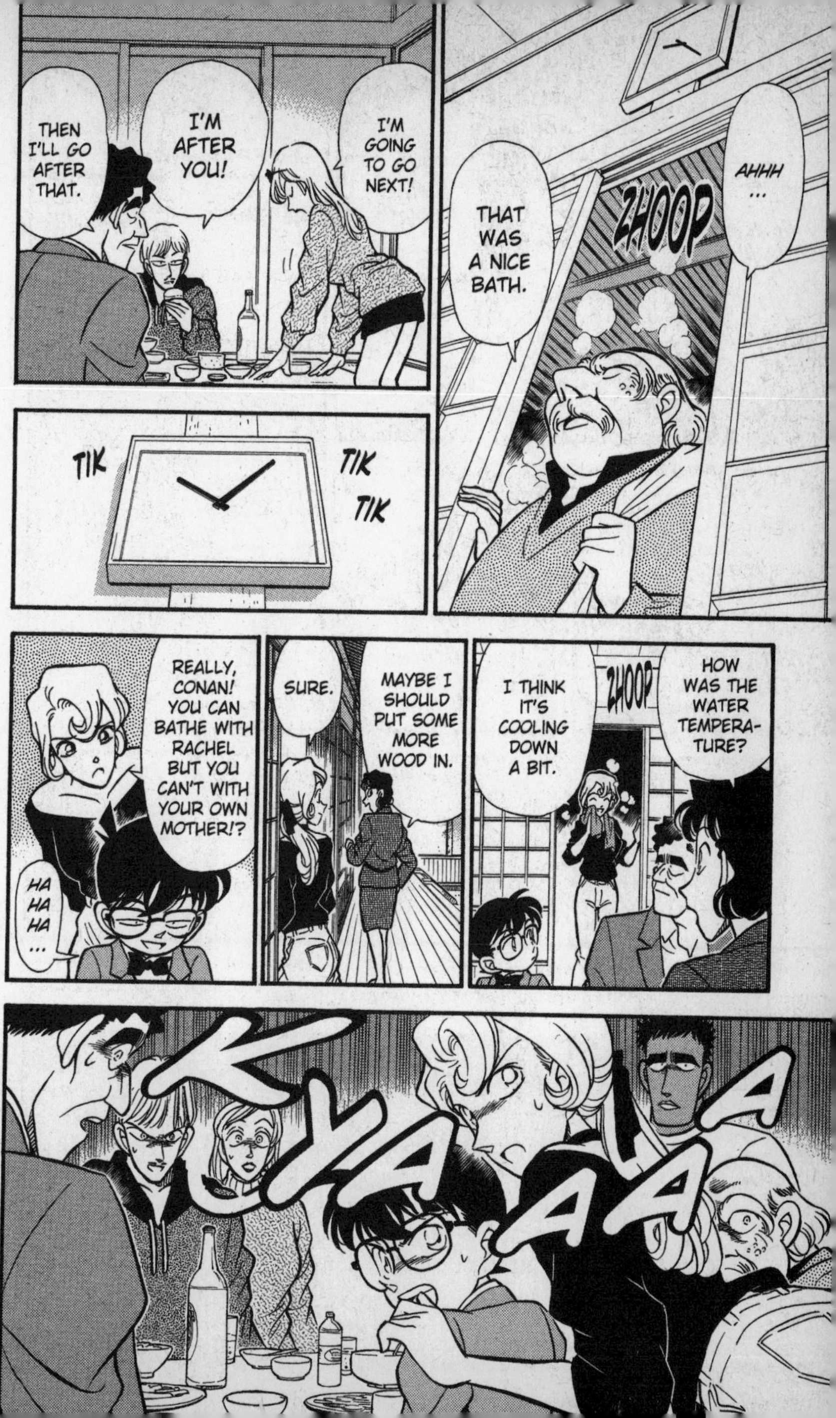
AHHH ...
ZHOOP
THAT WAS A NICE BATH.
I'M GOING TO GO NEXT!
I'M AFTER YOU!
THEN I'LL GO AFTER THAT.
TIK
TIK
TIK
HOW WAS THE WATER TEMPERA-TURE?
ZHOOP
I THINK IT'S COOLING DOWN A BIT.
MAYBE I SHOULD PUT SOME MORE WOOD IN.
SURE.
REALLY, CONAN! YOU CAN BATHE WITH RACHEL BUT YOU CAN'T WITH YOUR OWN MOTHER!?
HA HA HA ...
KYAAAAA

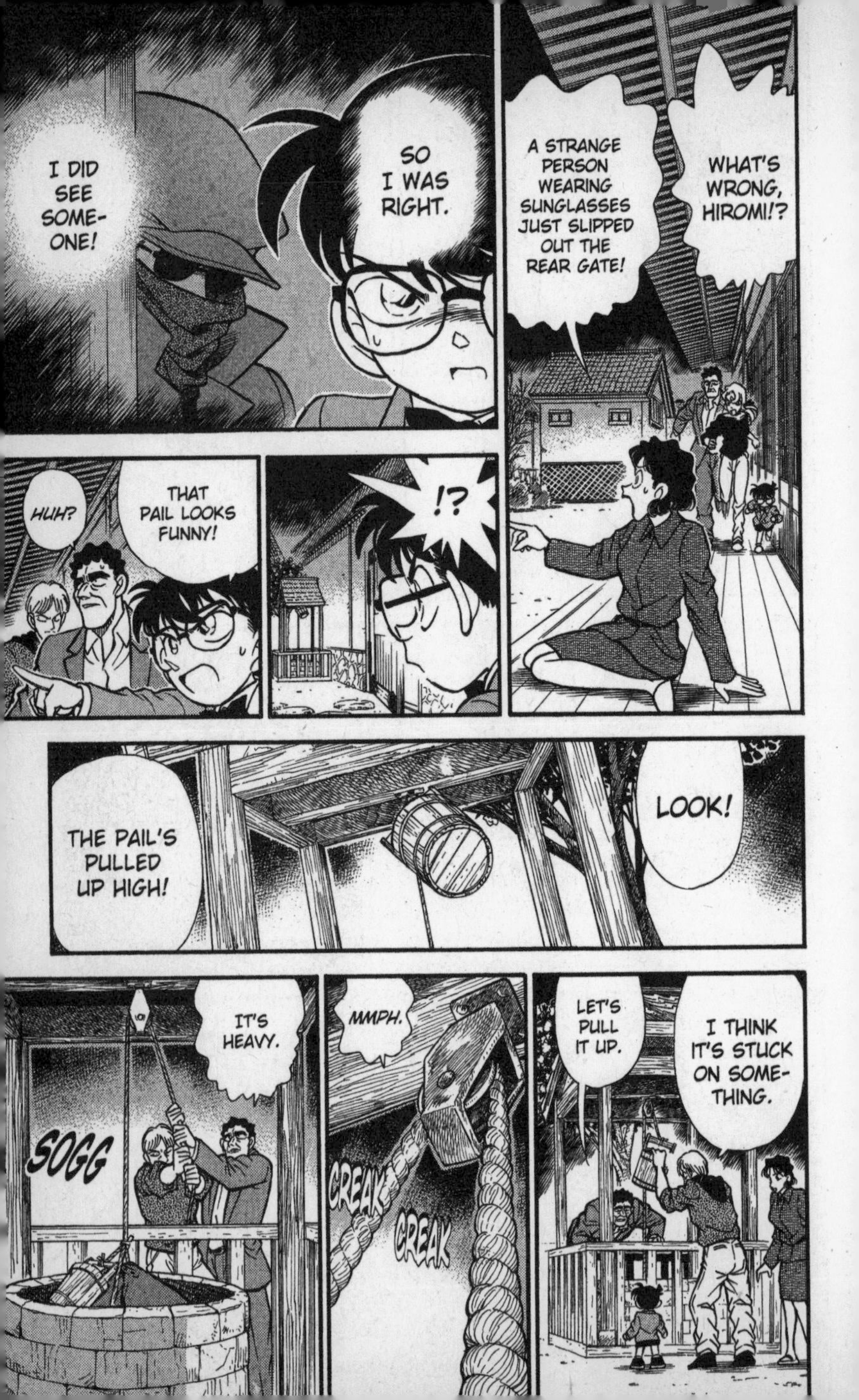
WHAT'S WRONG, HIROMI!?
A STRANGE PERSON WEARING SUNGLASSES JUST SLIPPED OUT THE REAR GATE!
SO I WAS RIGHT.
I DID SEE SOME-ONE!
!?
THAT PAIL LOOKS FUNNY!
HUH?
LOOK!
THE PAIL'S PULLED UP HIGH!
I THINK IT'S STUCK ON SOME-THING.
LET'S PULL IT UP.
MMPH.
CREAK
CREAK
IT'S HEAVY.
SOGG

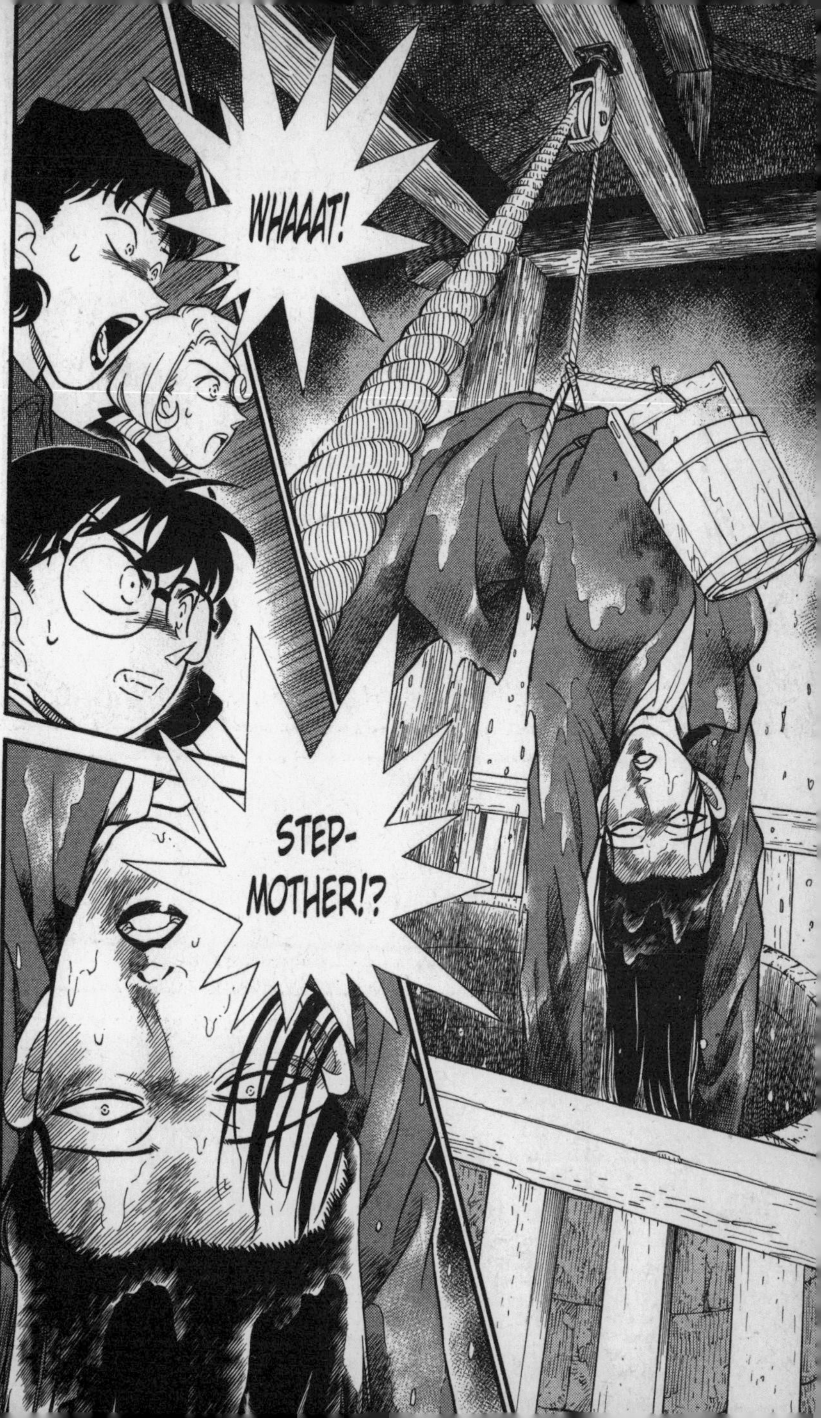
WHAAAT!
STEP-
MOTHER!?

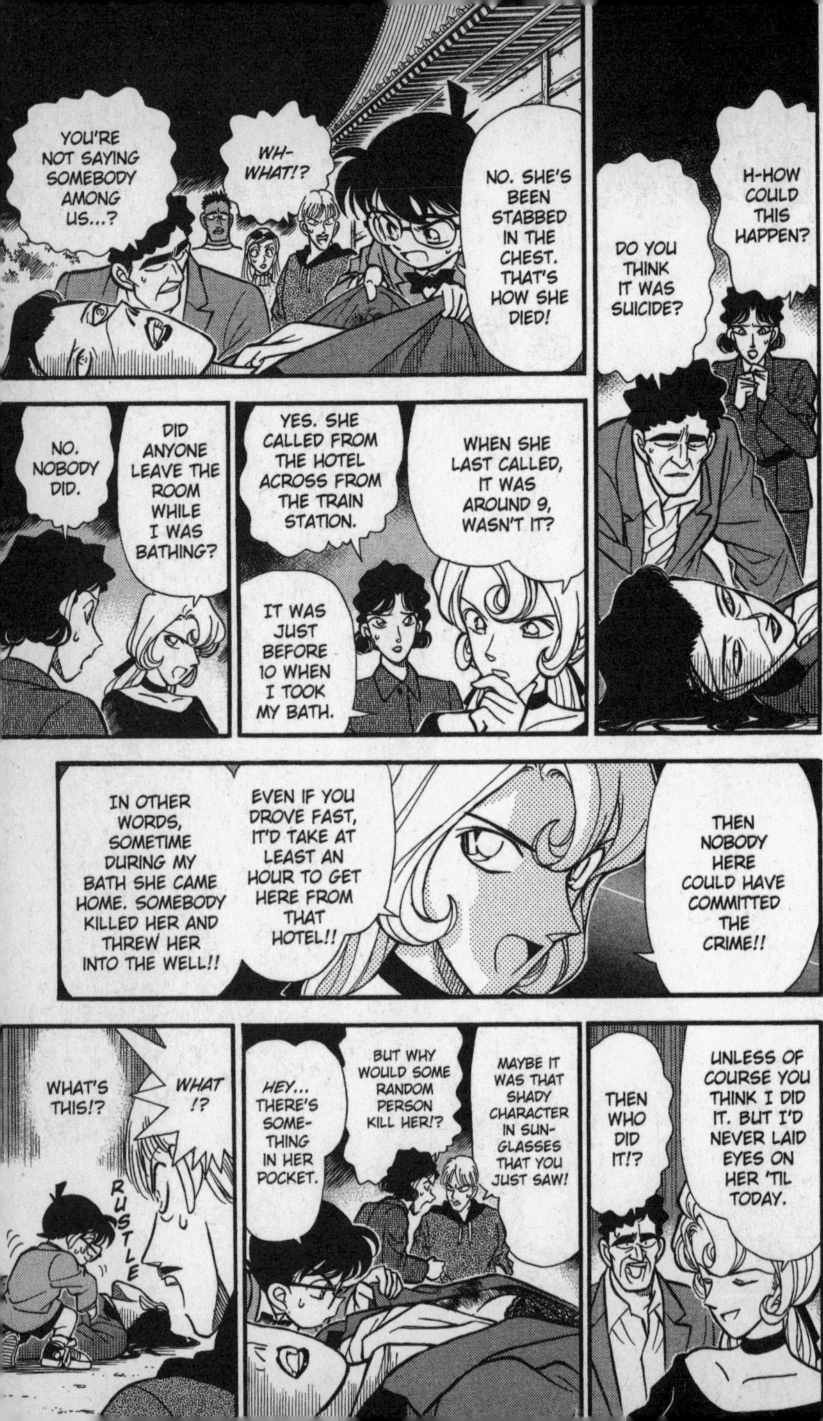
H-HOW COULD THIS HAPPEN?
DO YOU THINK IT WAS SUICIDE?
NO. SHE'S BEEN STABBED IN THE CHEST. THAT'S HOW SHE DIED!
WH-WHAT!?
YOU'RE NOT SAYING SOMEBODY AMONG US...?
WHEN SHE LAST CALLED, IT WAS AROUND 9, WASN'T IT?
YES. SHE CALLED FROM THE HOTEL ACROSS FROM THE TRAIN STATION.
IT WAS JUST BEFORE 10 WHEN I TOOK MY BATH.
DID ANYONE LEAVE THE ROOM WHILE I WAS BATHING?
NO. NOBODY DID.
THEN NOBODY HERE COULD HAVE COMMITTED THE CRIME!!
EVEN IF YOU DROVE FAST, IT'D TAKE AT LEAST AN HOUR TO GET HERE FROM THAT HOTEL!!
IN OTHER WORDS, SOMETIME DURING MY BATH SHE CAME HOME. SOMEBODY KILLED HER AND THREW HER INTO THE WELL!!
UNLESS OF COURSE YOU THINK I DID IT. BUT I'D NEVER LAID EYES ON HER 'TIL TODAY.
THEN WHO DID IT!?
MAYBE IT WAS THAT SHADY CHARACTER IN SUNGLASSES THAT YOU JUST SAW!
BUT WHY WOULD SOME RANDOM PERSON KILL HER!?
HEY... THERE'S SOMETHING IN HER POCKET.
WHAT!?
WHAT'S THIS!?
RUSTLE

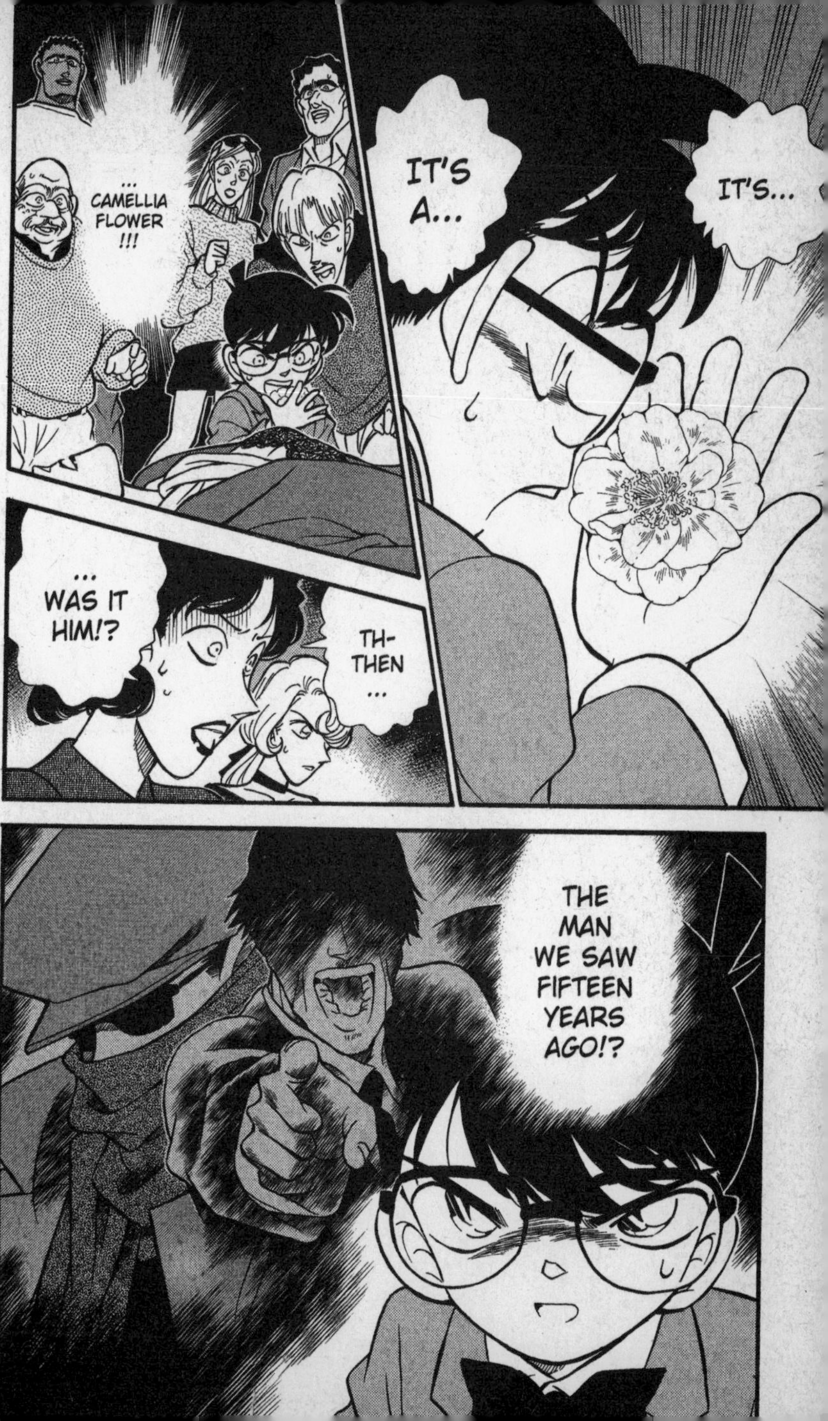
IT'S...
IT'S A...
... CAMELLIA FLOWER !!!
TH-THEN ...
... WAS IT HIM!?
THE MAN WE SAW FIFTEEN YEARS AGO!?

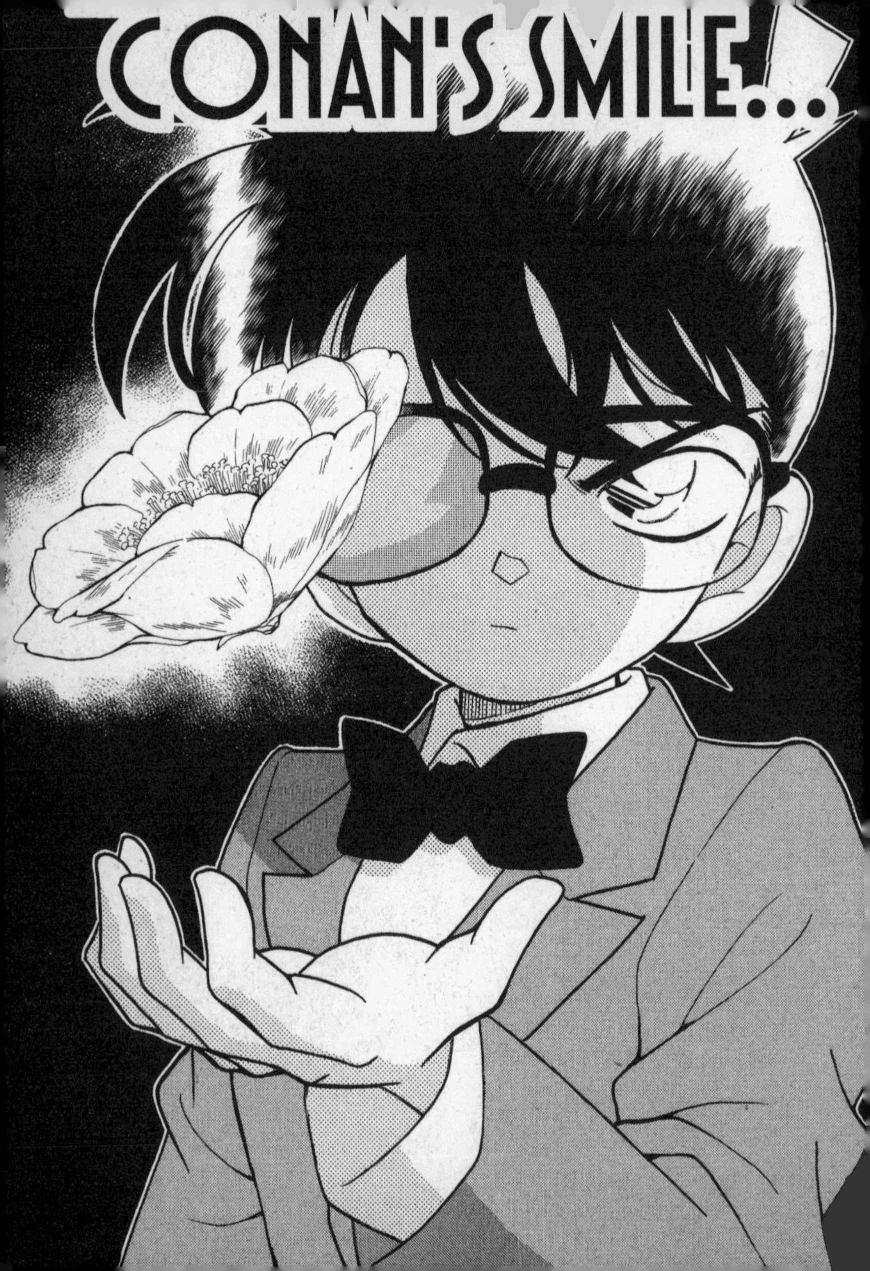
CONAN'S SMILE...

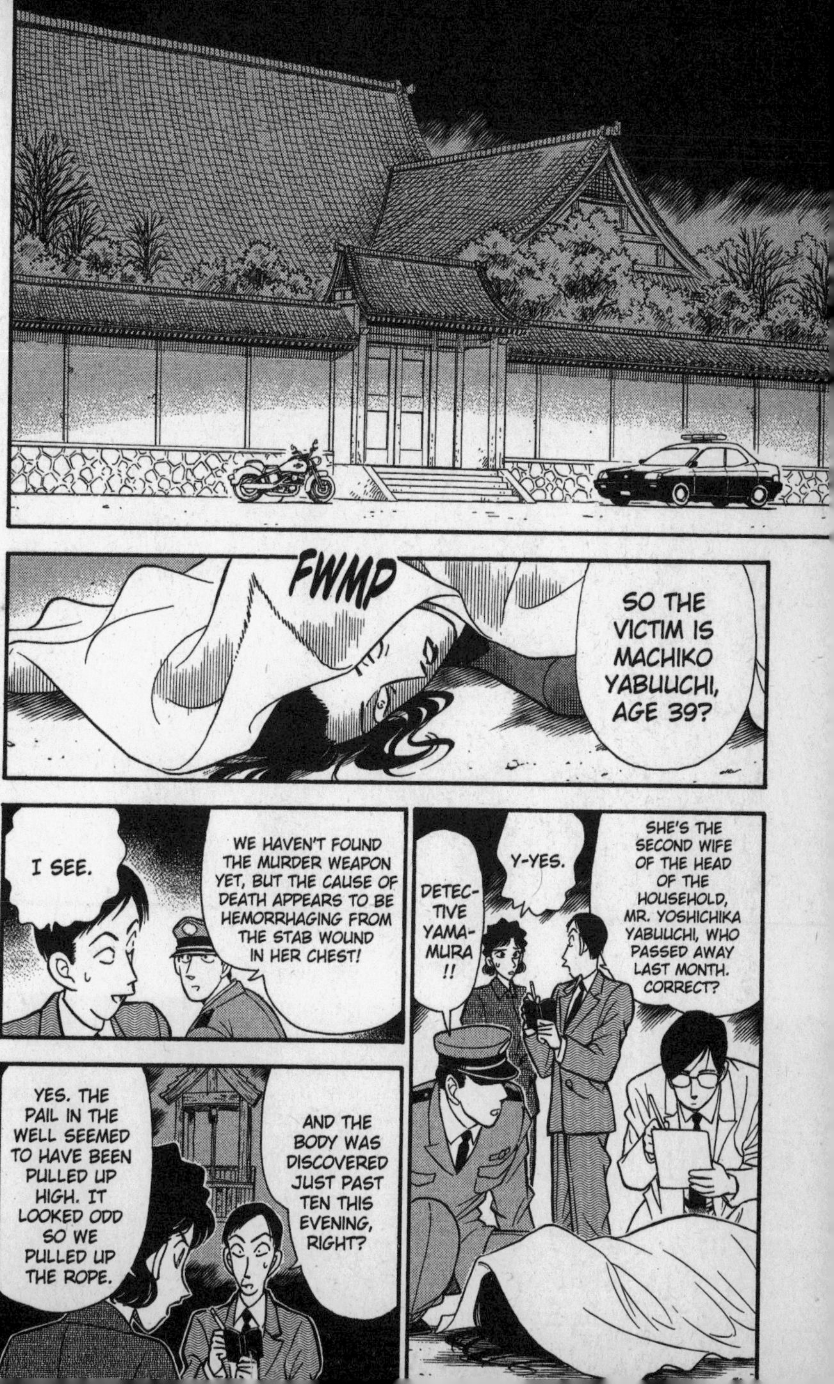
FWMP
SO THE VICTIM IS MACHIKO YABUUCHI, AGE 39?
SHE'S THE SECOND WIFE OF THE HEAD OF THE HOUSEHOLD, MR. YOSHICHIKA YABUUCHI, WHO PASSED AWAY LAST MONTH. CORRECT?
Y-YES.
DETECTIVE YAMAMURA!!
WE HAVEN'T FOUND THE MURDER WEAPON YET, BUT THE CAUSE OF DEATH APPEARS TO BE HEMORRHAGING FROM THE STAB WOUND IN HER CHEST!
I SEE.
AND THE BODY WAS DISCOVERED JUST PAST TEN THIS EVENING, RIGHT?
YES. THE PAIL IN THE WELL SEEMED TO HAVE BEEN PULLED UP HIGH. IT LOOKED ODD SO WE PULLED UP THE ROPE.

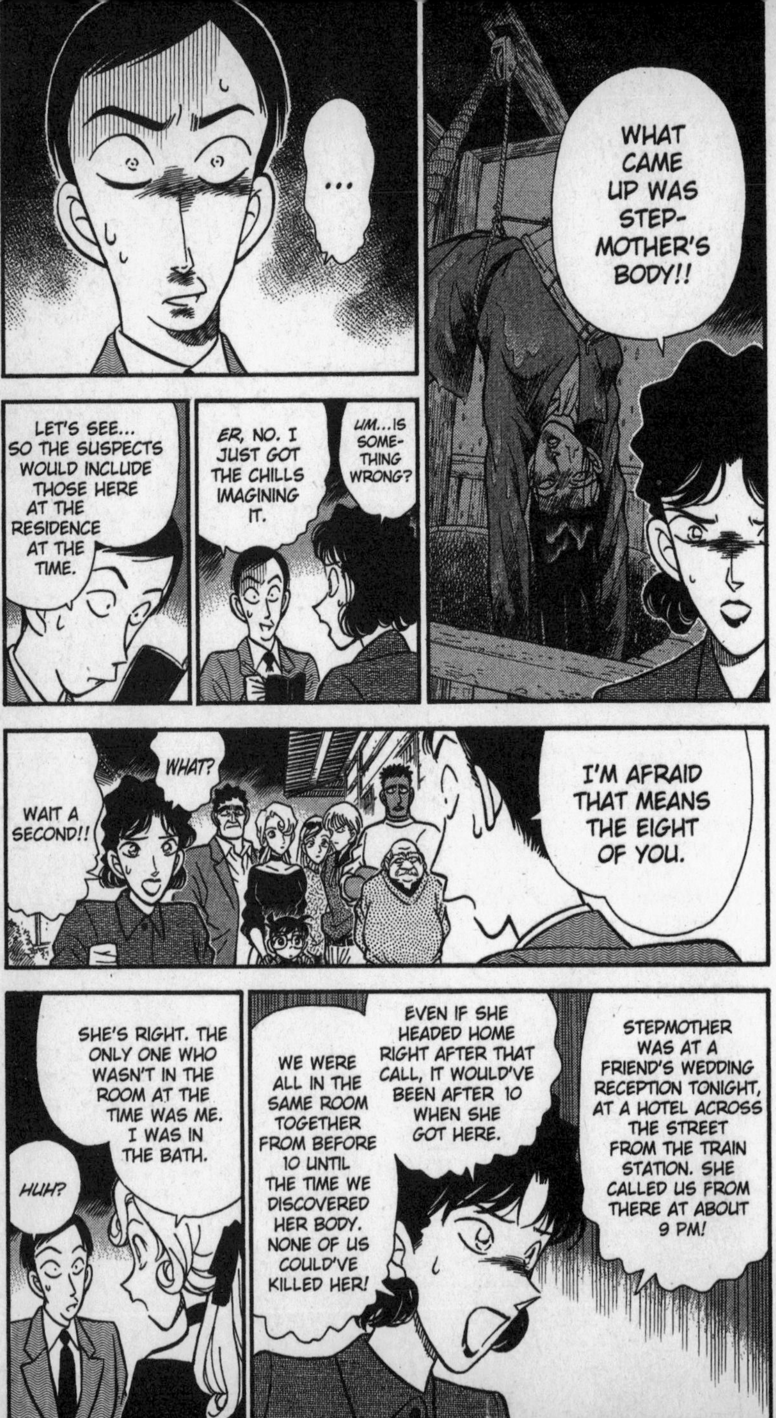
WHAT CAME UP WAS STEP-MOTHER'S BODY!!
...
UM...IS SOMETHING WRONG?
ER, NO. I JUST GOT THE CHILLS IMAGINING IT.
LET'S SEE... SO THE SUSPECTS WOULD INCLUDE THOSE HERE AT THE RESIDENCE AT THE TIME.
I'M AFRAID THAT MEANS THE EIGHT OF YOU.
WHAT?
WAIT A SECOND!!
STEPMOTHER WAS AT A FRIEND'S WEDDING RECEPTION TONIGHT, AT A HOTEL ACROSS THE STREET FROM THE TRAIN STATION. SHE CALLED US FROM THERE AT ABOUT 9 PM!
EVEN IF SHE HEADED HOME RIGHT AFTER THAT CALL, IT WOULD'VE BEEN AFTER 10 WHEN SHE GOT HERE.
WE WERE ALL IN THE SAME ROOM TOGETHER FROM BEFORE 10 UNTIL THE TIME WE DISCOVERED HER BODY. NONE OF US COULD'VE KILLED HER!
SHE'S RIGHT. THE ONLY ONE WHO WASN'T IN THE ROOM AT THE TIME WAS ME. I WAS IN THE BATH.
HUH?

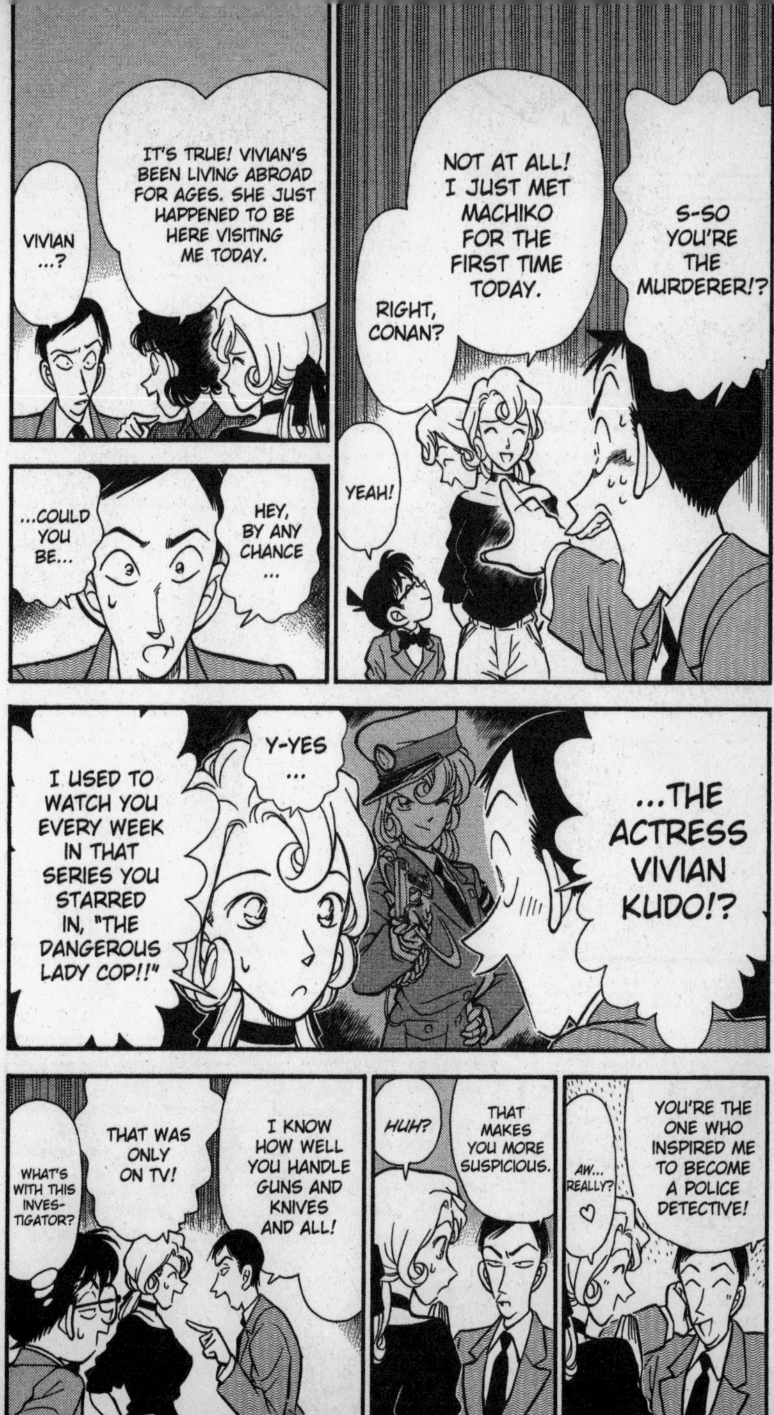
S-SO YOU'RE THE MURDERER!?
NOT AT ALL! I JUST MET MACHIKO FOR THE FIRST TIME TODAY.
RIGHT, CONAN?
YEAH!
IT'S TRUE! VIVIAN'S BEEN LIVING ABROAD FOR AGES. SHE JUST HAPPENED TO BE HERE VISITING ME TODAY.
VIVIAN ...?
HEY, BY ANY CHANCE ...
...COULD YOU BE...
...THE ACTRESS VIVIAN KUDO!?
Y-YES ...
I USED TO WATCH YOU EVERY WEEK IN THAT SERIES YOU STARRED IN, "THE DANGEROUS LADY COP!!"
YOU'RE THE ONE WHO INSPIRED ME TO BECOME A POLICE DETECTIVE!
AW... REALLY? ♡
THAT MAKES YOU MORE SUSPICIOUS.
HUH?
I KNOW HOW WELL YOU HANDLE GUNS AND KNIVES AND ALL!
THAT WAS ONLY ON TV!
WHAT'S WITH THIS INVES-TIGATOR?

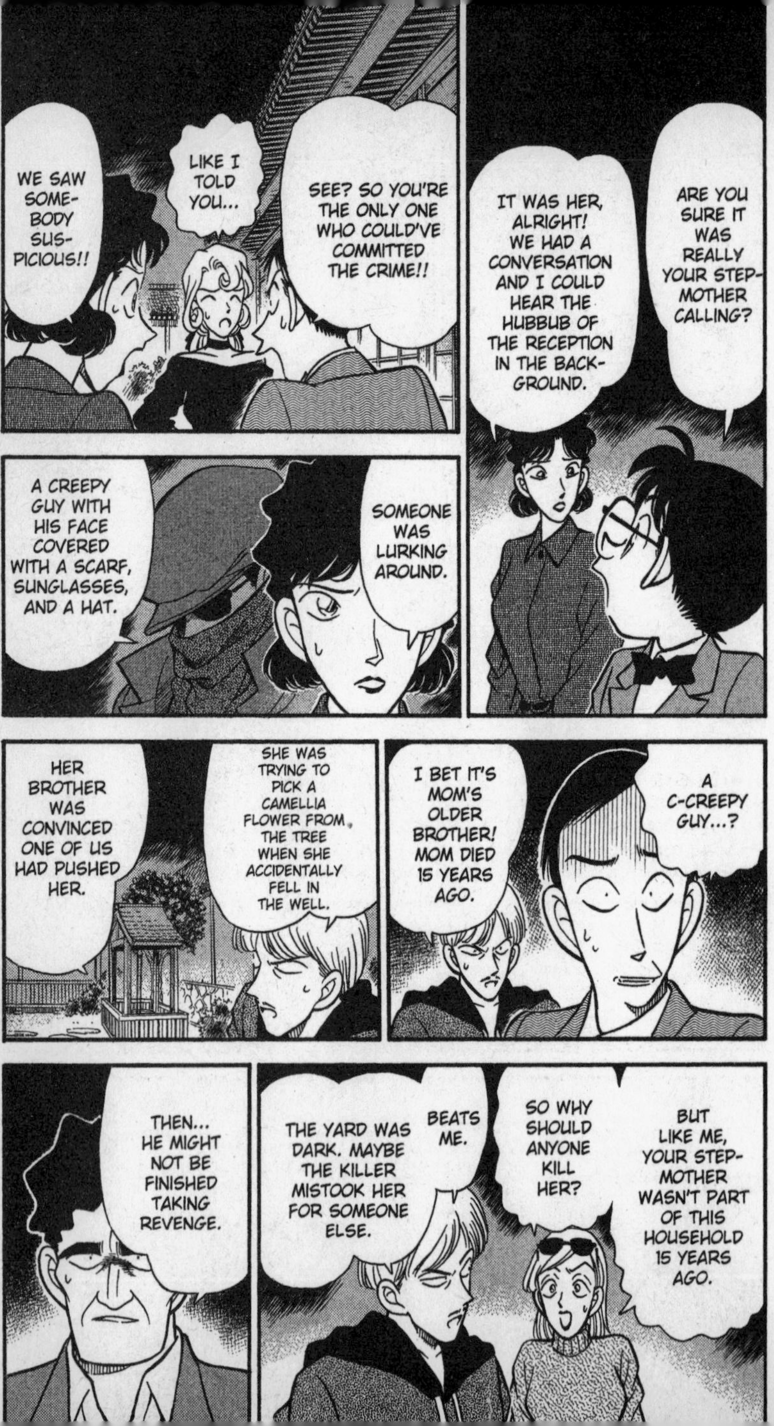
ARE YOU SURE IT WAS REALLY YOUR STEP-MOTHER CALLING?
IT WAS HER, ALRIGHT! WE HAD A CONVERSATION AND I COULD HEAR THE HUBBUB OF THE RECEPTION IN THE BACK-GROUND.
SEE? SO YOU'RE THE ONLY ONE WHO COULD'VE COMMITTED THE CRIME!!
LIKE I TOLD YOU...
WE SAW SOME-BODY SUS-PICIOUS!!
SOMEONE WAS LURKING AROUND.
A CREEPY GUY WITH HIS FACE COVERED WITH A SCARF, SUNGLASSES, AND A HAT.
A C-CREEPY GUY...?
I BET IT'S MOM'S OLDER BROTHER! MOM DIED 15 YEARS AGO.
SHE WAS TRYING TO PICK A CAMELLIA FLOWER FROM THE TREE WHEN SHE ACCIDENTALLY FELL IN THE WELL.
HER BROTHER WAS CONVINCED ONE OF US HAD PUSHED HER.
BUT LIKE ME, YOUR STEP-MOTHER WASN'T PART OF THIS HOUSEHOLD 15 YEARS AGO.
SO WHY SHOULD ANYONE KILL HER?
BEATS ME.
THE YARD WAS DARK. MAYBE THE KILLER MISTOOK HER FOR SOMEONE ELSE.
THEN... HE MIGHT NOT BE FINISHED TAKING REVENGE.

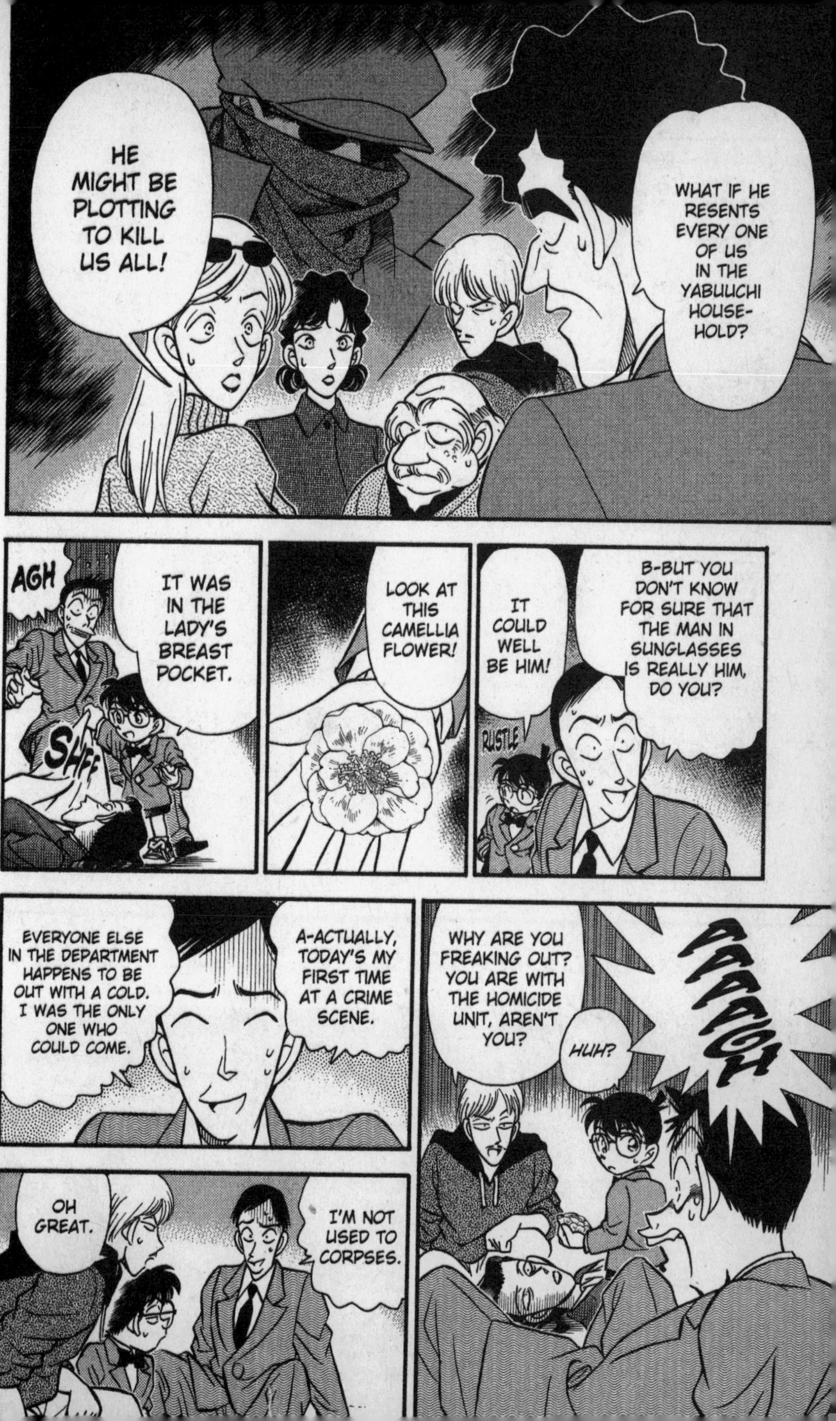
WHAT IF HE RESENTS EVERY ONE OF US IN THE YABUUCHI HOUSE-HOLD?
HE MIGHT BE PLOTTING TO KILL US ALL!
B-BUT YOU DON'T KNOW FOR SURE THAT THE MAN IN SUNGLASSES IS REALLY HIM, DO YOU?
IT COULD WELL BE HIM!
RUSTLE
LOOK AT THIS CAMELLIA FLOWER!
IT WAS IN THE LADY'S BREAST POCKET.
AGH
SHFF
WHY ARE YOU FREAKING OUT? YOU ARE WITH THE HOMICIDE UNIT, AREN'T YOU?
HUH?
A-ACTUALLY, TODAY'S MY FIRST TIME AT A CRIME SCENE.
EVERYONE ELSE IN THE DEPARTMENT HAPPENS TO BE OUT WITH A COLD. I WAS THE ONLY ONE WHO COULD COME.
I'M NOT USED TO CORPSES.
OH GREAT.

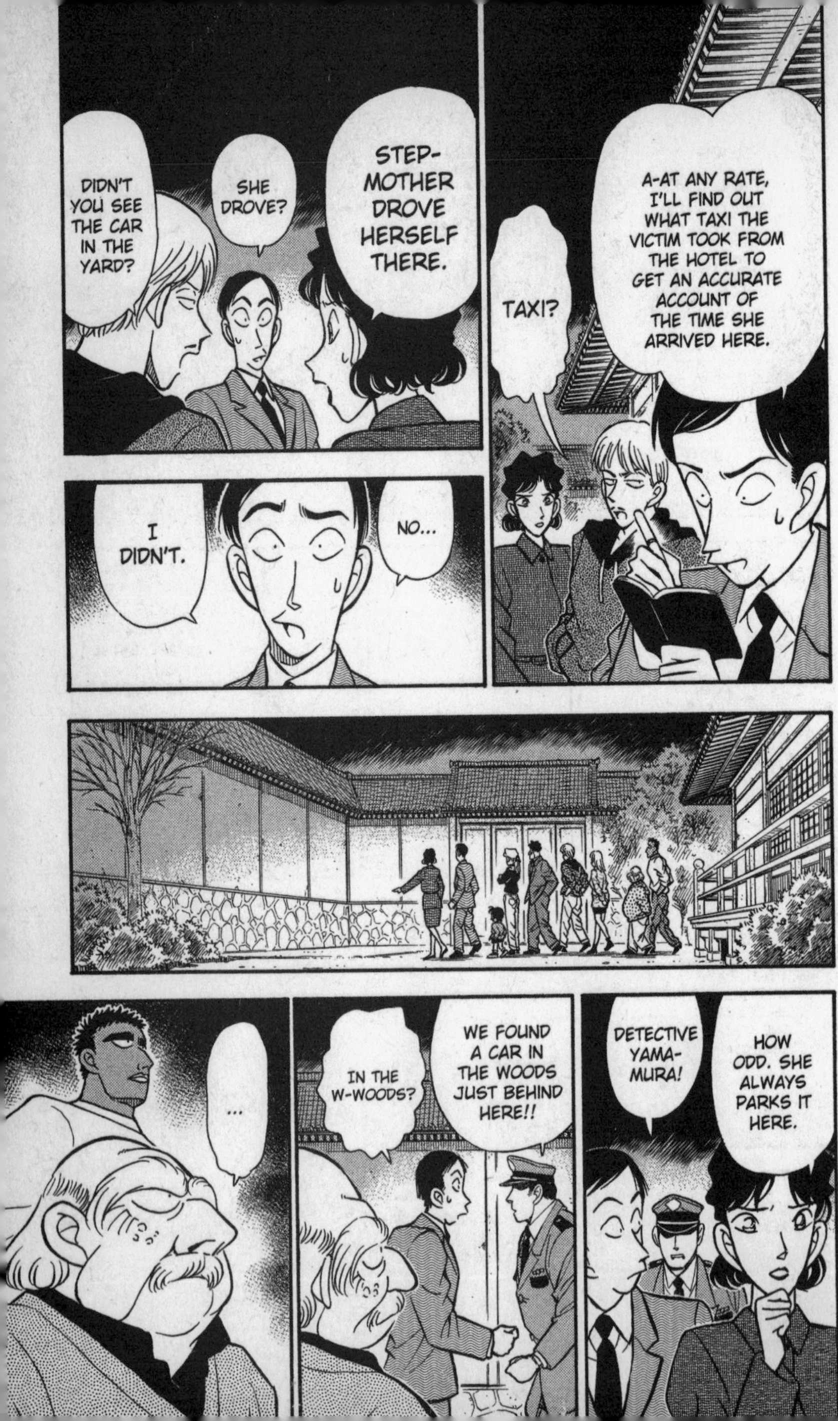
A-AT ANY RATE, I'LL FIND OUT WHAT TAXI THE VICTIM TOOK FROM THE HOTEL TO GET AN ACCURATE ACCOUNT OF THE TIME SHE ARRIVED HERE.
TAXI?
STEP-MOTHER DROVE HERSELF THERE.
SHE DROVE?
DIDN'T YOU SEE THE CAR IN THE YARD?
NO...
I DIDN'T.
HOW ODD. SHE ALWAYS PARKS IT HERE.
DETECTIVE YAMAMURA!
WE FOUND A CAR IN THE WOODS JUST BEHIND HERE!!
IN THE W-WOODS?
...

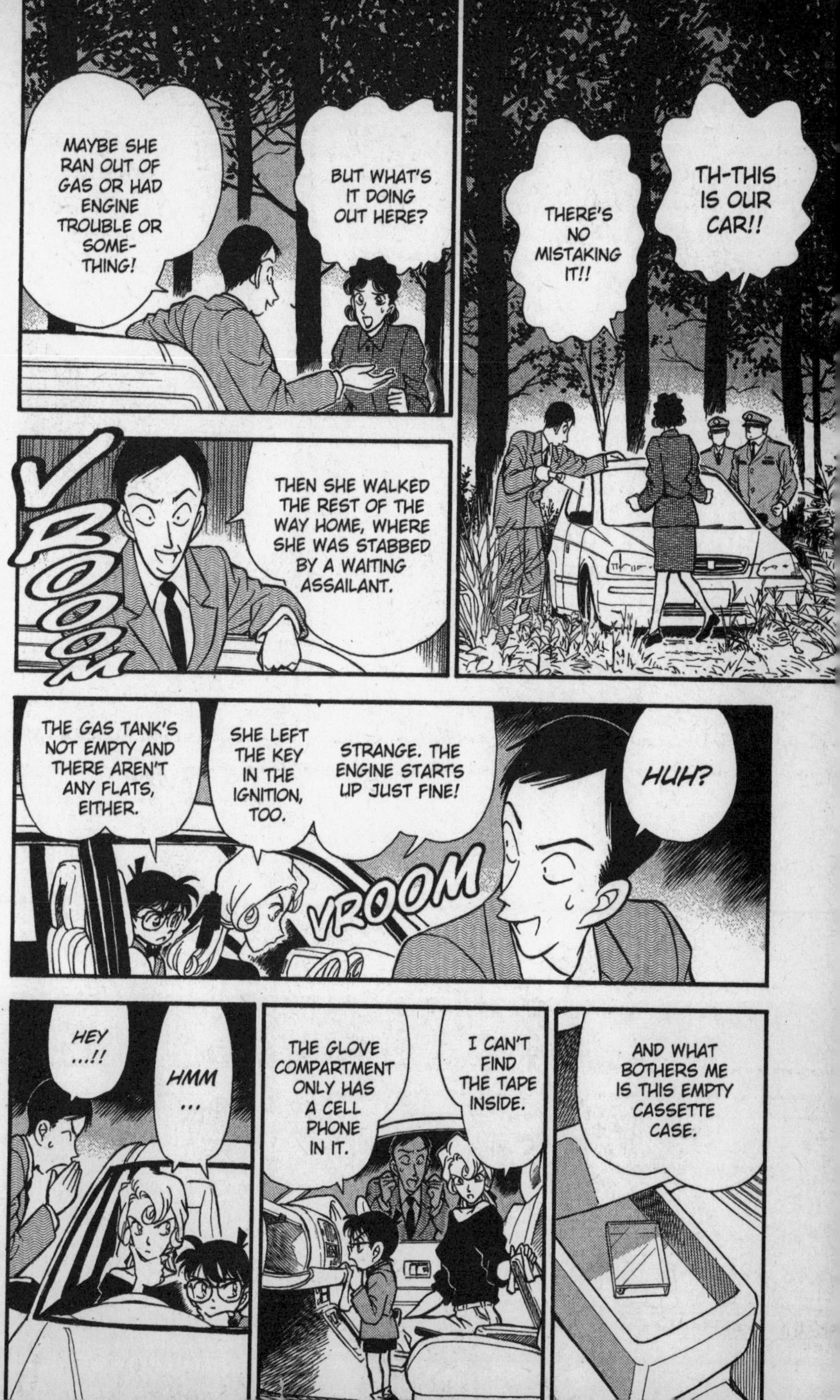
TH-THIS IS OUR CAR!!
THERE'S NO MISTAKING IT!!
BUT WHAT'S IT DOING OUT HERE?
MAYBE SHE RAN OUT OF GAS OR HAD ENGINE TROUBLE OR SOME-THING!
THEN SHE WALKED THE REST OF THE WAY HOME, WHERE SHE WAS STABBED BY A WAITING ASSAILANT.
VROOOOM
HUH?
STRANGE. THE ENGINE STARTS UP JUST FINE!
SHE LEFT THE KEY IN THE IGNITION, TOO.
THE GAS TANK'S NOT EMPTY AND THERE AREN'T ANY FLATS, EITHER.
VROOM
AND WHAT BOTHERS ME IS THIS EMPTY CASSETTE CASE.
I CAN'T FIND THE TAPE INSIDE.
THE GLOVE COMPARTMENT ONLY HAS A CELL PHONE IN IT.
HMM ...
HEY ...!!

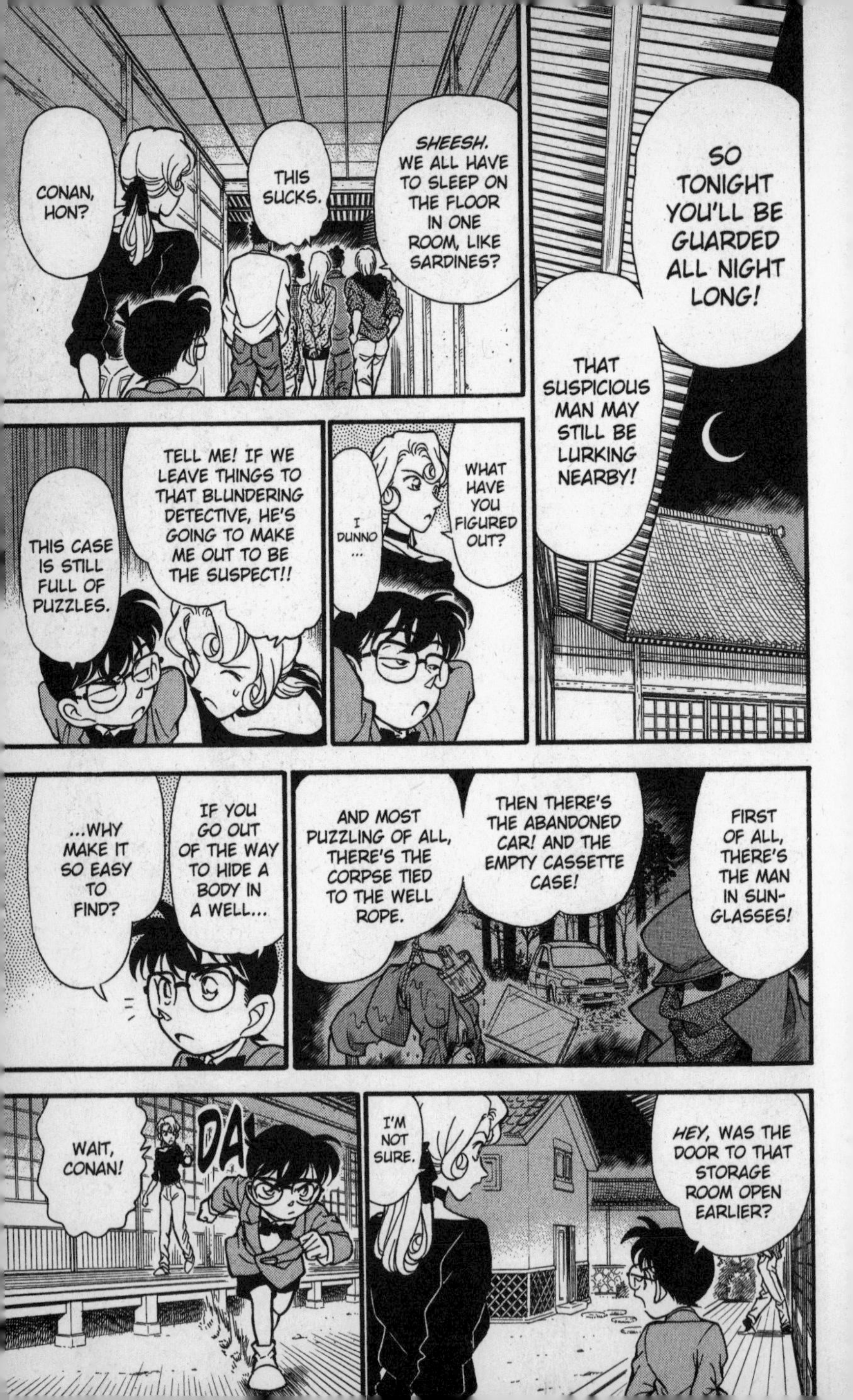
SO TONIGHT YOU'LL BE GUARDED ALL NIGHT LONG!
THAT SUSPICIOUS MAN MAY STILL BE LURKING NEARBY!
SHEESH. WE ALL HAVE TO SLEEP ON THE FLOOR IN ONE ROOM, LIKE SARDINES?
THIS SUCKS.
CONAN, HON?
WHAT HAVE YOU FIGURED OUT?
I DUNNO...
TELL ME! IF WE LEAVE THINGS TO THAT BLUNDERING DETECTIVE, HE'S GOING TO MAKE ME OUT TO BE THE SUSPECT!!
THIS CASE IS STILL FULL OF PUZZLES.
FIRST OF ALL, THERE'S THE MAN IN SUN-GLASSES!
THEN THERE'S THE ABANDONED CAR! AND THE EMPTY CASSETTE CASE!
AND MOST PUZZLING OF ALL, THERE'S THE CORPSE TIED TO THE WELL ROPE.
IF YOU GO OUT OF THE WAY TO HIDE A BODY IN A WELL...
...WHY MAKE IT SO EASY TO FIND?
HEY, WAS THE DOOR TO THAT STORAGE ROOM OPEN EARLIER?
I'M NOT SURE.
DA
WAIT, CONAN!

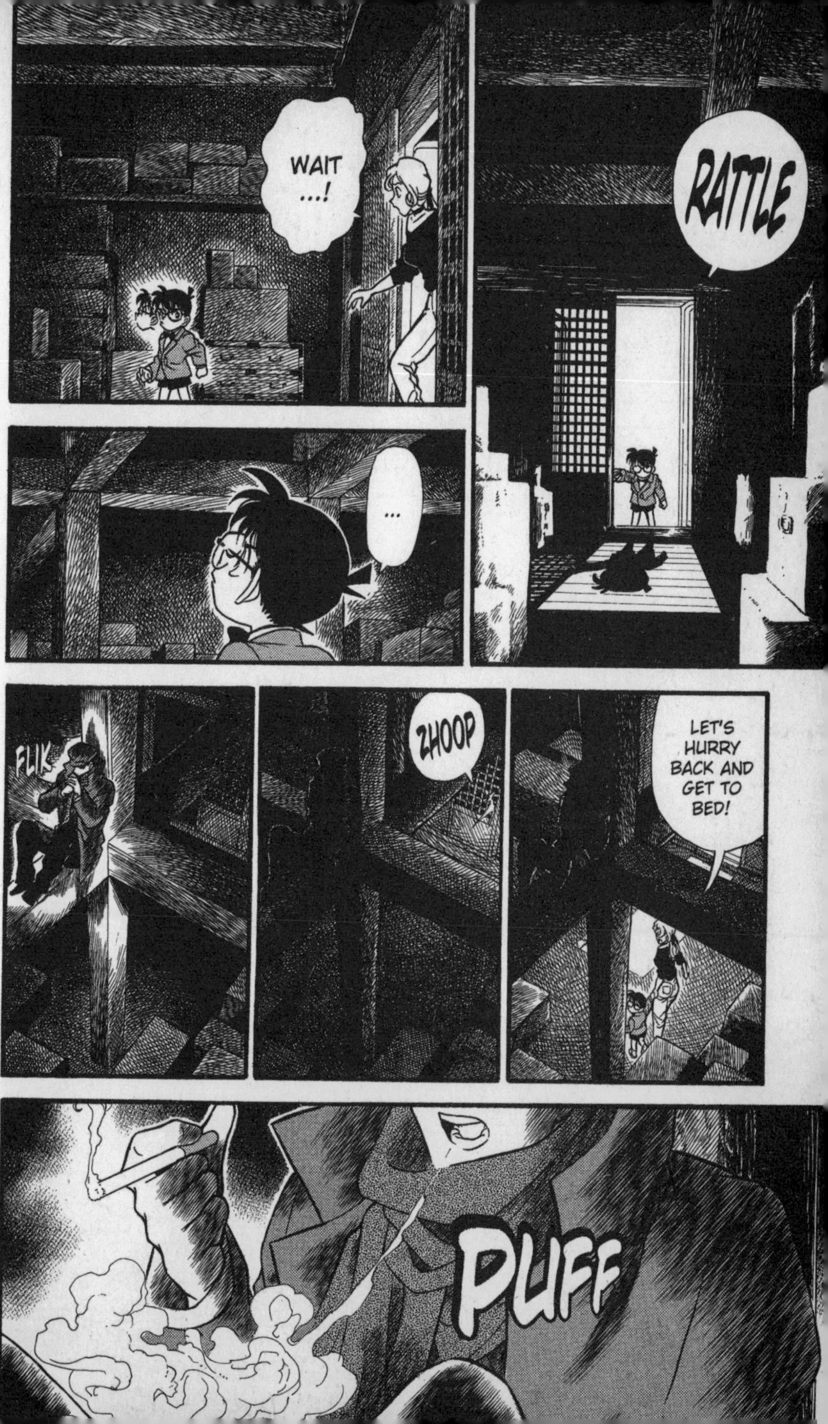
RATTLE
WAIT ...!
...
LET'S HURRY BACK AND GET TO BED!
ZHOOP
FLIK
PUFF

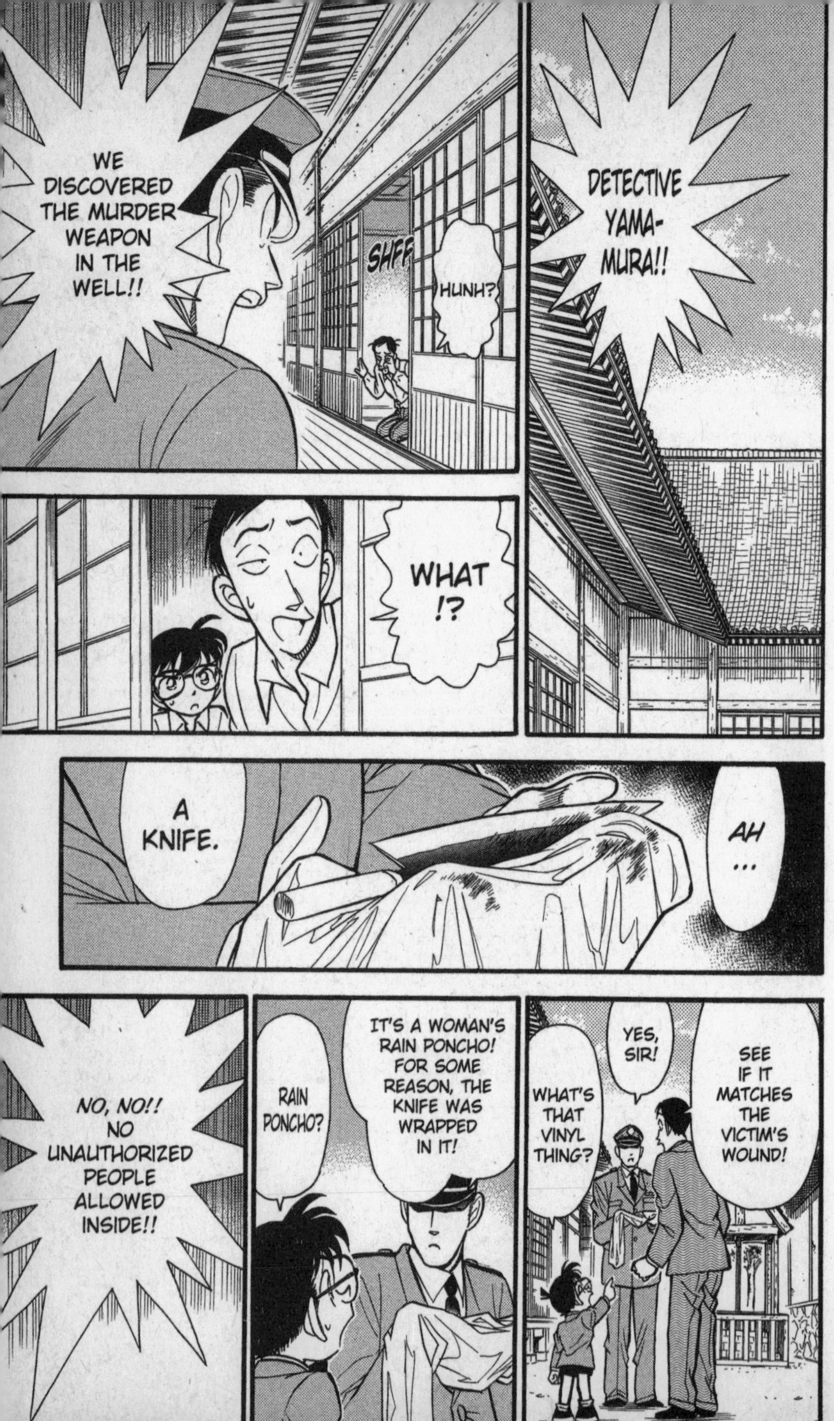
DETECTIVE YAMA-MURA!!
SHFF
HUNH?
WE DISCOVERED THE MURDER WEAPON IN THE WELL!!
WHAT!?
AH...
A KNIFE.
SEE IF IT MATCHES THE VICTIM'S WOUND!
YES, SIR!
WHAT'S THAT VINYL THING?
IT'S A WOMAN'S RAIN PONCHO! FOR SOME REASON, THE KNIFE WAS WRAPPED IN IT!
RAIN PONCHO?
NO, NO!! NO UNAUTHORIZED PEOPLE ALLOWED INSIDE!!

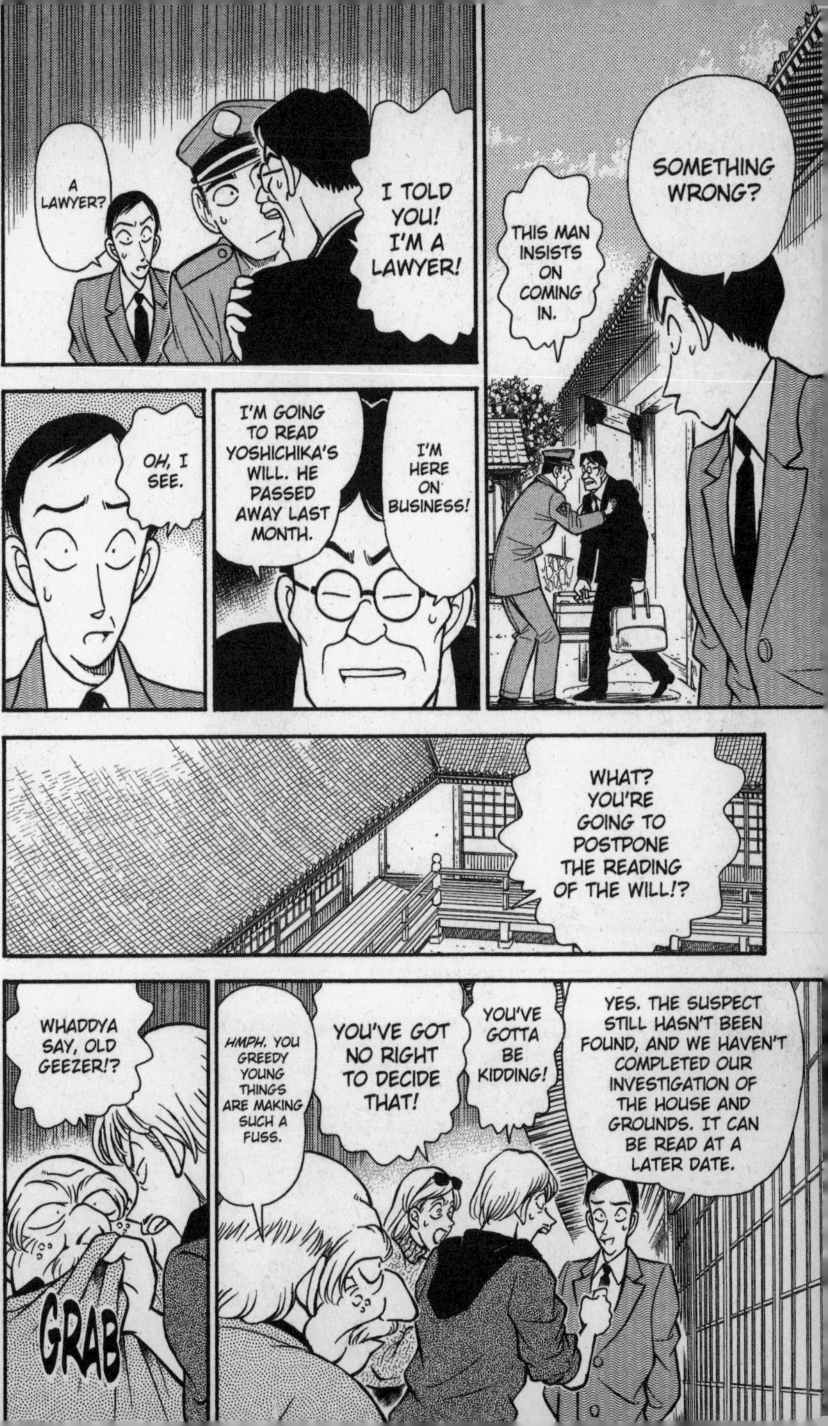
SOMETHING WRONG?
THIS MAN INSISTS ON COMING IN.
I TOLD YOU! I'M A LAWYER!
A LAWYER?
I'M HERE ON BUSINESS!
I'M GOING TO READ YOSHICHIKA'S WILL. HE PASSED AWAY LAST MONTH.
OH, I SEE.
WHAT? YOU'RE GOING TO POSTPONE THE READING OF THE WILL!?
YES. THE SUSPECT STILL HASN'T BEEN FOUND, AND WE HAVEN'T COMPLETED OUR INVESTIGATION OF THE HOUSE AND GROUNDS. IT CAN BE READ AT A LATER DATE.
YOU'VE GOTTA BE KIDDING!
YOU'VE GOT NO RIGHT TO DECIDE THAT!
HMPH. YOU GREEDY YOUNG THINGS ARE MAKING SUCH A FUSS.
WHADDYA SAY, OLD GEEZER!?
GRAB

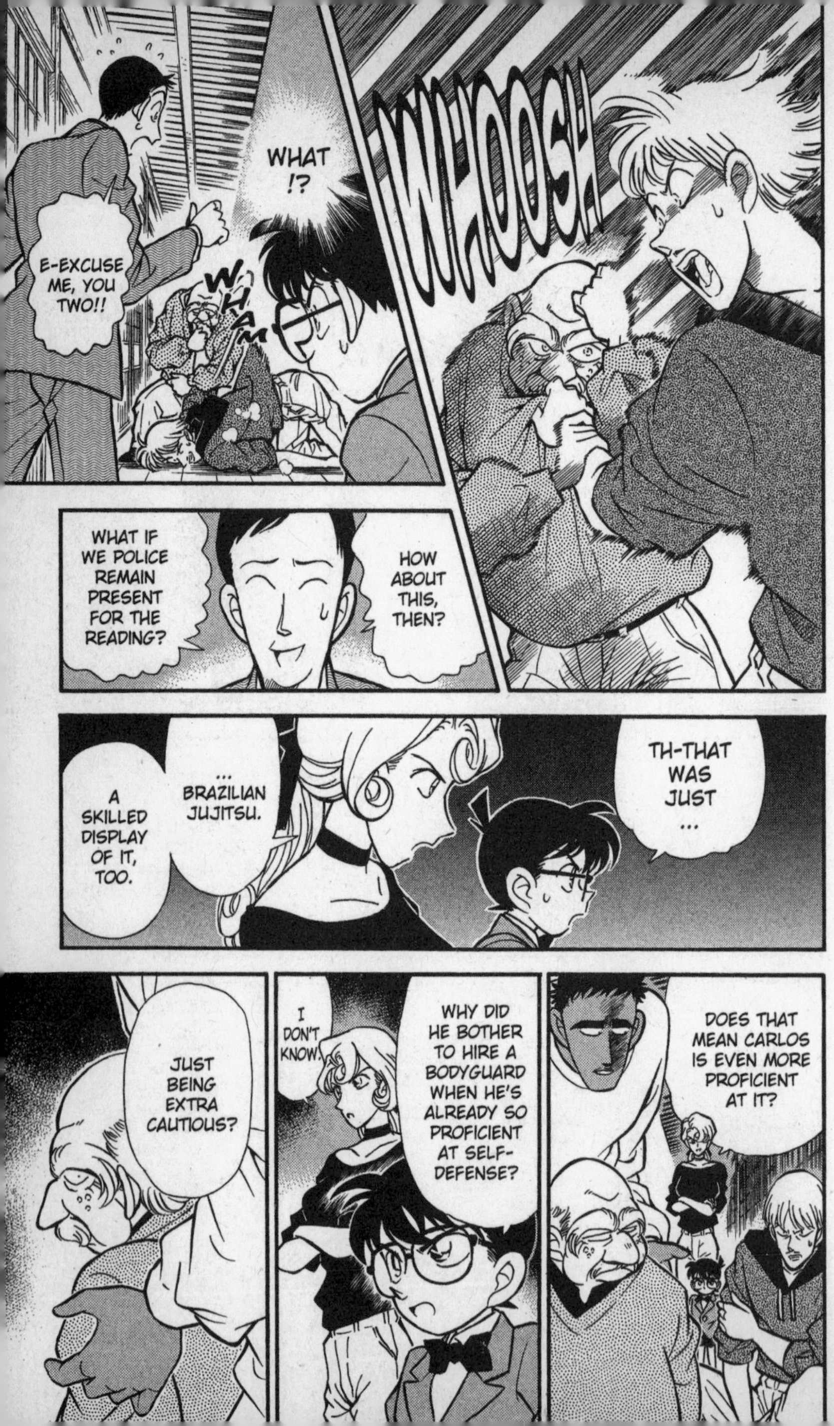
WHOOSH
WHAT !?
WHAM
E-EXCUSE ME, YOU TWO!!
HOW ABOUT THIS, THEN?
WHAT IF WE POLICE REMAIN PRESENT FOR THE READING?
TH-THAT WAS JUST ...
... BRAZILIAN JUJITSU.
A SKILLED DISPLAY OF IT, TOO.
DOES THAT MEAN CARLOS IS EVEN MORE PROFICIENT AT IT?
WHY DID HE BOTHER TO HIRE A BODYGUARD WHEN HE'S ALREADY SO PROFICIENT AT SELF-DEFENSE?
I DON'T KNOW.
JUST BEING EXTRA CAUTIOUS?

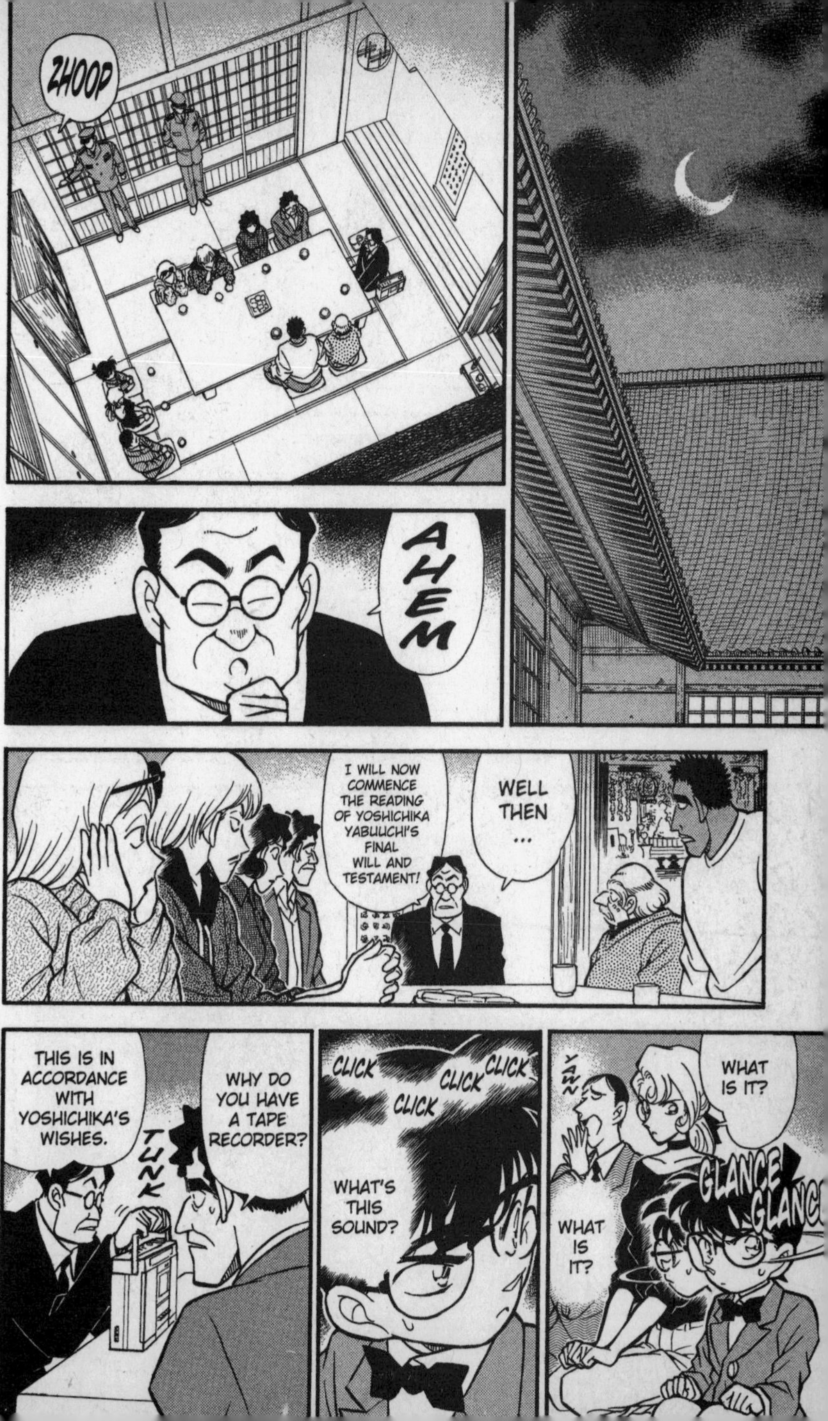
ZHOOP
AHEM
WELL THEN ...
I WILL NOW COMMENCE THE READING OF YOSHICHIKA YABUUCHI'S FINAL WILL AND TESTAMENT!
WHAT IS IT?
GLANCE GLANC
YAWN
WHAT IS IT?
CLICK CLICK
CLICK CLICK
WHAT'S THIS SOUND?
WHY DO YOU HAVE A TAPE RECORDER?
TUNK
THIS IS IN ACCORDANCE WITH YOSHICHIKA'S WISHES.

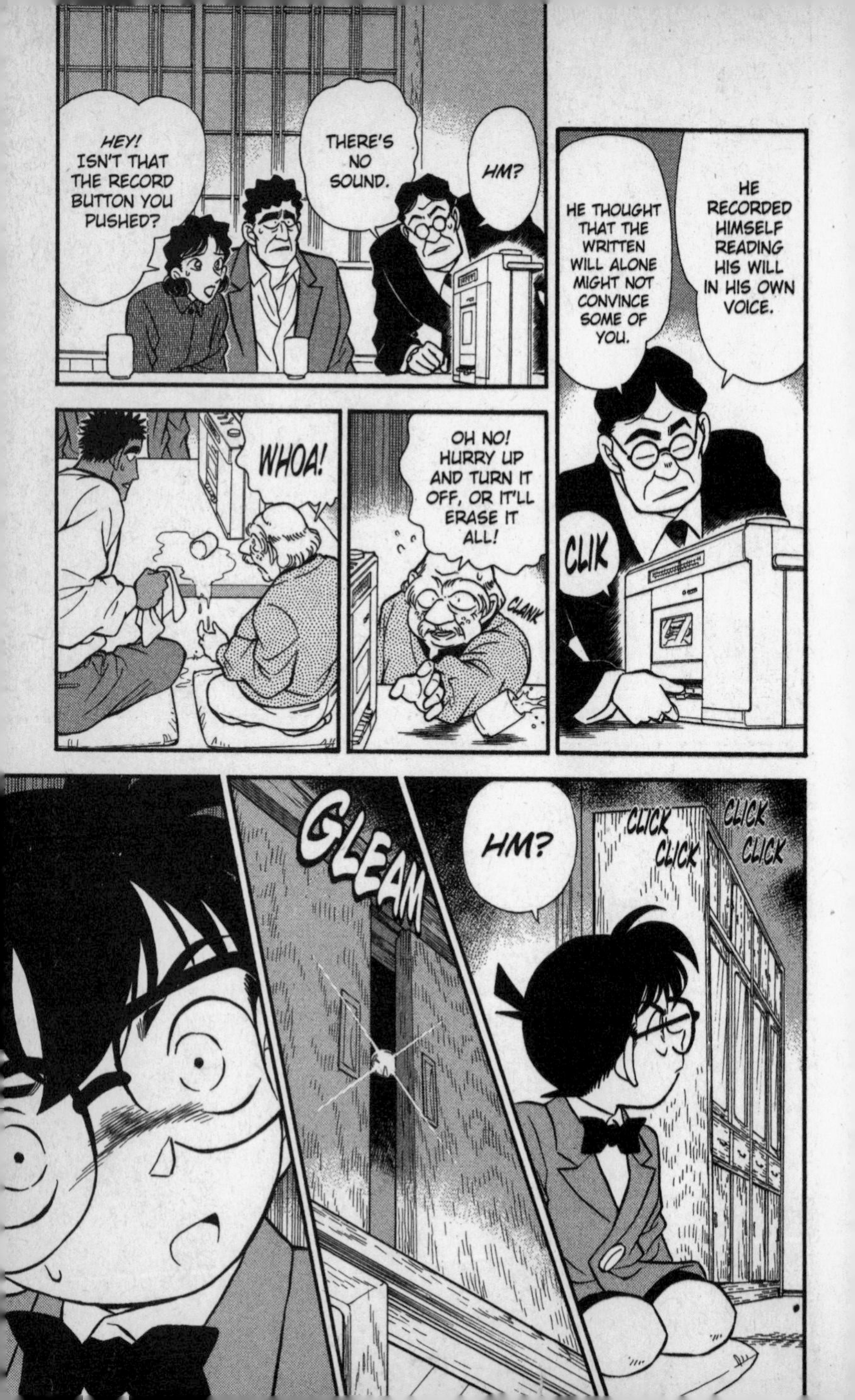
HE RECORDED HIMSELF READING HIS WILL IN HIS OWN VOICE.
HE THOUGHT THAT THE WRITTEN WILL ALONE MIGHT NOT CONVINCE SOME OF YOU.
CLIK
HM?
THERE'S NO SOUND.
HEY! ISN'T THAT THE RECORD BUTTON YOU PUSHED?
OH NO! HURRY UP AND TURN IT OFF, OR IT'LL ERASE IT ALL!
CLANK
WHOA!
CLICK CLICK
CLICK CLICK
HM?
GLEAM

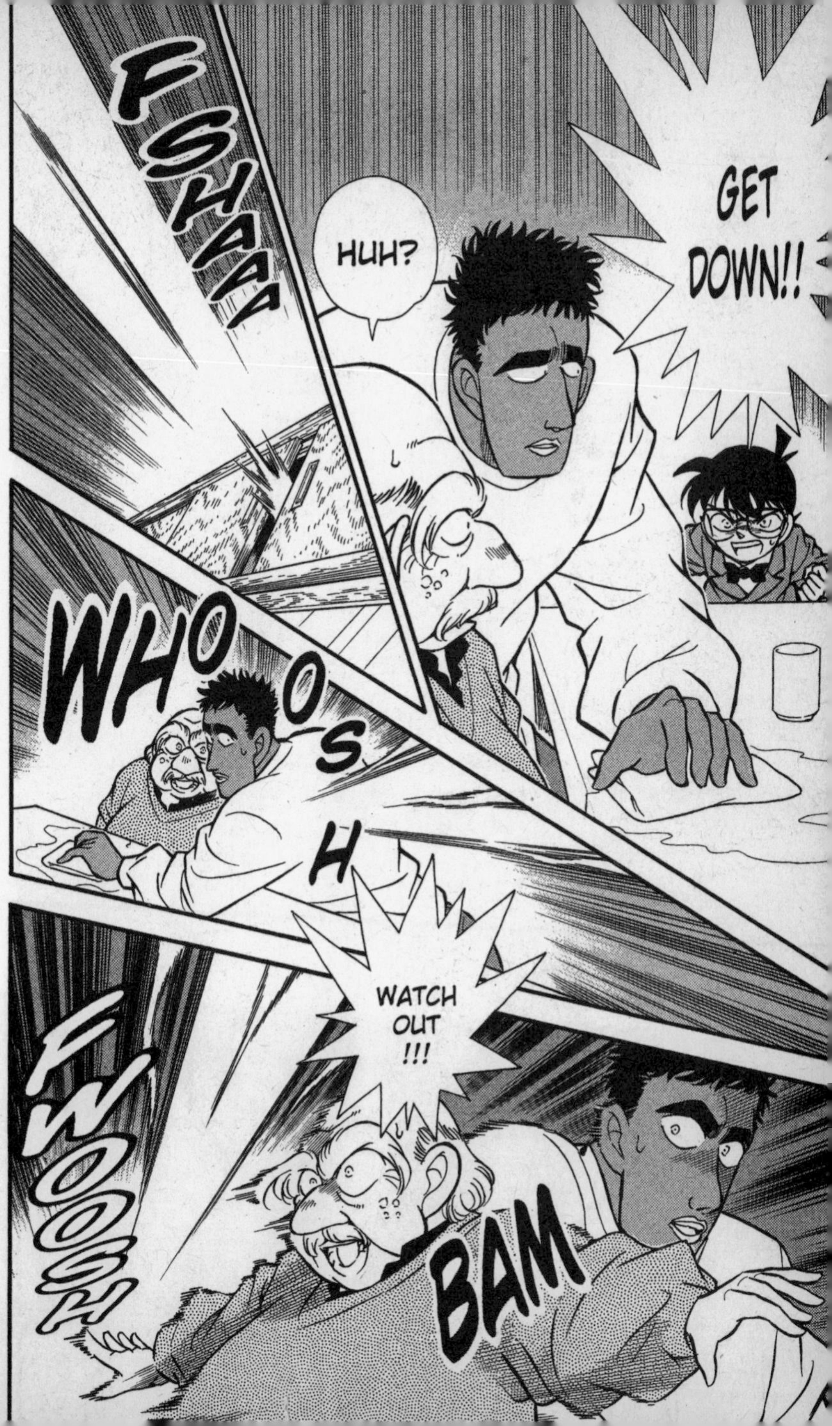
GET DOWN!!
HUH?
FSHAAA
WHOOSH
WATCH OUT!!!
BAM
FWOOOSH

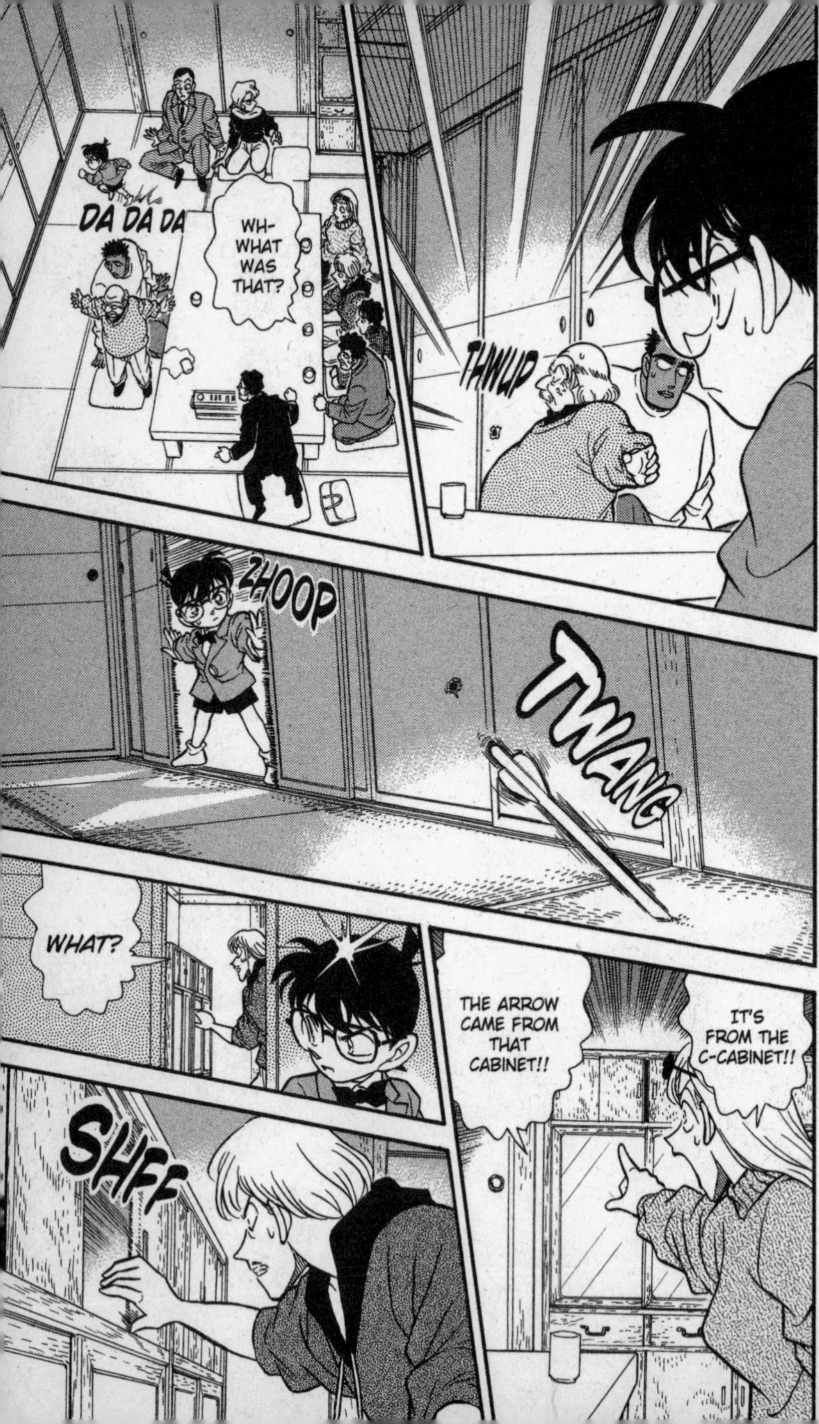
THWUP
WH-WHAT WAS THAT?
DA DA DA
TWANG
ZHOOP
IT'S FROM THE C-CABINET!!
THE ARROW CAME FROM THAT CABINET!!
WHAT?
SHFF

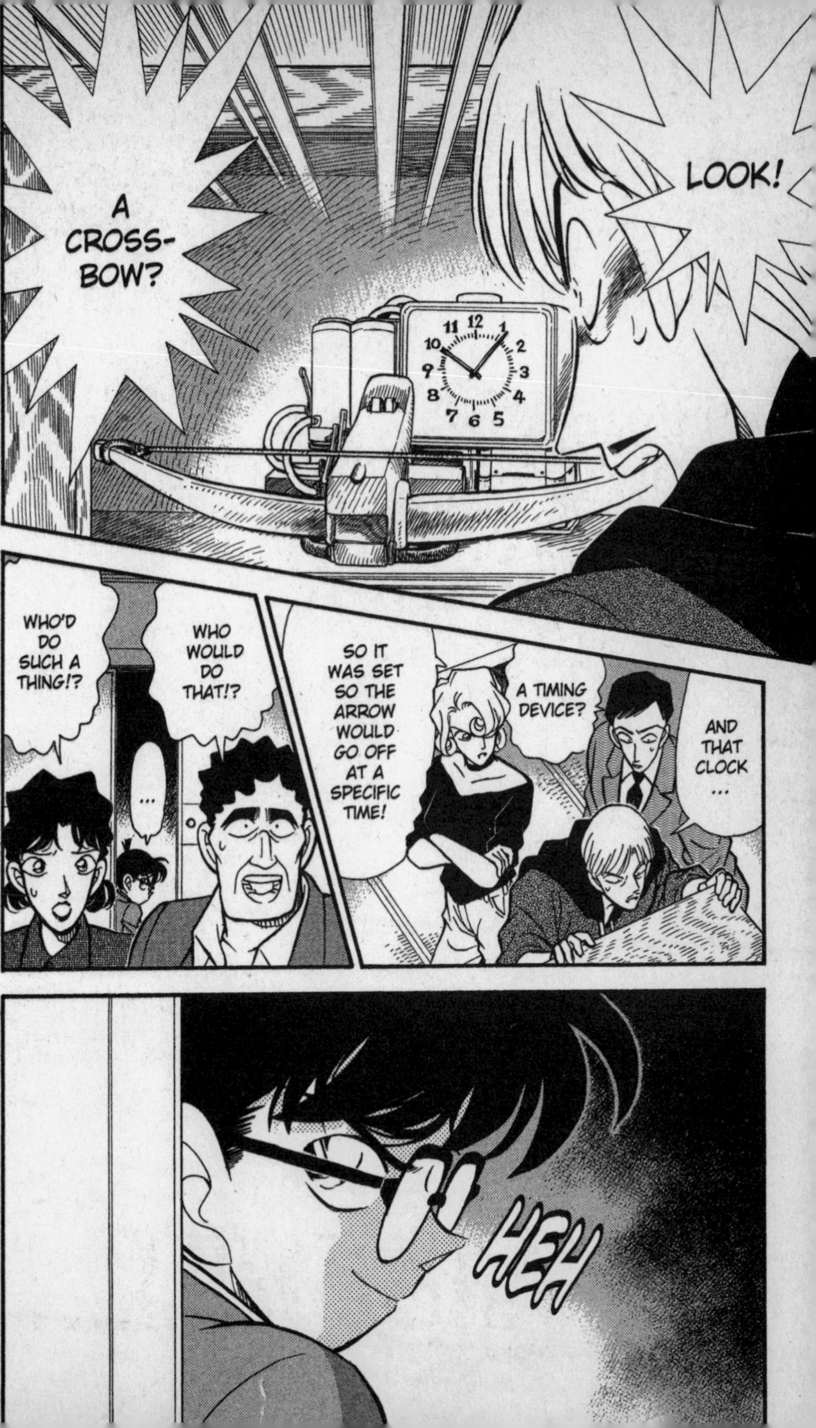

LOOK!
A CROSS-BOW?
AND THAT CLOCK ...
A TIMING DEVICE?
SO IT WAS SET SO THE ARROW WOULD GO OFF AT A SPECIFIC TIME!
WHO WOULD DO THAT!?
...
WHO'D DO SUCH A THING!?
HEH

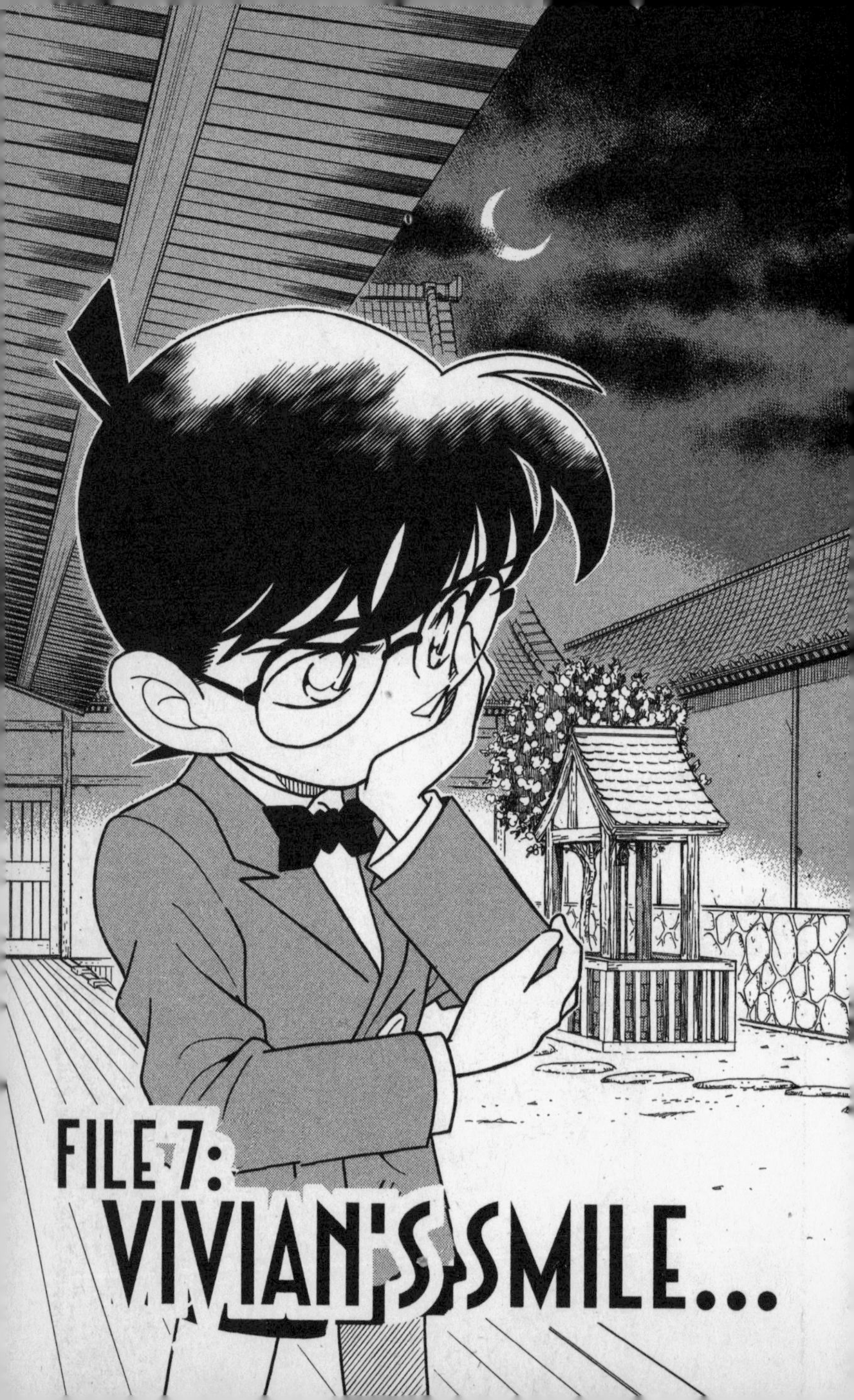
FILE 7:
VIVIAN'S SMILE...

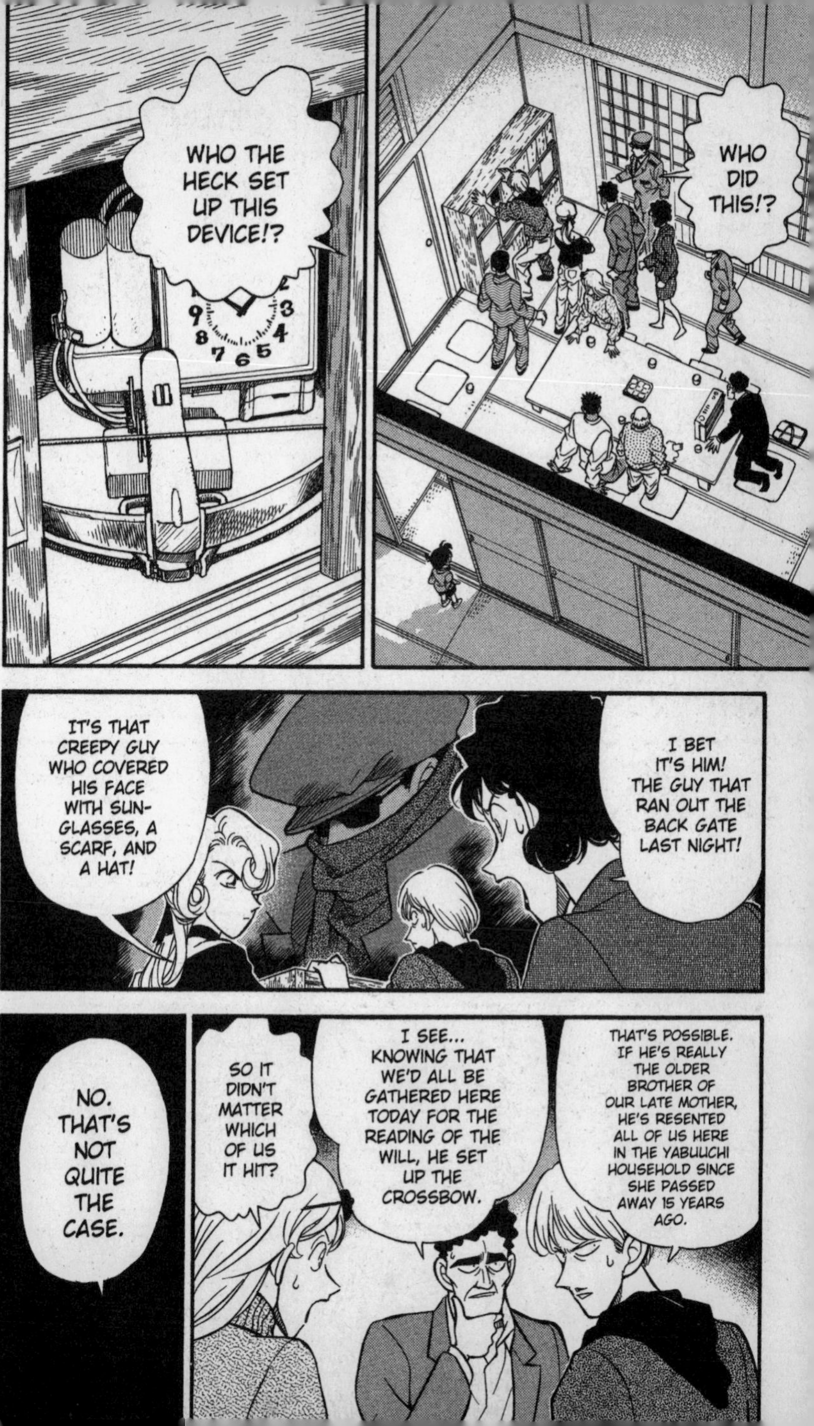
WHO DID THIS!?
WHO THE HECK SET UP THIS DEVICE!?
I BET IT'S HIM! THE GUY THAT RAN OUT THE BACK GATE LAST NIGHT!
IT'S THAT CREEPY GUY WHO COVERED HIS FACE WITH SUN-GLASSES, A SCARF, AND A HAT!
THAT'S POSSIBLE. IF HE'S REALLY THE OLDER BROTHER OF OUR LATE MOTHER, HE'S RESENTED ALL OF US HERE IN THE YABUUCHI HOUSEHOLD SINCE SHE PASSED AWAY 15 YEARS AGO.
I SEE... KNOWING THAT WE'D ALL BE GATHERED HERE TODAY FOR THE READING OF THE WILL, HE SET UP THE CROSSBOW.
SO IT DIDN'T MATTER WHICH OF US IT HIT?
NO. THAT'S NOT QUITE THE CASE.

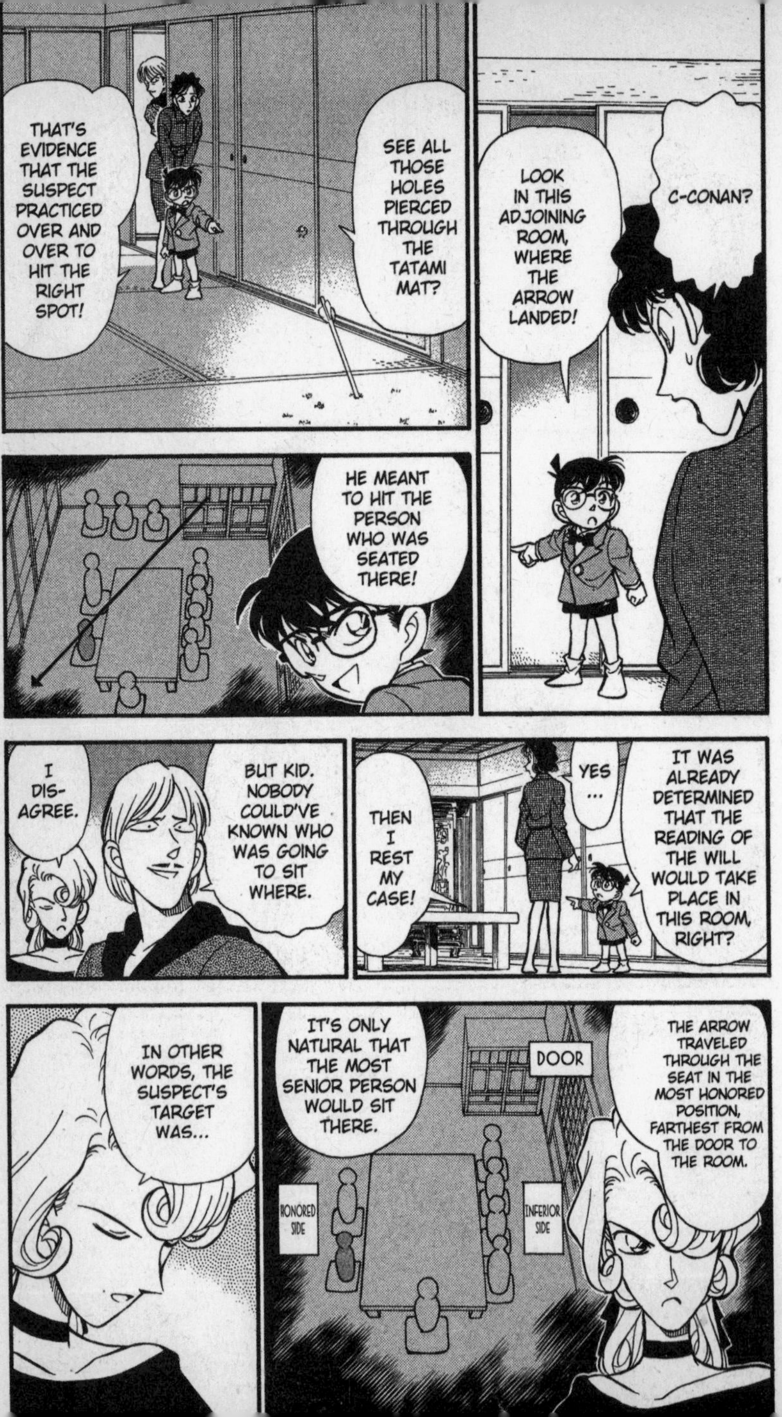
C-CONAN?
LOOK IN THIS ADJOINING ROOM, WHERE THE ARROW LANDED!
SEE ALL THOSE HOLES PIERCED THROUGH THE TATAMI MAT?
THAT'S EVIDENCE THAT THE SUSPECT PRACTICED OVER AND OVER TO HIT THE RIGHT SPOT!
HE MEANT TO HIT THE PERSON WHO WAS SEATED THERE!
IT WAS ALREADY DETERMINED THAT THE READING OF THE WILL WOULD TAKE PLACE IN THIS ROOM, RIGHT?
YES ...
THEN I REST MY CASE!
BUT KID. NOBODY COULD'VE KNOWN WHO WAS GOING TO SIT WHERE.
I DIS-AGREE.
THE ARROW TRAVELED THROUGH THE SEAT IN THE MOST HONORED POSITION, FARTHEST FROM THE DOOR TO THE ROOM.
DOOR
INFERIOR SIDE
HONORED SIDE
IT'S ONLY NATURAL THAT THE MOST SENIOR PERSON WOULD SIT THERE.
IN OTHER WORDS, THE SUSPECT'S TARGET WAS...

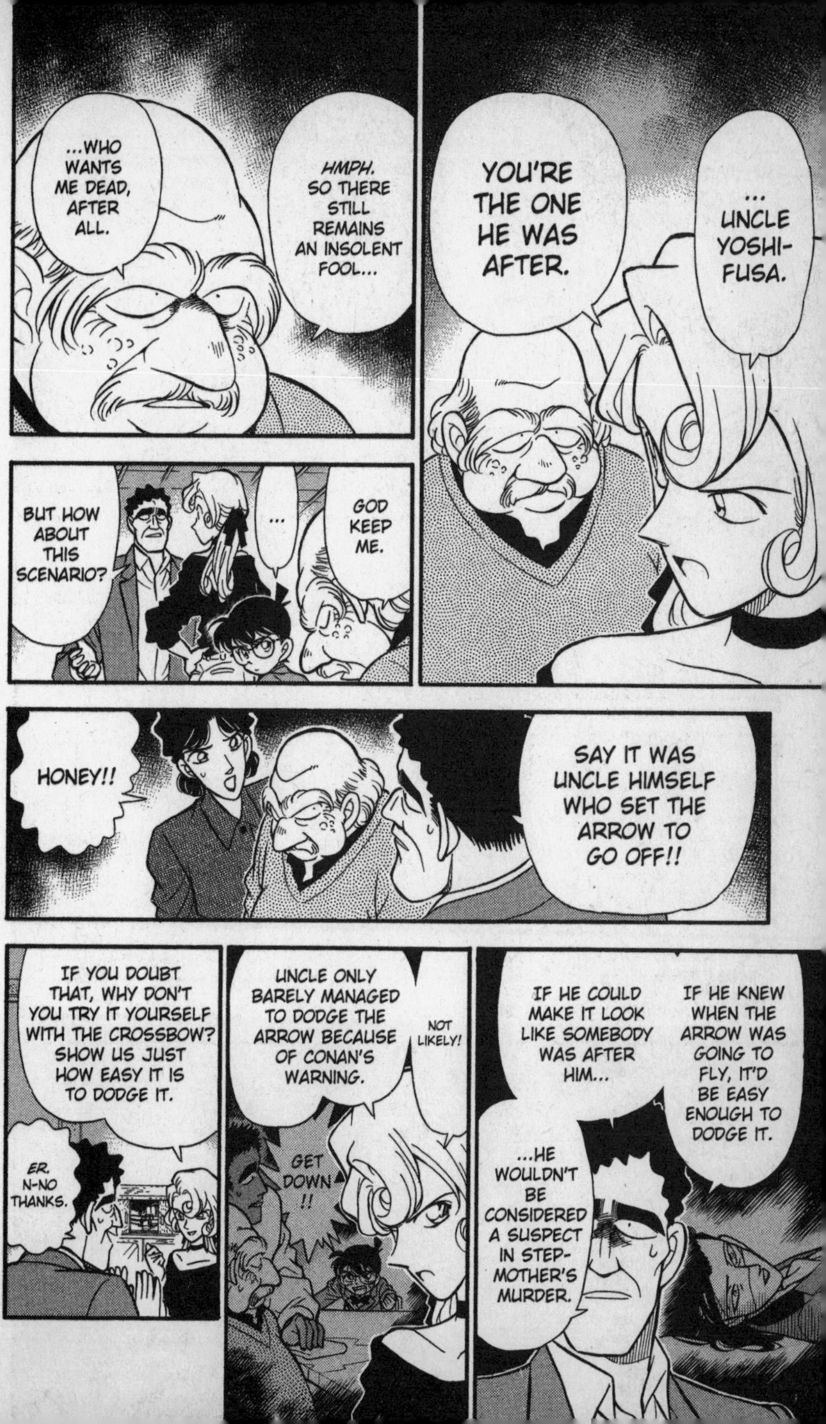
...UNCLE YOSHI-FUSA.
YOU'RE THE ONE HE WAS AFTER.
HMPH. SO THERE STILL REMAINS AN INSOLENT FOOL...
...WHO WANTS ME DEAD, AFTER ALL.
GOD KEEP ME.
...
BUT HOW ABOUT THIS SCENARIO?
SAY IT WAS UNCLE HIMSELF WHO SET THE ARROW TO GO OFF!!
HONEY!!
IF HE KNEW WHEN THE ARROW WAS GOING TO FLY, IT'D BE EASY ENOUGH TO DODGE IT.
IF HE COULD MAKE IT LOOK LIKE SOMEBODY WAS AFTER HIM...
...HE WOULDN'T BE CONSIDERED A SUSPECT IN STEP-MOTHER'S MURDER.
NOT LIKELY!
UNCLE ONLY BARELY MANAGED TO DODGE THE ARROW BECAUSE OF CONAN'S WARNING.
GET DOWN!!
IF YOU DOUBT THAT, WHY DON'T YOU TRY IT YOURSELF WITH THE CROSSBOW? SHOW US JUST HOW EASY IT IS TO DODGE IT.
ER. N-NO THANKS.

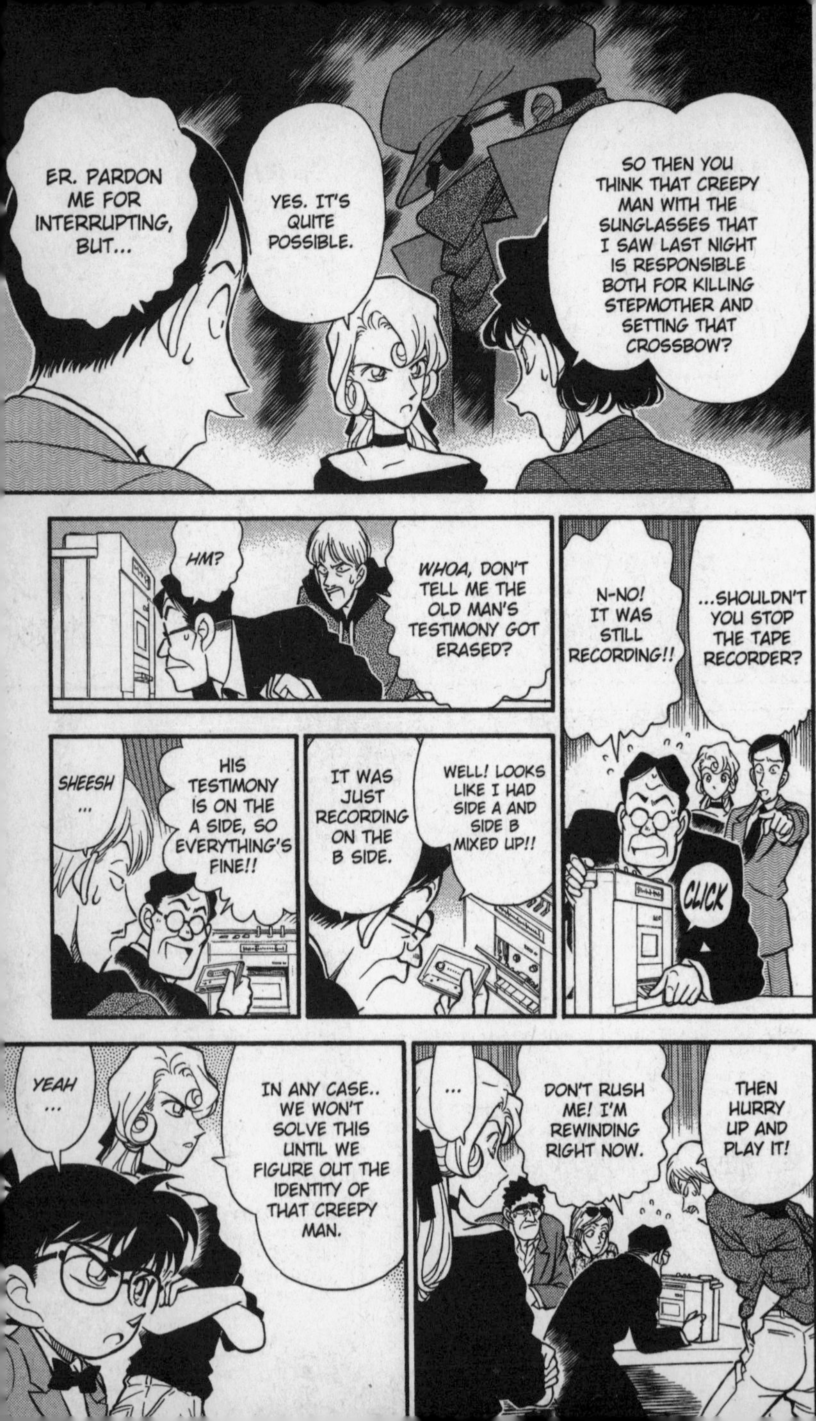
SO THEN YOU THINK THAT CREEPY MAN WITH THE SUNGLASSES THAT I SAW LAST NIGHT IS RESPONSIBLE BOTH FOR KILLING STEPMOTHER AND SETTING THAT CROSSBOW?
YES. IT'S QUITE POSSIBLE.
ER. PARDON ME FOR INTERRUPTING, BUT...
...SHOULDN'T YOU STOP THE TAPE RECORDER?
N-NO! IT WAS STILL RECORDING!!
CLICK
WHOA, DON'T TELL ME THE OLD MAN'S TESTIMONY GOT ERASED?
HM?
WELL! LOOKS LIKE I HAD SIDE A AND SIDE B MIXED UP!!
IT WAS JUST RECORDING ON THE B SIDE.
HIS TESTIMONY IS ON THE A SIDE, SO EVERYTHING'S FINE!!
SHEESH ...
THEN HURRY UP AND PLAY IT!
DON'T RUSH ME! I'M REWINDING RIGHT NOW.
...
IN ANY CASE.. WE WON'T SOLVE THIS UNTIL WE FIGURE OUT THE IDENTITY OF THAT CREEPY MAN.
YEAH ...

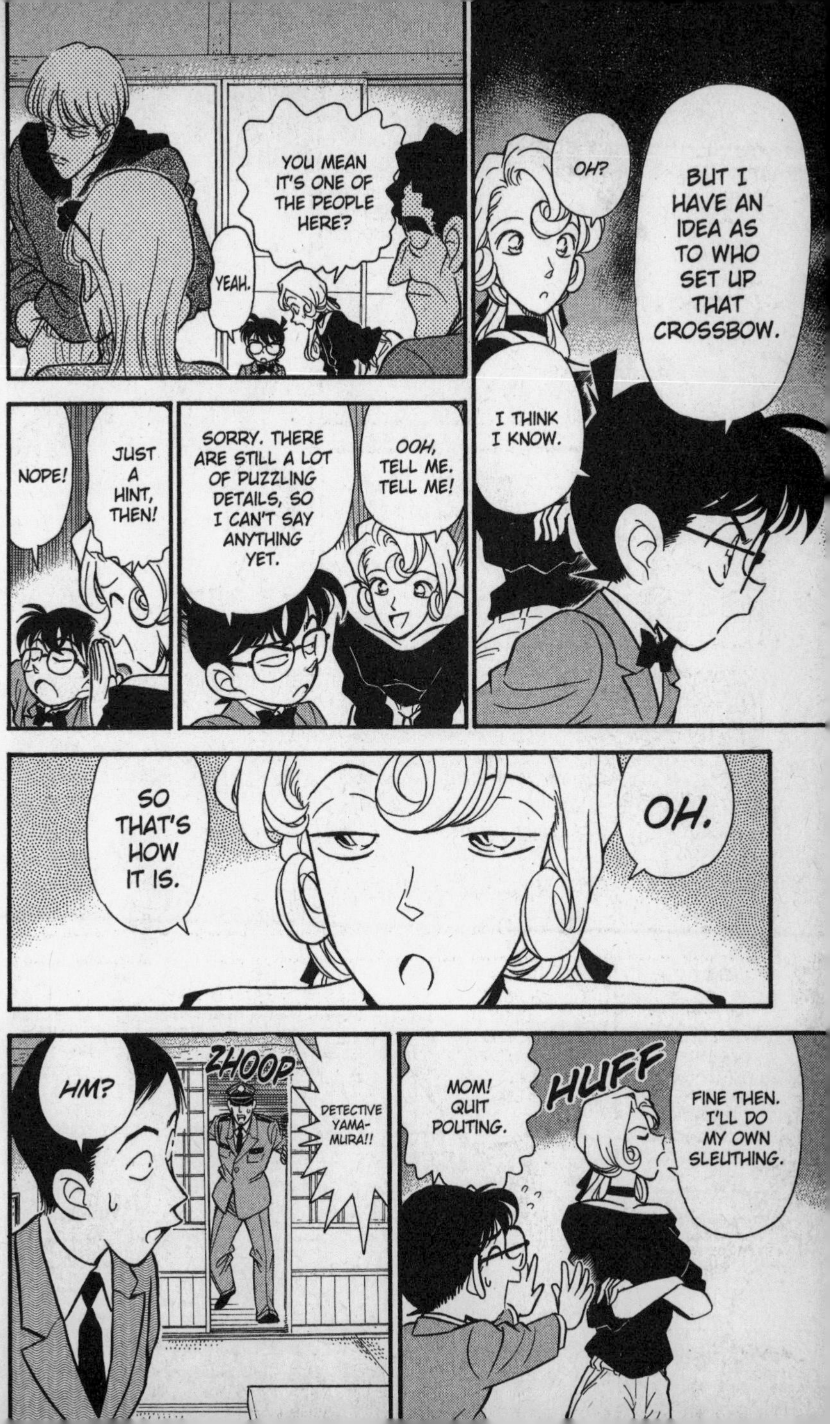
BUT I HAVE AN IDEA AS TO WHO SET UP THAT CROSSBOW.
OH?
I THINK I KNOW.
YOU MEAN IT'S ONE OF THE PEOPLE HERE?
YEAH.
OOH, TELL ME. TELL ME!
SORRY. THERE ARE STILL A LOT OF PUZZLING DETAILS, SO I CAN'T SAY ANYTHING YET.
JUST A HINT, THEN!
NOPE!
OH.
SO THAT'S HOW IT IS.
FINE THEN. I'LL DO MY OWN SLEUTHING.
HUFF
MOM! QUIT POUTING.
ZHOOP
DETECTIVE YAMA-MURA!!
HM?

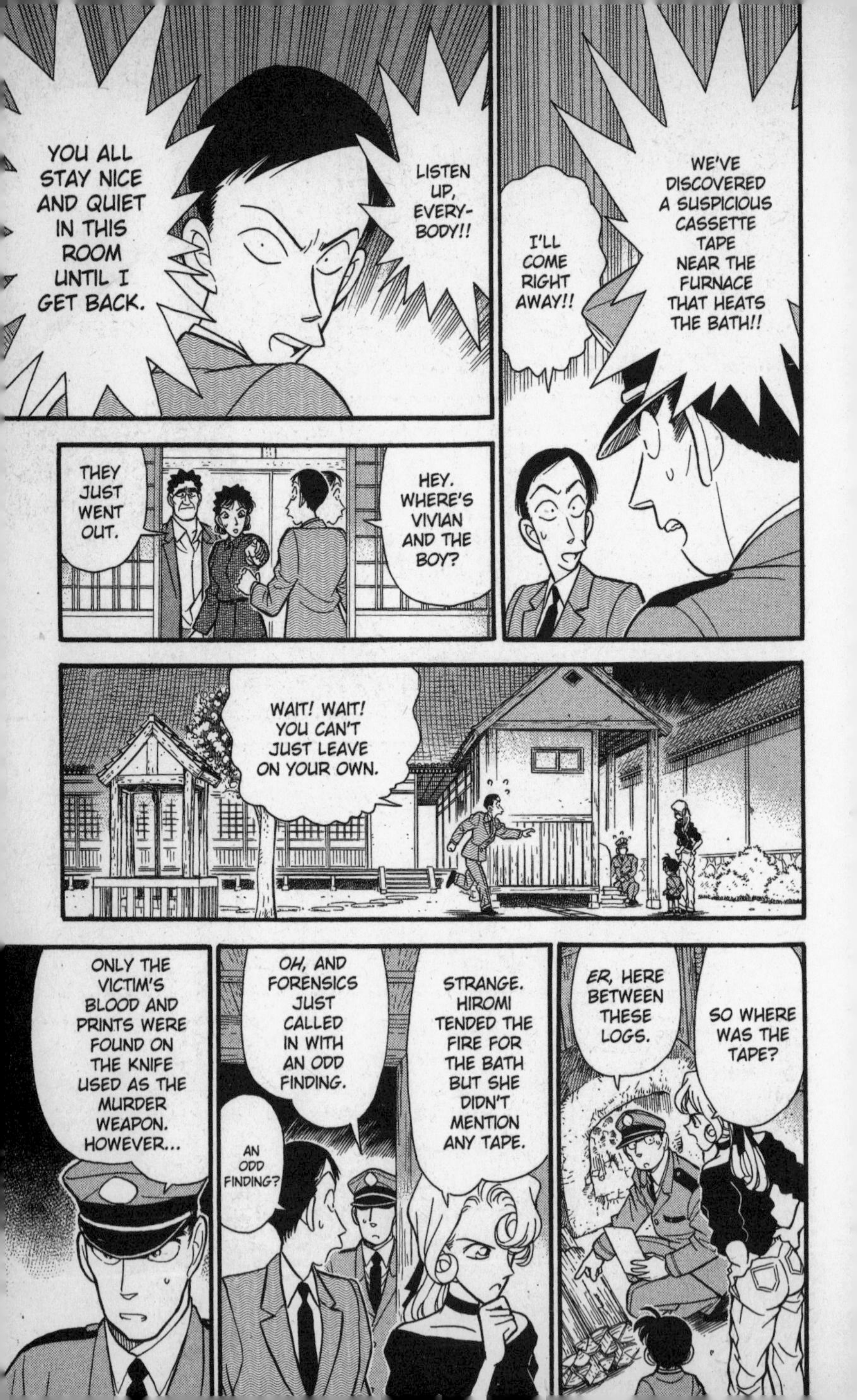
WE'VE DISCOVERED A SUSPICIOUS CASSETTE TAPE NEAR THE FURNACE THAT HEATS THE BATH!!
I'LL COME RIGHT AWAY!!
LISTEN UP, EVERYBODY!!
YOU ALL STAY NICE AND QUIET IN THIS ROOM UNTIL I GET BACK.
HEY. WHERE'S VIVIAN AND THE BOY?
THEY JUST WENT OUT.
WAIT! WAIT! YOU CAN'T JUST LEAVE ON YOUR OWN.
SO WHERE WAS THE TAPE?
ER, HERE BETWEEN THESE LOGS.
STRANGE. HIROMI TENDED THE FIRE FOR THE BATH BUT SHE DIDN'T MENTION ANY TAPE.
OH, AND FORENSICS JUST CALLED IN WITH AN ODD FINDING.
AN ODD FINDING?
ONLY THE VICTIM'S BLOOD AND PRINTS WERE FOUND ON THE KNIFE USED AS THE MURDER WEAPON. HOWEVER...

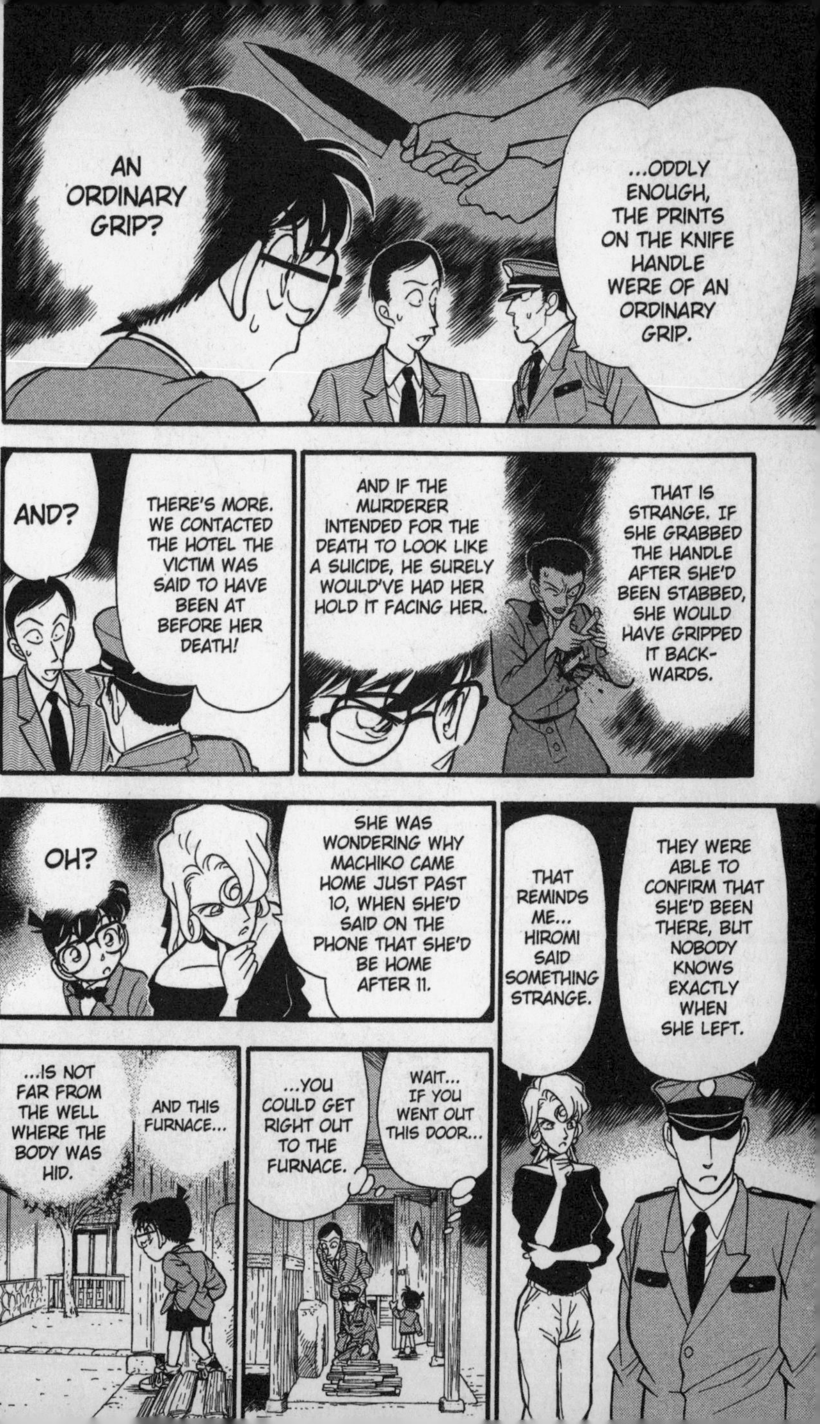
...ODDLY ENOUGH, THE PRINTS ON THE KNIFE HANDLE WERE OF AN ORDINARY GRIP.
AN ORDINARY GRIP?
THAT IS STRANGE. IF SHE GRABBED THE HANDLE AFTER SHE'D BEEN STABBED, SHE WOULD HAVE GRIPPED IT BACK-WARDS.
AND IF THE MURDERER INTENDED FOR THE DEATH TO LOOK LIKE A SUICIDE, HE SURELY WOULD'VE HAD HER HOLD IT FACING HER.
THERE'S MORE. WE CONTACTED THE HOTEL THE VICTIM WAS SAID TO HAVE BEEN AT BEFORE HER DEATH!
AND?
THEY WERE ABLE TO CONFIRM THAT SHE'D BEEN THERE, BUT NOBODY KNOWS EXACTLY WHEN SHE LEFT.
THAT REMINDS ME... HIROMI SAID SOMETHING STRANGE.
SHE WAS WONDERING WHY MACHIKO CAME HOME JUST PAST 10, WHEN SHE'D SAID ON THE PHONE THAT SHE'D BE HOME AFTER 11.
OH?
WAIT... IF YOU WENT OUT THIS DOOR...
...YOU COULD GET RIGHT OUT TO THE FURNACE.
AND THIS FURNACE...
...IS NOT FAR FROM THE WELL WHERE THE BODY WAS HID.

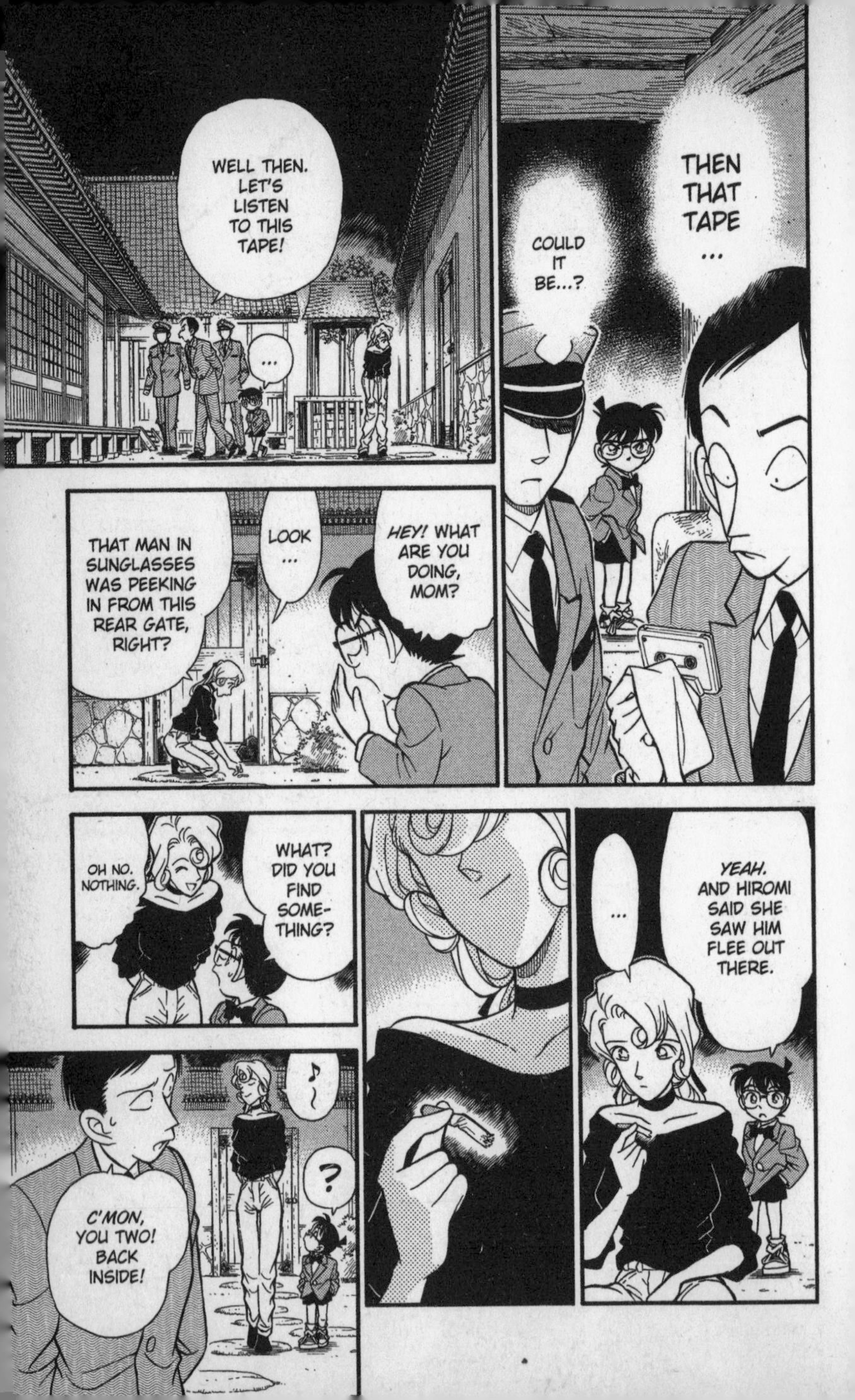
THEN THAT TAPE ...
COULD IT BE...?
WELL THEN. LET'S LISTEN TO THIS TAPE!
...
HEY! WHAT ARE YOU DOING, MOM?
LOOK ...
THAT MAN IN SUNGLASSES WAS PEEKING IN FROM THIS REAR GATE, RIGHT?
YEAH. AND HIROMI SAID SHE SAW HIM FLEE OUT THERE.
...
WHAT? DID YOU FIND SOME-THING?
OH NO. NOTHING.
♪ ~
?
C'MON, YOU TWO! BACK INSIDE!

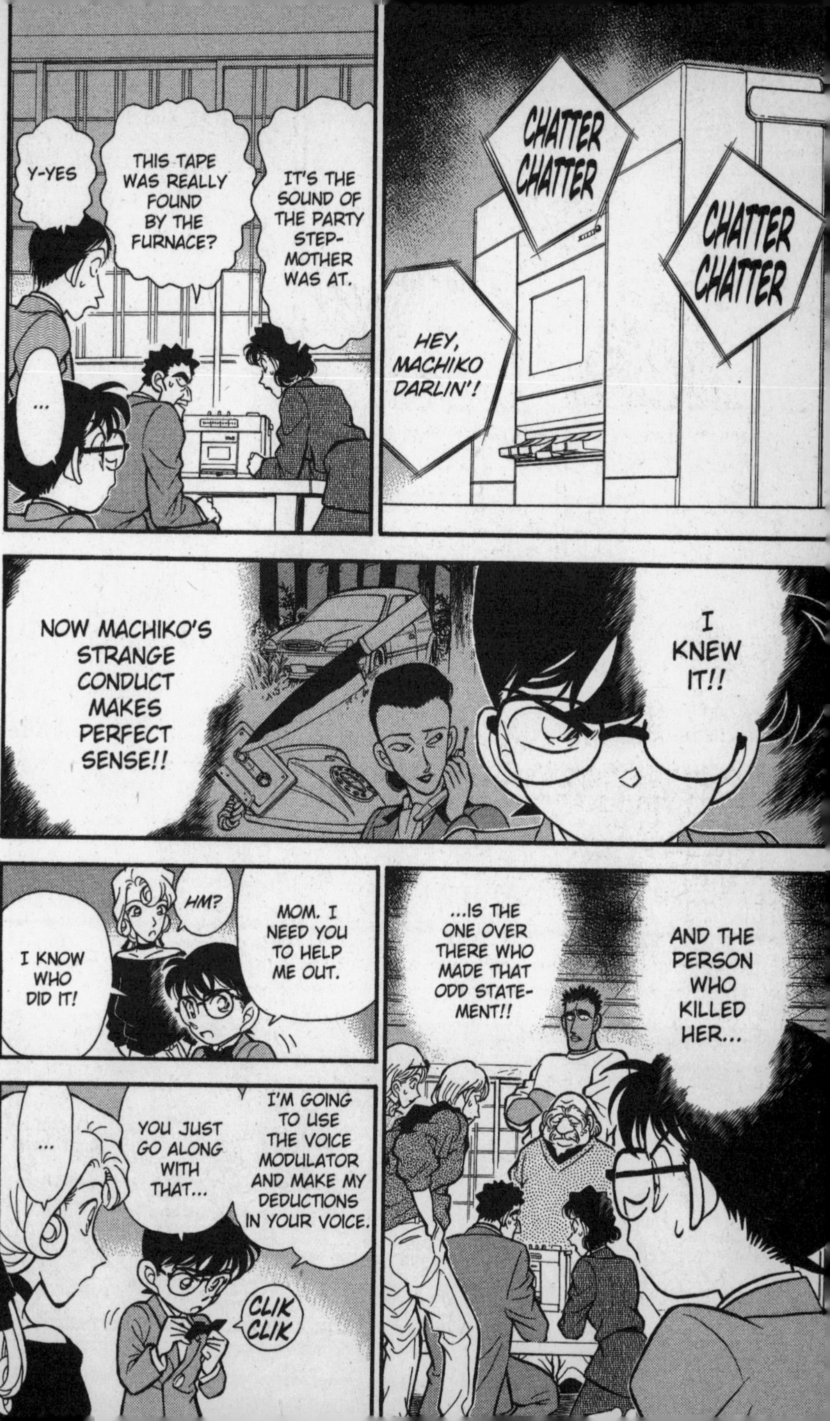
CHATTER CHATTER
CHATTER CHATTER
HEY, MACHIKO DARLIN'!
IT'S THE SOUND OF THE PARTY STEP-MOTHER WAS AT.
THIS TAPE WAS REALLY FOUND BY THE FURNACE?
Y-YES
...
I KNEW IT!!
NOW MACHIKO'S STRANGE CONDUCT MAKES PERFECT SENSE!!
AND THE PERSON WHO KILLED HER...
...IS THE ONE OVER THERE WHO MADE THAT ODD STATEMENT!!
MOM. I NEED YOU TO HELP ME OUT.
HM?
I KNOW WHO DID IT!
I'M GOING TO USE THE VOICE MODULATOR AND MAKE MY DEDUCTIONS IN YOUR VOICE.
YOU JUST GO ALONG WITH THAT...
...
CLIK CLIK

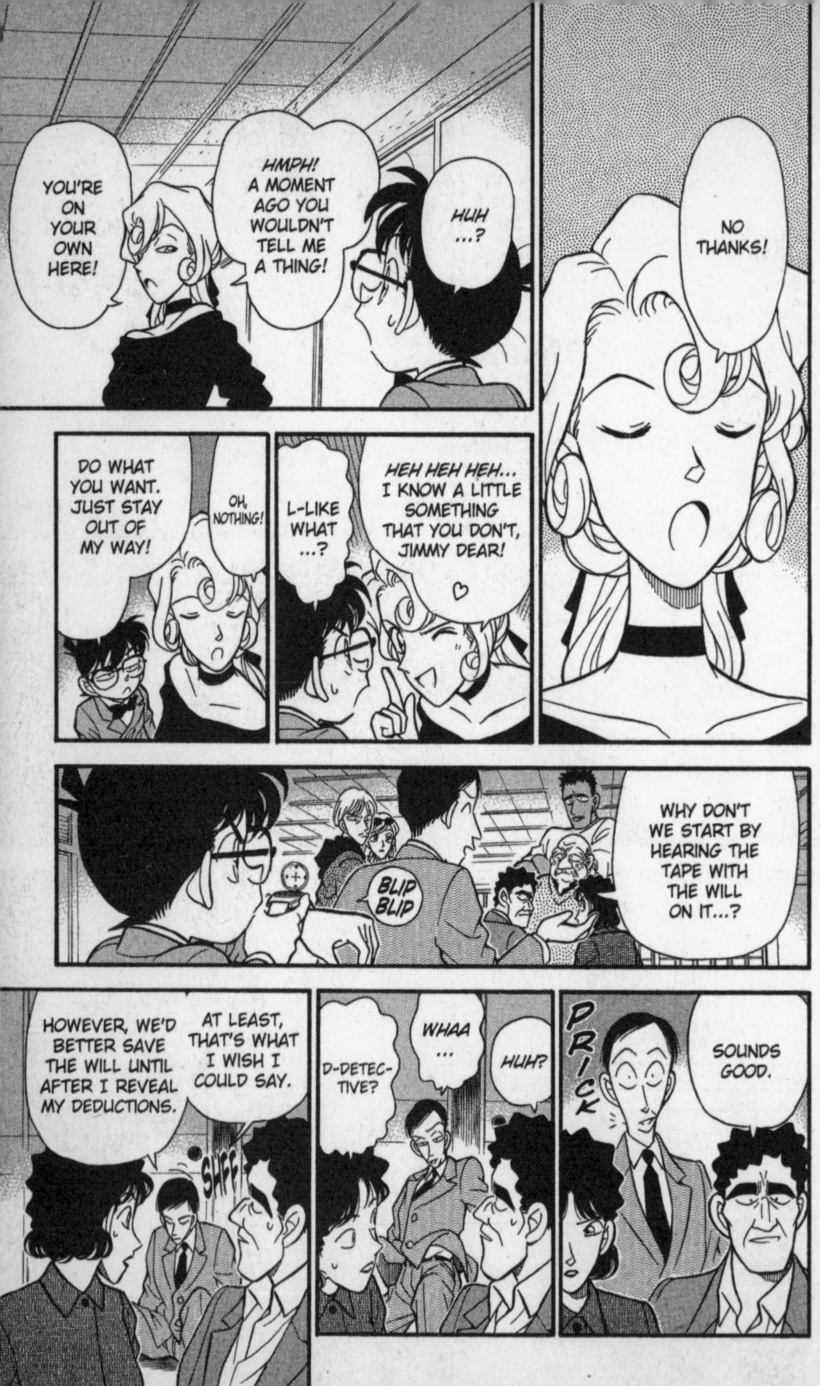
NO THANKS!
HUH ...?
HMPH! A MOMENT AGO YOU WOULDN'T TELL ME A THING!
YOU'RE ON YOUR OWN HERE!
HEH HEH HEH... I KNOW A LITTLE SOMETHING THAT YOU DON'T, JIMMY DEAR! ♡
L-LIKE WHAT ...?
OH, NOTHING!
DO WHAT YOU WANT. JUST STAY OUT OF MY WAY!
WHY DON'T WE START BY HEARING THE TAPE WITH THE WILL ON IT...?
BLIP BLIP
PRICK
SOUNDS GOOD.
HUH?
WHAA ...
D-DETEC-TIVE?
HOWEVER, WE'D BETTER SAVE THE WILL UNTIL AFTER I REVEAL MY DEDUCTIONS.
AT LEAST, THAT'S WHAT I WISH I COULD SAY.
SHFF

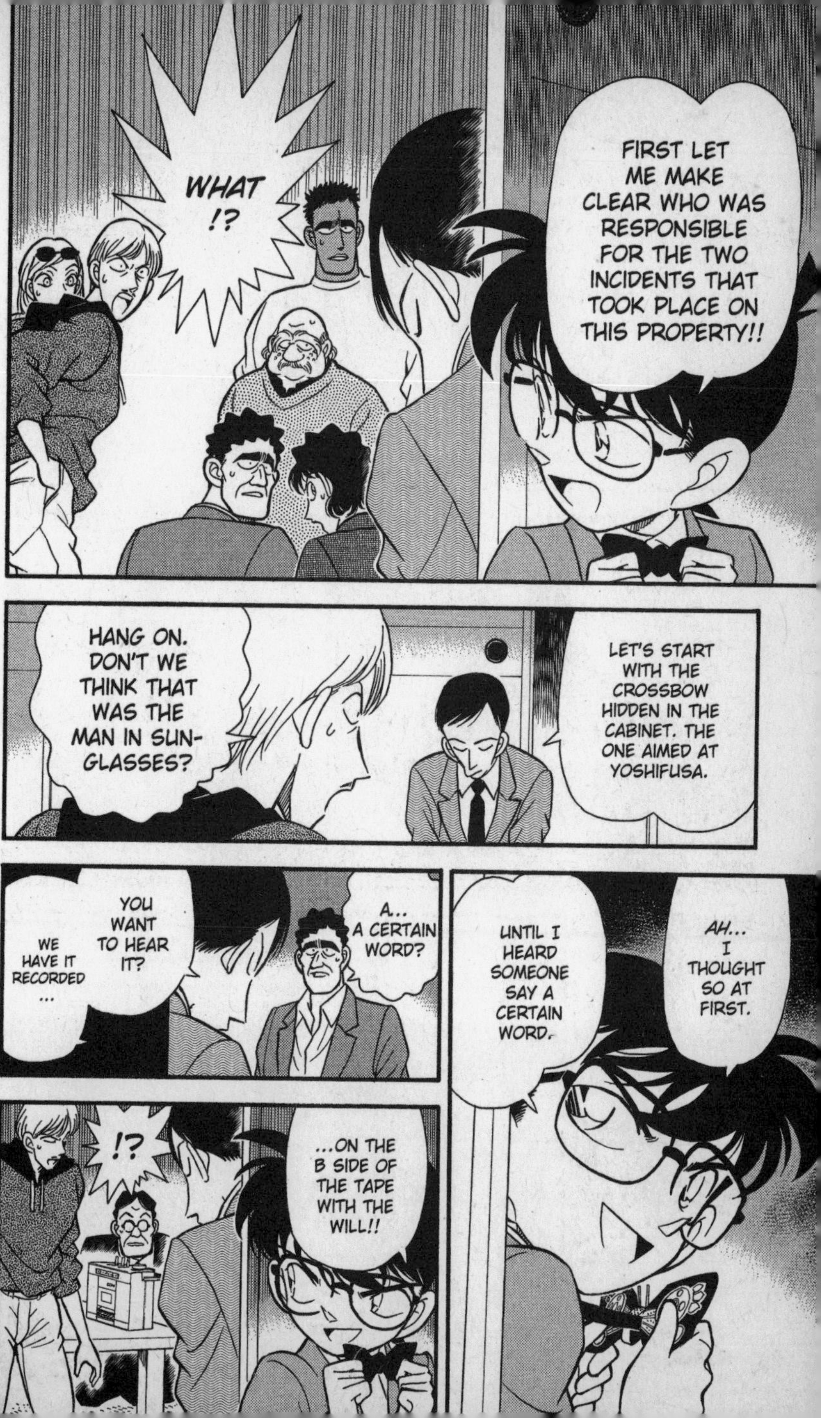
FIRST LET ME MAKE CLEAR WHO WAS RESPONSIBLE FOR THE TWO INCIDENTS THAT TOOK PLACE ON THIS PROPERTY!!
WHAT!?
LET'S START WITH THE CROSSBOW HIDDEN IN THE CABINET. THE ONE AIMED AT YOSHIFUSA.
HANG ON. DON'T WE THINK THAT WAS THE MAN IN SUN-GLASSES?
AH... I THOUGHT SO AT FIRST.
UNTIL I HEARD SOMEONE SAY A CERTAIN WORD.
A... A CERTAIN WORD?
YOU WANT TO HEAR IT?
WE HAVE IT RECORDED...
...ON THE B SIDE OF THE TAPE WITH THE WILL!!
!?

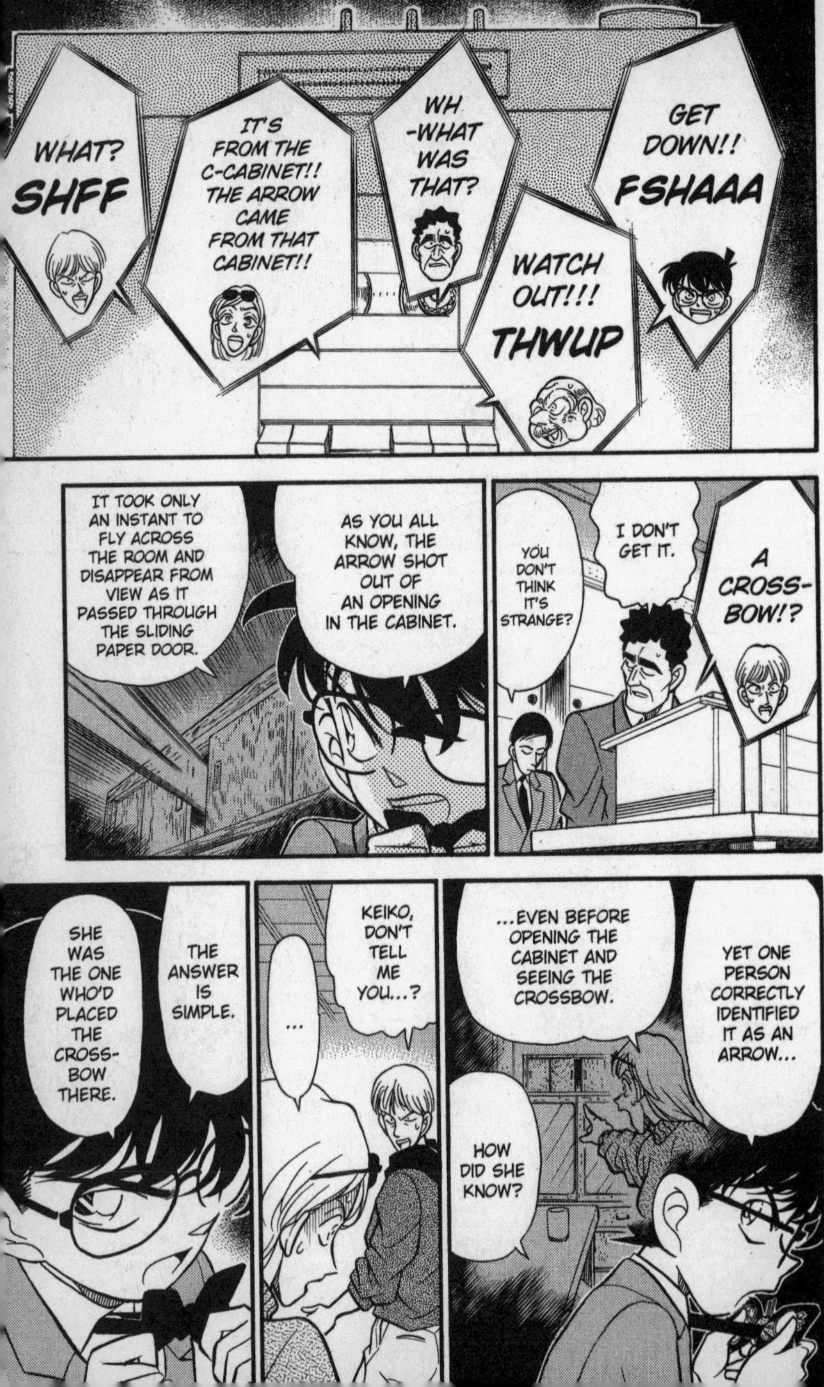
GET DOWN!! FSHAAA
WATCH OUT!!! THWUP
WH-WHAT WAS THAT?
IT'S FROM THE C-CABINET!! THE ARROW CAME FROM THAT CABINET!!
WHAT? SHFF
A CROSS-BOW!?
I DON'T GET IT.
YOU DON'T THINK IT'S STRANGE?
AS YOU ALL KNOW, THE ARROW SHOT OUT OF AN OPENING IN THE CABINET.
IT TOOK ONLY AN INSTANT TO FLY ACROSS THE ROOM AND DISAPPEAR FROM VIEW AS IT PASSED THROUGH THE SLIDING PAPER DOOR.
YET ONE PERSON CORRECTLY IDENTIFIED IT AS AN ARROW...
...EVEN BEFORE OPENING THE CABINET AND SEEING THE CROSSBOW.
HOW DID SHE KNOW?
KEIKO, DON'T TELL ME YOU...?
...
THE ANSWER IS SIMPLE.
SHE WAS THE ONE WHO'D PLACED THE CROSS-BOW THERE.

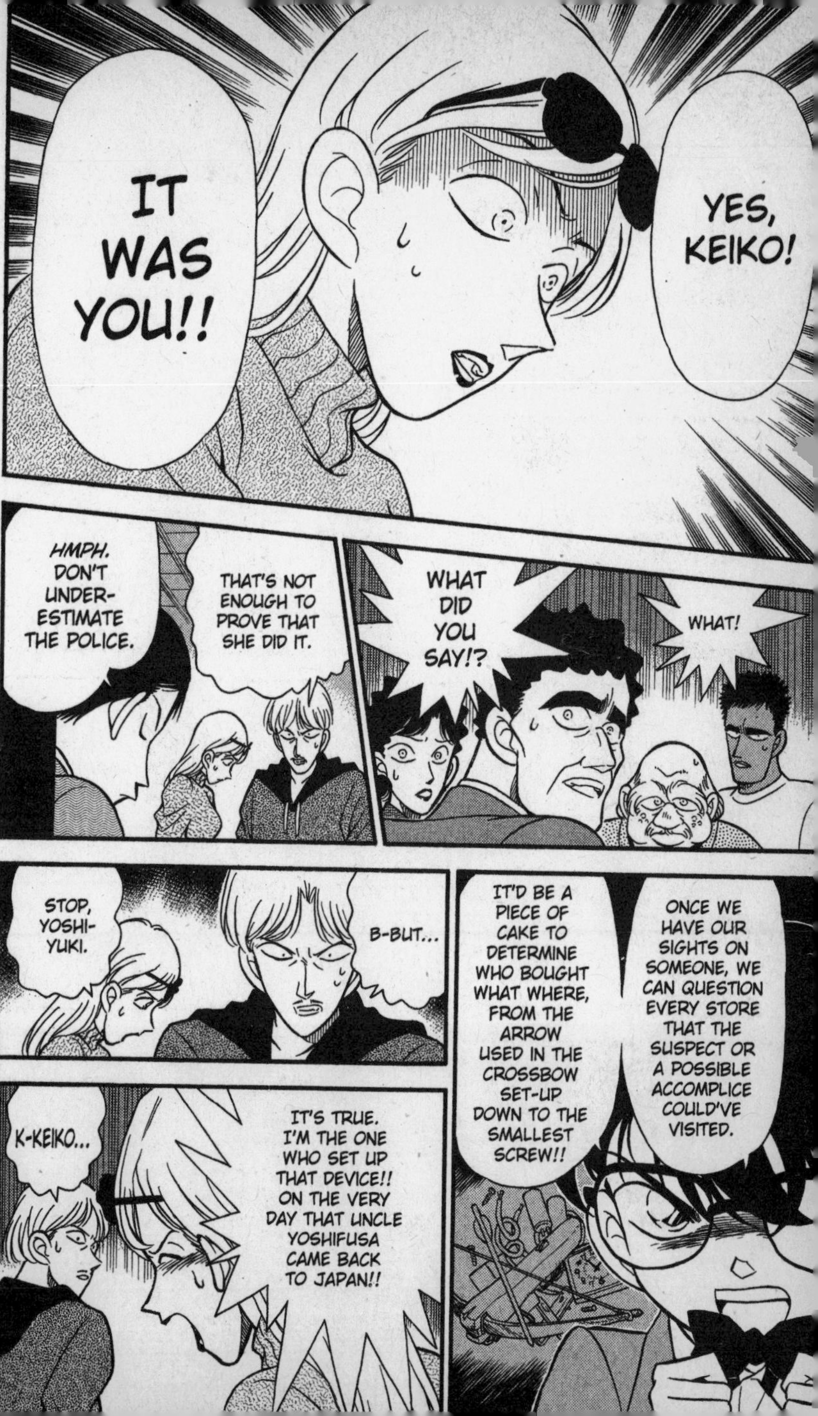
YES, KEIKO!
IT WAS YOU!!
WHAT!
WHAT DID YOU SAY!?
THAT'S NOT ENOUGH TO PROVE THAT SHE DID IT.
HMPH. DON'T UNDER-ESTIMATE THE POLICE.
ONCE WE HAVE OUR SIGHTS ON SOMEONE, WE CAN QUESTION EVERY STORE THAT THE SUSPECT OR A POSSIBLE ACCOMPLICE COULD'VE VISITED.
IT'D BE A PIECE OF CAKE TO DETERMINE WHO BOUGHT WHAT WHERE, FROM THE ARROW USED IN THE CROSSBOW SET-UP DOWN TO THE SMALLEST SCREW!!
STOP, YOSHI-YUKI.
B-BUT...
IT'S TRUE. I'M THE ONE WHO SET UP THAT DEVICE!! ON THE VERY DAY THAT UNCLE YOSHIFUSA CAME BACK TO JAPAN!!
K-KEIKO...

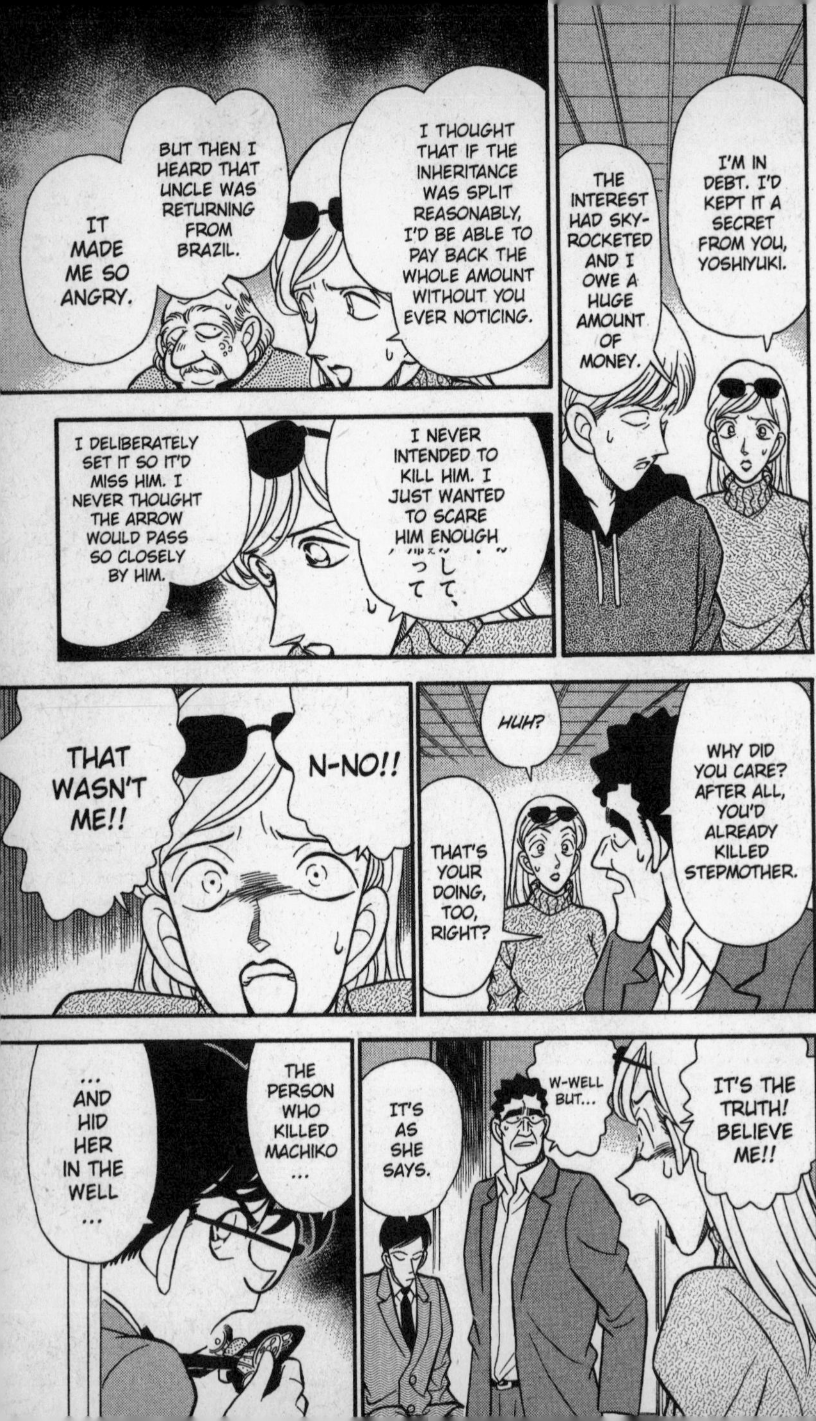
I'M IN DEBT. I'D KEPT IT A SECRET FROM YOU, YOSHIYUKI.
THE INTEREST HAD SKY-ROCKETED AND I OWE A HUGE AMOUNT OF MONEY.
I THOUGHT THAT IF THE INHERITANCE WAS SPLIT REASONABLY, I'D BE ABLE TO PAY BACK THE WHOLE AMOUNT WITHOUT YOU EVER NOTICING.
BUT THEN I HEARD THAT UNCLE WAS RETURNING FROM BRAZIL.
IT MADE ME SO ANGRY.
I NEVER INTENDED TO KILL HIM. I JUST WANTED TO SCARE HIM ENOUGH
I DELIBERATELY SET IT SO IT'D MISS HIM. I NEVER THOUGHT THE ARROW WOULD PASS SO CLOSELY BY HIM.
WHY DID YOU CARE? AFTER ALL, YOU'D ALREADY KILLED STEPMOTHER.
HUH?
THAT'S YOUR DOING, TOO, RIGHT?
N-NO!!
THAT WASN'T ME!!
IT'S THE TRUTH! BELIEVE ME!!
W-WELL BUT...
IT'S AS SHE SAYS.
THE PERSON WHO KILLED MACHIKO ...
... AND HID HER IN THE WELL ...

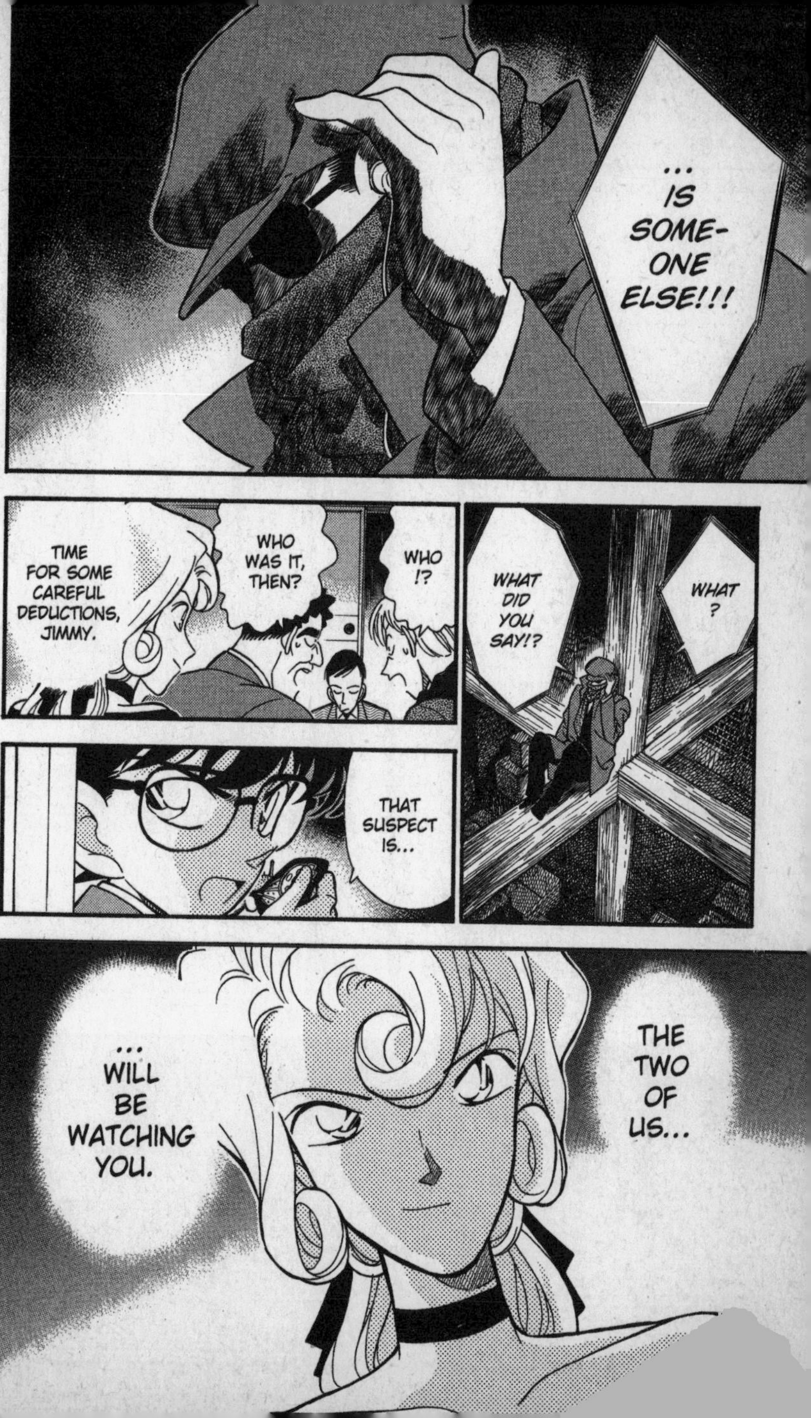
... IS SOMEONE ELSE!!!
WHAT ?
WHAT DID YOU SAY!?
WHO !?
WHO WAS IT, THEN?
TIME FOR SOME CAREFUL DEDUCTIONS, JIMMY.
THAT SUSPECT IS...
THE TWO OF US...
... WILL BE WATCHING YOU.

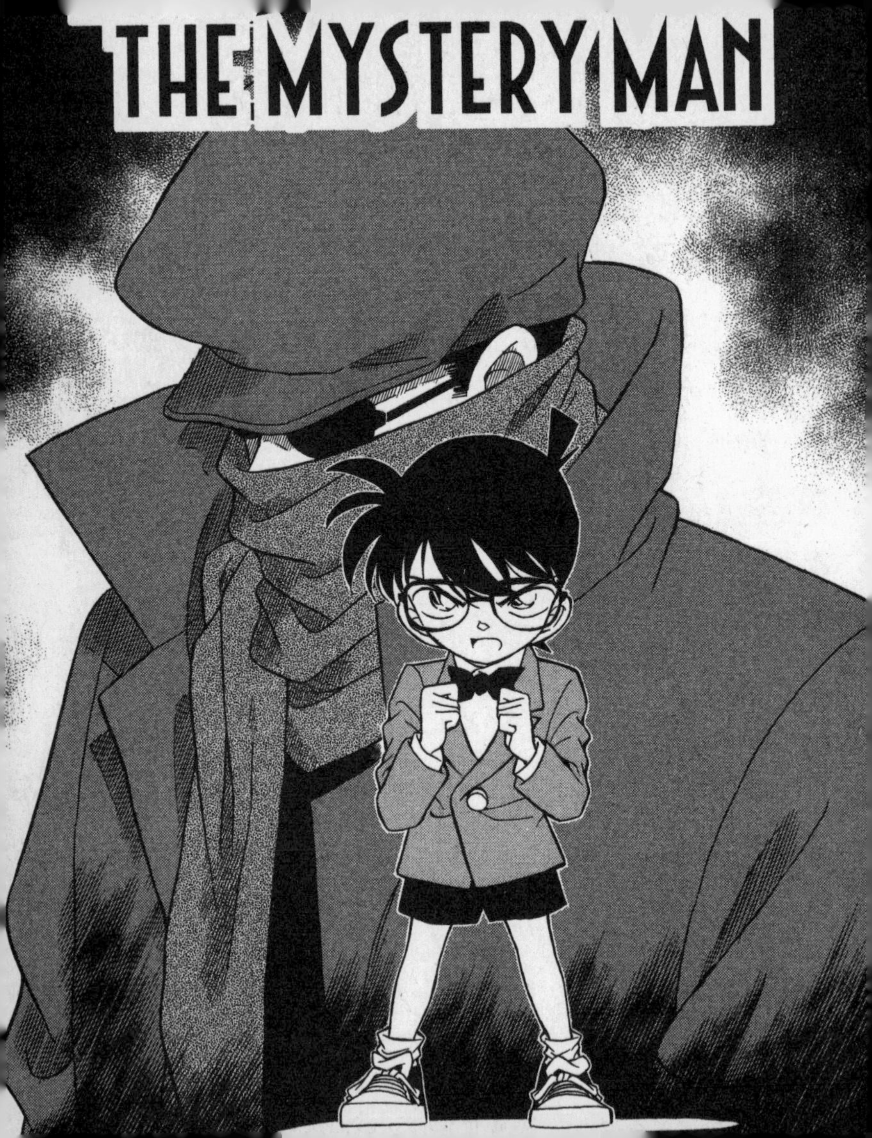
THE MYSTERY MAN

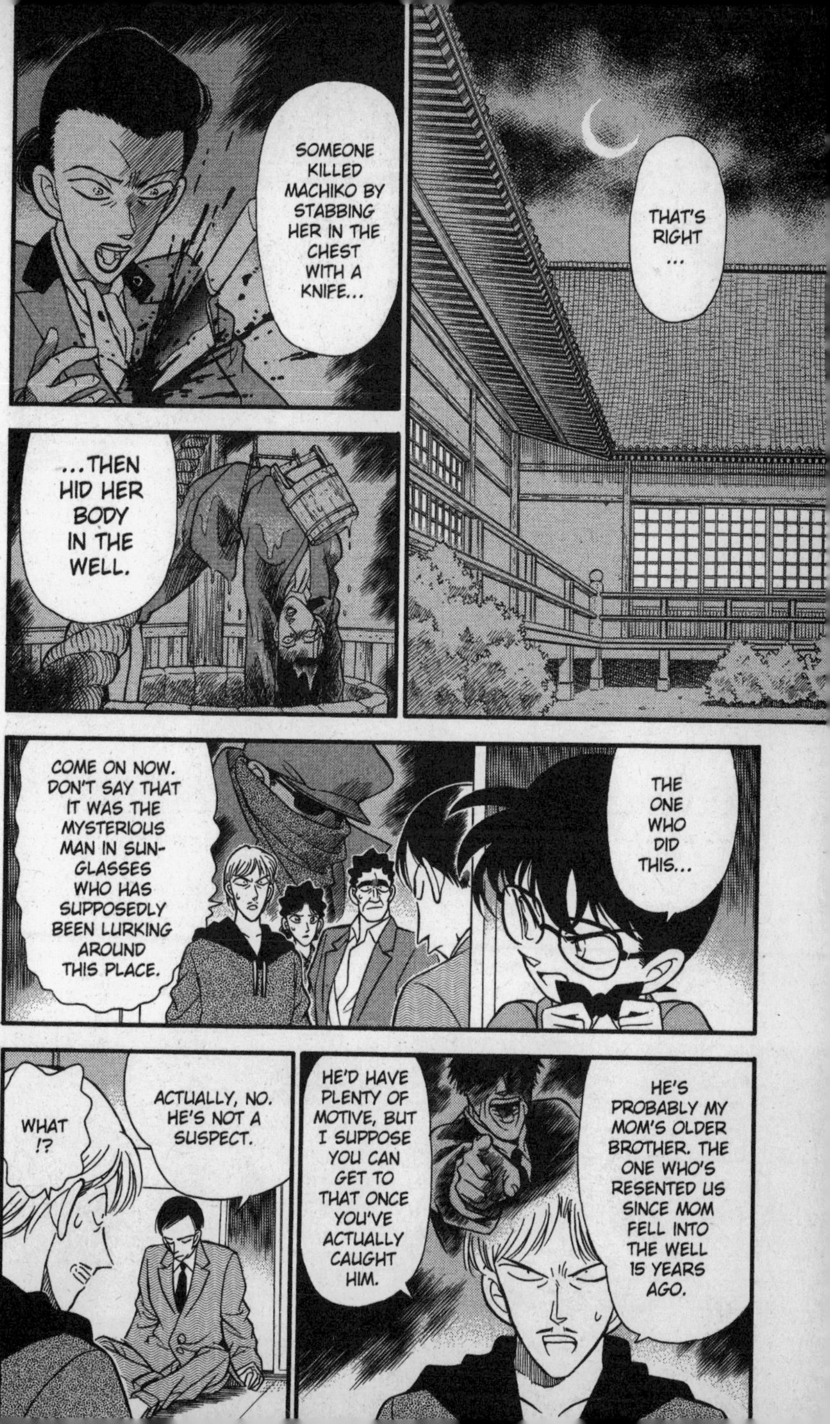
THAT'S RIGHT ...
SOMEONE KILLED MACHIKO BY STABBING HER IN THE CHEST WITH A KNIFE...
...THEN HID HER BODY IN THE WELL.
THE ONE WHO DID THIS...
COME ON NOW. DON'T SAY THAT IT WAS THE MYSTERIOUS MAN IN SUN-GLASSES WHO HAS SUPPOSEDLY BEEN LURKING AROUND THIS PLACE.
HE'S PROBABLY MY MOM'S OLDER BROTHER. THE ONE WHO'S RESENTED US SINCE MOM FELL INTO THE WELL 15 YEARS AGO.
HE'D HAVE PLENTY OF MOTIVE, BUT I SUPPOSE YOU CAN GET TO THAT ONCE YOU'VE ACTUALLY CAUGHT HIM.
ACTUALLY, NO. HE'S NOT A SUSPECT.
WHAT !?

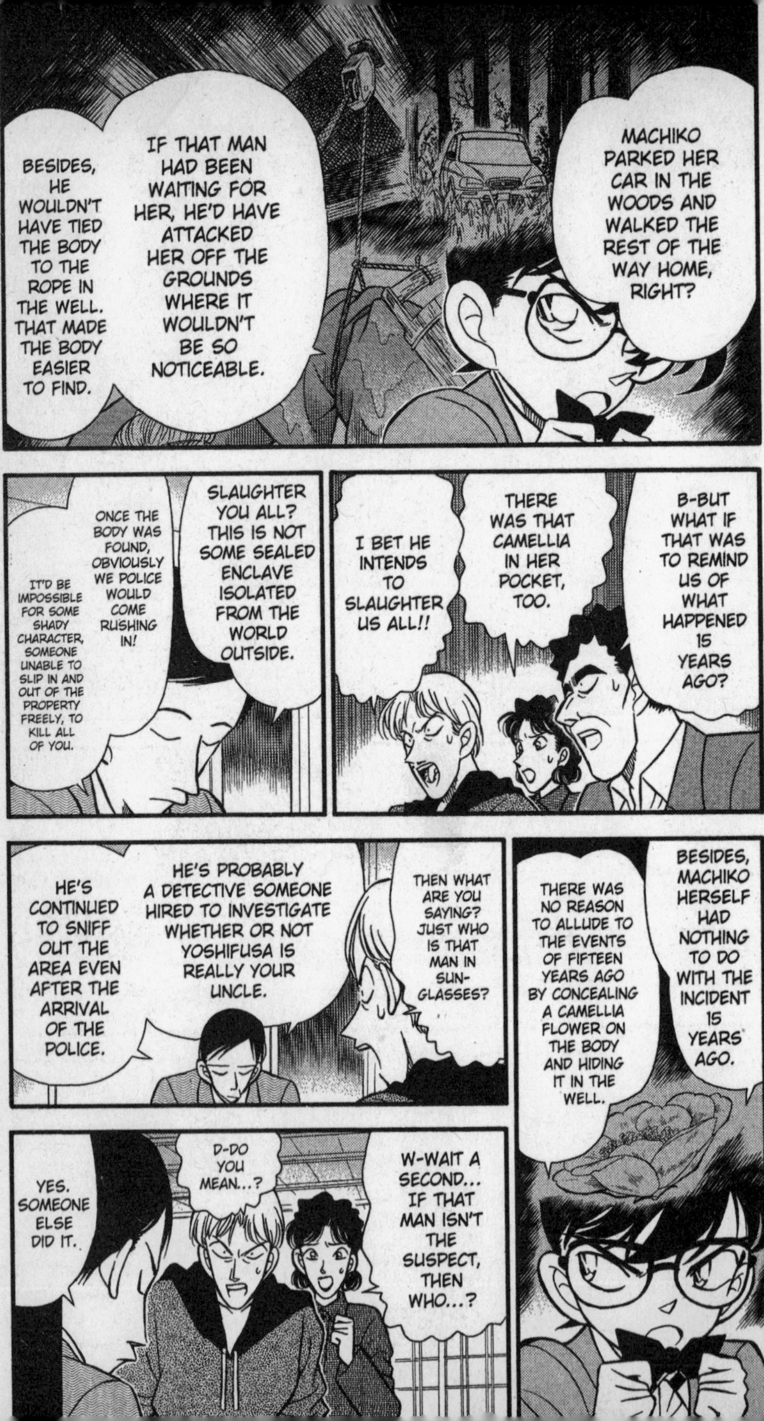

MACHIKO PARKED HER CAR IN THE WOODS AND WALKED THE REST OF THE WAY HOME, RIGHT?
IF THAT MAN HAD BEEN WAITING FOR HER, HE'D HAVE ATTACKED HER OFF THE GROUNDS WHERE IT WOULDN'T BE SO NOTICEABLE.
BESIDES, HE WOULDN'T HAVE TIED THE BODY TO THE ROPE IN THE WELL. THAT MADE THE BODY EASIER TO FIND.
B-BUT WHAT IF THAT WAS TO REMIND US OF WHAT HAPPENED 15 YEARS AGO?
THERE WAS THAT CAMELLIA IN HER POCKET, TOO.
I BET HE INTENDS TO SLAUGHTER US ALL!!
SLAUGHTER YOU ALL? THIS IS NOT SOME SEALED ENCLAVE ISOLATED FROM THE WORLD OUTSIDE.
ONCE THE BODY WAS FOUND, OBVIOUSLY WE POLICE WOULD COME RUSHING IN!
IT'D BE IMPOSSIBLE FOR SOME SHADY CHARACTER, SOMEONE UNABLE TO SLIP IN AND OUT OF THE PROPERTY FREELY, TO KILL ALL OF YOU.
BESIDES, MACHIKO HERSELF HAD NOTHING TO DO WITH THE INCIDENT 15 YEARS AGO.
THERE WAS NO REASON TO ALLUDE TO THE EVENTS OF FIFTEEN YEARS AGO BY CONCEALING A CAMELLIA FLOWER ON THE BODY AND HIDING IT IN THE WELL.
THEN WHAT ARE YOU SAYING? JUST WHO IS THAT MAN IN SUN-GLASSES?
HE'S PROBABLY A DETECTIVE SOMEONE HIRED TO INVESTIGATE WHETHER OR NOT YOSHIFUSA IS REALLY YOUR UNCLE.
HE'S CONTINUED TO SNIFF OUT THE AREA EVEN AFTER THE ARRIVAL OF THE POLICE.
W-WAIT A SECOND... IF THAT MAN ISN'T THE SUSPECT, THEN WHO...?
D-DO YOU MEAN...?
YES. SOMEONE ELSE DID IT.

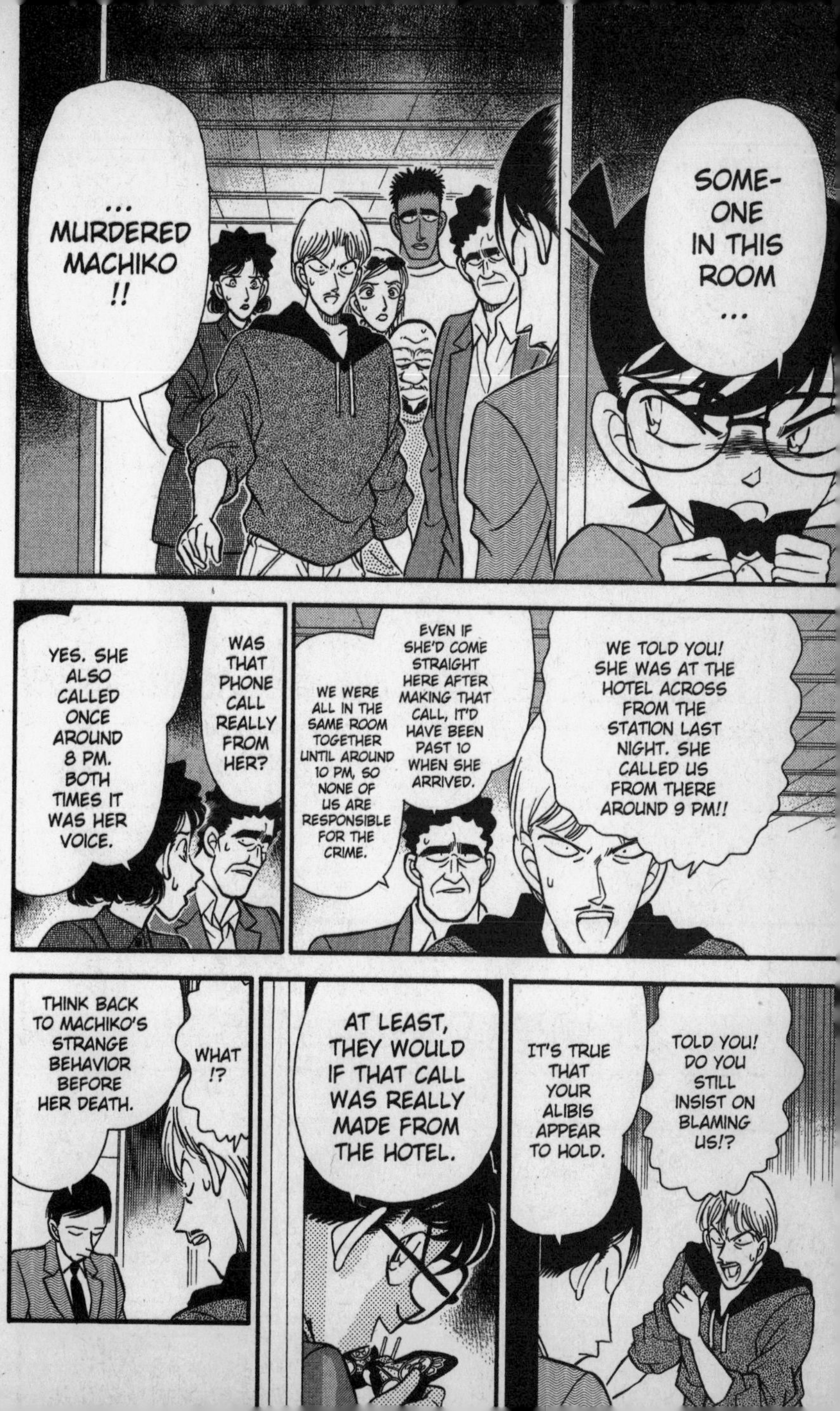
SOME-ONE IN THIS ROOM ...
... MURDERED MACHIKO !!
WE TOLD YOU! SHE WAS AT THE HOTEL ACROSS FROM THE STATION LAST NIGHT. SHE CALLED US FROM THERE AROUND 9 PM!!
EVEN IF SHE'D COME STRAIGHT HERE AFTER MAKING THAT CALL, IT'D HAVE BEEN PAST 10 WHEN SHE ARRIVED.
WE WERE ALL IN THE SAME ROOM TOGETHER UNTIL AROUND 10 PM, SO NONE OF US ARE RESPONSIBLE FOR THE CRIME.
WAS THAT PHONE CALL REALLY FROM HER?
YES. SHE ALSO CALLED ONCE AROUND 8 PM. BOTH TIMES IT WAS HER VOICE.
TOLD YOU! DO YOU STILL INSIST ON BLAMING US!?
IT'S TRUE THAT YOUR ALIBIS APPEAR TO HOLD.
AT LEAST, THEY WOULD IF THAT CALL WAS REALLY MADE FROM THE HOTEL.
WHAT !?
THINK BACK TO MACHIKO'S STRANGE BEHAVIOR BEFORE HER DEATH.

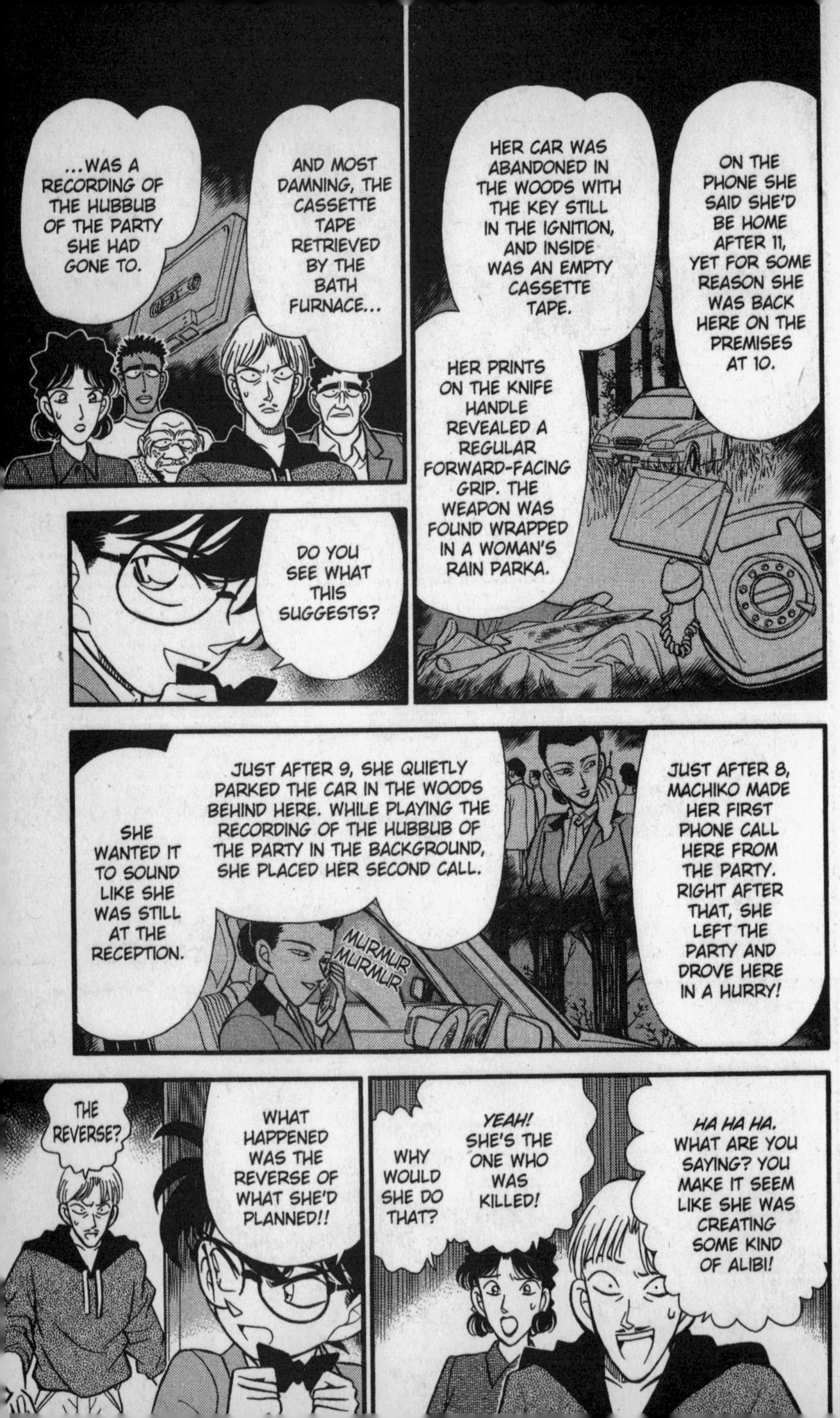
ON THE PHONE SHE SAID SHE'D BE HOME AFTER 11, YET FOR SOME REASON SHE WAS BACK HERE ON THE PREMISES AT 10.
HER CAR WAS ABANDONED IN THE WOODS WITH THE KEY STILL IN THE IGNITION, AND INSIDE WAS AN EMPTY CASSETTE TAPE.
HER PRINTS ON THE KNIFE HANDLE REVEALED A REGULAR FORWARD-FACING GRIP. THE WEAPON WAS FOUND WRAPPED IN A WOMAN'S RAIN PARKA.
AND MOST DAMNING, THE CASSETTE TAPE RETRIEVED BY THE BATH FURNACE...
...WAS A RECORDING OF THE HUBBUB OF THE PARTY SHE HAD GONE TO.
DO YOU SEE WHAT THIS SUGGESTS?
JUST AFTER 8, MACHIKO MADE HER FIRST PHONE CALL HERE FROM THE PARTY. RIGHT AFTER THAT, SHE LEFT THE PARTY AND DROVE HERE IN A HURRY!
JUST AFTER 9, SHE QUIETLY PARKED THE CAR IN THE WOODS BEHIND HERE. WHILE PLAYING THE RECORDING OF THE HUBBUB OF THE PARTY IN THE BACKGROUND, SHE PLACED HER SECOND CALL.
SHE WANTED IT TO SOUND LIKE SHE WAS STILL AT THE RECEPTION.
MURMUR MURMUR
HA HA HA. WHAT ARE YOU SAYING? YOU MAKE IT SEEM LIKE SHE WAS CREATING SOME KIND OF ALIBI!
YEAH! SHE'S THE ONE WHO WAS KILLED!
WHY WOULD SHE DO THAT?
WHAT HAPPENED WAS THE REVERSE OF WHAT SHE'D PLANNED!!
THE REVERSE?

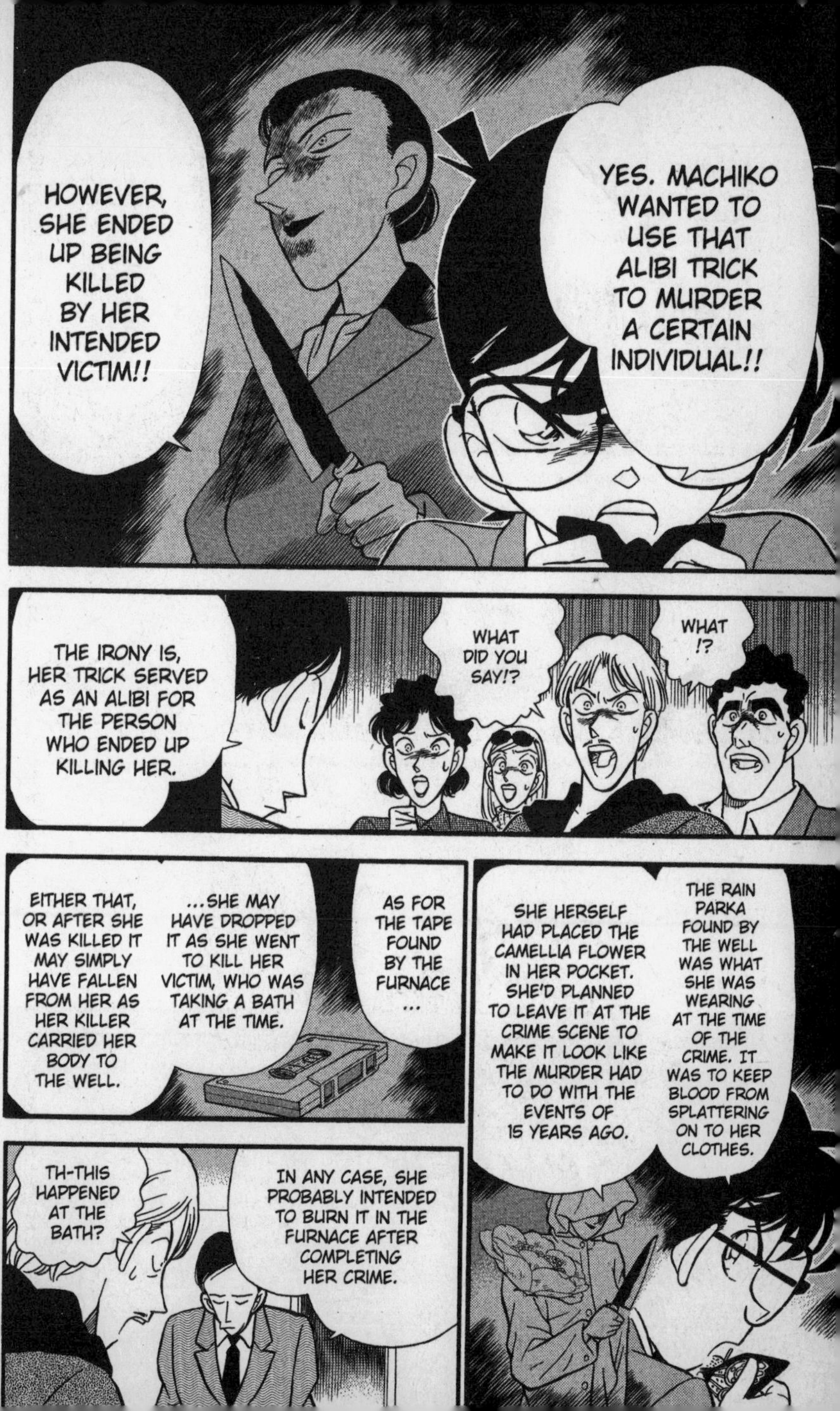
YES. MACHIKO WANTED TO USE THAT ALIBI TRICK TO MURDER A CERTAIN INDIVIDUAL!!
HOWEVER, SHE ENDED UP BEING KILLED BY HER INTENDED VICTIM!!
WHAT !?
WHAT DID YOU SAY!?
THE IRONY IS, HER TRICK SERVED AS AN ALIBI FOR THE PERSON WHO ENDED UP KILLING HER.
THE RAIN PARKA FOUND BY THE WELL WAS WHAT SHE WAS WEARING AT THE TIME OF THE CRIME. IT WAS TO KEEP BLOOD FROM SPLATTERING ON TO HER CLOTHES.
SHE HERSELF HAD PLACED THE CAMELLIA FLOWER IN HER POCKET. SHE'D PLANNED TO LEAVE IT AT THE CRIME SCENE TO MAKE IT LOOK LIKE THE MURDER HAD TO DO WITH THE EVENTS OF 15 YEARS AGO.
AS FOR THE TAPE FOUND BY THE FURNACE ...
...SHE MAY HAVE DROPPED IT AS SHE WENT TO KILL HER VICTIM, WHO WAS TAKING A BATH AT THE TIME.
EITHER THAT, OR AFTER SHE WAS KILLED IT MAY SIMPLY HAVE FALLEN FROM HER AS HER KILLER CARRIED HER BODY TO THE WELL.
IN ANY CASE, SHE PROBABLY INTENDED TO BURN IT IN THE FURNACE AFTER COMPLETING HER CRIME.
TH-THIS HAPPENED AT THE BATH?

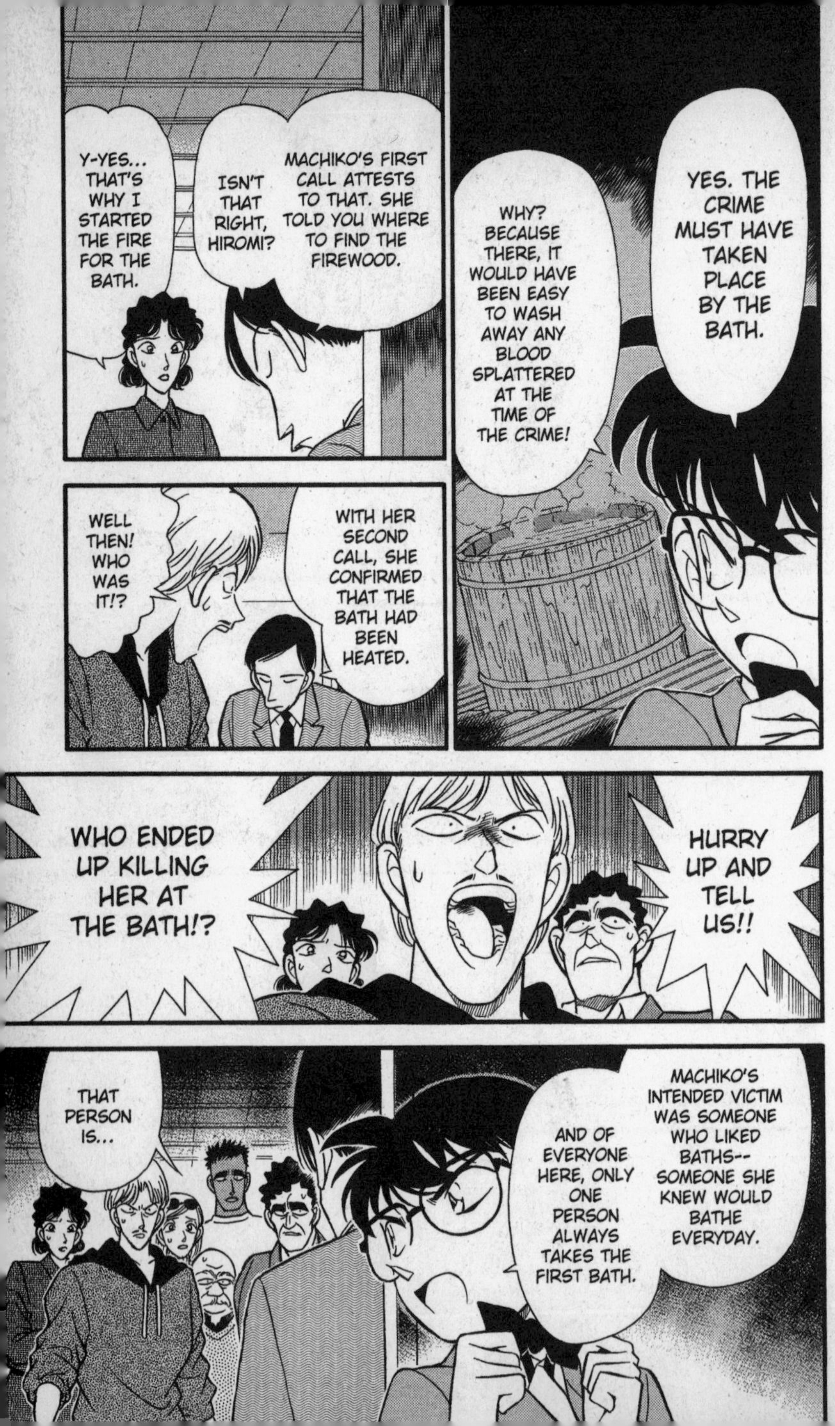
YES. THE CRIME MUST HAVE TAKEN PLACE BY THE BATH.
WHY? BECAUSE THERE, IT WOULD HAVE BEEN EASY TO WASH AWAY ANY BLOOD SPLATTERED AT THE TIME OF THE CRIME!
MACHIKO'S FIRST CALL ATTESTS TO THAT. SHE TOLD YOU WHERE TO FIND THE FIREWOOD.
ISN'T THAT RIGHT, HIROMI?
Y-YES... THAT'S WHY I STARTED THE FIRE FOR THE BATH.
WITH HER SECOND CALL, SHE CONFIRMED THAT THE BATH HAD BEEN HEATED.
WELL THEN! WHO WAS IT!?
HURRY UP AND TELL US!!
WHO ENDED UP KILLING HER AT THE BATH!?
MACHIKO'S INTENDED VICTIM WAS SOMEONE WHO LIKED BATHS-- SOMEONE SHE KNEW WOULD BATHE EVERYDAY.
AND OF EVERYONE HERE, ONLY ONE PERSON ALWAYS TAKES THE FIRST BATH.
THAT PERSON IS...

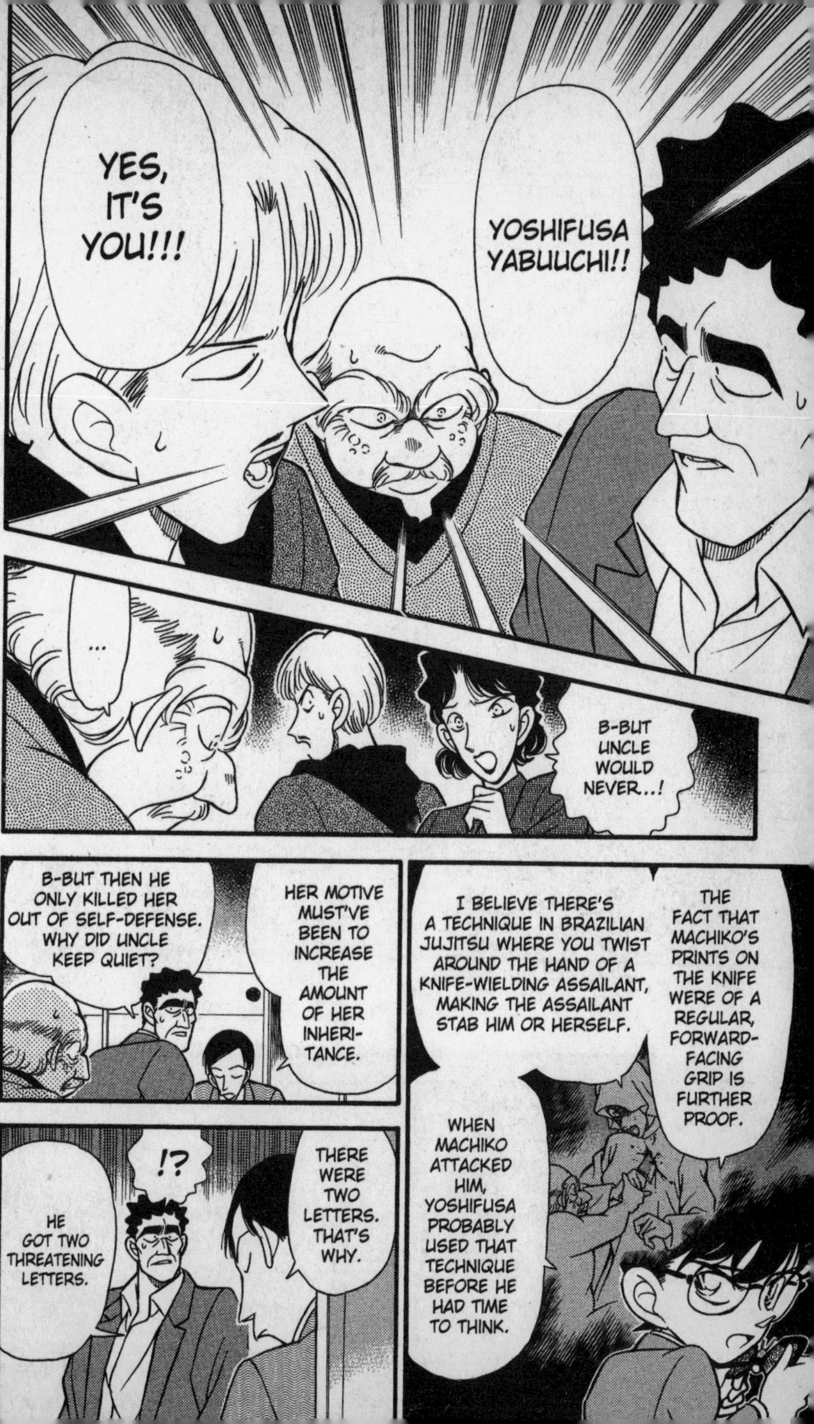
YOSHIFUSA YABUUCHI!!
YES, IT'S YOU!!!
B-BUT UNCLE WOULD NEVER...!
...
I BELIEVE THERE'S A TECHNIQUE IN BRAZILIAN JUJITSU WHERE YOU TWIST AROUND THE HAND OF A KNIFE-WIELDING ASSAILANT, MAKING THE ASSAILANT STAB HIM OR HERSELF.
WHEN MACHIKO ATTACKED HIM, YOSHIFUSA PROBABLY USED THAT TECHNIQUE BEFORE HE HAD TIME TO THINK.
THE FACT THAT MACHIKO'S PRINTS ON THE KNIFE WERE OF A REGULAR, FORWARD-FACING GRIP IS FURTHER PROOF.
HER MOTIVE MUST'VE BEEN TO INCREASE THE AMOUNT OF HER INHERITANCE.
B-BUT THEN HE ONLY KILLED HER OUT OF SELF-DEFENSE. WHY DID UNCLE KEEP QUIET?
THERE WERE TWO LETTERS. THAT'S WHY.
!?
HE GOT TWO THREATENING LETTERS.

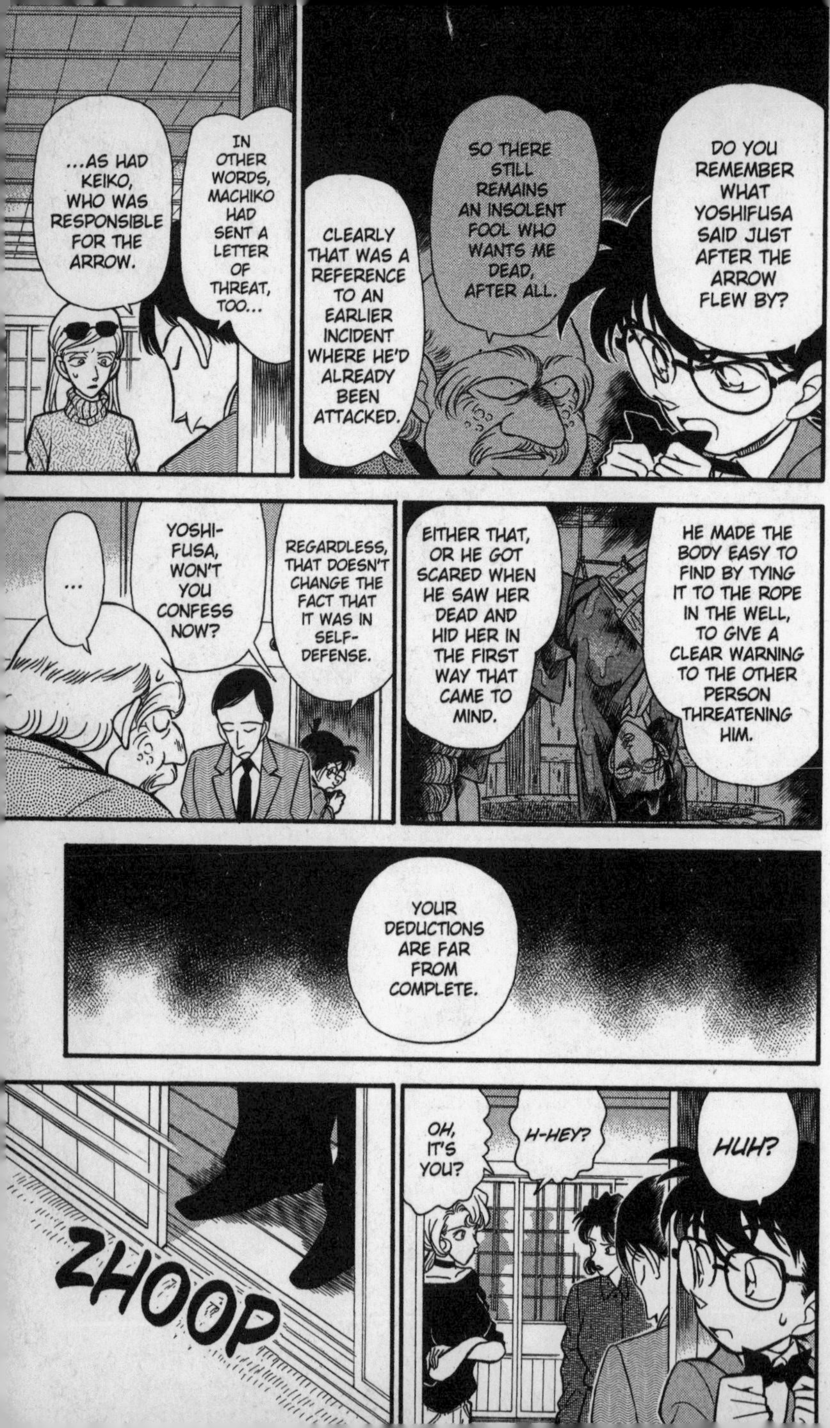
DO YOU REMEMBER WHAT YOSHIFUSA SAID JUST AFTER THE ARROW FLEW BY?
SO THERE STILL REMAINS AN INSOLENT FOOL WHO WANTS ME DEAD, AFTER ALL.
CLEARLY THAT WAS A REFERENCE TO AN EARLIER INCIDENT WHERE HE'D ALREADY BEEN ATTACKED.
IN OTHER WORDS, MACHIKO HAD SENT A LETTER OF THREAT, TOO...
...AS HAD KEIKO, WHO WAS RESPONSIBLE FOR THE ARROW.
HE MADE THE BODY EASY TO FIND BY TYING IT TO THE ROPE IN THE WELL, TO GIVE A CLEAR WARNING TO THE OTHER PERSON THREATENING HIM.
EITHER THAT, OR HE GOT SCARED WHEN HE SAW HER DEAD AND HID HER IN THE FIRST WAY THAT CAME TO MIND.
REGARDLESS, THAT DOESN'T CHANGE THE FACT THAT IT WAS IN SELF-DEFENSE.
YOSHI-FUSA, WON'T YOU CONFESS NOW?
...
YOUR DEDUCTIONS ARE FAR FROM COMPLETE.
HUH?
H-HEY?
OH, IT'S YOU?
ZHOOP

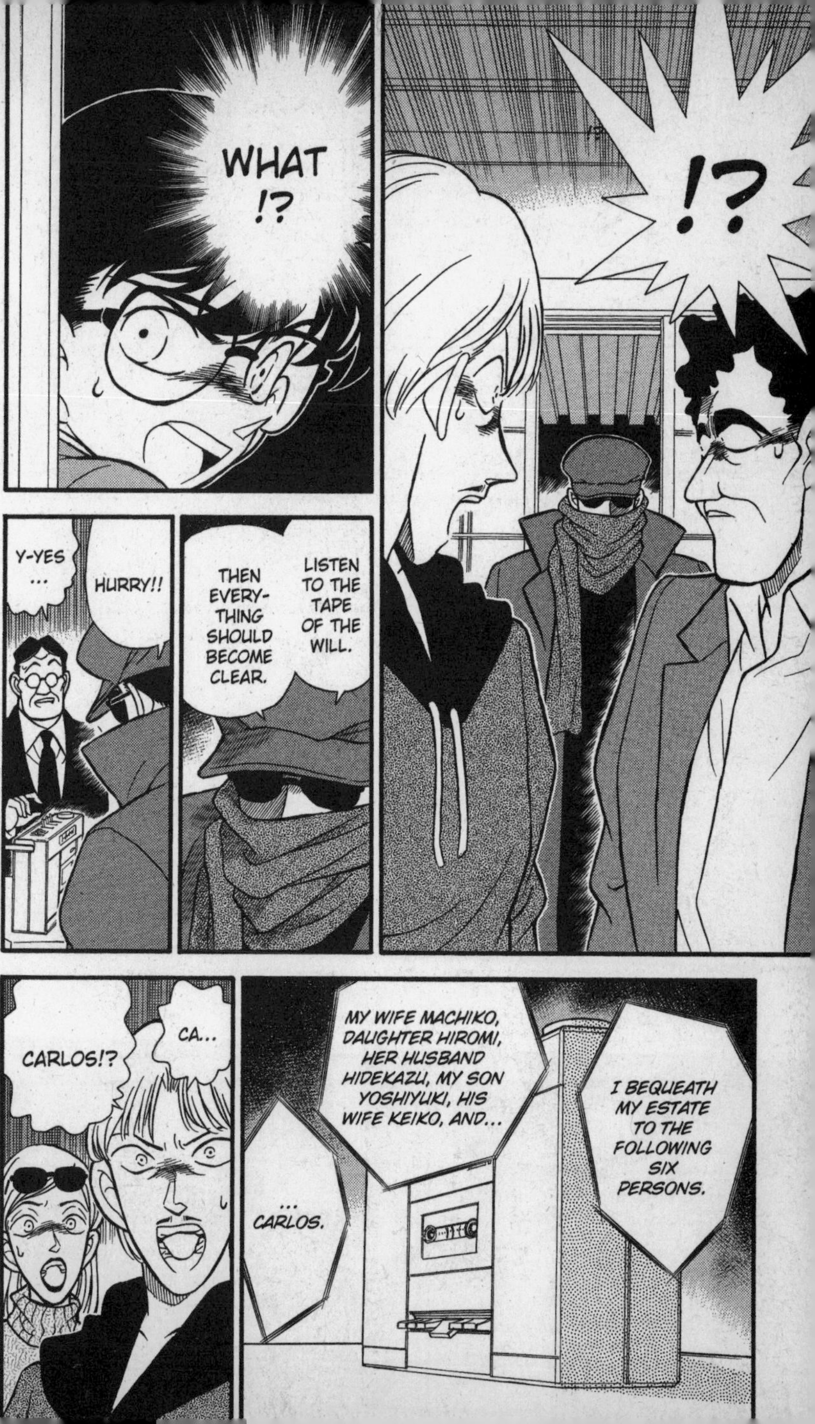
!?
!?
WHAT !?
LISTEN TO THE TAPE OF THE WILL.
THEN EVERY-THING SHOULD BECOME CLEAR.
HURRY!!
Y-YES ...
I BEQUEATH MY ESTATE TO THE FOLLOWING SIX PERSONS.
MY WIFE MACHIKO, DAUGHTER HIROMI, HER HUSBAND HIDEKAZU, MY SON YOSHIYUKI, HIS WIFE KEIKO, AND...
... CARLOS.
CA...
CARLOS!?

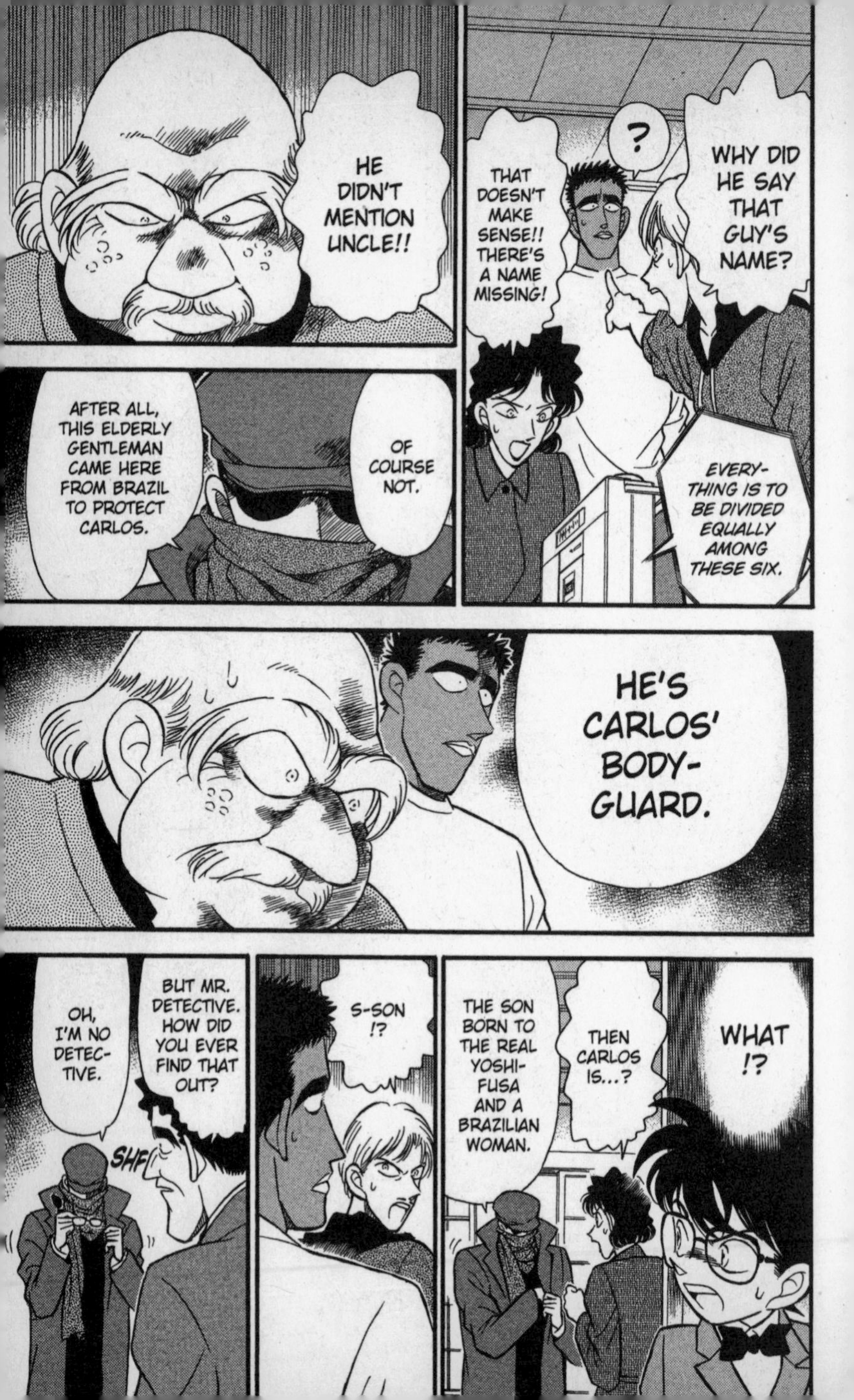
WHY DID HE SAY THAT GUY'S NAME?
?
THAT DOESN'T MAKE SENSE!! THERE'S A NAME MISSING!
EVERY-THING IS TO BE DIVIDED EQUALLY AMONG THESE SIX.
HE DIDN'T MENTION UNCLE!!
OF COURSE NOT.
AFTER ALL, THIS ELDERLY GENTLEMAN CAME HERE FROM BRAZIL TO PROTECT CARLOS.
HE'S CARLOS' BODY-GUARD.
WHAT !?
THEN CARLOS IS...?
THE SON BORN TO THE REAL YOSHI-FUSA AND A BRAZILIAN WOMAN.
S-SON !?
BUT MR. DETECTIVE. HOW DID YOU EVER FIND THAT OUT?
OH, I'M NO DETEC-TIVE.
SHF

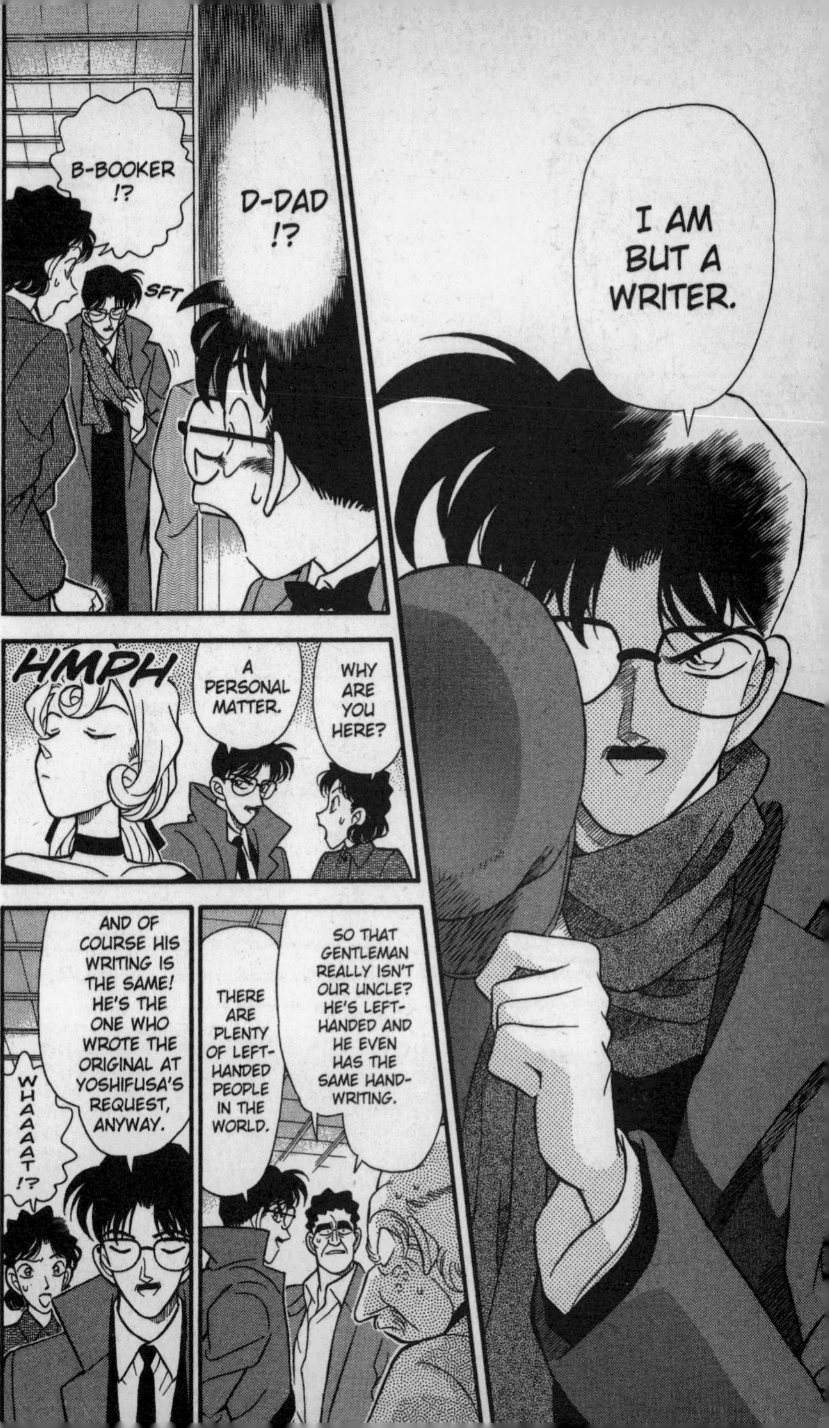
I AM BUT A WRITER.
D-DAD!?
B-BOOKER!?
SFT
WHY ARE YOU HERE?
A PERSONAL MATTER.
HMPH
SO THAT GENTLEMAN REALLY ISN'T OUR UNCLE? HE'S LEFT-HANDED AND HE EVEN HAS THE SAME HAND-WRITING.
THERE ARE PLENTY OF LEFT-HANDED PEOPLE IN THE WORLD.
AND OF COURSE HIS WRITING IS THE SAME! HE'S THE ONE WHO WROTE THE ORIGINAL AT YOSHIFUSA'S REQUEST, ANYWAY.
WHAAAAAT!?

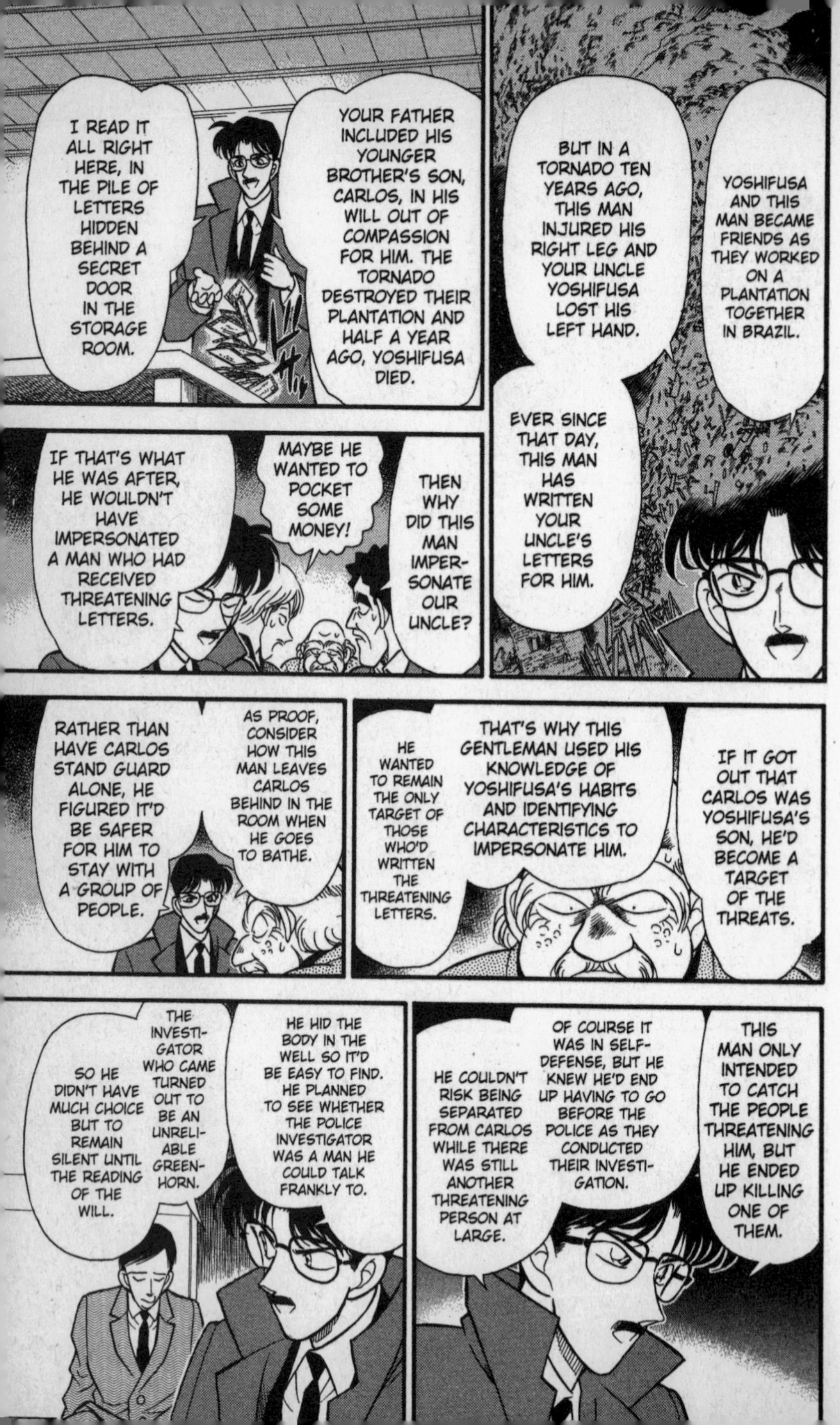
YOSHIFUSA AND THIS MAN BECAME FRIENDS AS THEY WORKED ON A PLANTATION TOGETHER IN BRAZIL.
BUT IN A TORNADO TEN YEARS AGO, THIS MAN INJURED HIS RIGHT LEG AND YOUR UNCLE YOSHIFUSA LOST HIS LEFT HAND.
EVER SINCE THAT DAY, THIS MAN HAS WRITTEN YOUR UNCLE'S LETTERS FOR HIM.
YOUR FATHER INCLUDED HIS YOUNGER BROTHER'S SON, CARLOS, IN HIS WILL OUT OF COMPASSION FOR HIM. THE TORNADO DESTROYED THEIR PLANTATION AND HALF A YEAR AGO, YOSHIFUSA DIED.
I READ IT ALL RIGHT HERE, IN THE PILE OF LETTERS HIDDEN BEHIND A SECRET DOOR IN THE STORAGE ROOM.
THEN WHY DID THIS MAN IMPER-SONATE OUR UNCLE?
MAYBE HE WANTED TO POCKET SOME MONEY!
IF THAT'S WHAT HE WAS AFTER, HE WOULDN'T HAVE IMPERSONATED A MAN WHO HAD RECEIVED THREATENING LETTERS.
IF IT GOT OUT THAT CARLOS WAS YOSHIFUSA'S SON, HE'D BECOME A TARGET OF THE THREATS.
THAT'S WHY THIS GENTLEMAN USED HIS KNOWLEDGE OF YOSHIFUSA'S HABITS AND IDENTIFYING CHARACTERISTICS TO IMPERSONATE HIM.
HE WANTED TO REMAIN THE ONLY TARGET OF THOSE WHO'D WRITTEN THE THREATENING LETTERS.
AS PROOF, CONSIDER HOW THIS MAN LEAVES CARLOS BEHIND IN THE ROOM WHEN HE GOES TO BATHE.
RATHER THAN HAVE CARLOS STAND GUARD ALONE, HE FIGURED IT'D BE SAFER FOR HIM TO STAY WITH A GROUP OF PEOPLE.
THIS MAN ONLY INTENDED TO CATCH THE PEOPLE THREATENING HIM, BUT HE ENDED UP KILLING ONE OF THEM.
OF COURSE IT WAS IN SELF-DEFENSE, BUT HE KNEW HE'D END UP HAVING TO GO BEFORE THE POLICE AS THEY CONDUCTED THEIR INVESTI-GATION.
HE COULDN'T RISK BEING SEPARATED FROM CARLOS WHILE THERE WAS STILL ANOTHER THREATENING PERSON AT LARGE.
HE HID THE BODY IN THE WELL SO IT'D BE EASY TO FIND. HE PLANNED TO SEE WHETHER THE POLICE INVESTIGATOR WAS A MAN HE COULD TALK FRANKLY TO.
THE INVESTI-GATOR WHO CAME TURNED OUT TO BE AN UNRELI-ABLE GREEN-HORN.
SO HE DIDN'T HAVE MUCH CHOICE BUT TO REMAIN SILENT UNTIL THE READING OF THE WILL.

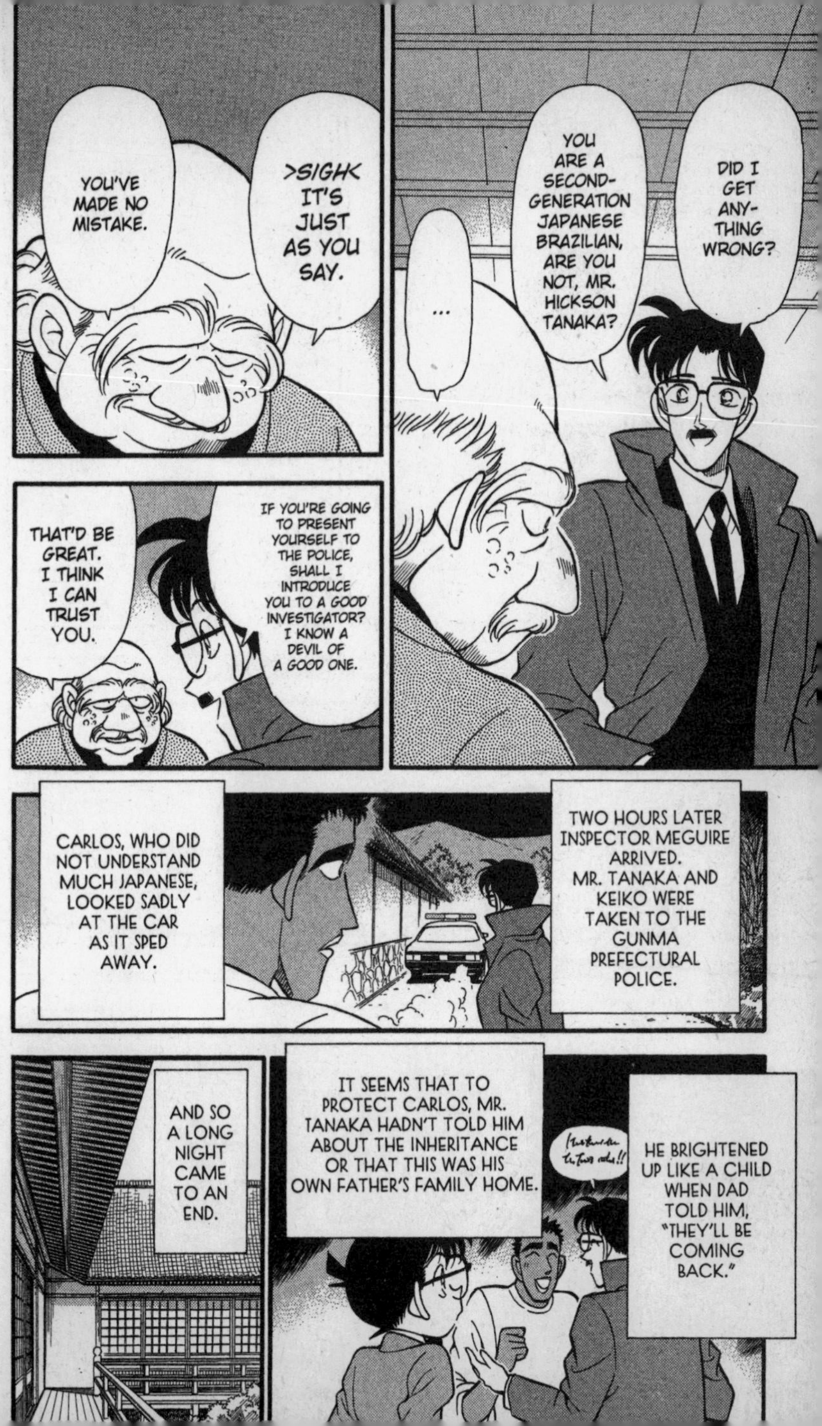
DID I GET ANY-THING WRONG?
YOU ARE A SECOND-GENERATION JAPANESE BRAZILIAN, ARE YOU NOT, MR. HICKSON TANAKA?
...
>SIGH< IT'S JUST AS YOU SAY.
YOU'VE MADE NO MISTAKE.
IF YOU'RE GOING TO PRESENT YOURSELF TO THE POLICE, SHALL I INTRODUCE YOU TO A GOOD INVESTIGATOR? I KNOW A DEVIL OF A GOOD ONE.
THAT'D BE GREAT. I THINK I CAN TRUST YOU.
TWO HOURS LATER INSPECTOR MEGUIRE ARRIVED. MR. TANAKA AND KEIKO WERE TAKEN TO THE GUNMA PREFECTURAL POLICE.
CARLOS, WHO DID NOT UNDERSTAND MUCH JAPANESE, LOOKED SADLY AT THE CAR AS IT SPED AWAY.
HE BRIGHTENED UP LIKE A CHILD WHEN DAD TOLD HIM, "THEY'LL BE COMING BACK."
IT SEEMS THAT TO PROTECT CARLOS, MR. TANAKA HADN'T TOLD HIM ABOUT THE INHERITANCE OR THAT THIS WAS HIS OWN FATHER'S FAMILY HOME.
AND SO A LONG NIGHT CAME TO AN END.

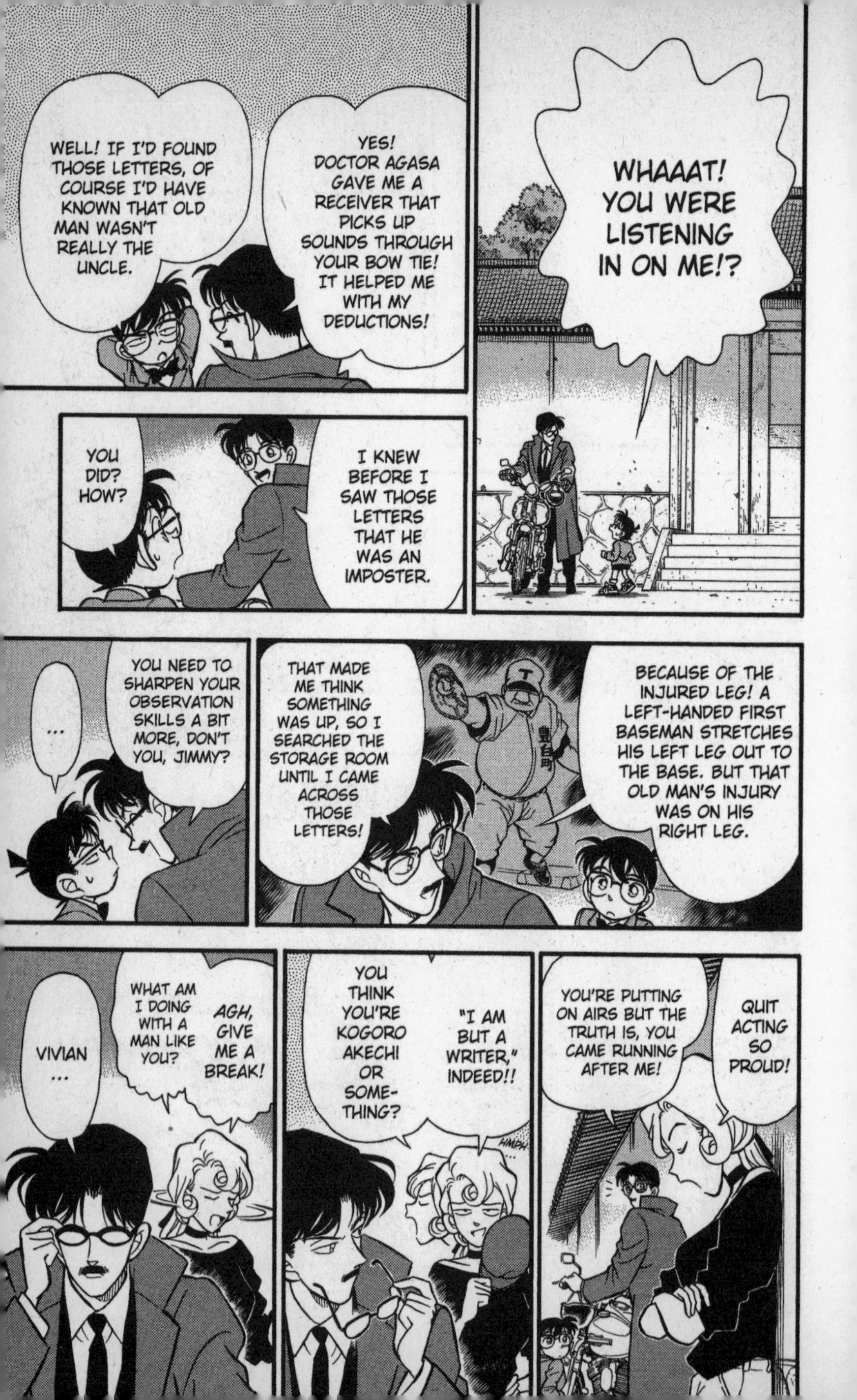
WHAAAT! YOU WERE LISTENING IN ON ME!?
YES! DOCTOR AGASA GAVE ME A RECEIVER THAT PICKS UP SOUNDS THROUGH YOUR BOW TIE! IT HELPED ME WITH MY DEDUCTIONS!
WELL! IF I'D FOUND THOSE LETTERS, OF COURSE I'D HAVE KNOWN THAT OLD MAN WASN'T REALLY THE UNCLE.
I KNEW BEFORE I SAW THOSE LETTERS THAT HE WAS AN IMPOSTER.
YOU DID? HOW?
BECAUSE OF THE INJURED LEG! A LEFT-HANDED FIRST BASEMAN STRETCHES HIS LEFT LEG OUT TO THE BASE. BUT THAT OLD MAN'S INJURY WAS ON HIS RIGHT LEG.
THAT MADE ME THINK SOMETHING WAS UP, SO I SEARCHED THE STORAGE ROOM UNTIL I CAME ACROSS THOSE LETTERS!
YOU NEED TO SHARPEN YOUR OBSERVATION SKILLS A BIT MORE, DON'T YOU, JIMMY?
...
QUIT ACTING SO PROUD!
YOU'RE PUTTING ON AIRS BUT THE TRUTH IS, YOU CAME RUNNING AFTER ME!
"I AM BUT A WRITER," INDEED!!
YOU THINK YOU'RE KOGORO AKECHI OR SOME-THING?
HMPH...
AGH, GIVE ME A BREAK!
WHAT AM I DOING WITH A MAN LIKE YOU?
VIVIAN ...

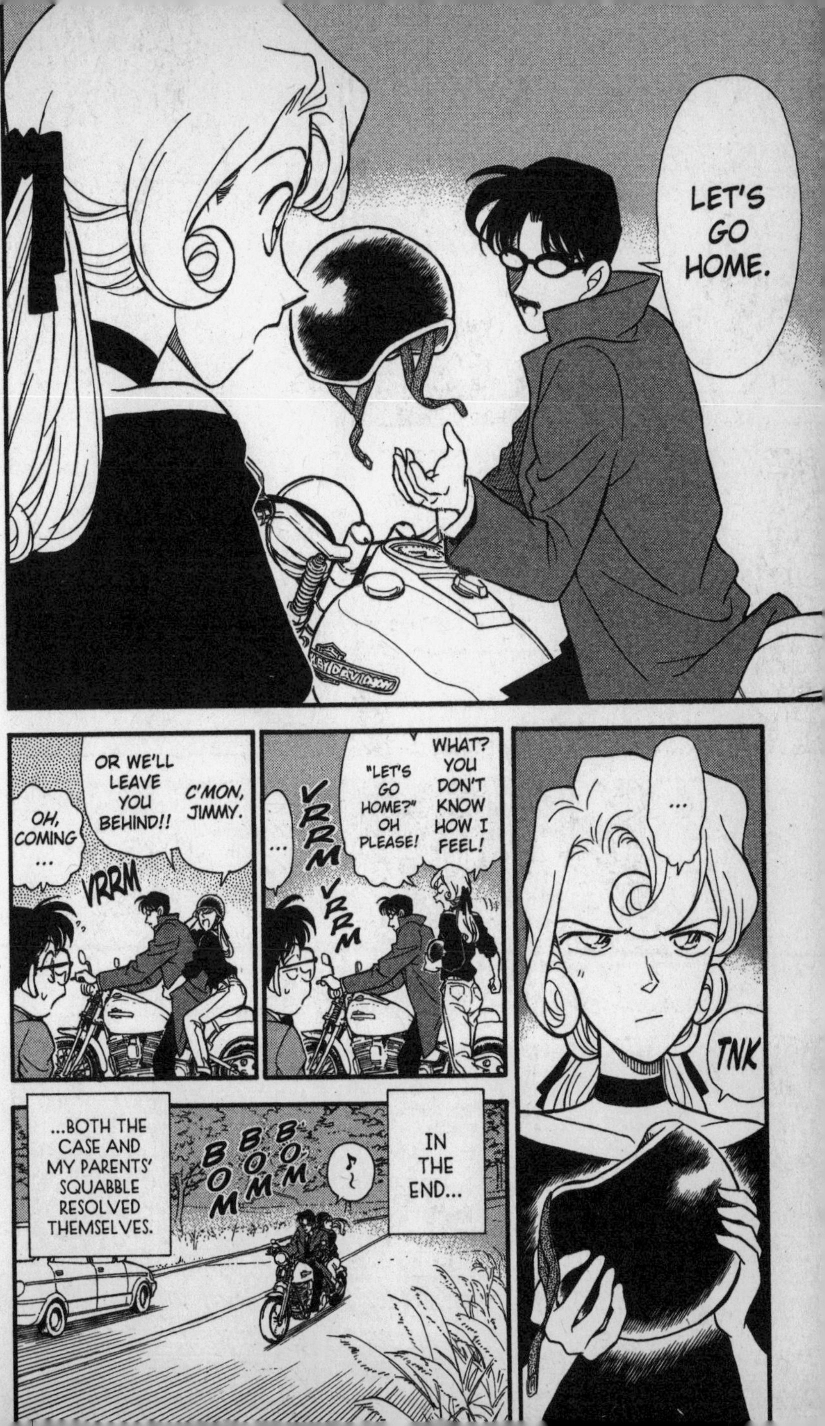
LET'S GO HOME.
...
TNK
WHAT? YOU DON'T KNOW HOW I FEEL!
"LET'S GO HOME?" OH PLEASE!
VRRM VRRM
...
C'MON, JIMMY.
OR WE'LL LEAVE YOU BEHIND!!
OH, COMING ...
VRRM
IN THE END...
♪~
BOM BOM BOM
...BOTH THE CASE AND MY PARENTS' SQUABBLE RESOLVED THEMSELVES.

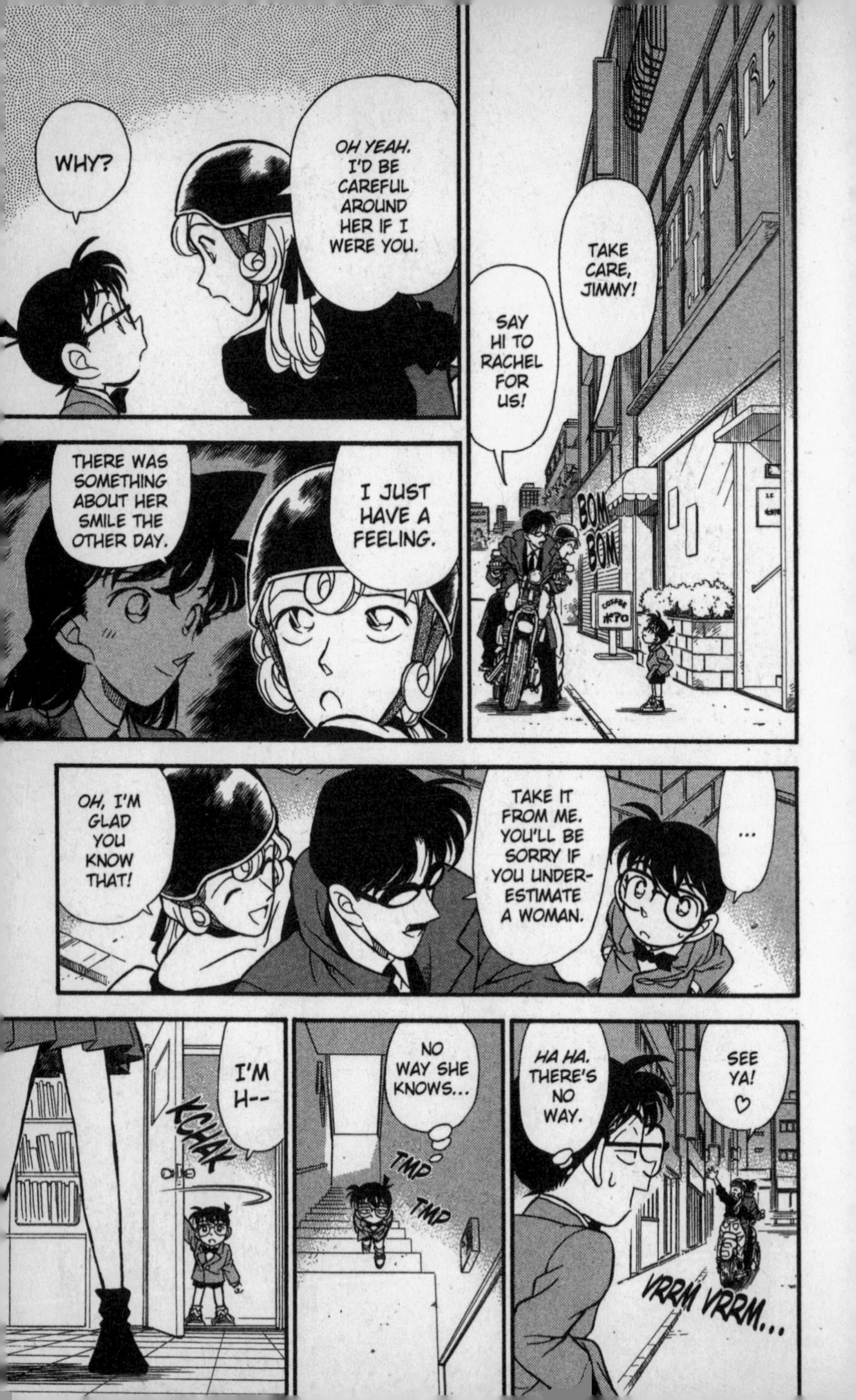
TAKE CARE, JIMMY!
SAY HI TO RACHEL FOR US!
BOM BOM
OH YEAH. I'D BE CAREFUL AROUND HER IF I WERE YOU.
WHY?
I JUST HAVE A FEELING.
THERE WAS SOMETHING ABOUT HER SMILE THE OTHER DAY.
...
TAKE IT FROM ME. YOU'LL BE SORRY IF YOU UNDER-ESTIMATE A WOMAN.
OH, I'M GLAD YOU KNOW THAT!
SEE YA! ♡
HA HA. THERE'S NO WAY.
VRRM VRRM...
NO WAY SHE KNOWS...
TMP
TMP
I'M H--
KCHAK

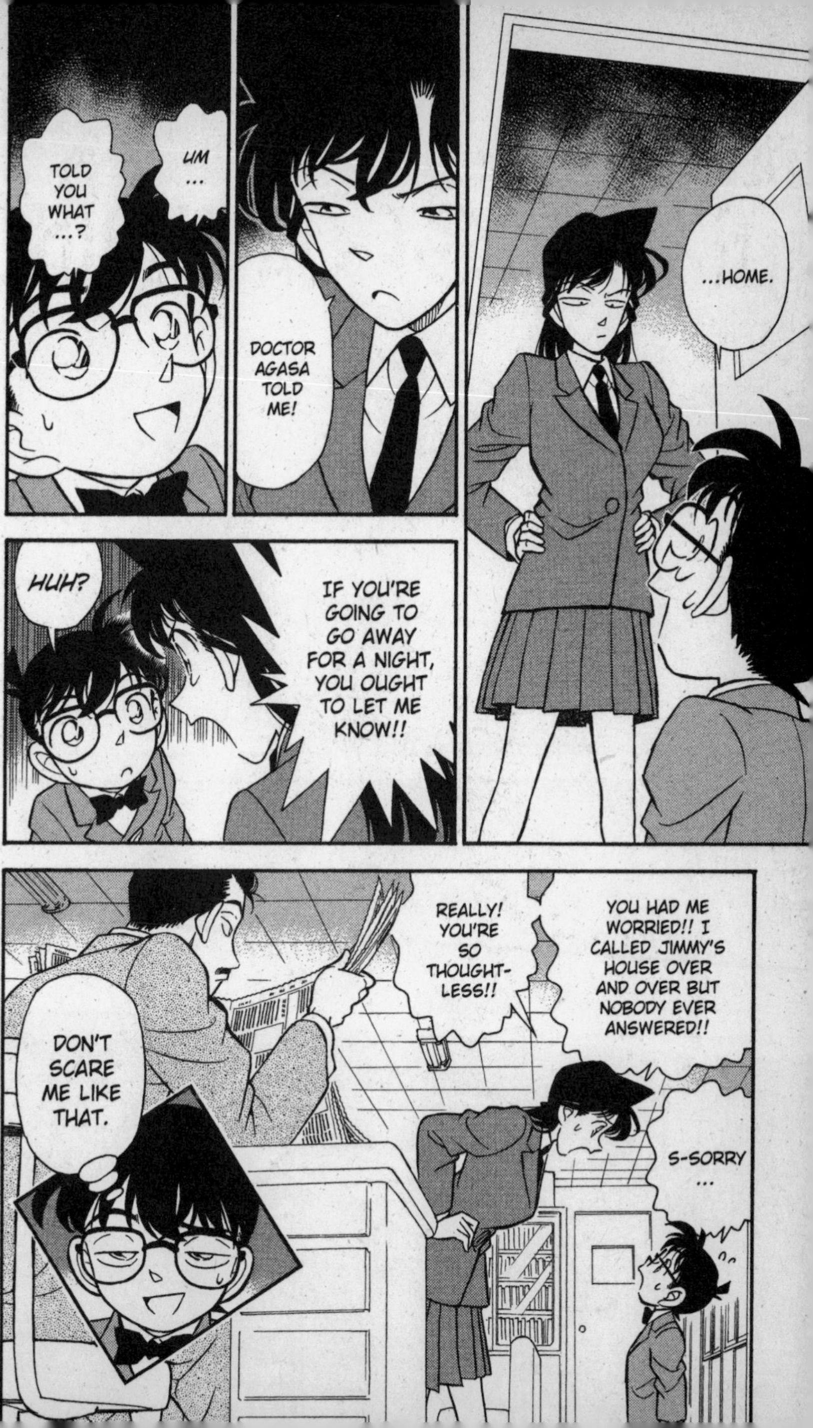
...HOME.
DOCTOR AGASA TOLD ME!
UM ...
TOLD YOU WHAT ...?
IF YOU'RE GOING TO GO AWAY FOR A NIGHT, YOU OUGHT TO LET ME KNOW!!
HUH?
YOU HAD ME WORRIED!! I CALLED JIMMY'S HOUSE OVER AND OVER BUT NOBODY EVER ANSWERED!!
REALLY! YOU'RE SO THOUGHT-LESS!!
S-SORRY ...
DON'T SCARE ME LIKE THAT.

FILE 9: A STRANGE GATHERING

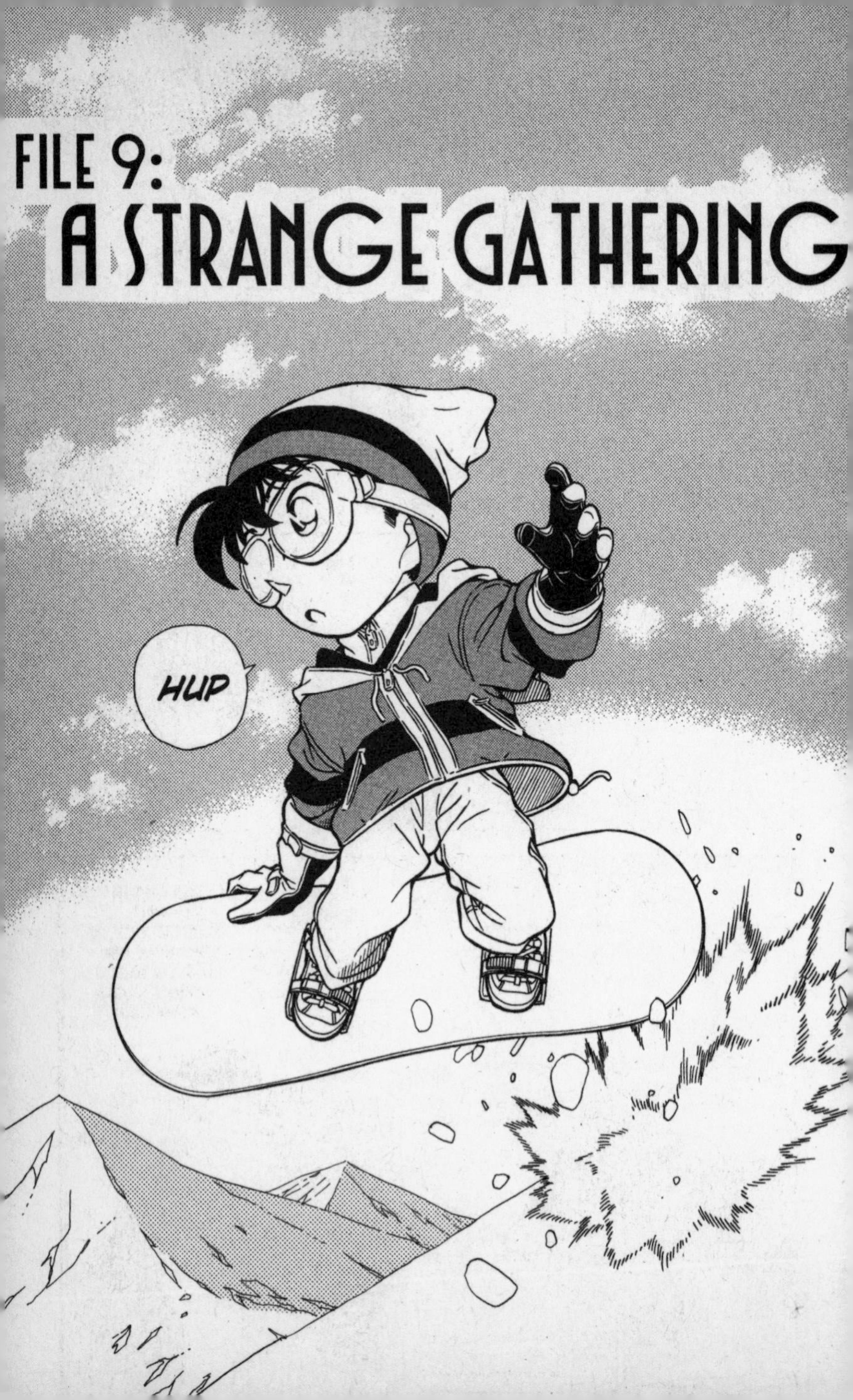
HUP

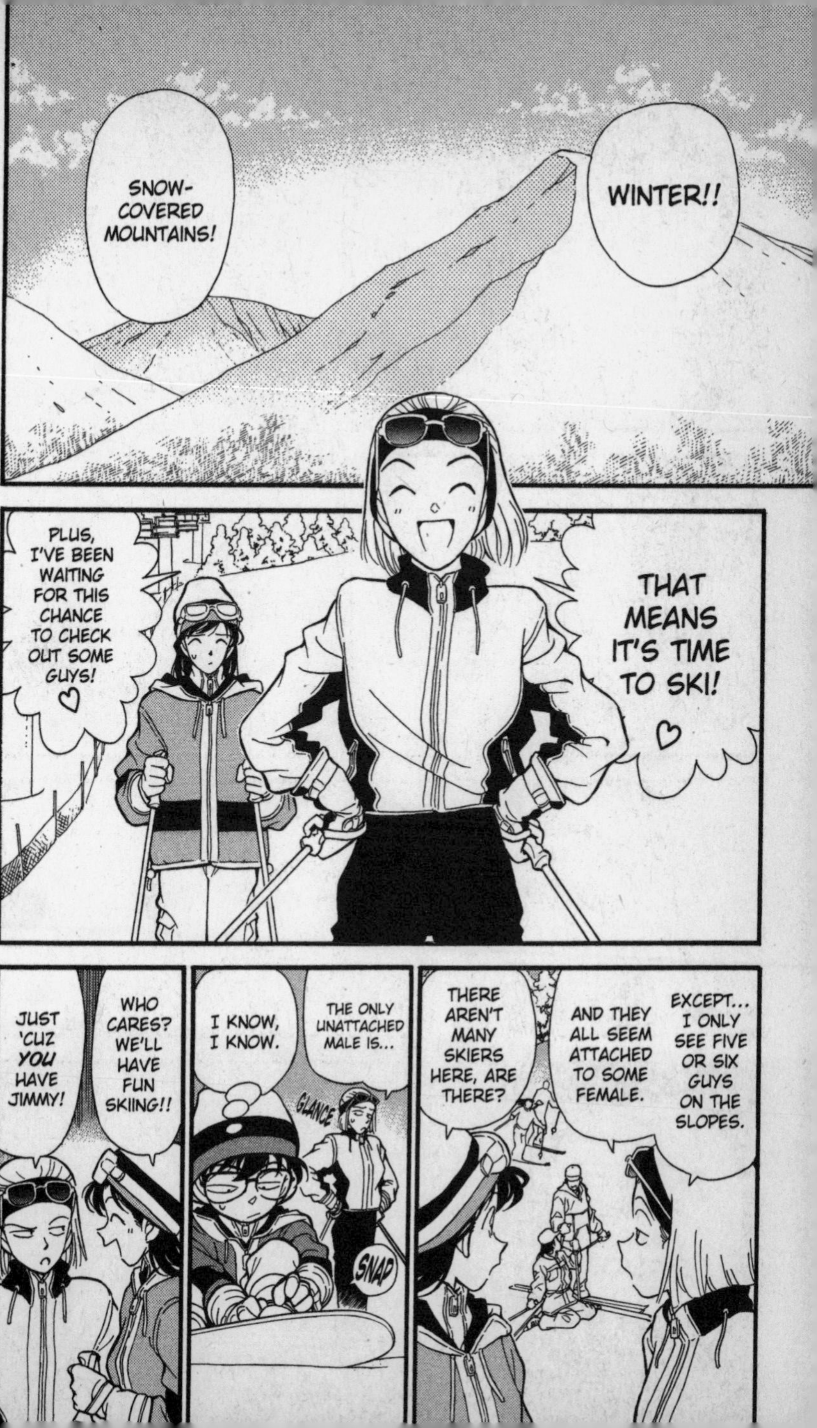
WINTER!!
SNOW-COVERED MOUNTAINS!
THAT MEANS IT'S TIME TO SKI! ♡
PLUS, I'VE BEEN WAITING FOR THIS CHANCE TO CHECK OUT SOME GUYS! ♡
EXCEPT... I ONLY SEE FIVE OR SIX GUYS ON THE SLOPES.
AND THEY ALL SEEM ATTACHED TO SOME FEMALE.
THERE AREN'T MANY SKIERS HERE, ARE THERE?
THE ONLY UNATTACHED MALE IS...
GLANCE
I KNOW, I KNOW.
SNAP
WHO CARES? WE'LL HAVE FUN SKIING!!
JUST 'CUZ *YOU* HAVE JIMMY!

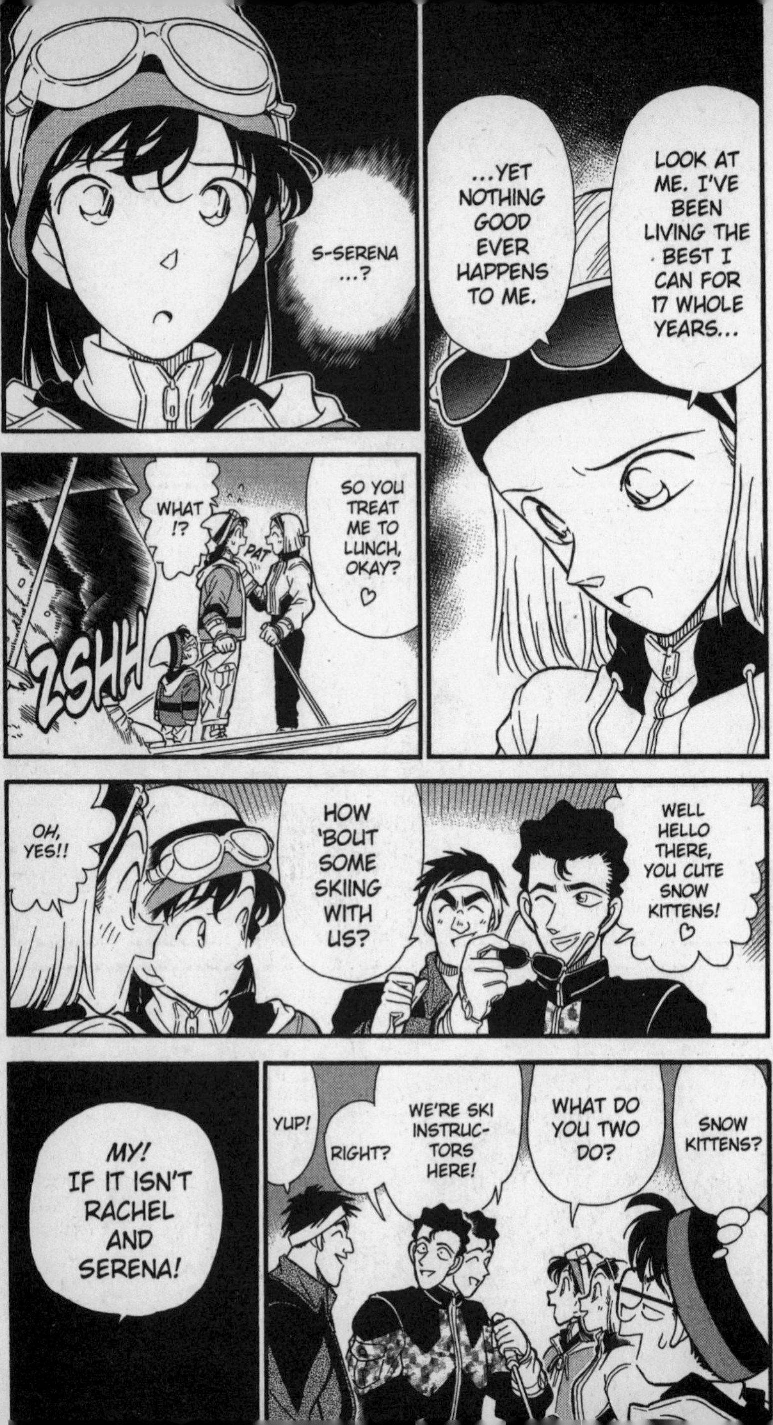
LOOK AT ME. I'VE BEEN LIVING THE BEST I CAN FOR 17 WHOLE YEARS...
...YET NOTHING GOOD EVER HAPPENS TO ME.
S-SERENA ...?
SO YOU TREAT ME TO LUNCH, OKAY? ♡
WHAT !?
PAT
ZSHH
WELL HELLO THERE, YOU CUTE SNOW KITTENS! ♡
HOW 'BOUT SOME SKIING WITH US?
OH, YES!!
SNOW KITTENS?
WHAT DO YOU TWO DO?
WE'RE SKI INSTRUC- TORS HERE!
RIGHT?
YUP!
MY! IF IT ISN'T RACHEL AND SERENA!

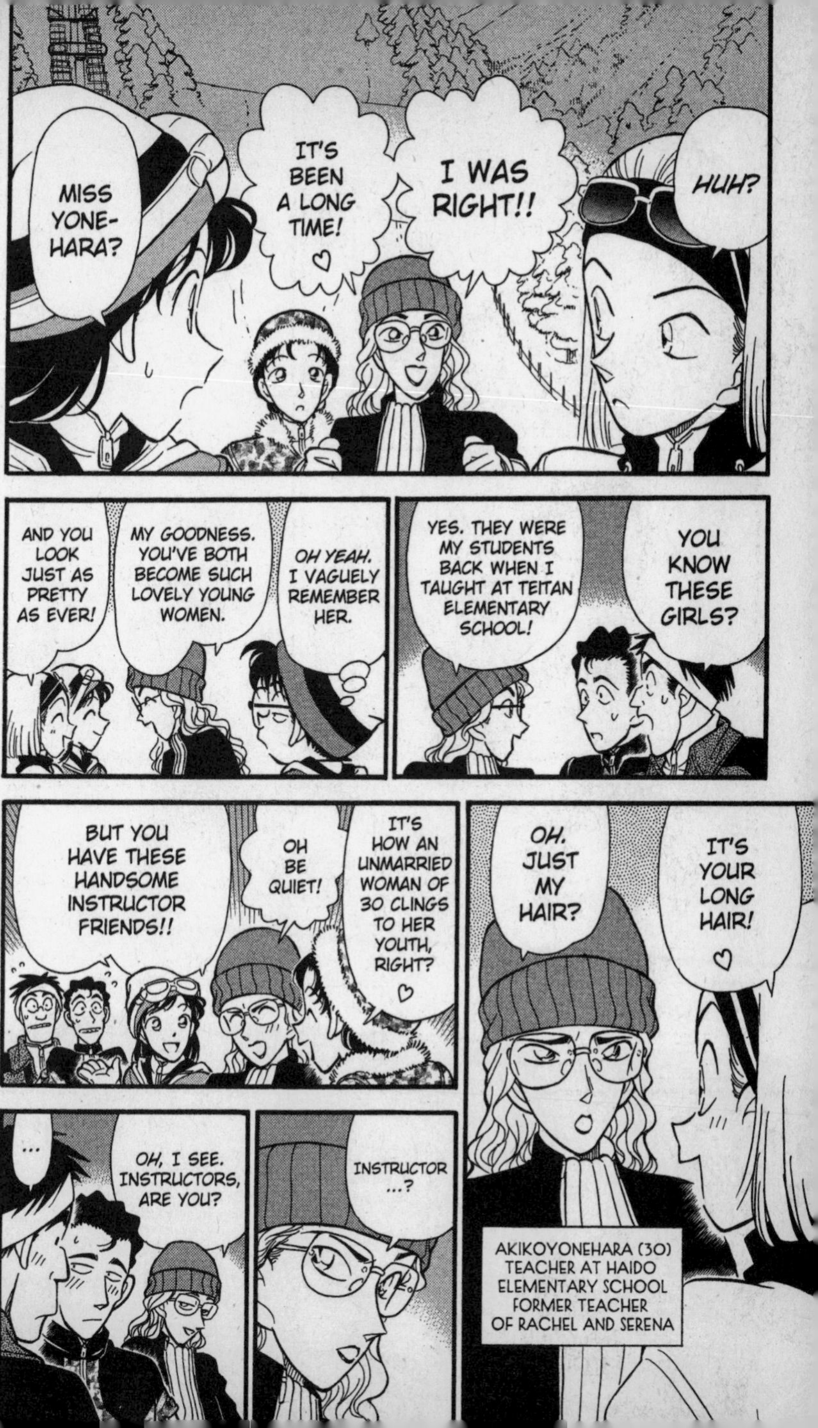
HUH?
I WAS RIGHT!!
IT'S BEEN A LONG TIME! ♡
MISS YONE-HARA?
YOU KNOW THESE GIRLS?
YES. THEY WERE MY STUDENTS BACK WHEN I TAUGHT AT TEITAN ELEMENTARY SCHOOL!
OH YEAH. I VAGUELY REMEMBER HER.
MY GOODNESS. YOU'VE BOTH BECOME SUCH LOVELY YOUNG WOMEN.
AND YOU LOOK JUST AS PRETTY AS EVER!
IT'S YOUR LONG HAIR! ♡
OH. JUST MY HAIR?
AKIKOYONEHARA (30) TEACHER AT HAIDO ELEMENTARY SCHOOL FORMER TEACHER OF RACHEL AND SERENA
IT'S HOW AN UNMARRIED WOMAN OF 30 CLINGS TO HER YOUTH, RIGHT? ♡
OH BE QUIET!
BUT YOU HAVE THESE HANDSOME INSTRUCTOR FRIENDS!!
INSTRUCTOR ...?
OH, I SEE. INSTRUCTORS, ARE YOU?
...

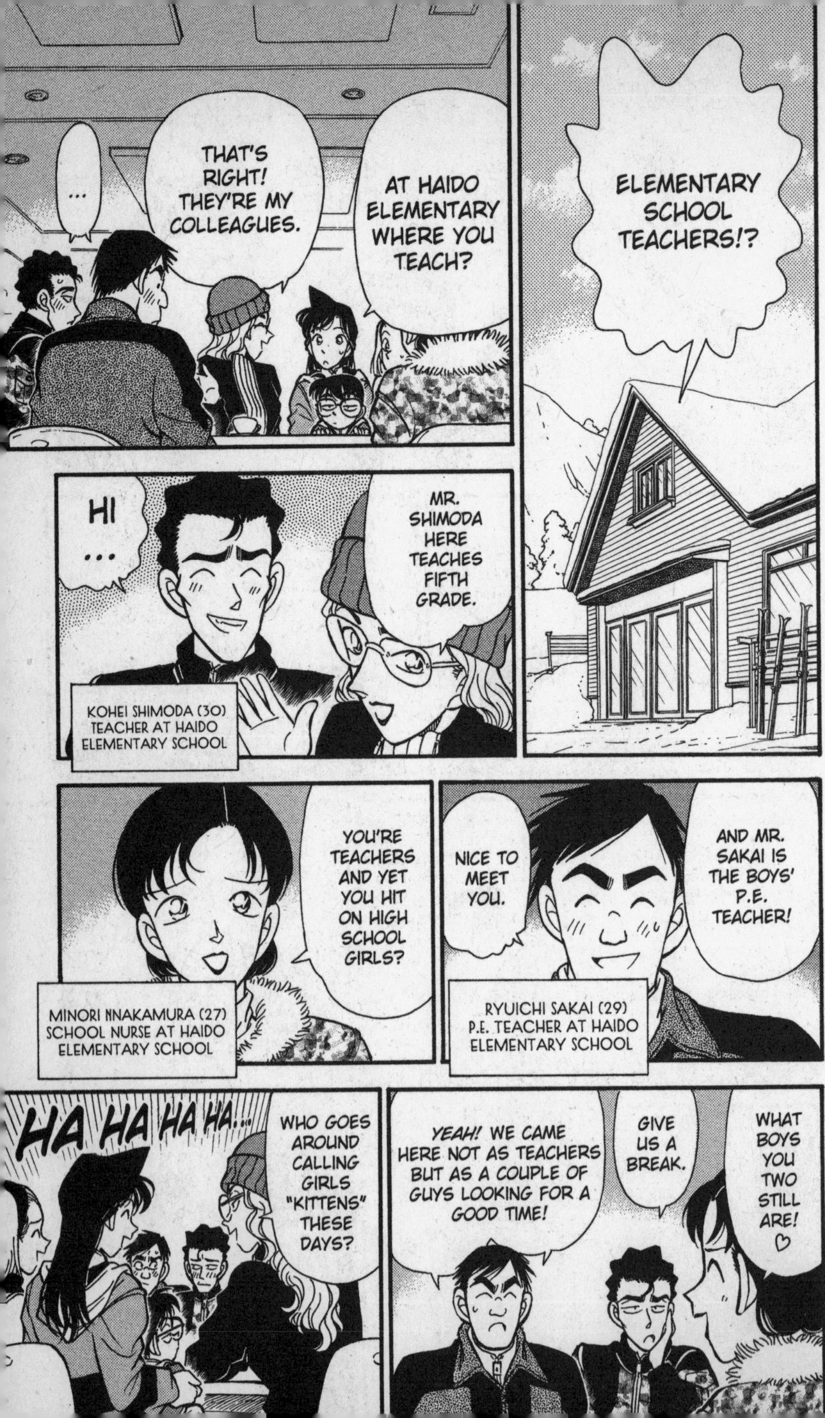
ELEMENTARY SCHOOL TEACHERS!?
AT HAIDO ELEMENTARY WHERE YOU TEACH?
THAT'S RIGHT! THEY'RE MY COLLEAGUES.
...
MR. SHIMODA HERE TEACHES FIFTH GRADE.
HI ...
KOHEI SHIMODA (30) TEACHER AT HAIDO ELEMENTARY SCHOOL
AND MR. SAKAI IS THE BOYS' P.E. TEACHER!
NICE TO MEET YOU.
RYUICHI SAKAI (29) P.E. TEACHER AT HAIDO ELEMENTARY SCHOOL
YOU'RE TEACHERS AND YET YOU HIT ON HIGH SCHOOL GIRLS?
MINORI NNAKAMURA (27) SCHOOL NURSE AT HAIDO ELEMENTARY SCHOOL
WHAT BOYS YOU TWO STILL ARE! ♥
GIVE US A BREAK.
YEAH! WE CAME HERE NOT AS TEACHERS BUT AS A COUPLE OF GUYS LOOKING FOR A GOOD TIME!
WHO GOES AROUND CALLING GIRLS "KITTENS" THESE DAYS?
HA HA HA HA...

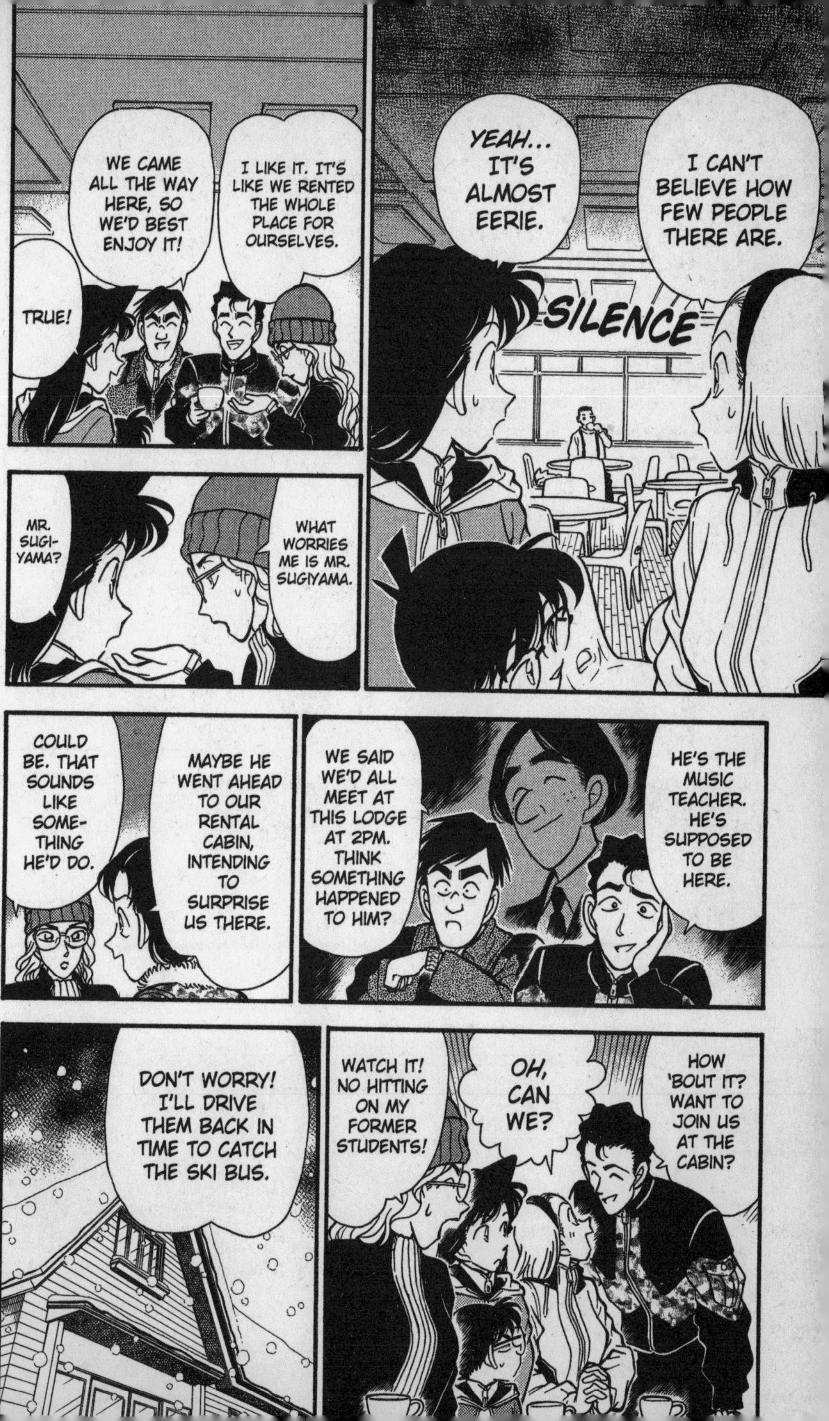
I CAN'T BELIEVE HOW FEW PEOPLE THERE ARE.
YEAH... IT'S ALMOST EERIE.
SILENCE
I LIKE IT. IT'S LIKE WE RENTED THE WHOLE PLACE FOR OURSELVES.
WE CAME ALL THE WAY HERE, SO WE'D BEST ENJOY IT!
TRUE!
WHAT WORRIES ME IS MR. SUGIYAMA.
MR. SUGI-YAMA?
HE'S THE MUSIC TEACHER. HE'S SUPPOSED TO BE HERE.
WE SAID WE'D ALL MEET AT THIS LODGE AT 2PM. THINK SOMETHING HAPPENED TO HIM?
MAYBE HE WENT AHEAD TO OUR RENTAL CABIN, INTENDING TO SURPRISE US THERE.
COULD BE. THAT SOUNDS LIKE SOME-THING HE'D DO.
HOW 'BOUT IT? WANT TO JOIN US AT THE CABIN?
OH, CAN WE?
WATCH IT! NO HITTING ON MY FORMER STUDENTS!
DON'T WORRY! I'LL DRIVE THEM BACK IN TIME TO CATCH THE SKI BUS.

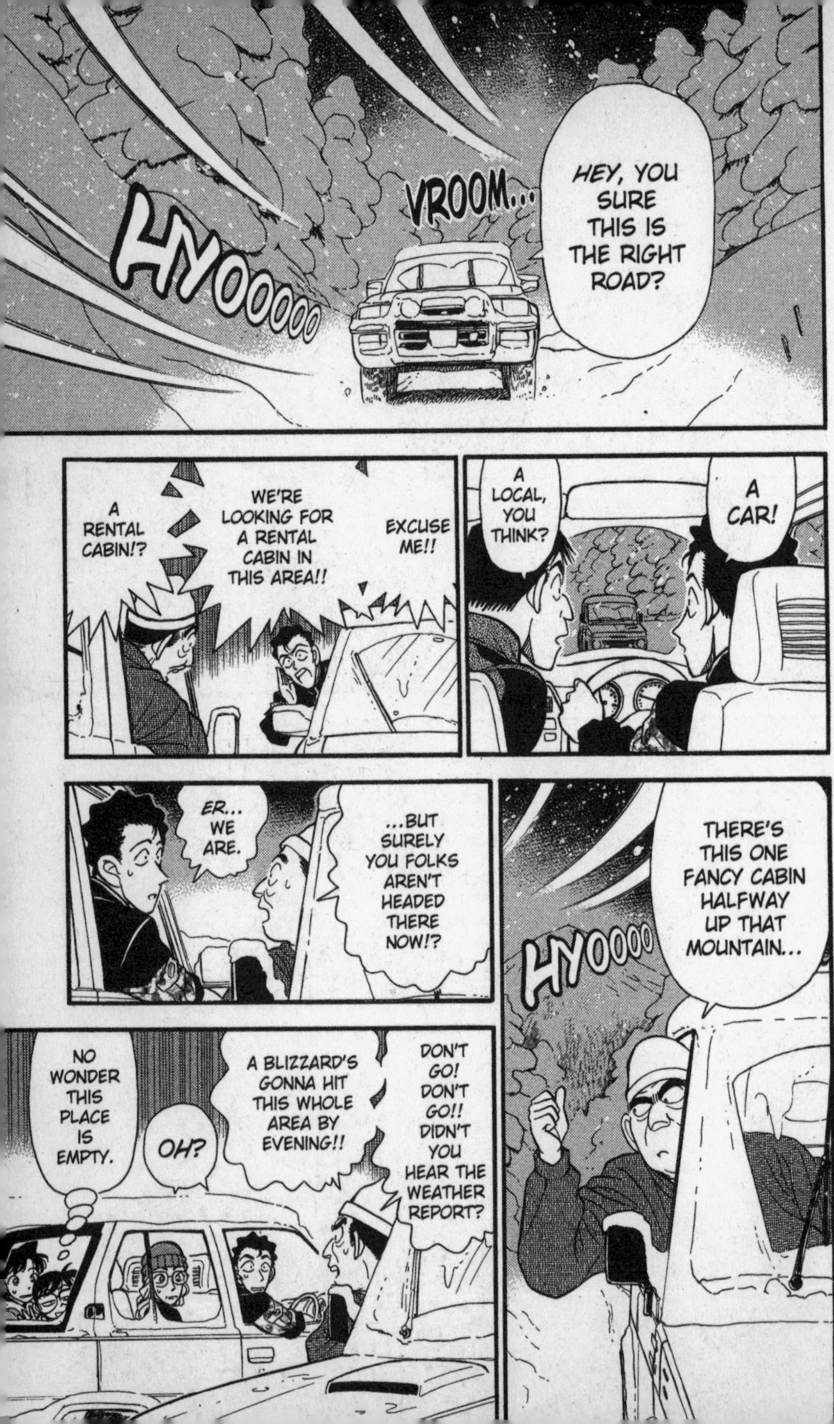
HEY, YOU SURE THIS IS THE RIGHT ROAD?
VROOM...
HYOOOOO
A CAR!
A LOCAL, YOU THINK?
EXCUSE ME!!
WE'RE LOOKING FOR A RENTAL CABIN IN THIS AREA!!
A RENTAL CABIN!?
THERE'S THIS ONE FANCY CABIN HALFWAY UP THAT MOUNTAIN...
HYOOOO
...BUT SURELY YOU FOLKS AREN'T HEADED THERE NOW!?
ER... WE ARE.
DON'T GO! DON'T GO!! DIDN'T YOU HEAR THE WEATHER REPORT?
A BLIZZARD'S GONNA HIT THIS WHOLE AREA BY EVENING!!
OH?
NO WONDER THIS PLACE IS EMPTY.

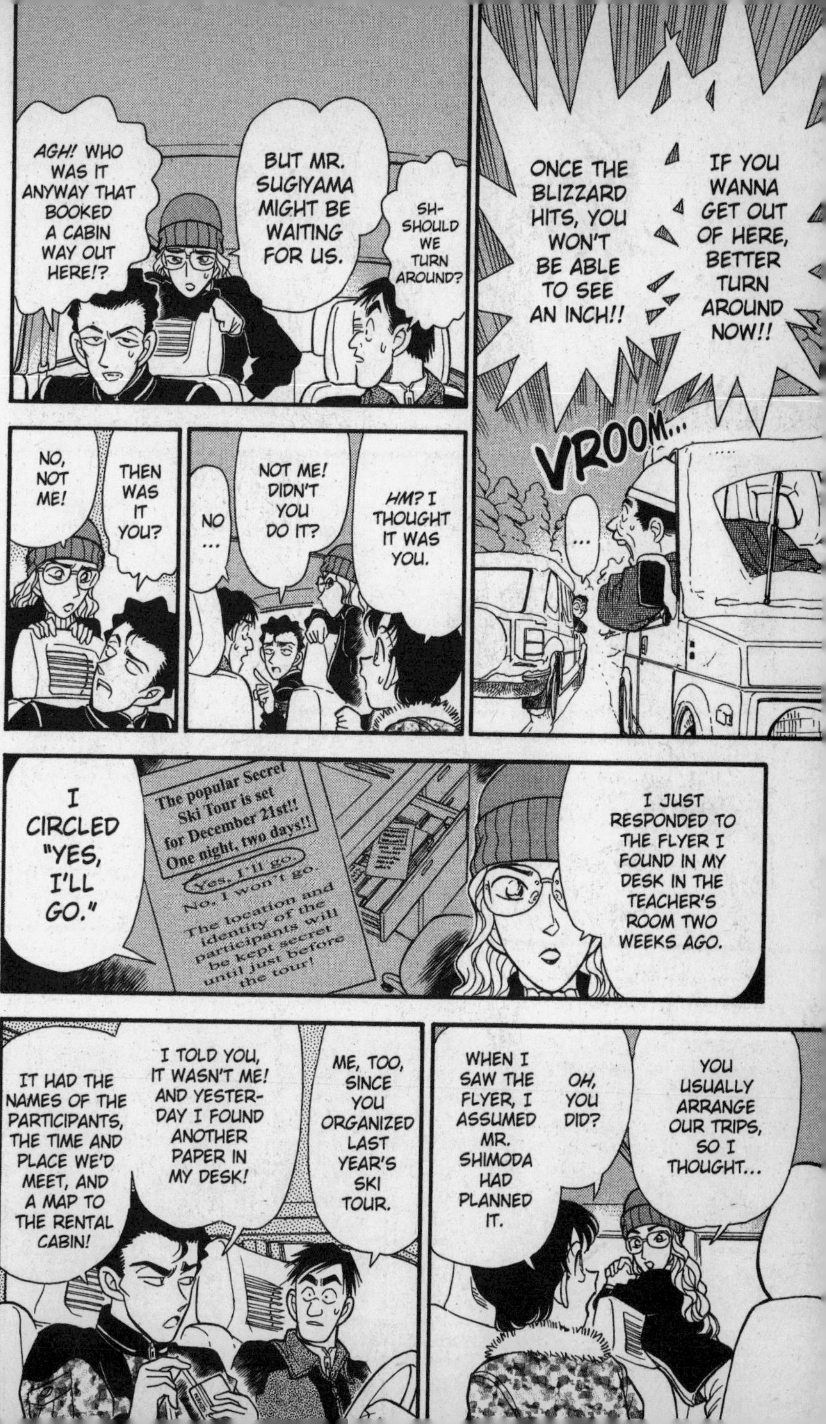
IF YOU WANNA GET OUT OF HERE, BETTER TURN AROUND NOW!!
ONCE THE BLIZZARD HITS, YOU WON'T BE ABLE TO SEE AN INCH!!
VROOM...
...
SH-SHOULD WE TURN AROUND?
BUT MR. SUGIYAMA MIGHT BE WAITING FOR US.
AGH! WHO WAS IT ANYWAY THAT BOOKED A CABIN WAY OUT HERE!?
HM? I THOUGHT IT WAS YOU.
NOT ME! DIDN'T YOU DO IT?
NO ...
THEN WAS IT YOU?
NO, NOT ME!
I JUST RESPONDED TO THE FLYER I FOUND IN MY DESK IN THE TEACHER'S ROOM TWO WEEKS AGO.
The popular Secret Ski Tour is set for December 21st!! One night, two days!!
Yes, I'll go.
No, I won't go.
The location and identity of the participants will be kept secret until just before the tour!
I CIRCLED "YES, I'LL GO."
YOU USUALLY ARRANGE OUR TRIPS, SO I THOUGHT...
OH, YOU DID?
WHEN I SAW THE FLYER, I ASSUMED MR. SHIMODA HAD PLANNED IT.
ME, TOO, SINCE YOU ORGANIZED LAST YEAR'S SKI TOUR.
I TOLD YOU, IT WASN'T ME! AND YESTERDAY I FOUND ANOTHER PAPER IN MY DESK!
IT HAD THE NAMES OF THE PARTICIPANTS, THE TIME AND PLACE WE'D MEET, AND A MAP TO THE RENTAL CABIN!

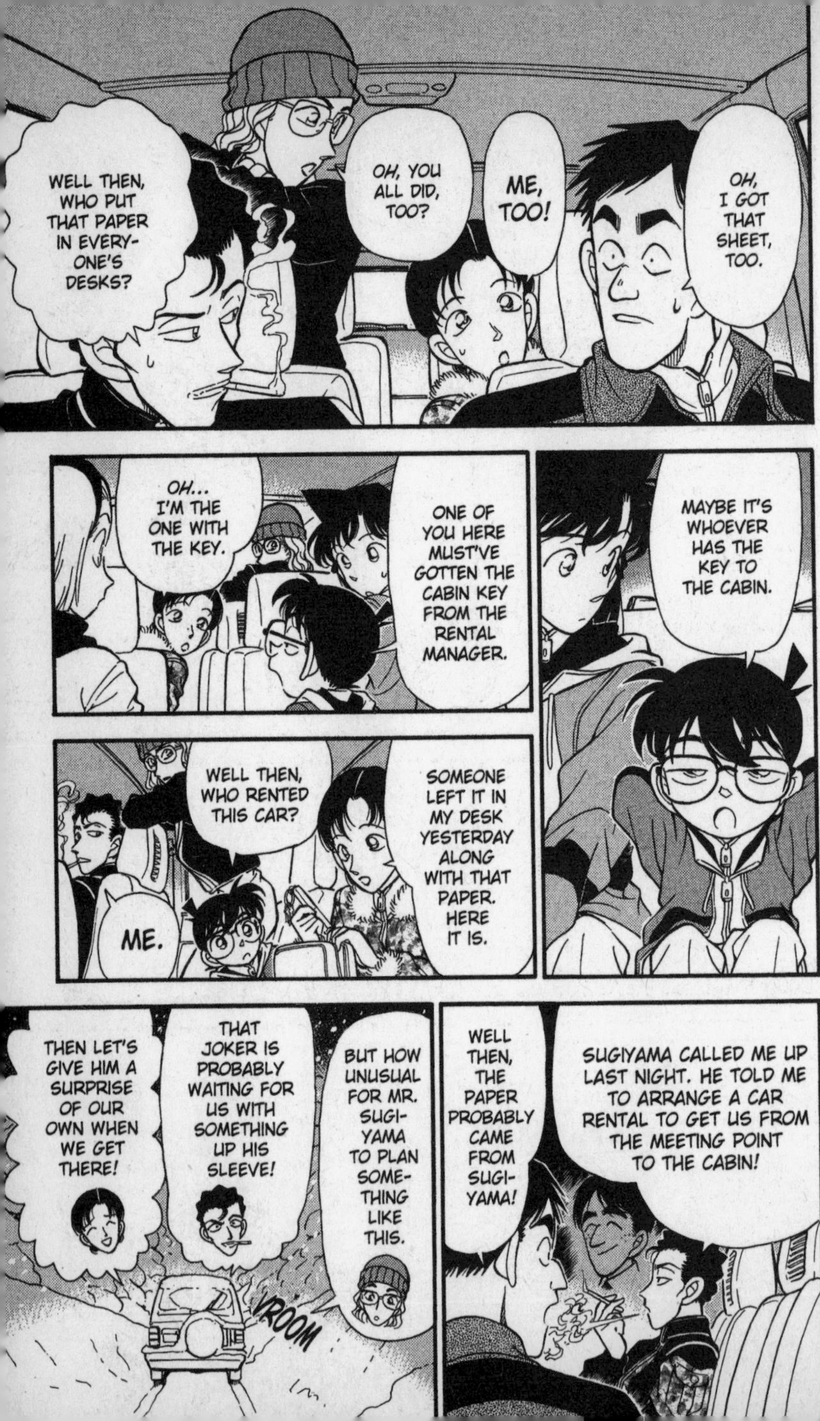
OH, I GOT THAT SHEET, TOO.
ME, TOO!
OH, YOU ALL DID, TOO?
WELL THEN, WHO PUT THAT PAPER IN EVERY-ONE'S DESKS?
MAYBE IT'S WHOEVER HAS THE KEY TO THE CABIN.
ONE OF YOU HERE MUST'VE GOTTEN THE CABIN KEY FROM THE RENTAL MANAGER.
OH... I'M THE ONE WITH THE KEY.
SOMEONE LEFT IT IN MY DESK YESTERDAY ALONG WITH THAT PAPER. HERE IT IS.
WELL THEN, WHO RENTED THIS CAR?
ME.
SUGIYAMA CALLED ME UP LAST NIGHT. HE TOLD ME TO ARRANGE A CAR RENTAL TO GET US FROM THE MEETING POINT TO THE CABIN!
WELL THEN, THE PAPER PROBABLY CAME FROM SUGI-YAMA!
BUT HOW UNUSUAL FOR MR. SUGI-YAMA TO PLAN SOME-THING LIKE THIS.
THAT JOKER IS PROBABLY WAITING FOR US WITH SOMETHING UP HIS SLEEVE!
THEN LET'S GIVE HIM A SURPRISE OF OUR OWN WHEN WE GET THERE!
VROOM

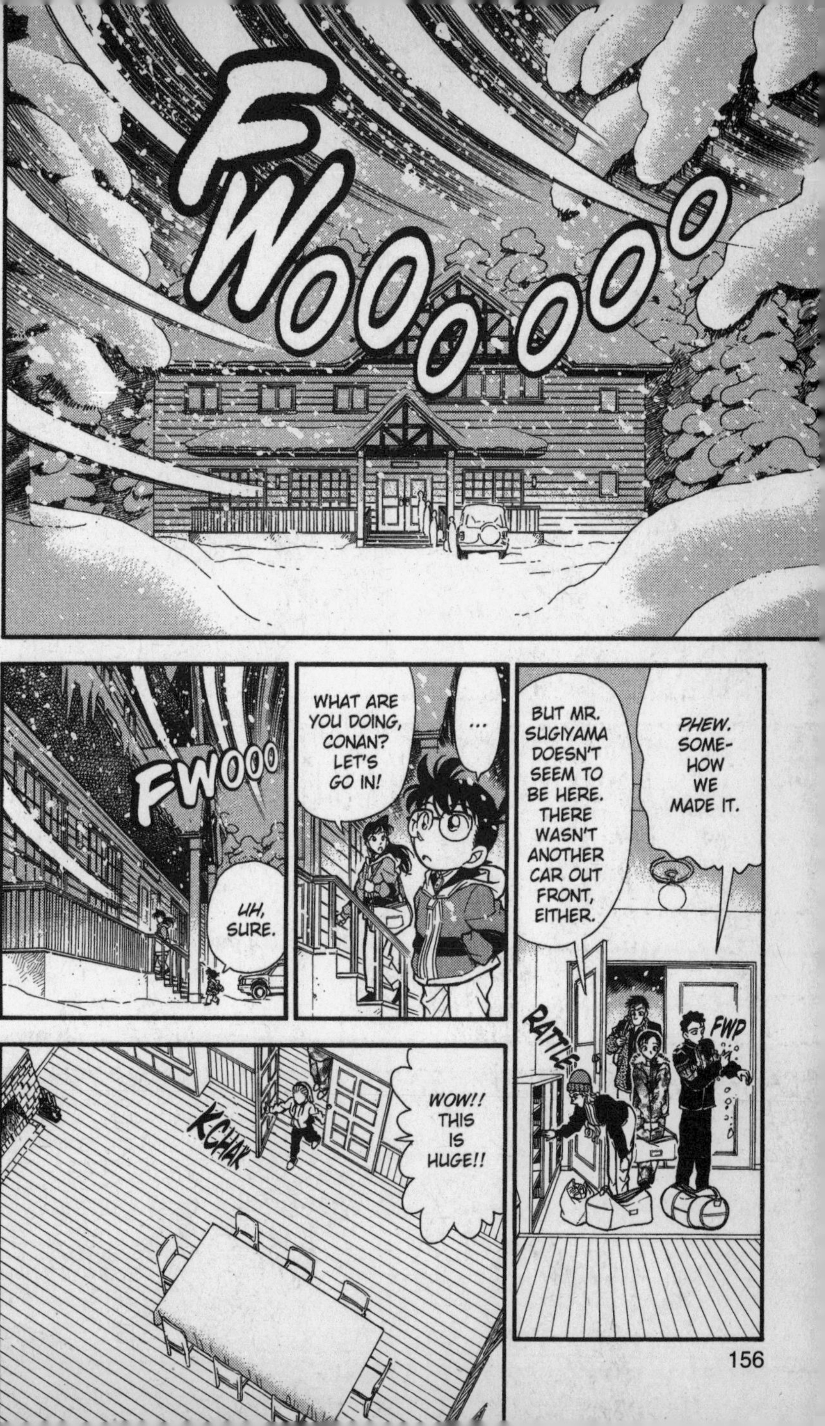
FWOOOOOOOO
PHEW. SOME-HOW WE MADE IT.
BUT MR. SUGIYAMA DOESN'T SEEM TO BE HERE. THERE WASN'T ANOTHER CAR OUT FRONT, EITHER.
RATTLE
FWP
...
WHAT ARE YOU DOING, CONAN? LET'S GO IN!
FWOOO
UH, SURE.
WOW!! THIS IS HUGE!!
K-CHAK

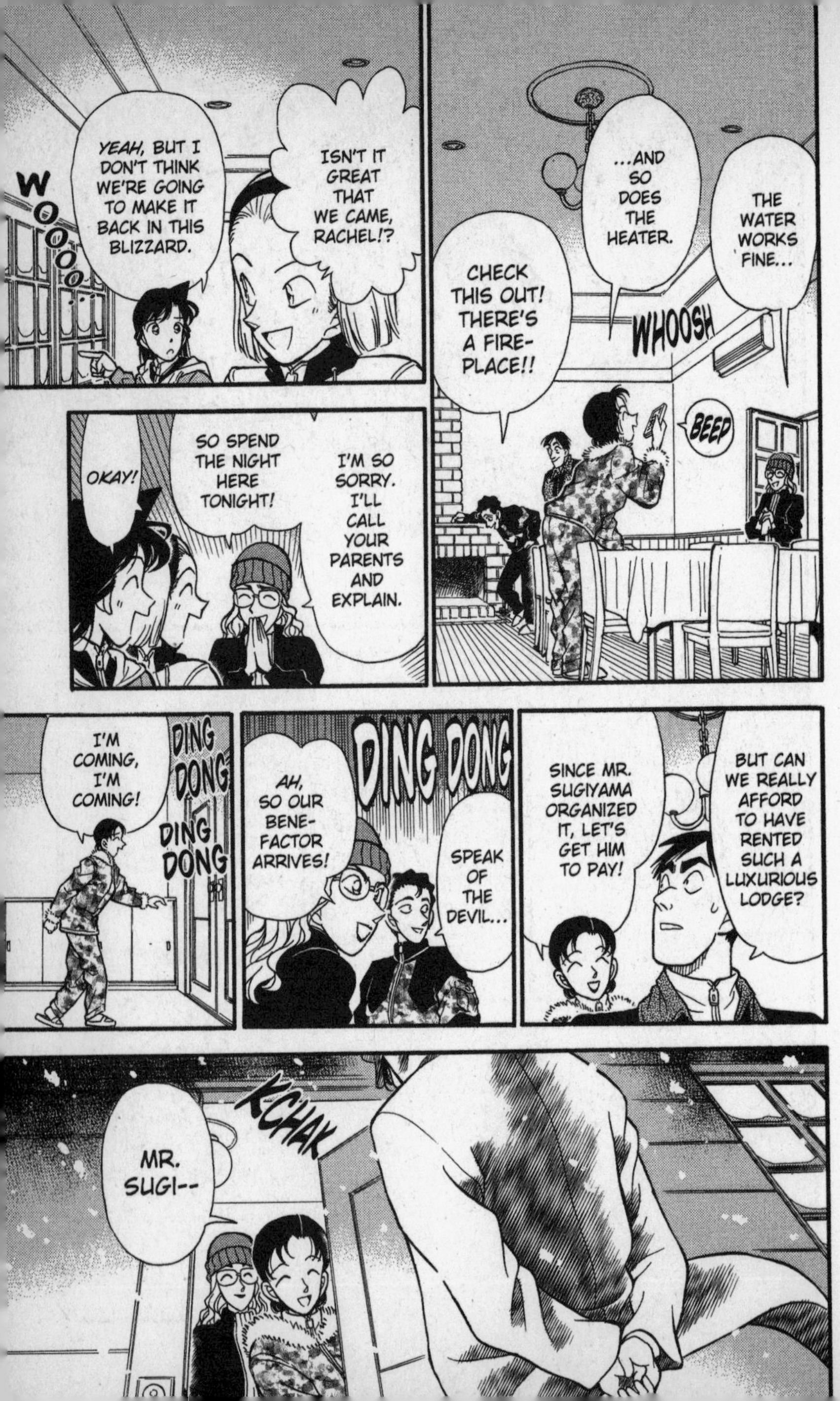
THE WATER WORKS FINE...
...AND SO DOES THE HEATER.
WHOOSH
CHECK THIS OUT! THERE'S A FIRE-PLACE!!
BEEP
ISN'T IT GREAT THAT WE CAME, RACHEL!?
YEAH, BUT I DON'T THINK WE'RE GOING TO MAKE IT BACK IN THIS BLIZZARD.
WOOOOO...
I'M SO SORRY. I'LL CALL YOUR PARENTS AND EXPLAIN.
SO SPEND THE NIGHT HERE TONIGHT!
OKAY!
BUT CAN WE REALLY AFFORD TO HAVE RENTED SUCH A LUXURIOUS LODGE?
SINCE MR. SUGIYAMA ORGANIZED IT, LET'S GET HIM TO PAY!
DING DONG
SPEAK OF THE DEVIL...
AH, SO OUR BENE-FACTOR ARRIVES!
DING DONG
DING DONG
I'M COMING, I'M COMING!
KCHAK
MR. SUGI--

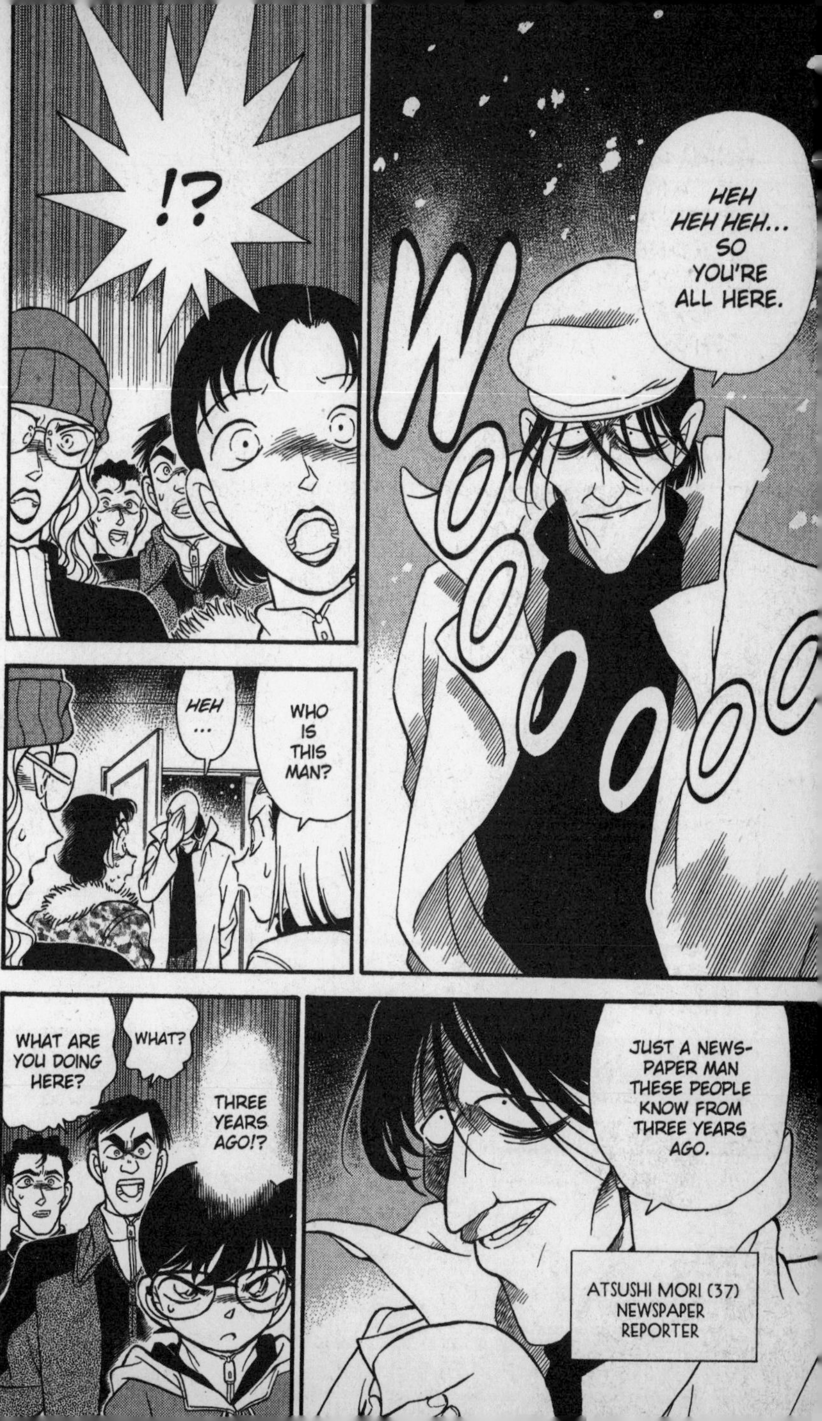
HEH HEH HEH... SO YOU'RE ALL HERE.
WOOOOOOO
!?
WHO IS THIS MAN?
HEH ...
JUST A NEWS-PAPER MAN THESE PEOPLE KNOW FROM THREE YEARS AGO.
ATSUSHI MORI (37) NEWSPAPER REPORTER
WHAT?
WHAT ARE YOU DOING HERE?
THREE YEARS AGO!?

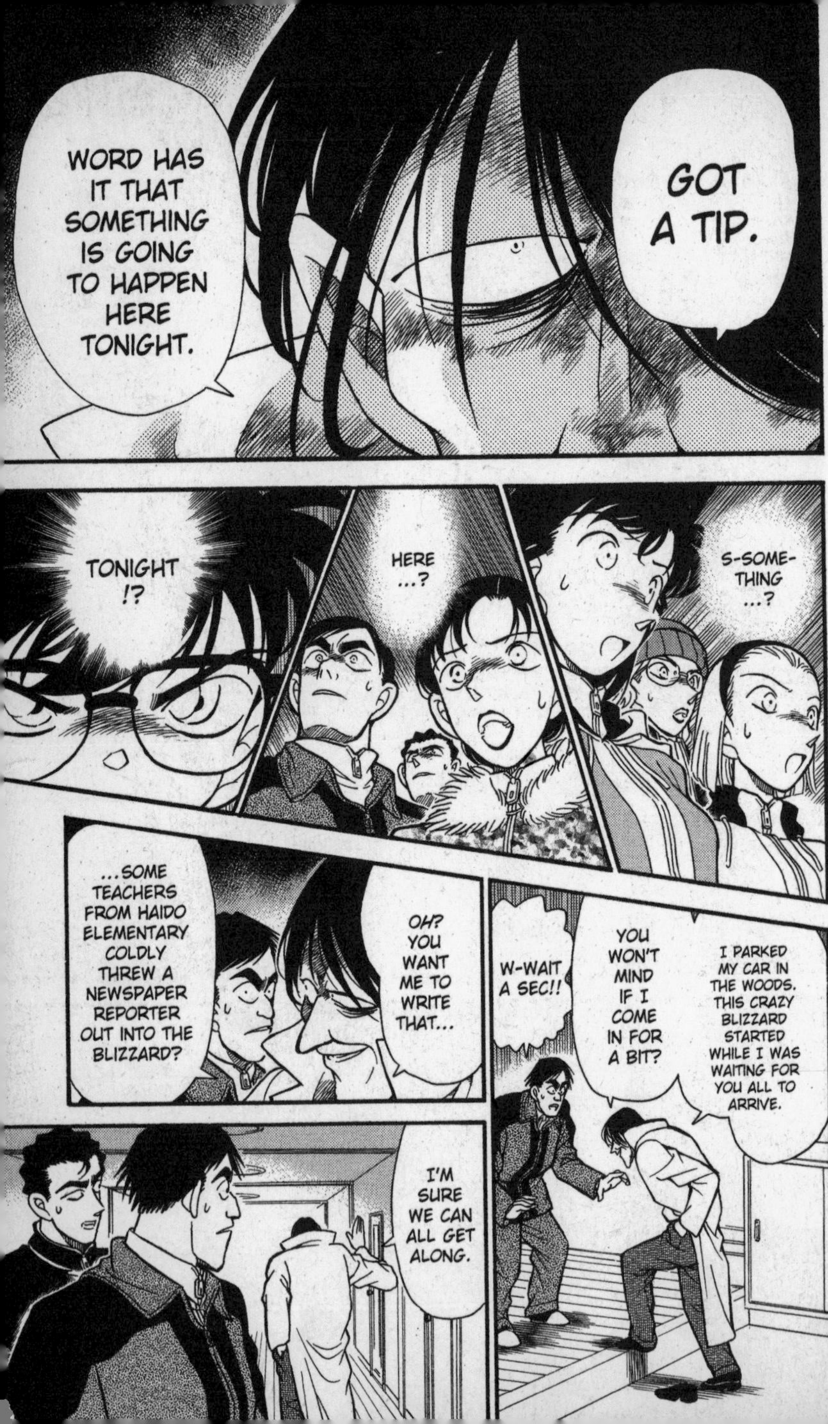
GOT A TIP.
WORD HAS IT THAT SOMETHING IS GOING TO HAPPEN HERE TONIGHT.
S-SOME-THING ...?
HERE ...?
TONIGHT !?
I PARKED MY CAR IN THE WOODS. THIS CRAZY BLIZZARD STARTED WHILE I WAS WAITING FOR YOU ALL TO ARRIVE.
YOU WON'T MIND IF I COME IN FOR A BIT?
W-WAIT A SEC!!
OH? YOU WANT ME TO WRITE THAT...
...SOME TEACHERS FROM HAIDO ELEMENTARY COLDLY THREW A NEWSPAPER REPORTER OUT INTO THE BLIZZARD?
I'M SURE WE CAN ALL GET ALONG.

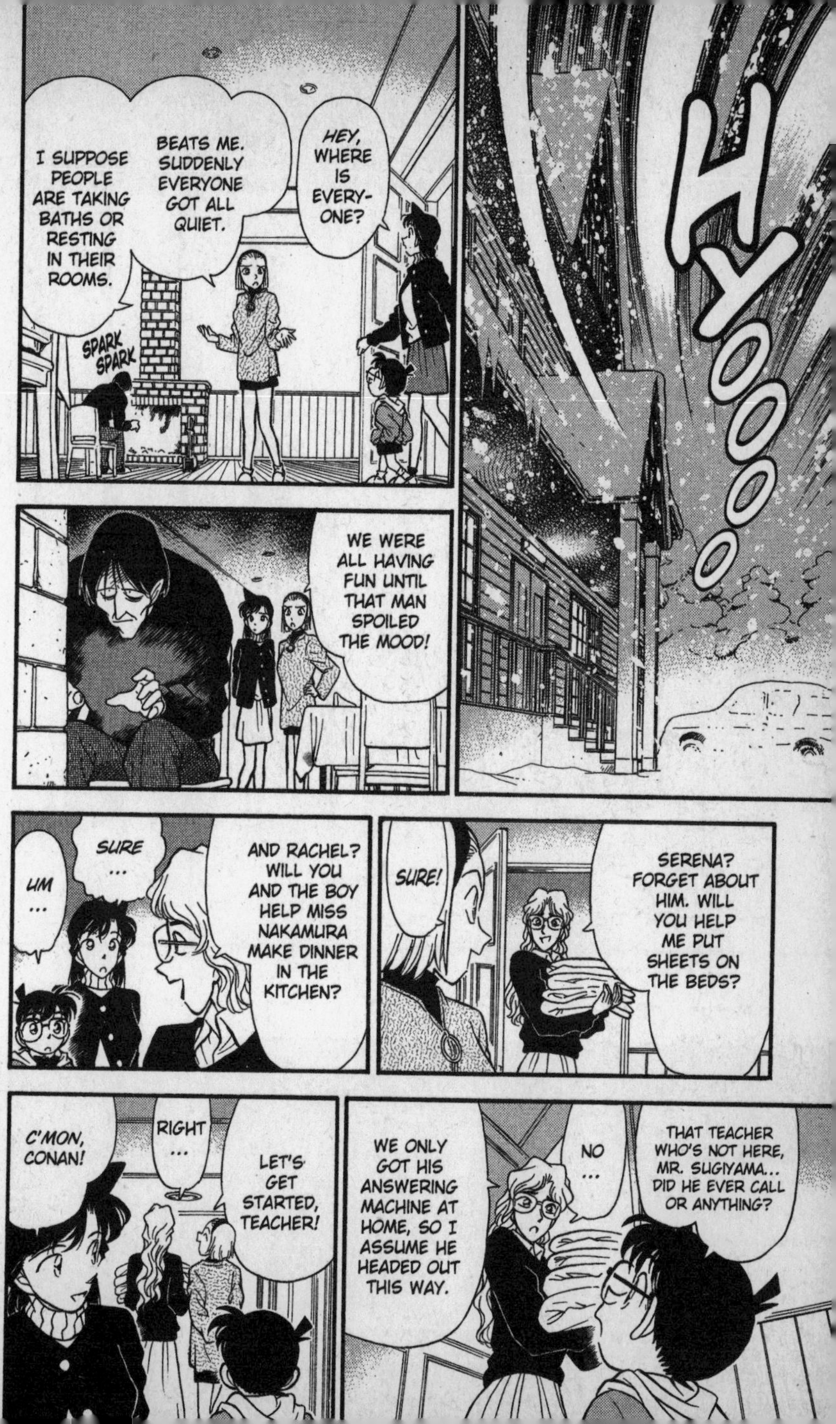
HYOOOOO
HEY, WHERE IS EVERYONE?
BEATS ME. SUDDENLY EVERYONE GOT ALL QUIET.
I SUPPOSE PEOPLE ARE TAKING BATHS OR RESTING IN THEIR ROOMS.
SPARK SPARK
WE WERE ALL HAVING FUN UNTIL THAT MAN SPOILED THE MOOD!
SERENA? FORGET ABOUT HIM. WILL YOU HELP ME PUT SHEETS ON THE BEDS?
SURE!
AND RACHEL? WILL YOU AND THE BOY HELP MISS NAKAMURA MAKE DINNER IN THE KITCHEN?
SURE ...
UM ...
THAT TEACHER WHO'S NOT HERE, MR. SUGIYAMA... DID HE EVER CALL OR ANYTHING?
NO ...
WE ONLY GOT HIS ANSWERING MACHINE AT HOME, SO I ASSUME HE HEADED OUT THIS WAY.
LET'S GET STARTED, TEACHER!
RIGHT ...
C'MON, CONAN!

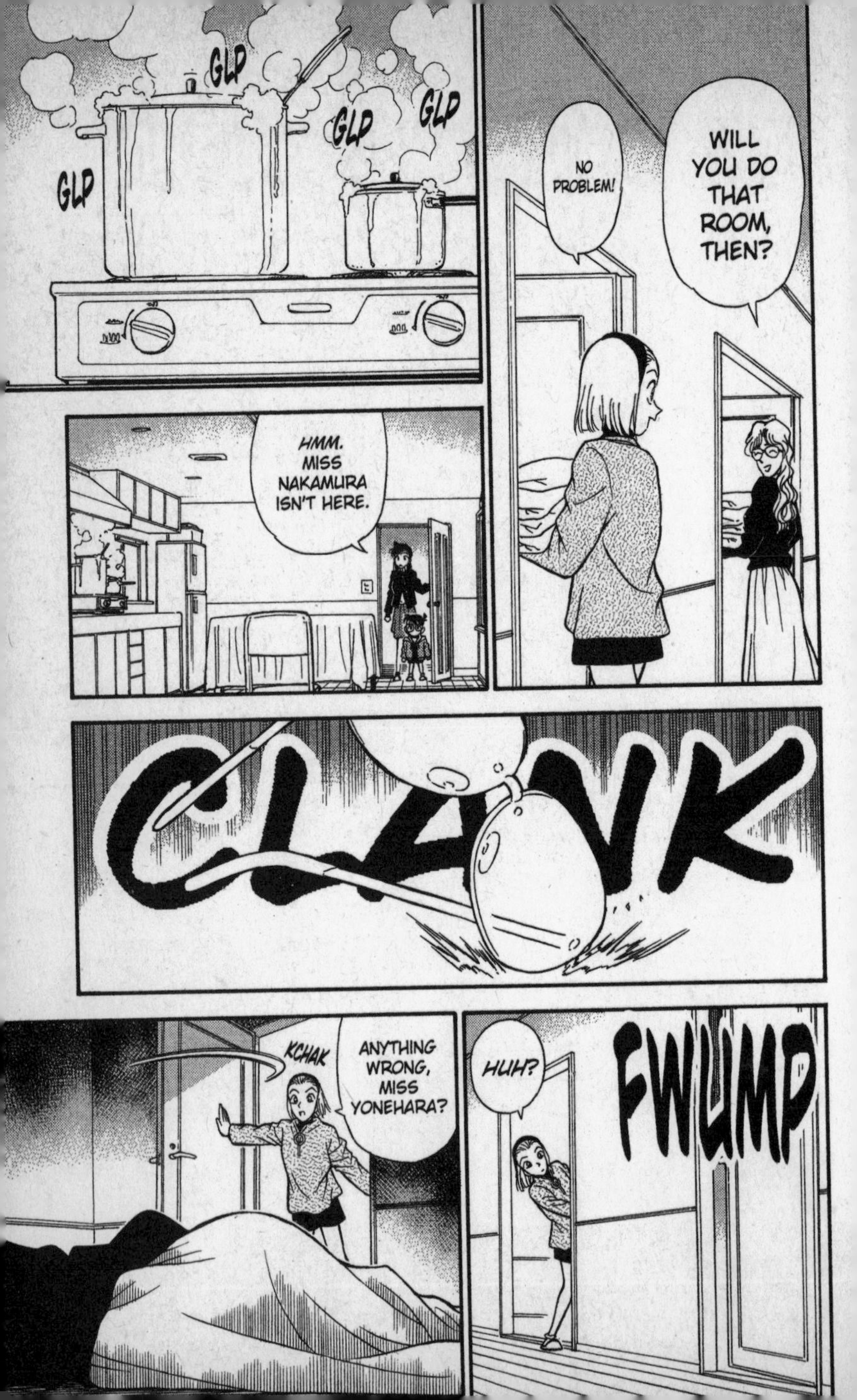
WILL YOU DO THAT ROOM, THEN?
NO PROBLEM!
GLP
GLP
GLP
GLP
HMM. MISS NAKAMURA ISN'T HERE.
CLANK
FWUMP
HUH?
KCHAK
ANYTHING WRONG, MISS YONEHARA?

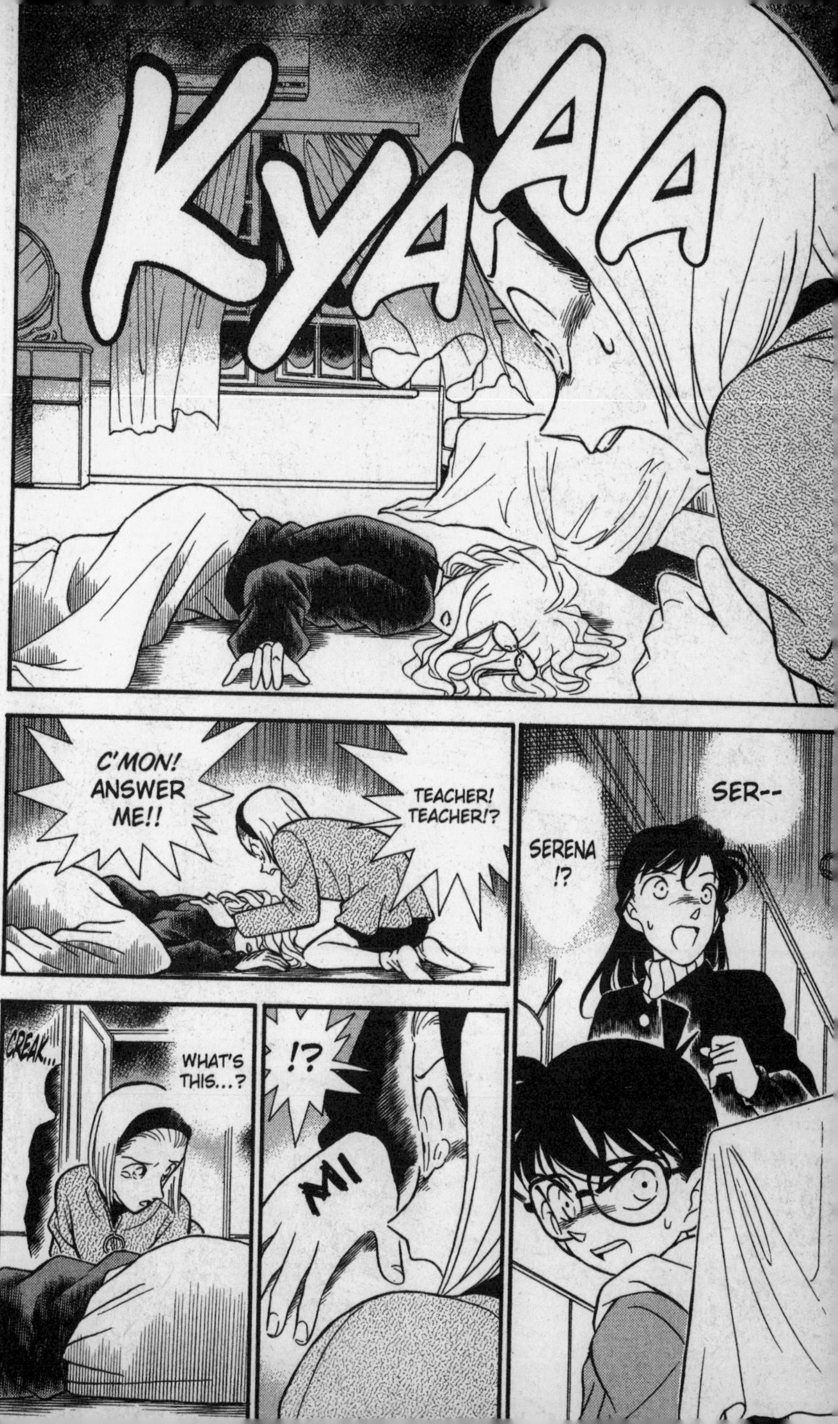
KYAAA
SER--
SERENA !?
TEACHER! TEACHER!?
C'MON! ANSWER ME!!
!?
MI
CREAK...
WHAT'S THIS...?

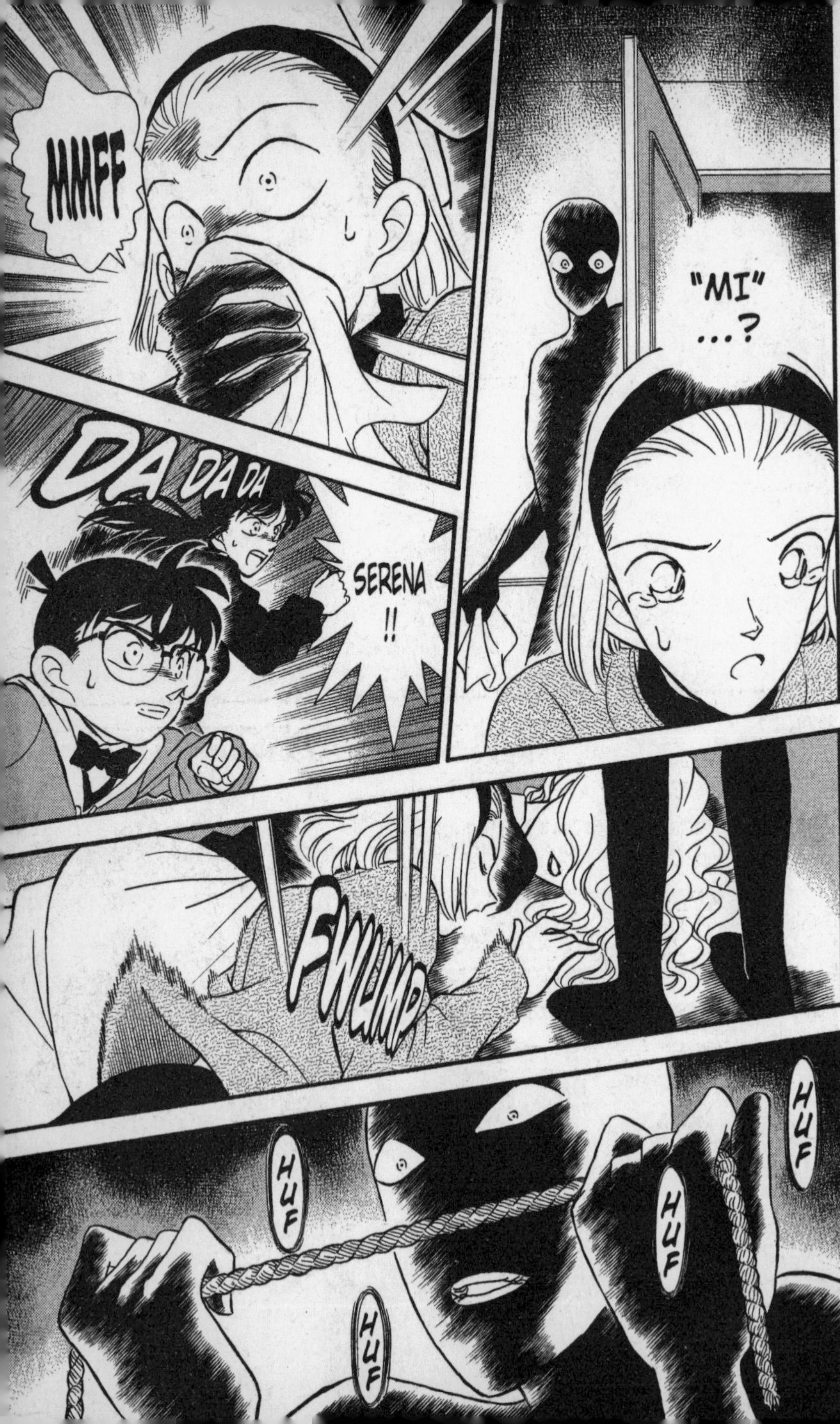
"MI"
...?
MMFF
DA DA DA
SERENA
!!
FWUMP
HUF
HUF HUF
HUF
HUF

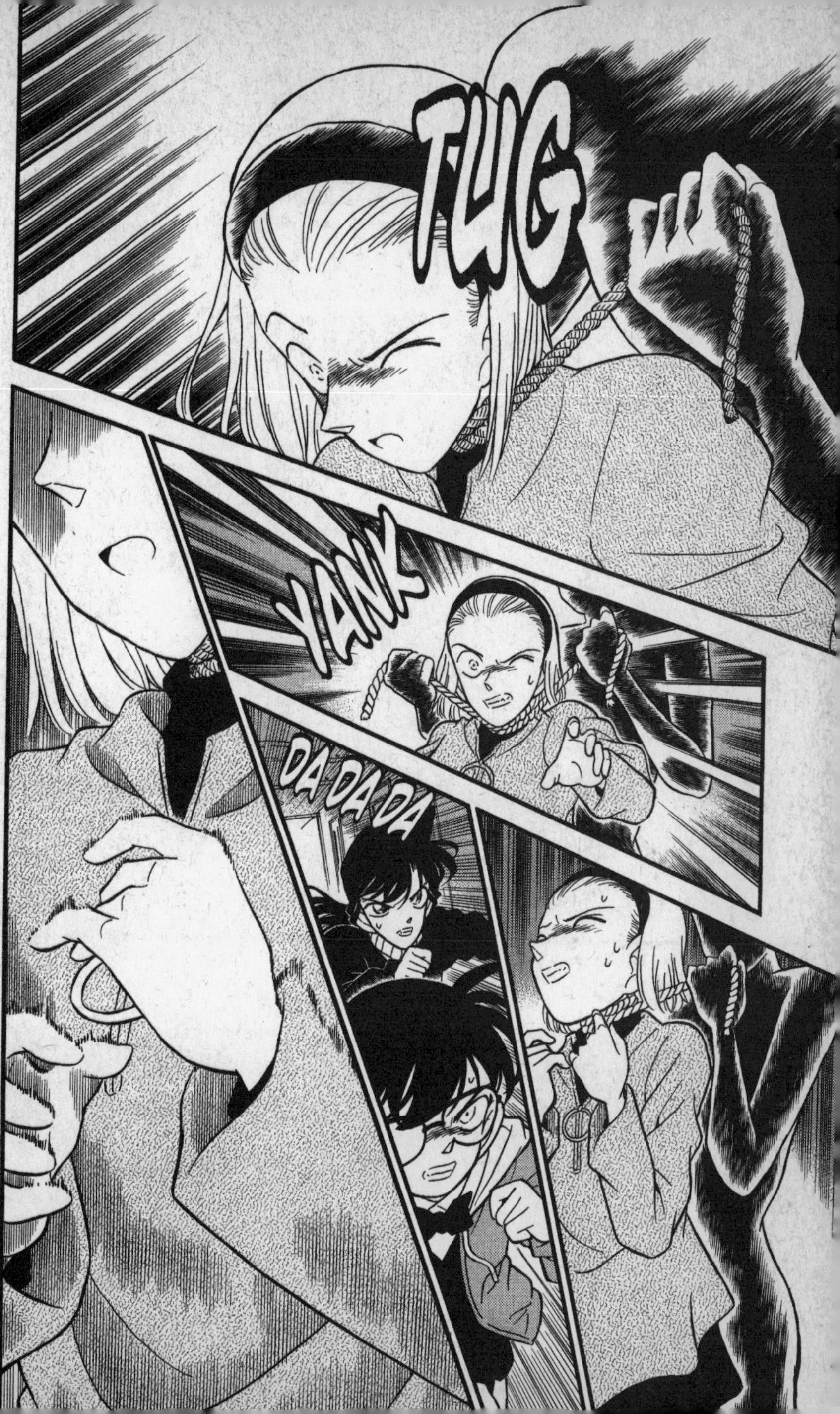
TUG
YANK
DA DA DA

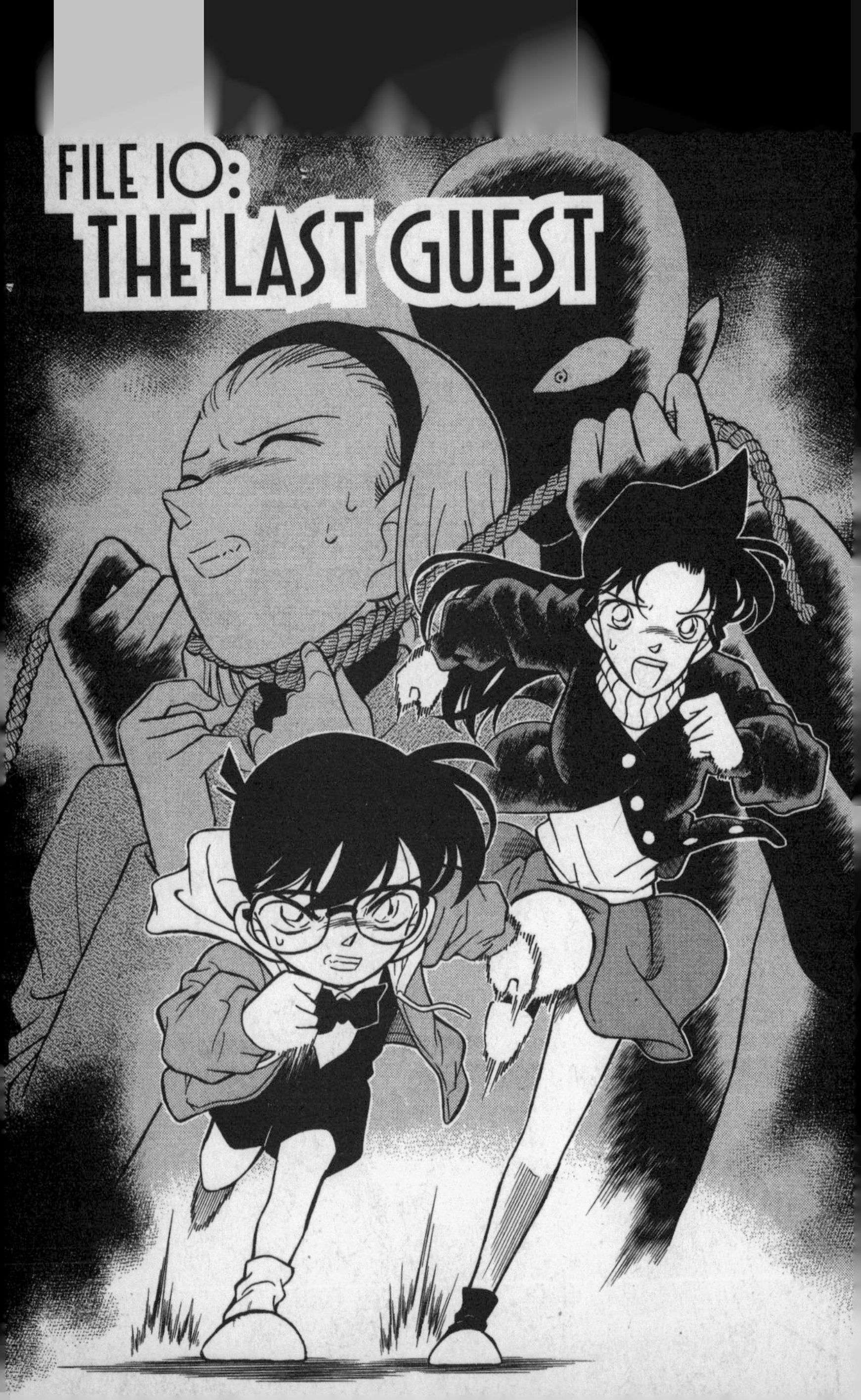
FILE 10:
THE LAST GUEST

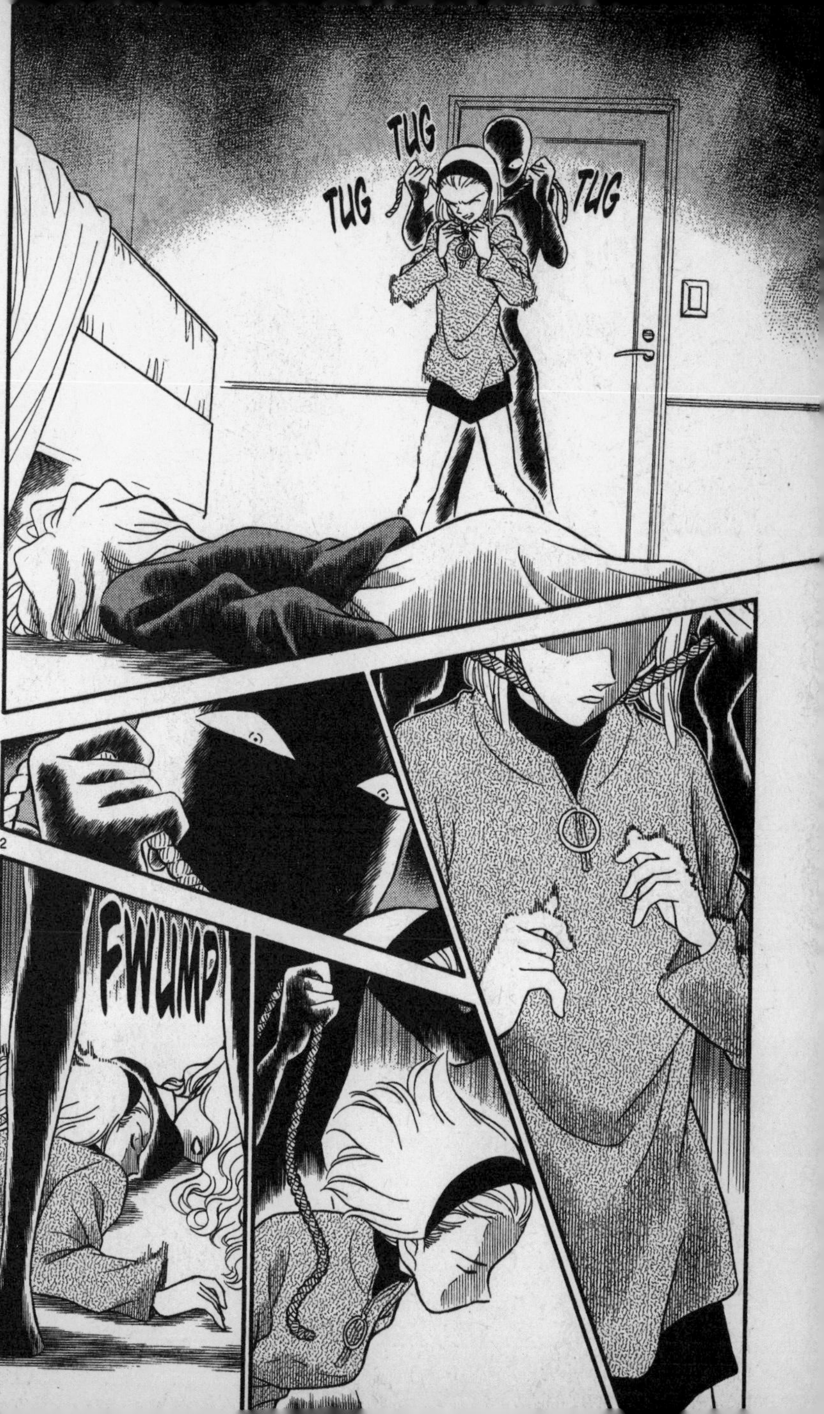
TUG
TUG
TUG
FWLUMP
2

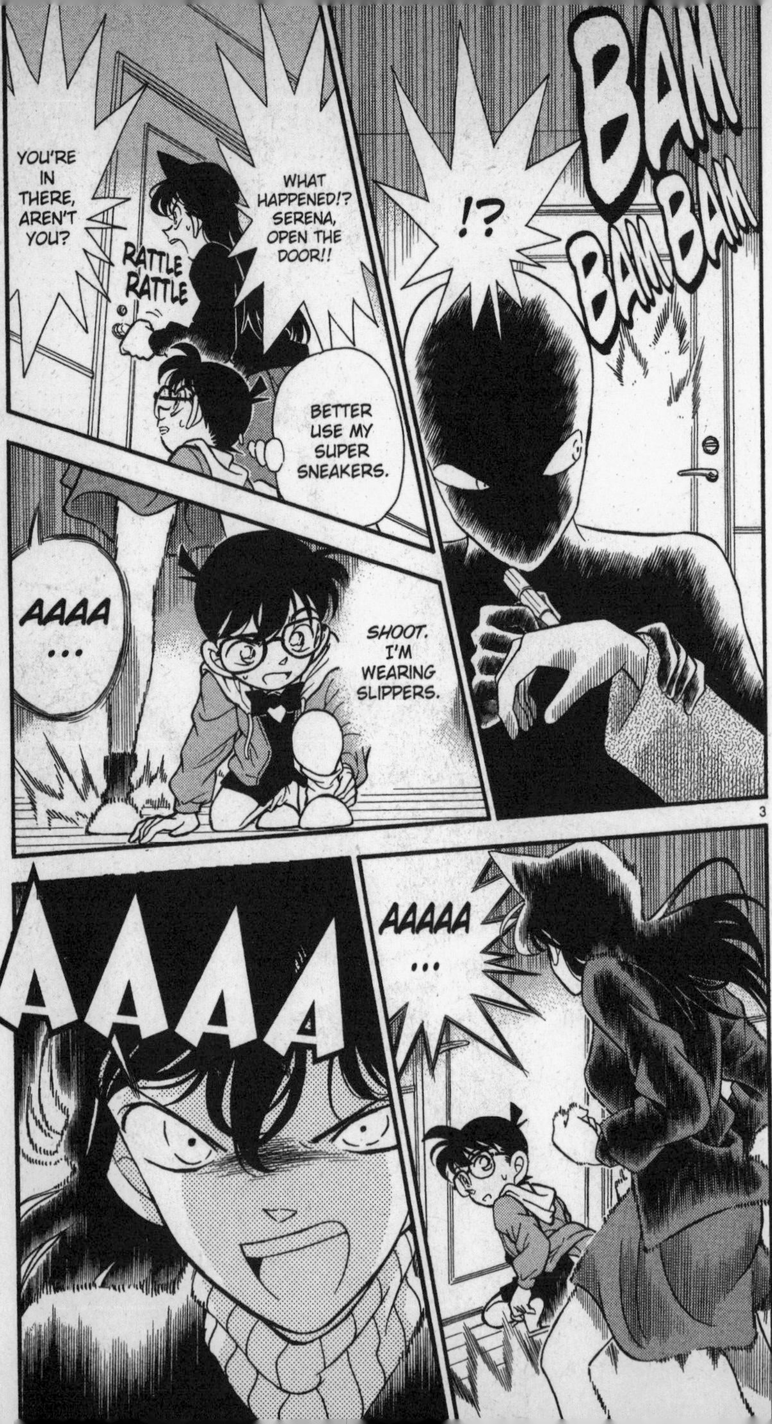
BAM BAM BAM
!?
WHAT HAPPENED!? SERENA, OPEN THE DOOR!!
RATTLE RATTLE
YOU'RE IN THERE, AREN'T YOU?
BETTER USE MY SUPER SNEAKERS.
SHOOT. I'M WEARING SLIPPERS.
AAAA ...
AAAAA ...
AAAA

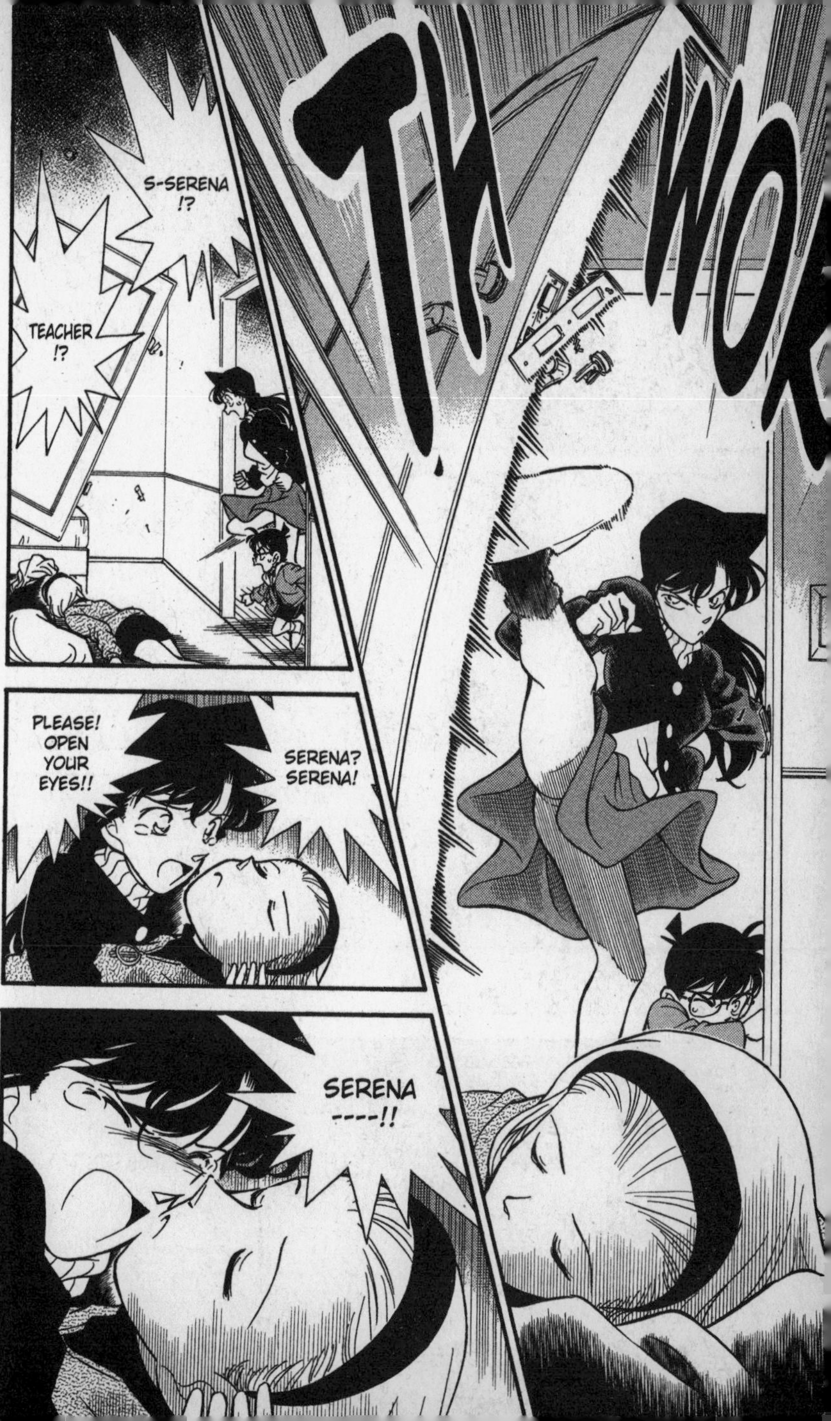
THWOK
S-SERENA !?
TEACHER !?
SERENA? SERENA!
PLEASE! OPEN YOUR EYES!!
SERENA ----!!

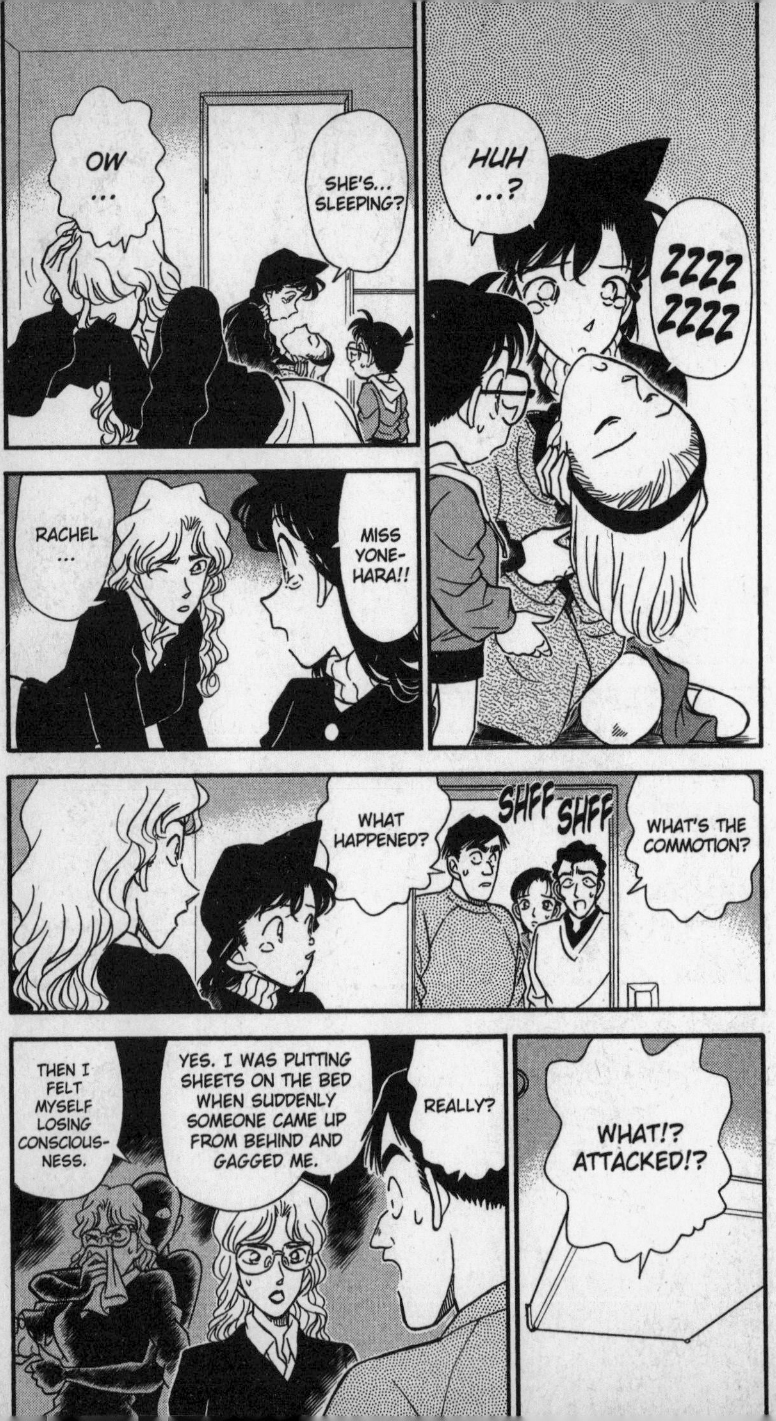
HUH ...?
ZZZZ ZZZZ
SHE'S... SLEEPING?
OW ...
MISS YONE-HARA!!
RACHEL ...
WHAT'S THE COMMOTION?
SHFF SHFF
WHAT HAPPENED?
WHAT!? ATTACKED!?
REALLY?
YES. I WAS PUTTING SHEETS ON THE BED WHEN SUDDENLY SOMEONE CAME UP FROM BEHIND AND GAGGED ME.
THEN I FELT MYSELF LOSING CONSCIOUS-NESS.

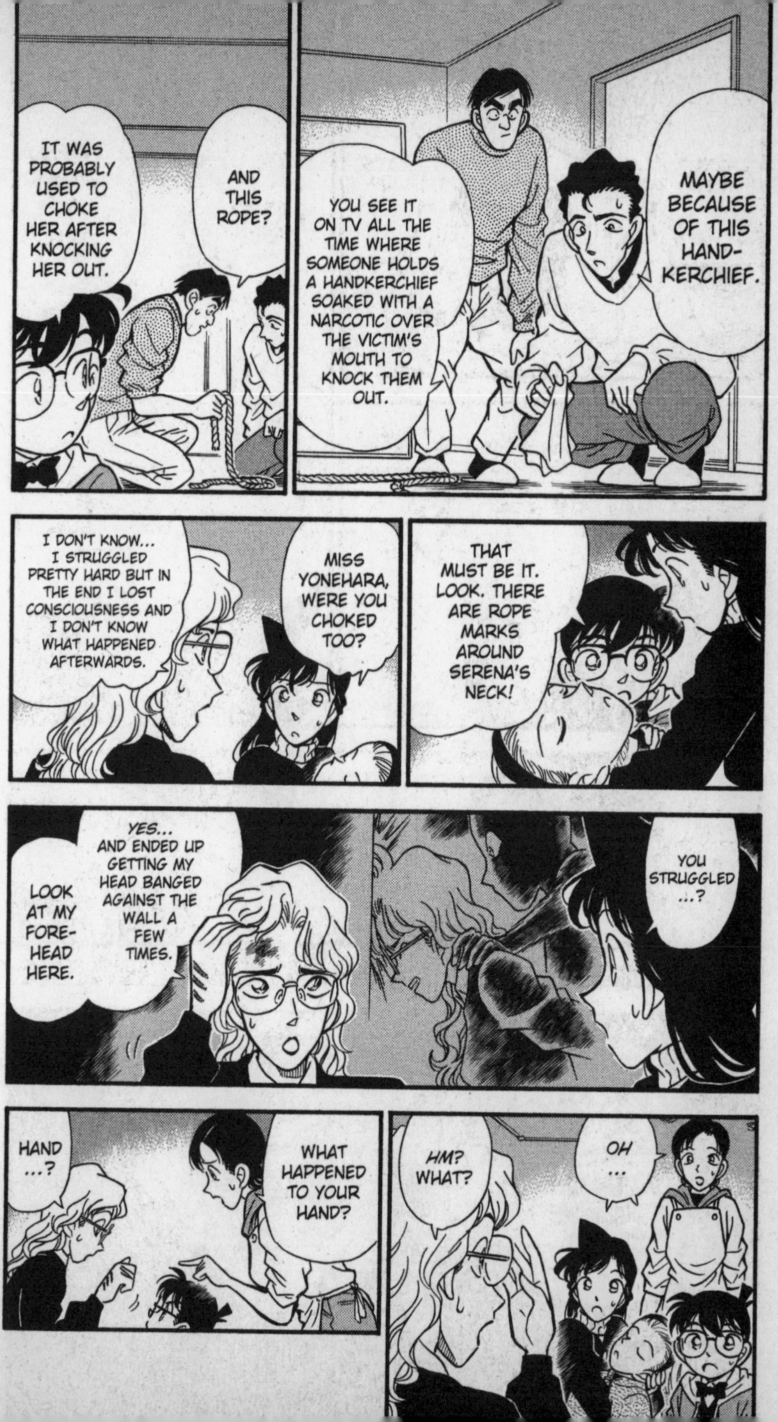
MAYBE BECAUSE OF THIS HAND-KERCHIEF.
YOU SEE IT ON TV ALL THE TIME WHERE SOMEONE HOLDS A HANDKERCHIEF SOAKED WITH A NARCOTIC OVER THE VICTIM'S MOUTH TO KNOCK THEM OUT.
AND THIS ROPE?
IT WAS PROBABLY USED TO CHOKE HER AFTER KNOCKING HER OUT.
THAT MUST BE IT. LOOK. THERE ARE ROPE MARKS AROUND SERENA'S NECK!
MISS YONEHARA, WERE YOU CHOKED TOO?
I DON'T KNOW... I STRUGGLED PRETTY HARD BUT IN THE END I LOST CONSCIOUSNESS AND I DON'T KNOW WHAT HAPPENED AFTERWARDS.
YOU STRUGGLED ...?
YES... AND ENDED UP GETTING MY HEAD BANGED AGAINST THE WALL A FEW TIMES.
LOOK AT MY FORE-HEAD HERE.
OH ...
HM? WHAT?
WHAT HAPPENED TO YOUR HAND?
HAND ...?

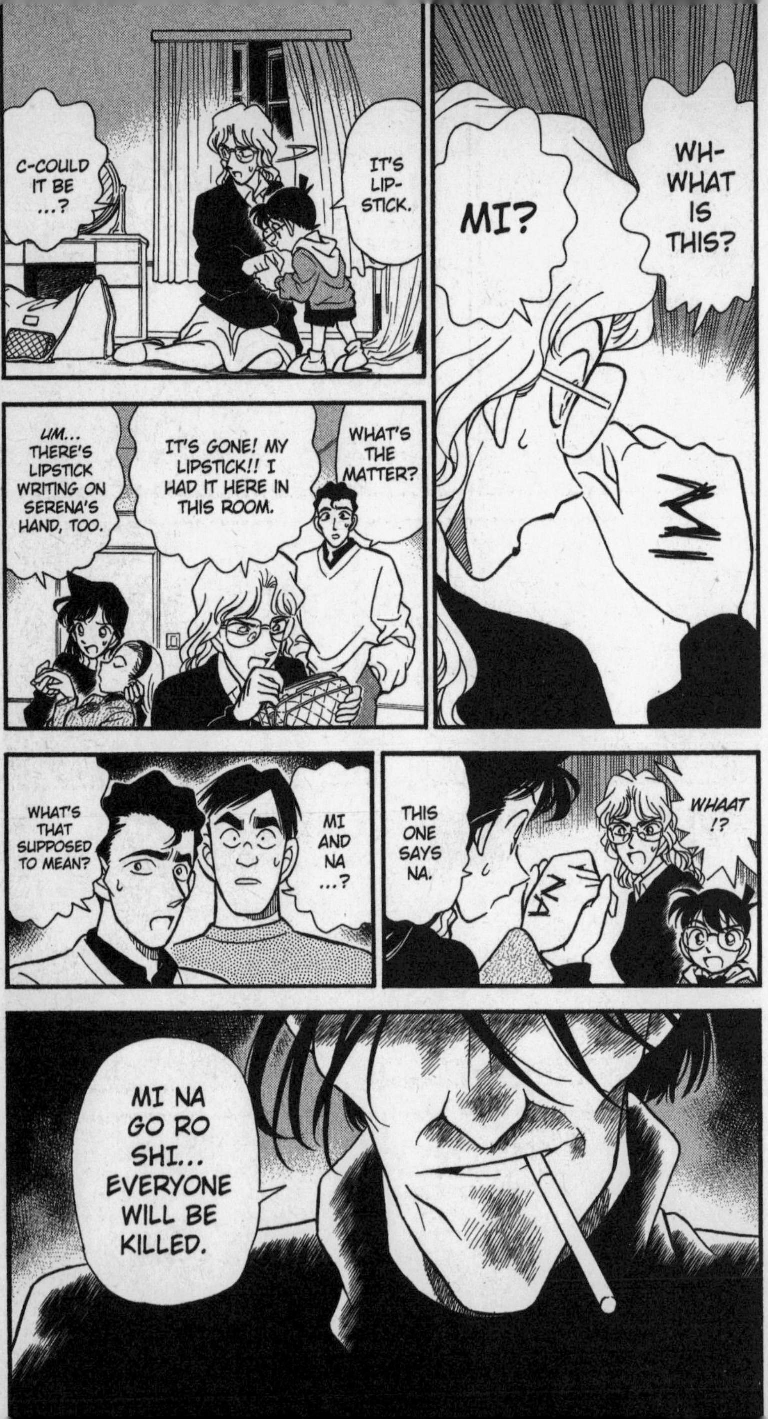
WH-WHAT IS THIS?
MI?
IT'S LIP-STICK.
C-COULD IT BE ...?
WHAT'S THE MATTER?
IT'S GONE! MY LIPSTICK!! I HAD IT HERE IN THIS ROOM.
UM... THERE'S LIPSTICK WRITING ON SERENA'S HAND, TOO.
WHAAT!?
THIS ONE SAYS NA.
MI AND NA ...?
WHAT'S THAT SUPPOSED TO MEAN?
MI NA GO RO SHI... EVERYONE WILL BE KILLED.

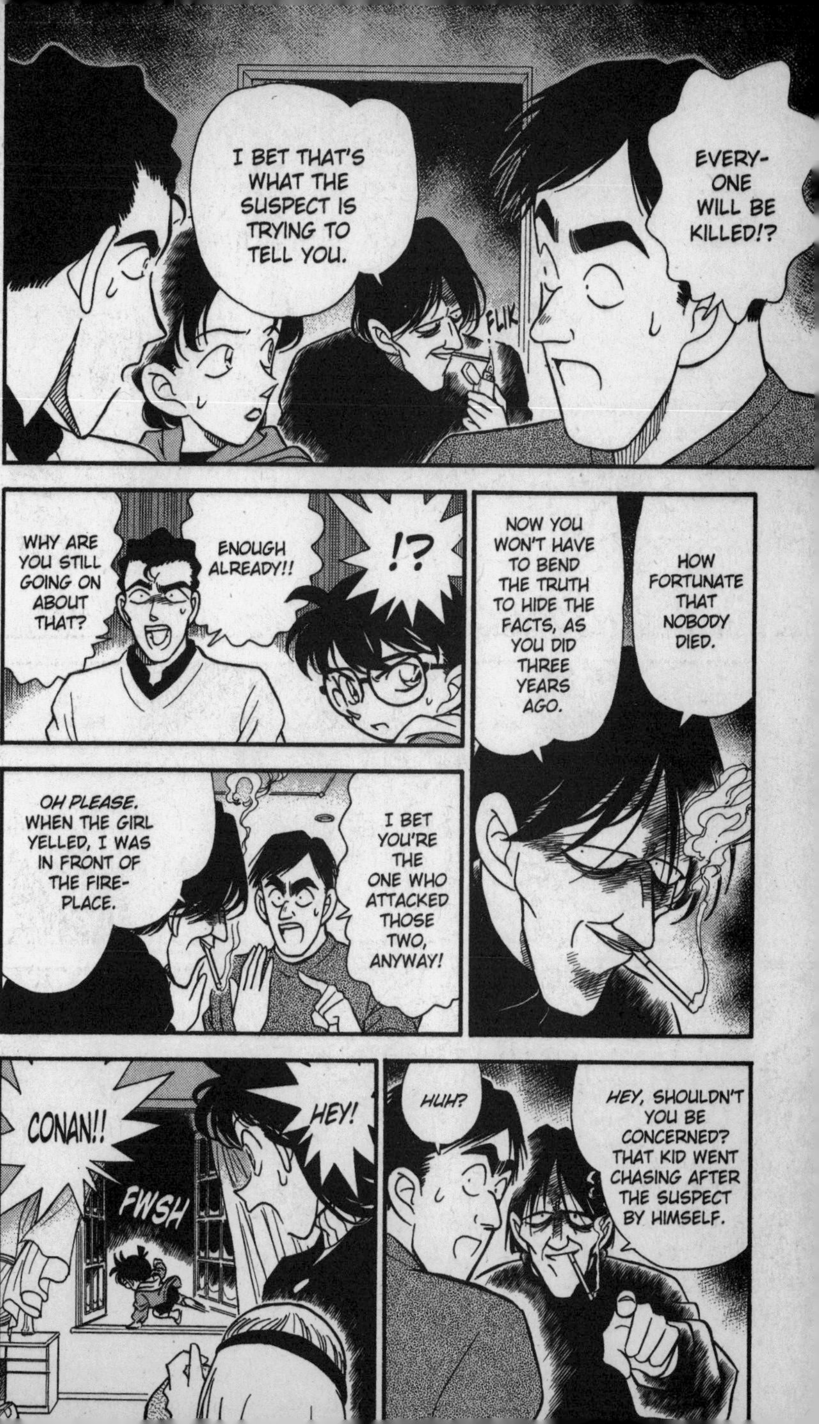
EVERY-ONE WILL BE KILLED!?
I BET THAT'S WHAT THE SUSPECT IS TRYING TO TELL YOU.
FLIK
HOW FORTUNATE THAT NOBODY DIED.
NOW YOU WON'T HAVE TO BEND THE TRUTH TO HIDE THE FACTS, AS YOU DID THREE YEARS AGO.
!?
ENOUGH ALREADY!!
WHY ARE YOU STILL GOING ON ABOUT THAT?
I BET YOU'RE THE ONE WHO ATTACKED THOSE TWO, ANYWAY!
OH PLEASE. WHEN THE GIRL YELLED, I WAS IN FRONT OF THE FIRE-PLACE.
HEY, SHOULDN'T YOU BE CONCERNED? THAT KID WENT CHASING AFTER THE SUSPECT BY HIMSELF.
HUH?
HEY!
CONAN!!
FWSH

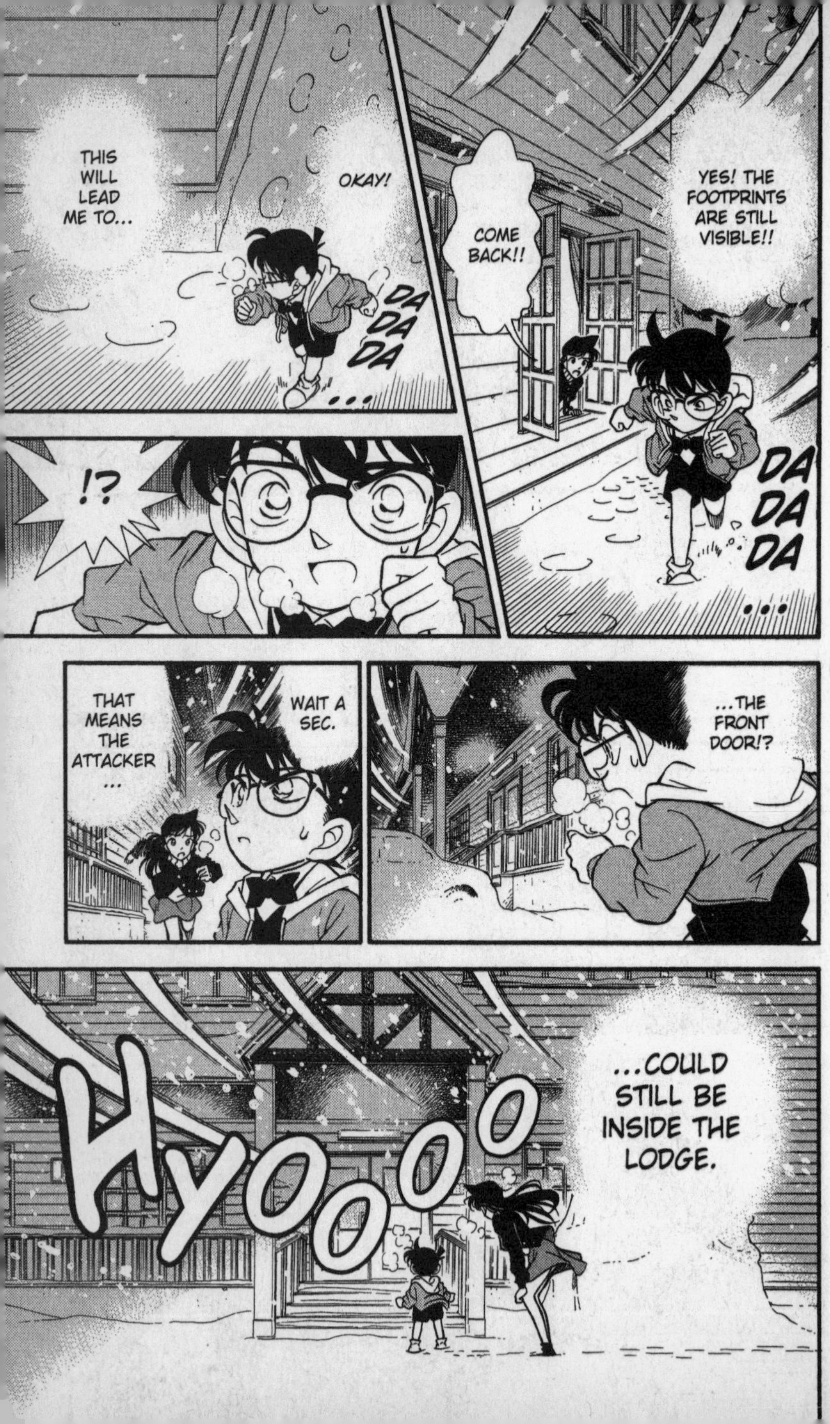
YES! THE FOOTPRINTS ARE STILL VISIBLE!!
COME BACK!!
DA DA DA ...
OKAY!
THIS WILL LEAD ME TO...
DA DA DA ...
!?
...THE FRONT DOOR!?
WAIT A SEC.
THAT MEANS THE ATTACKER ...
...COULD STILL BE INSIDE THE LODGE.
HYOOOO

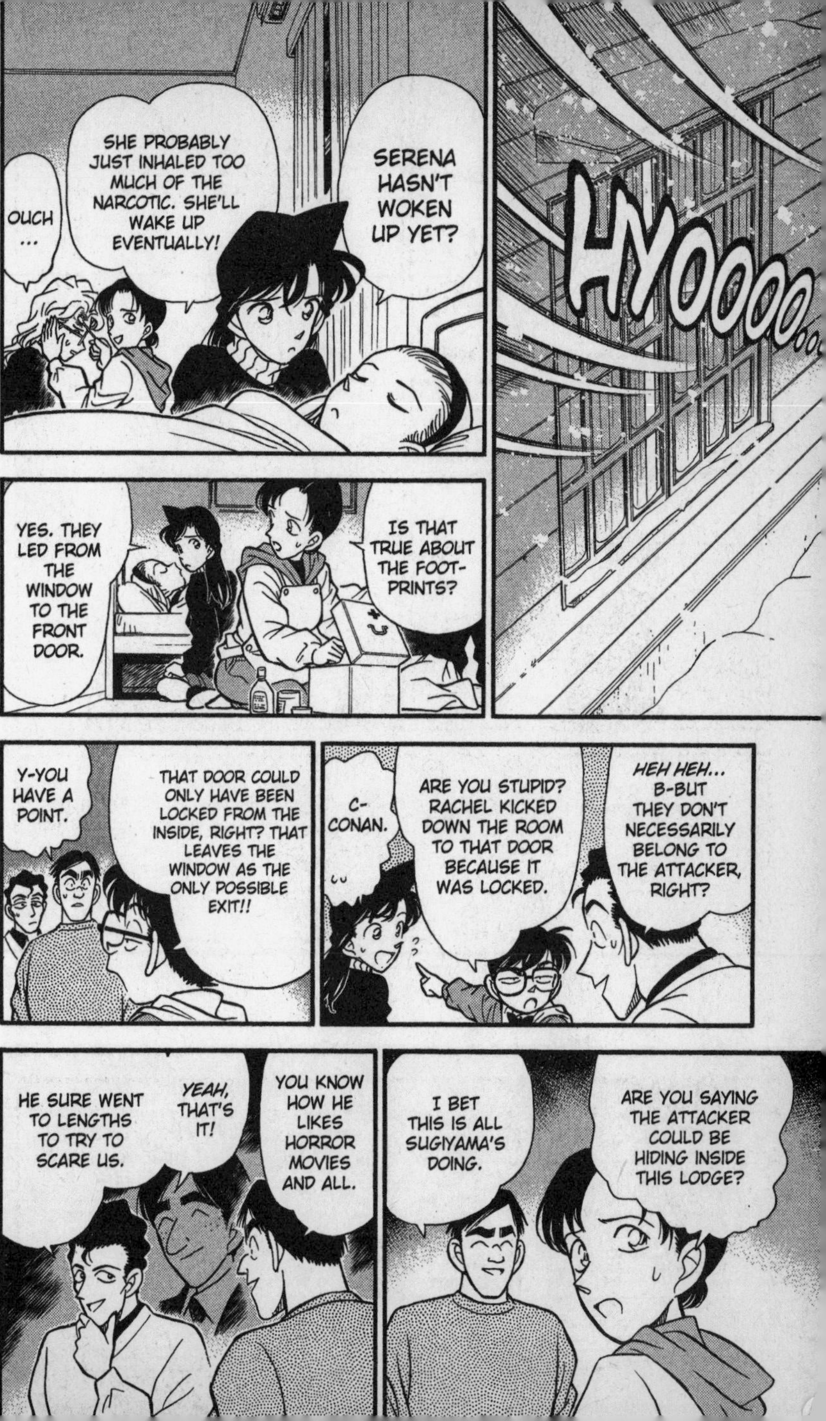
HYOOOO...
SERENA HASN'T WOKEN UP YET?
SHE PROBABLY JUST INHALED TOO MUCH OF THE NARCOTIC. SHE'LL WAKE UP EVENTUALLY!
OUCH ...
IS THAT TRUE ABOUT THE FOOT-PRINTS?
YES. THEY LED FROM THE WINDOW TO THE FRONT DOOR.
HEH HEH... B-BUT THEY DON'T NECESSARILY BELONG TO THE ATTACKER, RIGHT?
ARE YOU STUPID? RACHEL KICKED DOWN THE ROOM TO THAT DOOR BECAUSE IT WAS LOCKED.
C-CONAN.
THAT DOOR COULD ONLY HAVE BEEN LOCKED FROM THE INSIDE, RIGHT? THAT LEAVES THE WINDOW AS THE ONLY POSSIBLE EXIT!!
Y-YOU HAVE A POINT.
ARE YOU SAYING THE ATTACKER COULD BE HIDING INSIDE THIS LODGE?
I BET THIS IS ALL SUGIYAMA'S DOING.
YOU KNOW HOW HE LIKES HORROR MOVIES AND ALL.
YEAH, THAT'S IT!
HE SURE WENT TO LENGTHS TO TRY TO SCARE US.

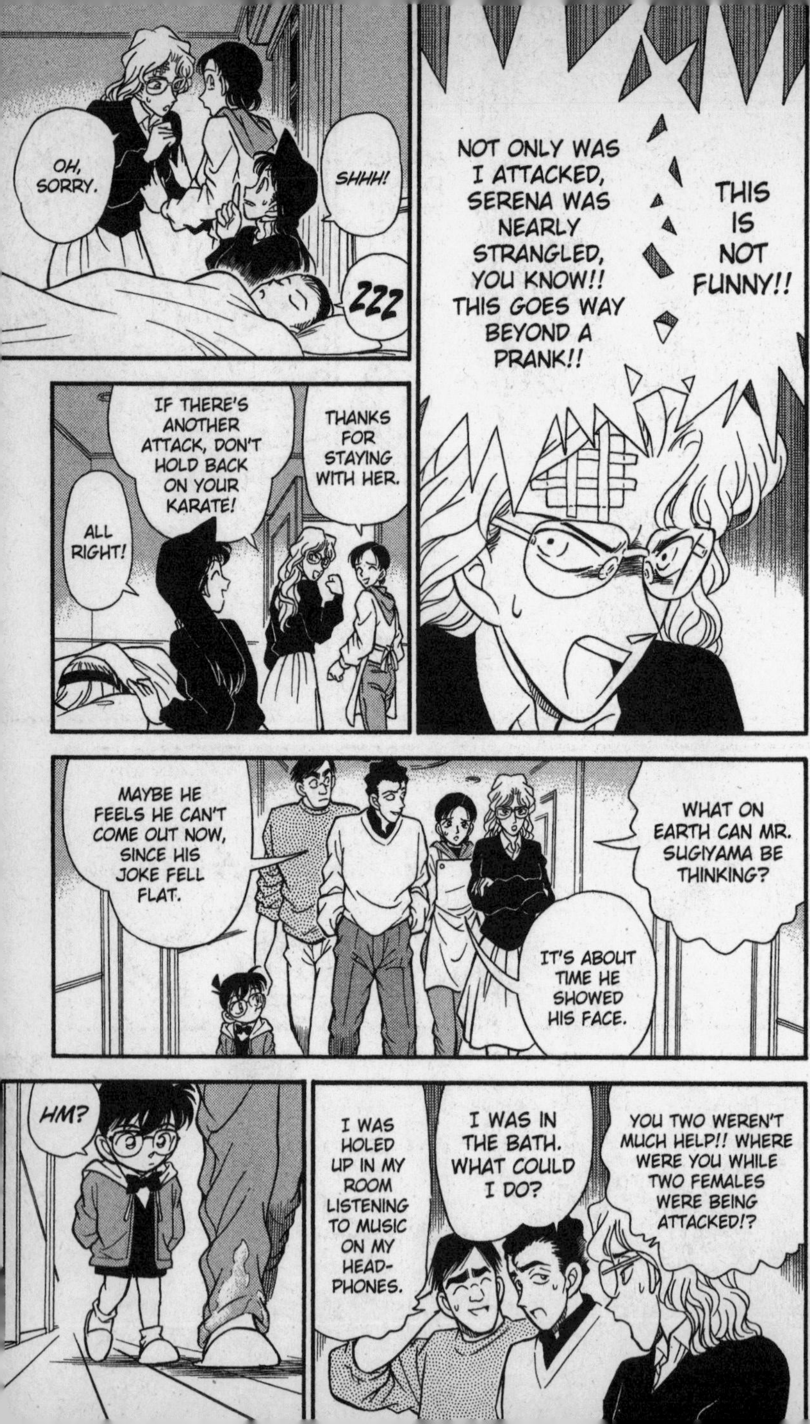
THIS IS NOT FUNNY!!
NOT ONLY WAS I ATTACKED, SERENA WAS NEARLY STRANGLED, YOU KNOW!! THIS GOES WAY BEYOND A PRANK!!
SHHH!
OH, SORRY.
ZZZ
THANKS FOR STAYING WITH HER.
IF THERE'S ANOTHER ATTACK, DON'T HOLD BACK ON YOUR KARATE!
ALL RIGHT!
WHAT ON EARTH CAN MR. SUGIYAMA BE THINKING?
IT'S ABOUT TIME HE SHOWED HIS FACE.
MAYBE HE FEELS HE CAN'T COME OUT NOW, SINCE HIS JOKE FELL FLAT.
YOU TWO WEREN'T MUCH HELP!! WHERE WERE YOU WHILE TWO FEMALES WERE BEING ATTACKED!?
I WAS IN THE BATH. WHAT COULD I DO?
I WAS HOLED UP IN MY ROOM LISTENING TO MUSIC ON MY HEAD-PHONES.
HM?

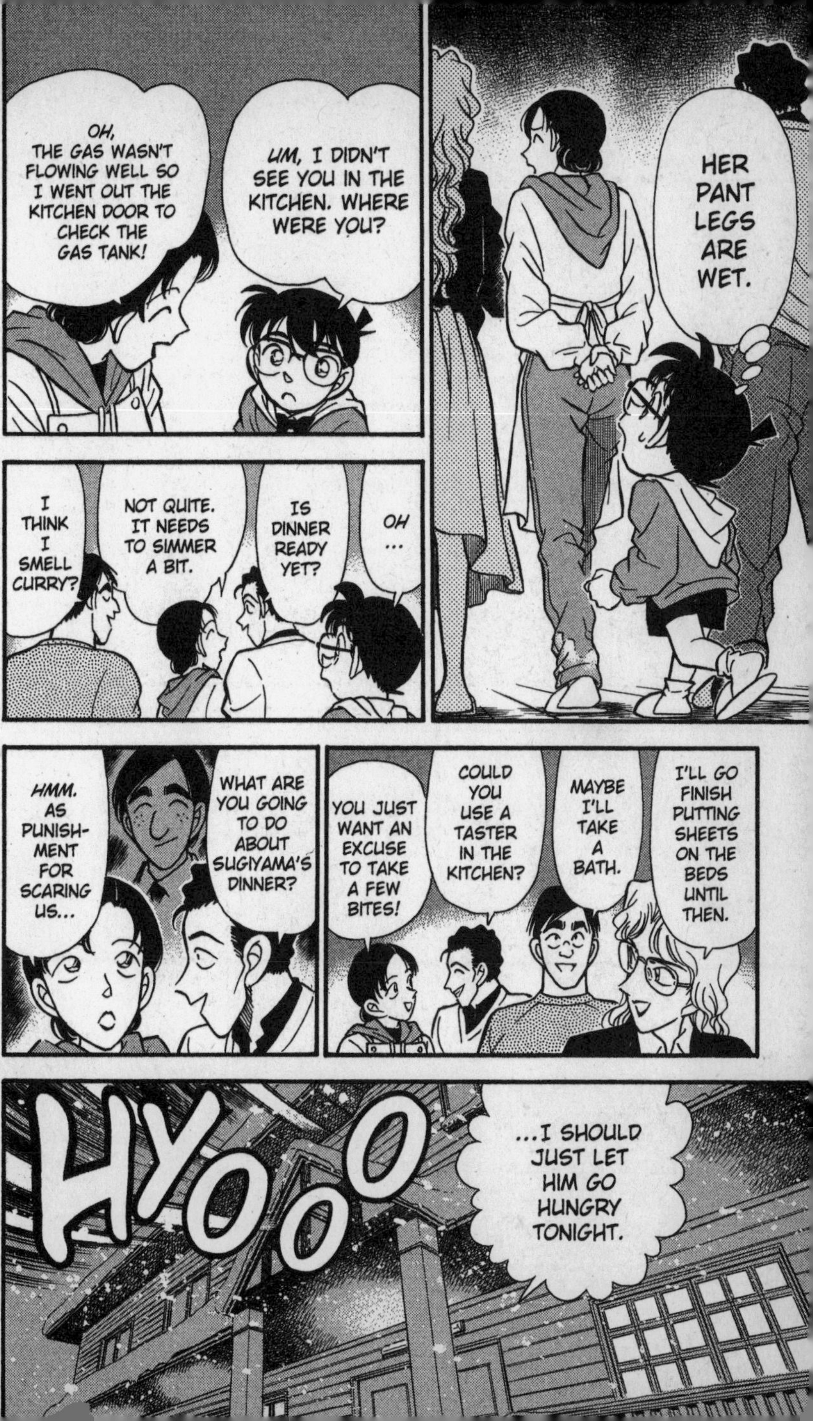
HER PANT LEGS ARE WET.
UM, I DIDN'T SEE YOU IN THE KITCHEN. WHERE WERE YOU?
OH, THE GAS WASN'T FLOWING WELL SO I WENT OUT THE KITCHEN DOOR TO CHECK THE GAS TANK!
OH ...
IS DINNER READY YET?
NOT QUITE. IT NEEDS TO SIMMER A BIT.
I THINK I SMELL CURRY?
I'LL GO FINISH PUTTING SHEETS ON THE BEDS UNTIL THEN.
MAYBE I'LL TAKE A BATH.
COULD YOU USE A TASTER IN THE KITCHEN?
YOU JUST WANT AN EXCUSE TO TAKE A FEW BITES!
WHAT ARE YOU GOING TO DO ABOUT SUGIYAMA'S DINNER?
HMM. AS PUNISH-MENT FOR SCARING US...
...I SHOULD JUST LET HIM GO HUNGRY TONIGHT.
HYOOOO

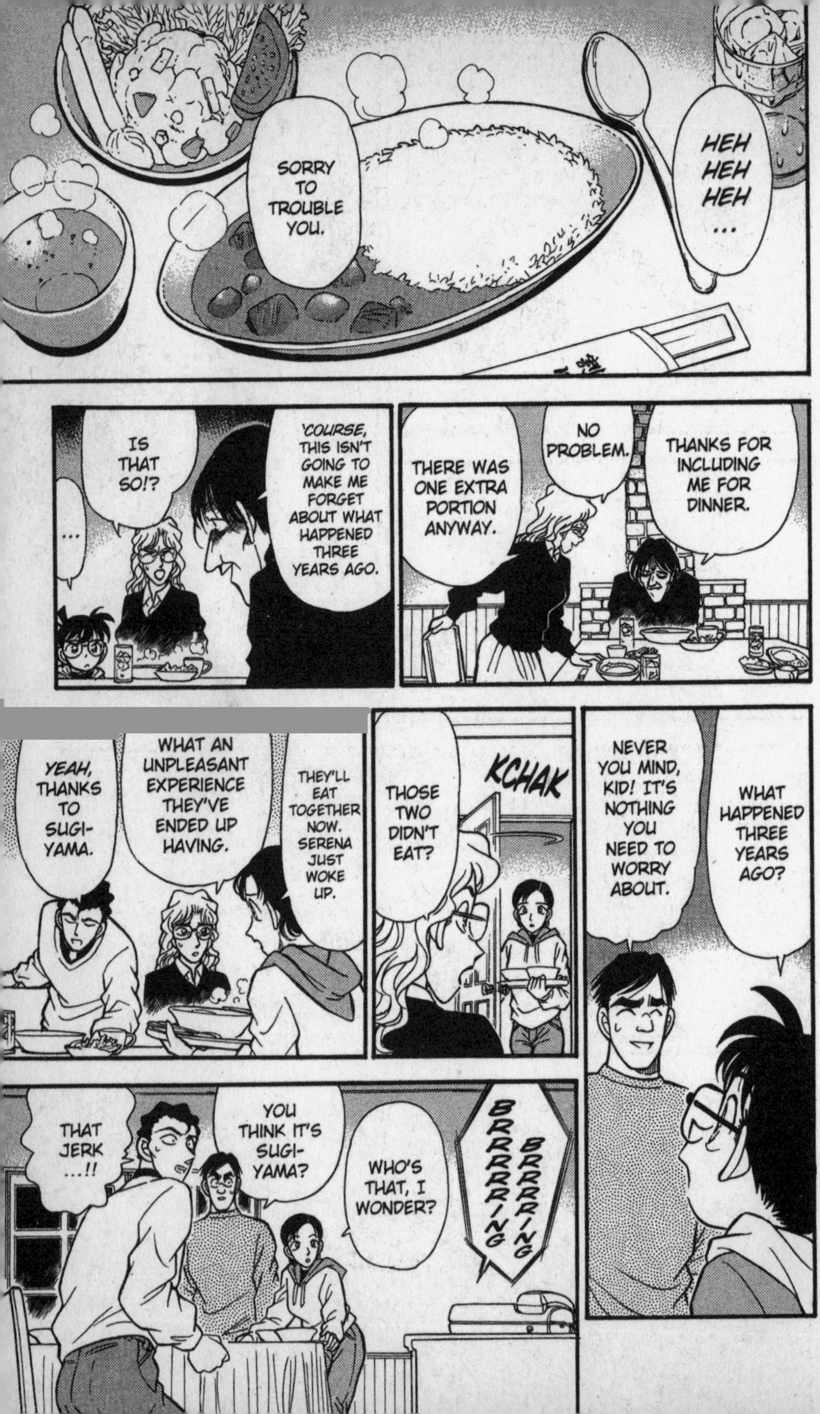
HEH HEH HEH...
SORRY TO TROUBLE YOU.
THANKS FOR INCLUDING ME FOR DINNER.
NO PROBLEM.
THERE WAS ONE EXTRA PORTION ANYWAY.
'COURSE, THIS ISN'T GOING TO MAKE ME FORGET ABOUT WHAT HAPPENED THREE YEARS AGO.
IS THAT SO!?
...
WHAT HAPPENED THREE YEARS AGO?
NEVER YOU MIND, KID! IT'S NOTHING YOU NEED TO WORRY ABOUT.
KCHAK
THOSE TWO DIDN'T EAT?
THEY'LL EAT TOGETHER NOW. SERENA JUST WOKE UP.
WHAT AN UNPLEASANT EXPERIENCE THEY'VE ENDED UP HAVING.
YEAH, THANKS TO SUGI-YAMA.
BRRRRING
BRRRRING
WHO'S THAT, I WONDER?
YOU THINK IT'S SUGI-YAMA?
THAT JERK ...!!

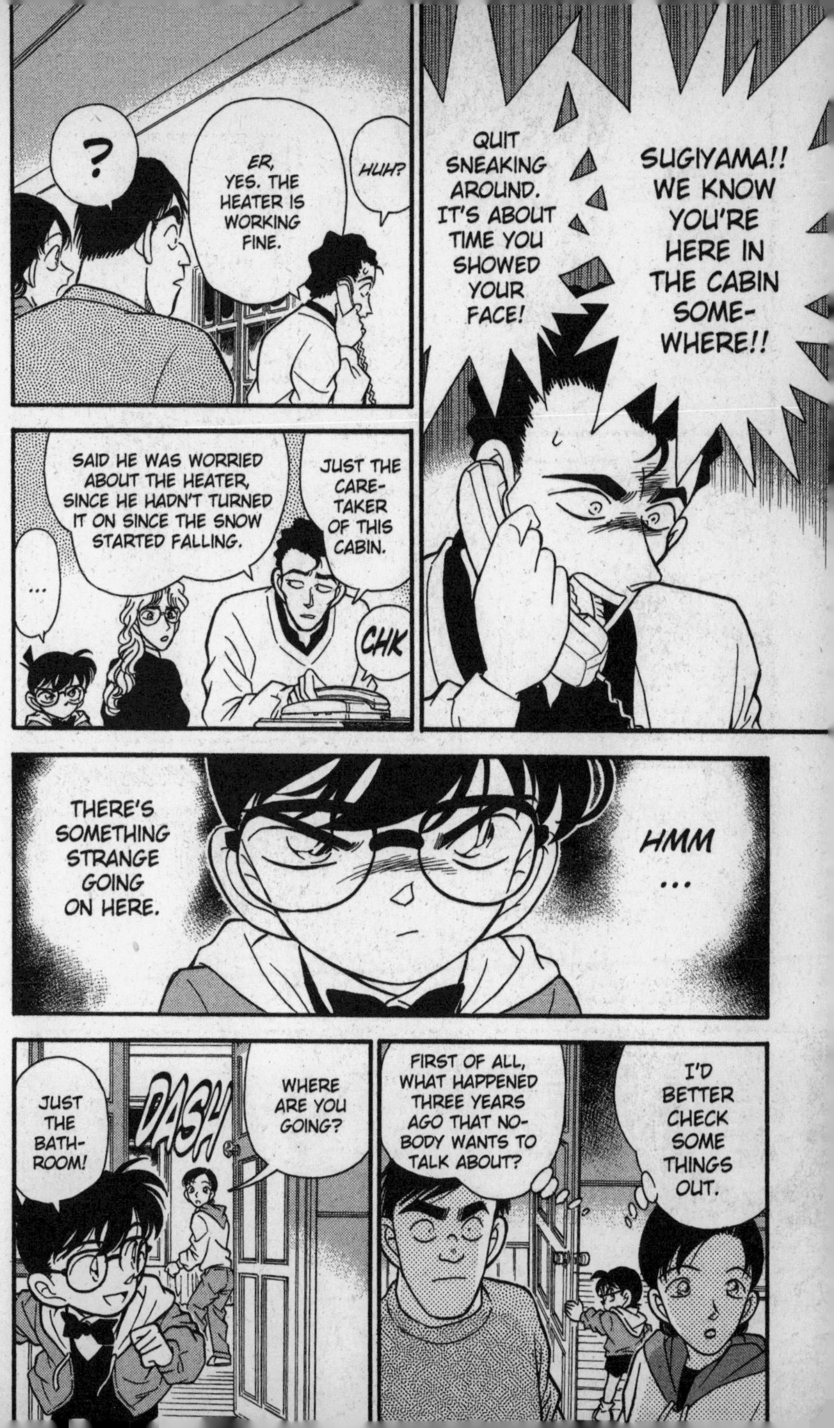
SUGIYAMA!! WE KNOW YOU'RE HERE IN THE CABIN SOME-WHERE!!
QUIT SNEAKING AROUND. IT'S ABOUT TIME YOU SHOWED YOUR FACE!
HUH?
ER, YES. THE HEATER IS WORKING FINE.
?
JUST THE CARE-TAKER OF THIS CABIN.
SAID HE WAS WORRIED ABOUT THE HEATER, SINCE HE HADN'T TURNED IT ON SINCE THE SNOW STARTED FALLING.
CHK
...
HMM ...
THERE'S SOMETHING STRANGE GOING ON HERE.
I'D BETTER CHECK SOME THINGS OUT.
FIRST OF ALL, WHAT HAPPENED THREE YEARS AGO THAT NO-BODY WANTS TO TALK ABOUT?
WHERE ARE YOU GOING?
DASH
JUST THE BATH-ROOM!

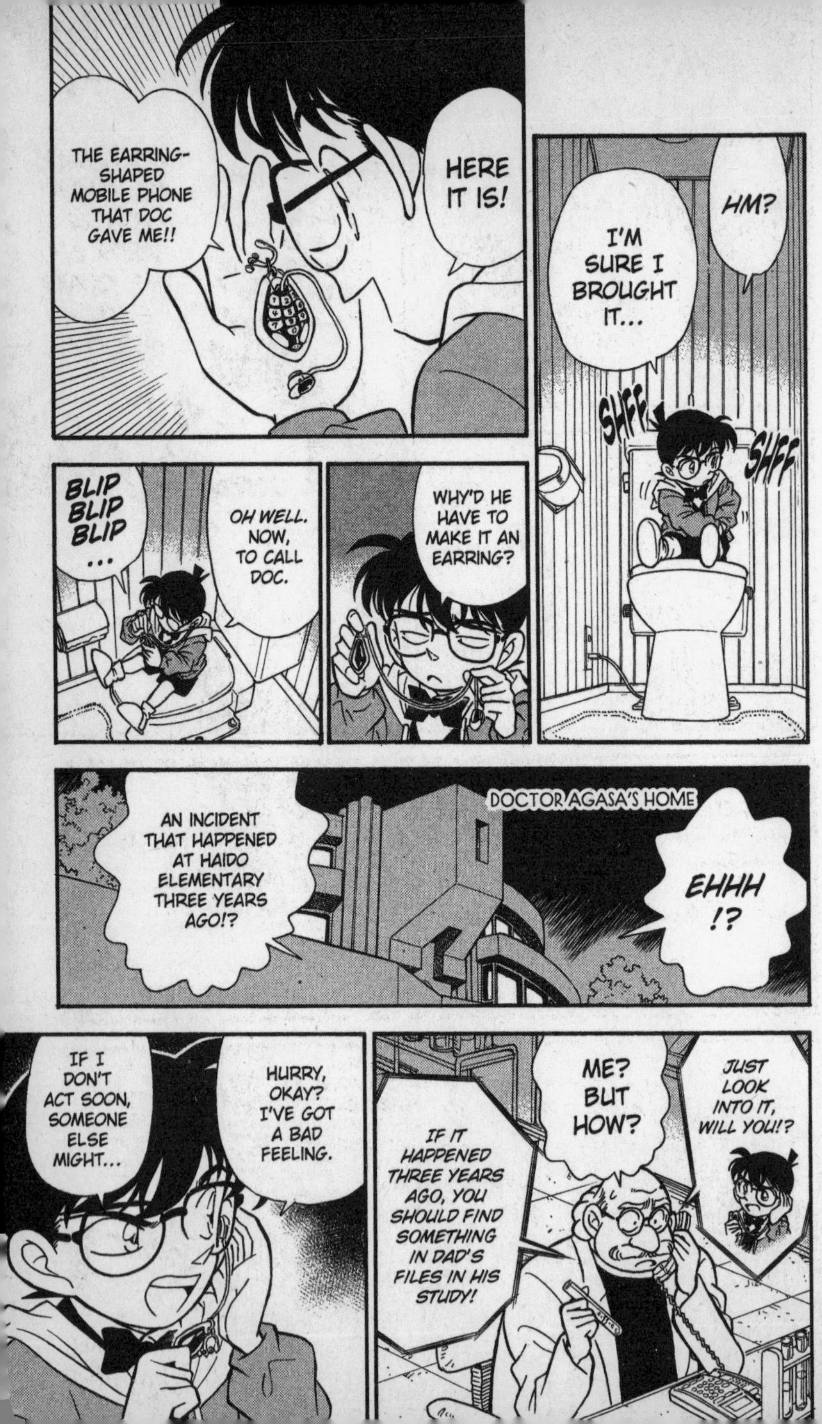
HM?
I'M SURE I BROUGHT IT...
SHFF
SHFF
HERE IT IS!
THE EARRING-SHAPED MOBILE PHONE THAT DOC GAVE ME!!
WHY'D HE HAVE TO MAKE IT AN EARRING?
OH WELL. NOW, TO CALL DOC.
BLIP BLIP BLIP ...
DOCTOR AGASA'S HOME
EHHH !?
AN INCIDENT THAT HAPPENED AT HAIDO ELEMENTARY THREE YEARS AGO!?
JUST LOOK INTO IT, WILL YOU!?
ME? BUT HOW?
IF IT HAPPENED THREE YEARS AGO, YOU SHOULD FIND SOMETHING IN DAD'S FILES IN HIS STUDY!
HURRY, OKAY? I'VE GOT A BAD FEELING.
IF I DON'T ACT SOON, SOMEONE ELSE MIGHT...

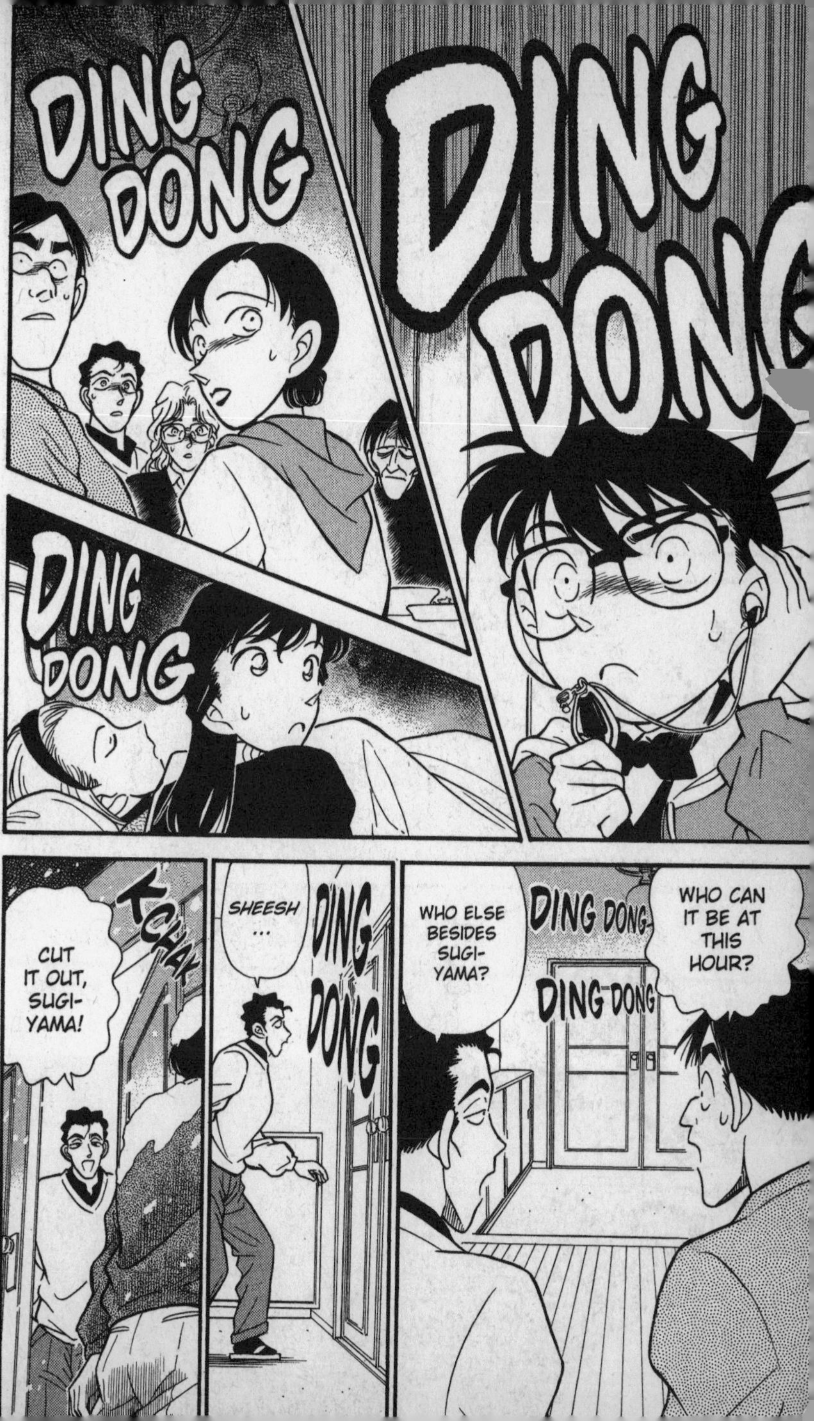
DING DONG
DING DONG
DING DONG
WHO CAN IT BE AT THIS HOUR?
DING DONG
DING DONG
WHO ELSE BESIDES SUGI-YAMA?
DING DONG
SHEESH ...
KCHAK
CUT IT OUT, SUGI-YAMA!

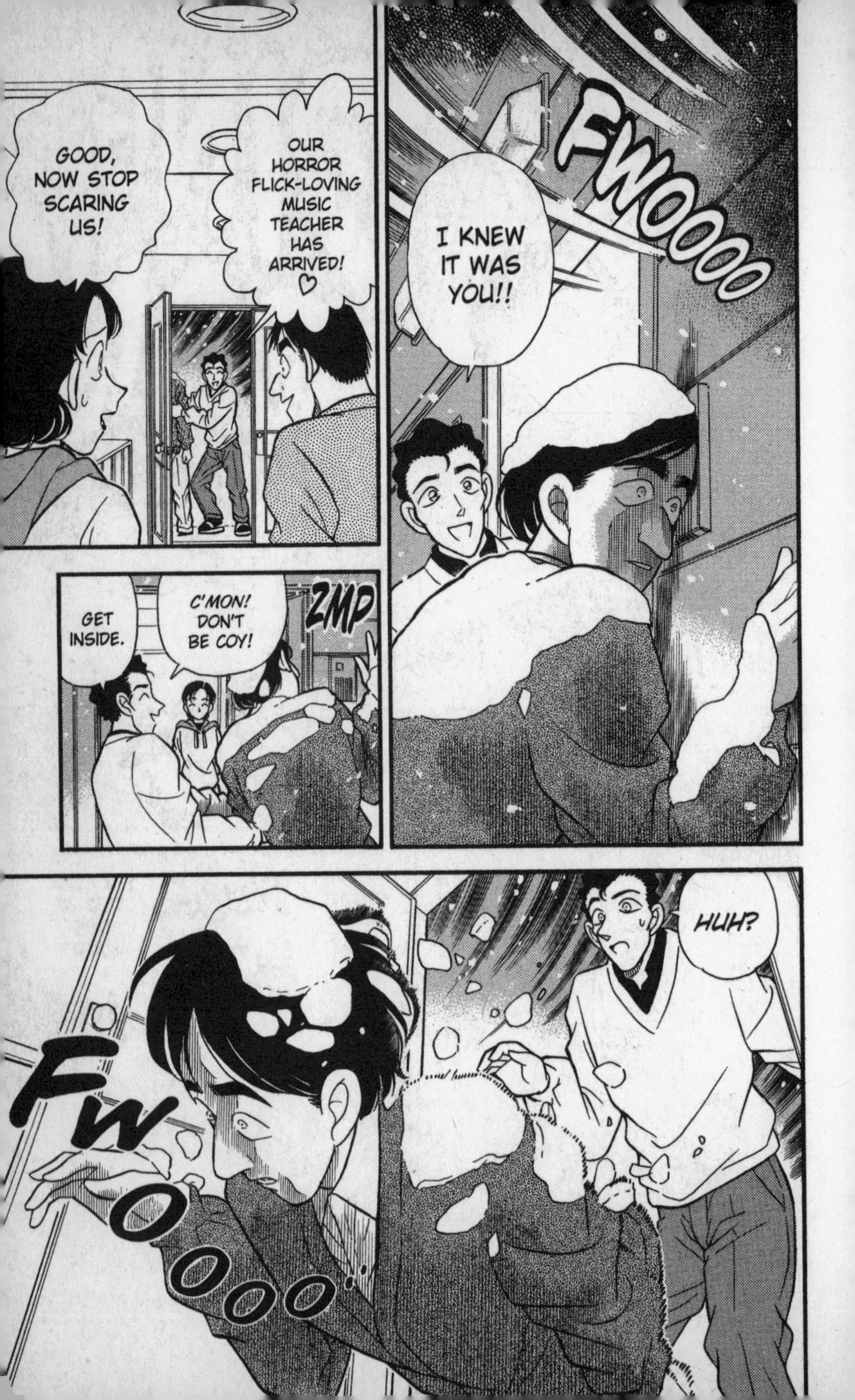
FWOOOO
I KNEW IT WAS YOU!!
OUR HORROR FLICK-LOVING MUSIC TEACHER HAS ARRIVED! ♡
GOOD, NOW STOP SCARING US!
ZMP
C'MON! DON'T BE COY!
GET INSIDE.
HUH?
FWOOOOO

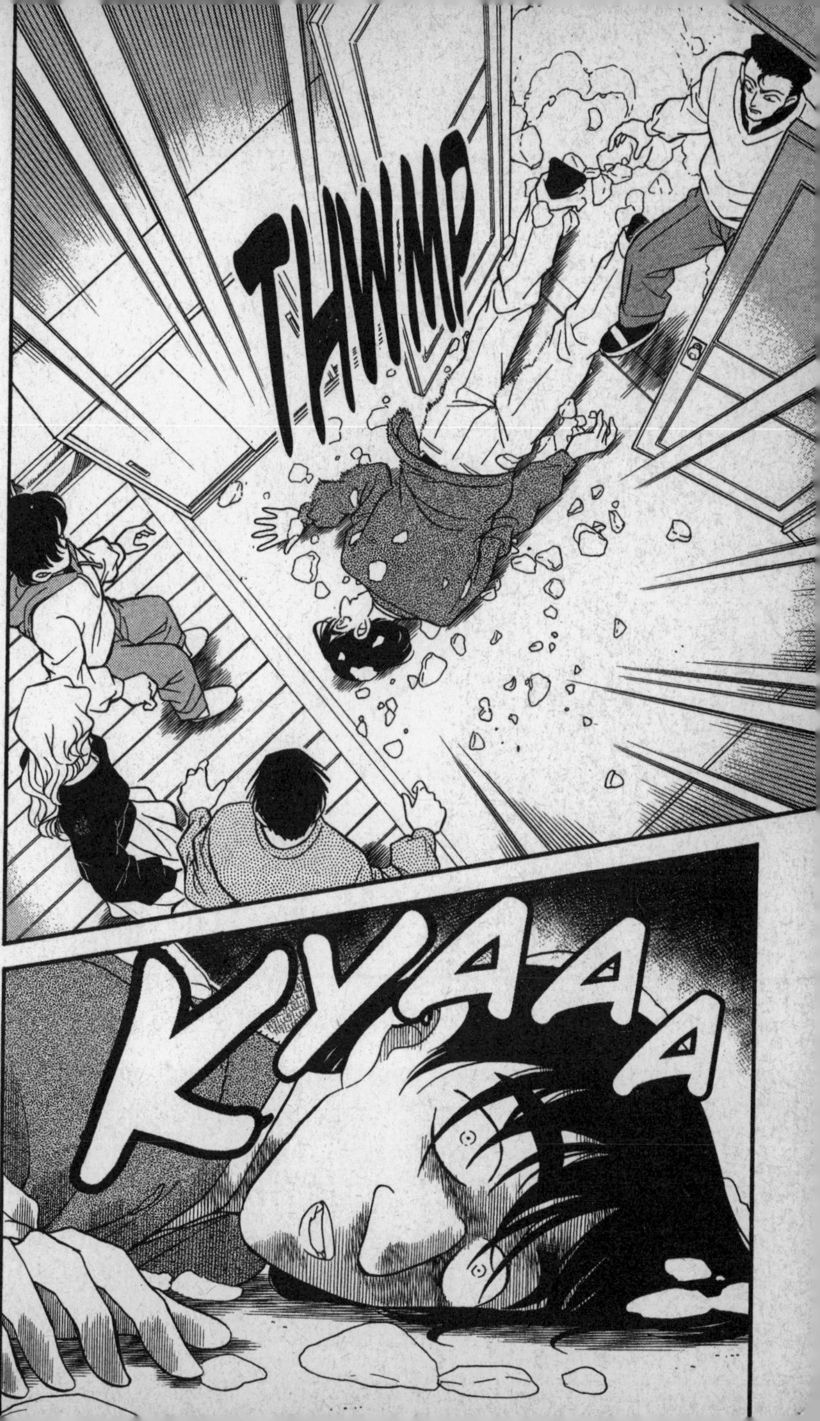
THWMP
KYAAA

Hello, Aoyama here.

Yesss! Finally my hopes of a *Case Closed* movie [in Japan] have come true!! It's really special – for the last scene they even used an episode I'd wanted to use in the manga!! Plus, I got to draw the originals myself ♥. Now, all you detective ladies and gentlemen: Get yourselves to a theater. Sharpen your powers of observation and try to figure out which images I personally drew!!

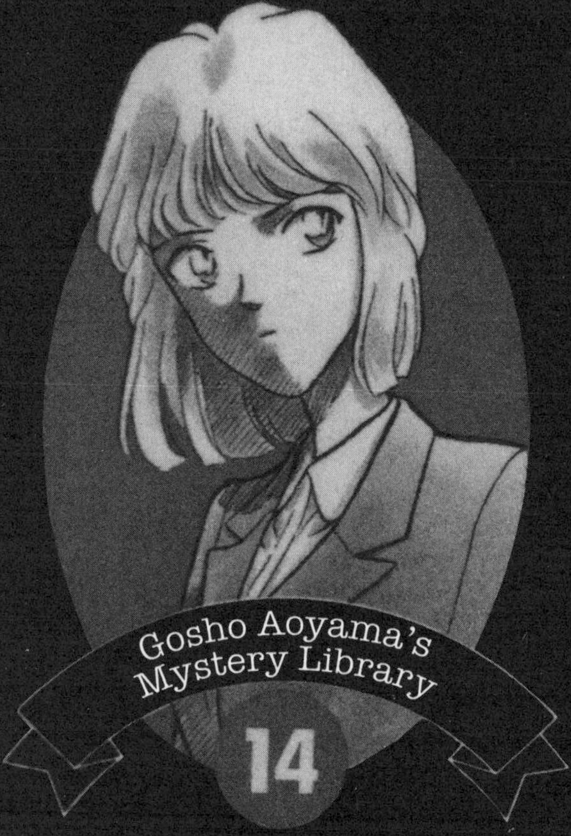
Gosho Aoyama's
Mystery Library
14

CORDELIA GRAY

Barely 22 years old, Cordelia Gray takes over an entire detective agency when her ill partner commits suicide. With light brown hair and big green eyes, she gives the impression of a cat. And like a feline, her slender body conceals hidden strength. She has no family, and now that she's lost her partner, the only things she can depend on are her trusty Mini and the .38 semi-automatic that belonged to her partner.

The Cordelia book was a spin-off from the police detective Dalgliesh series by the same author, P.D. James. There are only two Cordelia books to date, but the brave Cordelia left a strong impression on me. Despite being told that being an investigator is a man's job, she still goes into dangerous situations alone as she unravels her cases. (I recommend *An Unsuitable Job for a Woman.*)

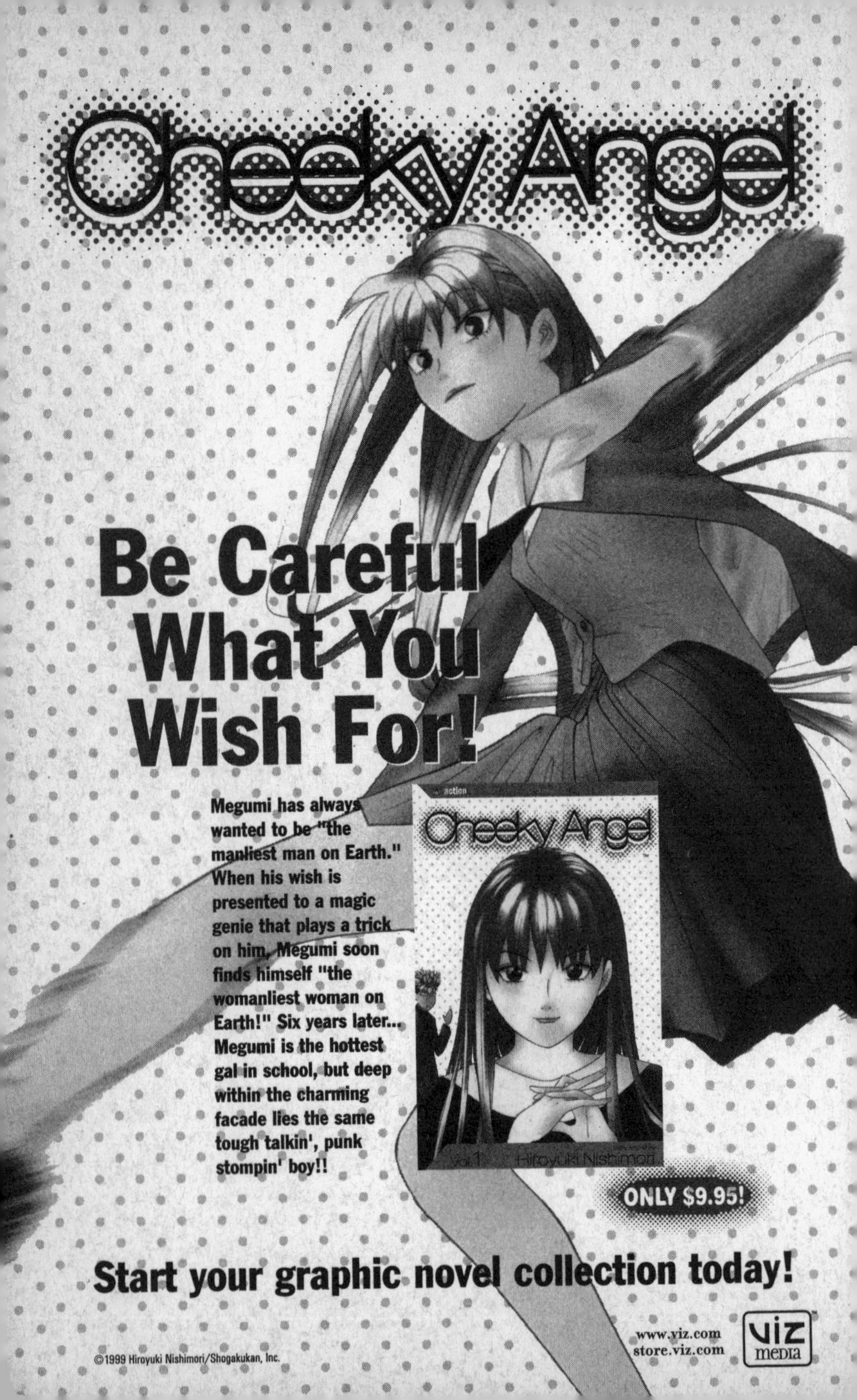

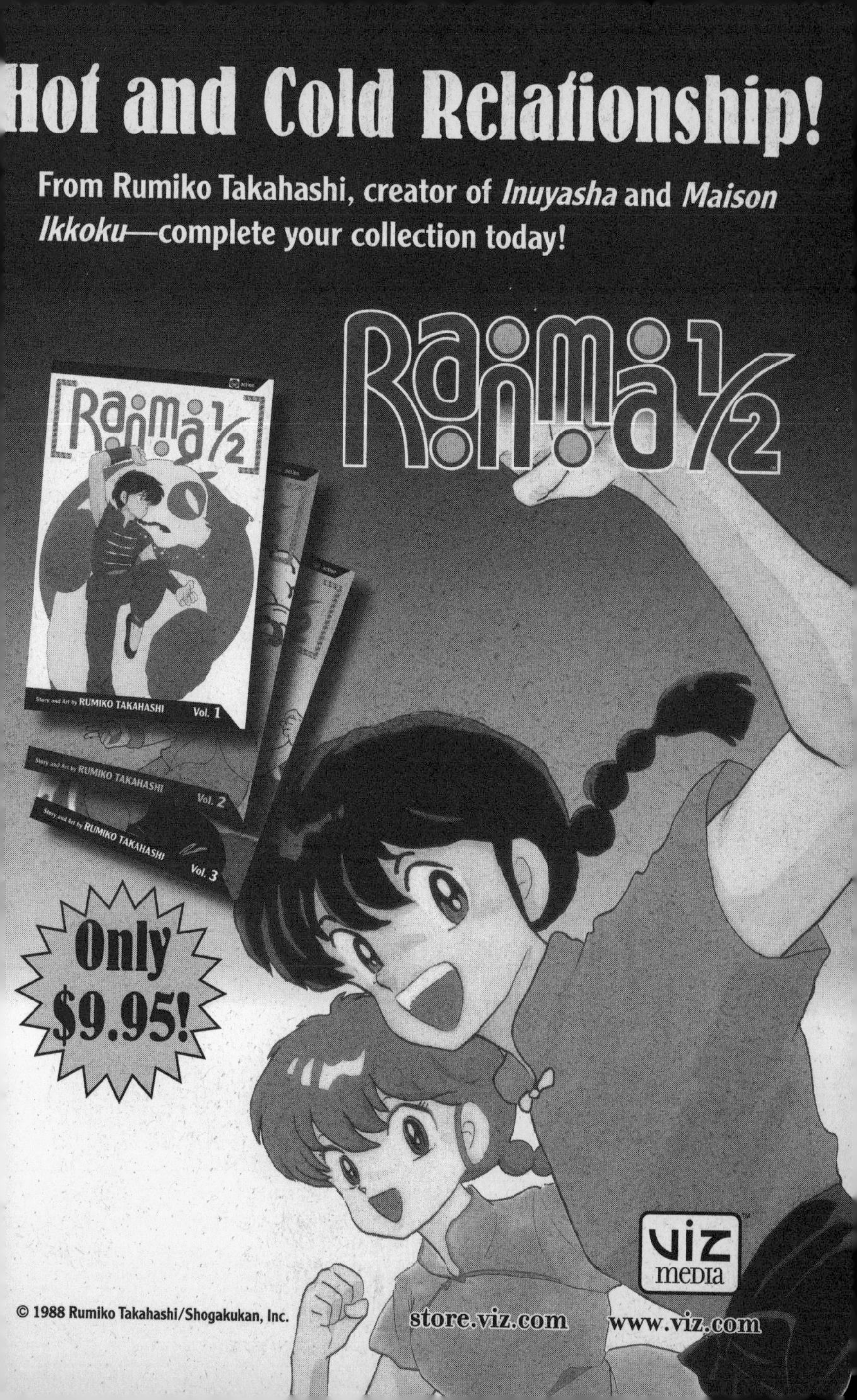
Hot and Cold Relationship!
From Rumiko Takahashi, creator of Inuyasha and Maison Ikkoku—complete your collection today!
Ranma 1/2
Ranma 1/2
Story and Art by RUMIKO TAKAHASHI
Vol. 1
Story and Art by RUMIKO TAKAHASHI
Vol. 2
Story and Art by RUMIKO TAKAHASHI
Vol. 3
Only $9.95!
viz media
© 1988 Rumiko Takahashi/Shogakukan, Inc.
store.viz.com
www.viz.com

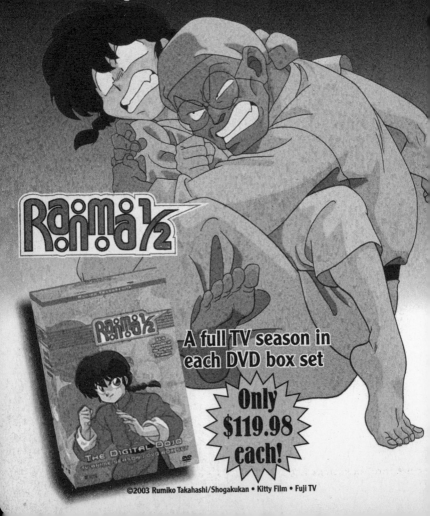

A Comedy that Redefines a

Due to an unfortunate accident, when martial artist Ranma gets splashed with cold water, he becomes a buxom young girl! Hot water reverses the effect, but when blamed for offenses both real and imagined, and pursued by lovesick suitors of both genders, what's a half-boy, half-girl to do?

A full TV season in each DVD box set

Only $119.98 each!

Half Human, Half

When Kagome discovers a well that transports her to feudal era Japan, she unwittingly frees a half-demon, Inuyasha, and shatters the sacred Jewel of Four Souls. Now they must work together to restore the jewel before it falls into the wrong hands...

INUYASHA

The manga that inspired a phenomenon!

FULL COLOR adaptation of the TV series!

Only $9.95!

Only $11.95!

HELP US MAKE THE MANGA
YOU LOVE BETTER!